A PRACTICAL REVIEW
OF GERMAN GRAMMAR

A PRACTICAL REVIEW OF GERMAN GRAMMAR

Third Edition

Gerda Dippmann

Johanna Watzinger-Tharp

University of Utah

Prentice Hall, Upper Saddle River, New Jersey 07458

Library of Congress Cataloging in Publication Data

Dippmann, Gerda.
  A practical review of German grammar / Gerda Dippmann, Johanna
Watzinger-Tharp. — 3rd ed.
      p. cm.
    Includes index
    ISBN 0-13-938143-0
    1. German language — Grammar. 2. German language — Textbooks
for foreign speakers—English. I. Watzinger-Tharp, Johanna.
II. Title.
PF3112 .D56 1999
438.2'421—dc21

                                            98-32226
                                               CIP

Editor-in-Chief: Rosemary Bradley
Executive Marketing Manager: Ilse Wolfe
Marketing Coordinator: Kathryn Sheehan
Editorial Assistant: Nadejda Rozeva
Editorial/Production and Interior Design: TSI Graphics
Project Manager: Claudia Dukeshire
Executive Managing Editor: Ann Marie McCarthy
Cover Design: Bruce Killmer
Creative Design Director: Leslie Osher
Buyer: Tricia Kenny

This book was set in 10/12 Meridien by TSI Graphics and was printed and
bound by Courier Companies, Inc. The cover was printed by Courier
Companies, Inc.

©2000 by Prentice-Hall, Inc.
Upper Saddle River, New Jersey   07458

Printed in the United States of America
10 9 8 7 6 5 4 3 2

ISBN 0-13-938143-0

Prentice-Hall International (UK) Limited, *London*
Prentice-Hall of Australia Pty. Limited, *Sydney*
Prentice-Hall Canada Inc., *Toronto*
Prentice-Hall Hispanoamericana, S. A., *Mexico*
Prentice-Hall of India Private Limited, *New Delhi*
Prentice-Hall of Japan, Inc., *Tokyo*
Pearson Education Asia Pte. Ltd., *Singapore*
Editora Prentice-Hall do Brasil, Ltda., *Rio de Janeiro*

ISBN 0-13-938143-0

90000

9 780139 381430

Contents

3 VERBS IN THE PAST AND FUTURE TENSES   *38*

4 MODAL AUXILIARIES   *65*

5 THE NOUNS 83

6 *der*-WORDS AND *ein*-WORDS; PERSONAL PRONOUNS 100

13 THE SUBJUNCTIVE PART II   236

14 *der*-WORDS AND *ein*-WORDS AS PRONOUNS; INDEFINITE PRONOUNS; RELATIVE CLAUSES   257

Preface

College students enrolled in intermediate or advanced-intermediate courses usually vary in their grasp of German grammar, and there is often limited class time for grammar review. We were delighted by the success of *A Practical Review of German Grammar* and are excited to share this *Third Edition* with you.

A Practical Review of German Grammar is arranged so that the instructor can assign the major portion of it as work outside of class. Before work on the *Third Edition* was begun, a survey was sent to instructors using or familiar with the *Second Edition*. Replies indicated that the book was in use in a variety of intermediate and post-intermediate courses, generally in combination with reading, conversation, and writing materials. Instructors and students underscored the value of the "self-study" feature of the book—the more grammar studies can be done outside the classroom, the more class time can be reserved for speaking and reading German.

As we worked on the *Third Edition*, Germany implemented a spelling reform. *A Practical Review of German Grammar* observes the new rules for spelling and punctuation. Section 1 of the Appendix explains and provides examples for the main features of the spelling reform.

Grammar Presentation and Explanation

The grammar is presented in manageable blocks and followed immediately by practice exercises. The foremost consideration has been to facilitate comprehension by the students. Explanations are basic enough that even students with little formal knowledge of grammar will be able to understand them. Students with deficient backgrounds will appreciate the detailed treatment; those with strong backgrounds will be able to work through the review rapidly.

Exercises

The exercises (**Übungen**) range from short-answer questions (**Verstehen**) to personalized questions (**Anwenden**). Whenever appropriate, the practice exercises are placed in situational contexts. Summarizing exercises (**Zusammenfassung**) at the end of a section or chapter review larger units of grammar. All exercises are in natural German and are frequently in conversational form.

Vocabulary

Each chapter concludes with a thematically organized vocabulary section (**Themen und Vokabular**). Throughout the book, students will find hints on particular lexical uses (**Vokabulartip**). Instructors may assign chapters in any sequence, as the vocabulary for each chapter is largely self-contained.

Appendix

The Appendix begins with a summary of the recently implemented German spelling reform (**Rechtschreibreform**) and a summary of German punctuation rules. It also includes lists of the principal parts of all strong and irregular verbs, followed by sections on adjectives and flavoring particles. The four final sections of the Appendix explain German measurements, punctuation, present letter-writing conventions, and illustrate the German alphabet.

Glossary

A German-English glossary and a glossary of grammatical terms follow the Appendix.

Acknowledgments

We would like to extend our gratitude to the professors who took time to assist us with comments and suggestions over the course of development of all three editions of *A Practical Review of German Grammar*. We thank each of the following colleagues for their invaluable suggestions and recommendations:

Judith Ricker-Aberhalden,
University of Arkansas

Annemarie Arnold, Wesleyan University

Elizabeth Bredeck,
University of California, San Diego

Christa W. Britt, Thunderbird University

Joan Keck Campbell, Dartmouth College

Ruth I. Cape, Skidmore College

Roger Crockett,
Washington and Lee University

Nancy Decker, Rollins College

Tom DiNapoli, Louisiana State University

Dinah Dodds, Lewis and Clark College

Lynn R. Eliason, Utah State University

Peter R. Erspamer, Winona State University

Henning Falkenstein, Valparaiso University

Jeffrey B. Gardiner,
Western Michigan University

Eberhard Geyer, Hillsdale College

Margaret Gonglewski,
The George Washington University

Anna Gramberg, Auburn University

Frauke A. Harvey, Baylor University

Kent Hooper, University of Puget Sound

James F. Hyde, Jr., Ripon College

Susan M. Johnson, Susquehanna University

Gudrun Tabbert-Jones,
Santa Clara University

Kenneth E. Keeton, Eckerd College

Charles J. Kenlan,
Washington State University

Astrid Klocke, Indiana University

Frauke Loewensen,
Monterey Institute of International Studies

Carla J. Love,
University of Wisconsin–Madison

Hans K. Musslee, Utah State University

Walke von Reinhart,
University of Rhode Island

Claus Reschke, University of Houston

Ferrel Rose, Grinnell College

Karen Six, University of California, Berkeley

Mark Southern, Carthage College

Wallace Sue, Michigan State University

Gerlinde Thompson, University of Oklahoma

Mary Wauchope, San Diego State University

Hendrik H. Winterstein,
University of Houston

Robert B. Youngblood,
Washington and Lee University

Cecile Cazort Zorach,
Franklin and Marshall College

At Prentice Hall, we extend our thanks to the publishing team: Rosemary Bradley, Editor-in-Chief; Claudia Dukeshire, Project Manager; Ilse Wolfe, Executive Marketing Manager; Kathryn Sheehan, Marketing Coordinator; and Nadejda Rozeva, Editorial Assistant. We also extend our thanks to our copyeditor, Douglas Guy, and to the editorial team at TSI Graphics, Lee Uehling and Liz Gabbard.

1 Preliminary Remarks about German Word Order

This chapter deals with some basic aspects of German word order. Those aspects not discussed in this chapter will be treated in subsequent chapters.

Word Order in Statements

§1 Subject — Inflected Verb

In a clause that stands alone (main clause), the subject commonly appears in the first position, followed by the inflected (conjugated) verb. The inflected verb takes a personal ending that agrees with the subject.

Der Student liest die Zeitung.   *The student is reading the newspaper.*
SUBJECT   VERB   DIRECT OBJECT

In English an adverb may be placed between the subject and the verb. This cannot be done in German. The verb must be the second element.

Ich lese oft die Zeitung.   *I often read the newspaper.*
VERB

§2 Inverted Word Order:
Element X — Inflected Verb — Subject

To emphasize information and to establish a topic, elements other than the subject often appear in the first position. These elements are most commonly adverbial expressions. For stylistic reasons, it is important that you vary the elements in the first position and avoid beginning too many sentences with the subject when you write in German. Note that in German, such elements are not set off by a comma as they are in English.

Heute liest die Studentin die Zeitung.
| | | |
TIME   VERB   SUBJECT   DIRECT
EXPRESSION   OBJECT

Today, the student is reading the newspaper.

In der Mensa essen viele Studenten.
| | |
PLACE   VERB   SUBJECT
EXPRESSION

Many students eat in the cafeteria.

Other elements, such as the grammatical object or a participle, occasionally also occur in the first position. They may be used to connect sentences effectively, to respond directly to a previous statement, or to emphasize.

Ihre Freundin besucht die Studentin morgen.
| | | |
DIRECT   VERB   SUBJECT   TIME
OBJECT   EXPRESSION

The student will visit her friend tomorrow.

Gelernt hat sie diese Woche nicht viel.
| | | |
PARTICIPLE VERB SUBJECT TIME EXPRESSION

She hasn't studied much this week.

When an element other than the subject occurs in first position, the inflected verb remains in second position. The subject *follows* the inflected verb. In summation, the subject of a statement usually appears first, but if another element appears in the first position, the subject must appear immediately after the verb.

Übung 1-1

VERSTEHEN Identify the subject in each sentence.

1. Den Kurs besucht Hannelore jeden Dienstag.
2. Die Freunde besuchen Hannelore am Wochenende.
3. Abends geht Christine oft mit Hannelore ins Kino.
4. Andi feiert am Sonntag seinen 30. Geburtstag.
5. Den Kuchen bringen Kerstin und Erika.
6. Die Getränke holt Bernhard.

Übung 1-2

ANWENDEN Restate the following sentences, using the boldface words at the beginning.

MODEL: Ich gehe **heute Abend** mit Hans ins Kino.
          Heute Abend gehe ich mit Hans ins Kino.

Erika beschreibt ihre Pläne für die nächste Woche.

1. Ich besuche **morgen** meine Oma.
2. Meine Schwester und ich wollen **am Dienstagabend** essen gehen.

3. Wir spielen **am Nachmittag** vielleicht Tennis.
4. Wir gehen am Freitagabend **vielleicht** ins Kino.
5. Ich gehe mit meinen Eltern am Samstag **ins Konzert**.

Erika erklärt, was sie schenkt und verleiht.

6. Ich kaufe **meinem Bruder** eine CD. Er hat nächste Woche Geburtstag.
7. Ich schreibe **meinen Eltern und Geschwistern** Briefe.
8. Ich schicke Freunden **Postkarten**.
9. Meine Mutti und ich backen **meinem Vater** zum Jubiläum einen Kuchen.
10. Man leiht **sein Auto** niemandem!

Elements that have no effect on word order

The most common elements that do not affect the Subject–Inflected Verb word order are listed below.

1. Elements set off by a comma

ja	Ja, ich verstehe Sie.
nein	Nein, ich verstehe Sie nicht.
(form of address)	Frau Böhme, ich verstehe Sie nicht.

2. Elements not set off by a comma

aber (*but*)
denn (*for*)
oder (*or*)
und (*and*)

Aber, denn, oder, and **und** are coordinating conjunctions that usually connect two equal clauses (cf. Kap. 11 §1).

Die Post ist heute geschlossen, **aber** viele Leute wissen das nicht.
The post office is closed today, **but** *many people don't know that.*

§3 Dependent Word Order: Inflected Verb Stands Last

Dependent word order occurs in dependent clauses. Such clauses cannot stand alone; they are dependent on a main clause. They are always introduced by subordinating conjunctions, such as **dass** (*that*), **weil** (*because*), or **wenn** (*when, if*) and are separated from the main clause by a comma. (cf. Kap 11 §3). Sentences that contain a main and a dependent clause are often called *complex sentences.*

⌐Es ist sicher,¬	⌐dass viele Leute zu der Feier kommen.¬
∟ MAIN CLAUSE ⌡	∟———— DEPENDENT CLAUSE ————⌡
It is certain	*that a lot of people will come to the party.*

In the dependent clause, the subject usually immediately follows the subordinating conjunction (**dass**). The inflected verb is always in final position in the dependent clause.

Übung 1-3

ANWENDEN Convert the following sentences to complex sentences, with a dependent clause. Begin with a phrase that contains the word in parentheses.

> MODEL: Wir fahren jeden Tag Fahrrad. (möglich)
> <u>Es ist möglich, dass wir jeden Tag Fahrrad fahren.</u>

Peter erzählt, was seine Familie in den Ferien macht. Sie verbringt ihren Urlaub in einem Ferienhaus.

1. Wir schwimmen täglich im Meer. (möglich)
2. Meine Mutter wandert viel. (sicher)
3. Sabine und Petra joggen jeden Morgen. (wahrscheinlich)
4. Mein Vater frühstückt gemütlich. (sicher)
5. Meine Familie diskutiert viel. (sicher)
6. Meine Eltern essen manchmal im Restaurant. (möglich)
7. Meine Geschwister und ich kochen oft. (wahrscheinlich)
8. Ich gehe früh ins Bett! (unwahrscheinlich)

Word order without **dass**

When **dass** is omitted, the clause operates like a main clause. The first element after the comma may be the subject or some other element, such as a time expression.

> Ich weiß, Müllers sind jetzt nicht zu Hause.
> Ich glaube, jetzt sind Müllers nicht zu Hause.

The dependent clause preceding the main clause

Compare:

The main clause has inverted word order when it is preceded by a dependent clause. The dependent clause at the beginning of a sentence is treated as the first element of the main clause. Compare:

Übung 1-4

ANWENDEN Restate each of the following sentences, beginning with the dependent clause.

> MODEL: Wir kaufen ein neues Auto, wenn wir genug Geld haben.
>   Wenn wir genug Geld haben, kaufen wir ein neues Auto.

Kerstin spricht über Gesundheit und über ihre Gefühle.

1. Man soll viel trinken, wenn man Sport treibt.
2. Meine Freunde und ich kaufen viel Gemüse, weil es frisch ist.
3. Ich trinke eine Tasse Kaffee, wenn ich müde werde.
4. Ich schlafe viel, wenn ich krank bin.
5. Ich höre laute Musik, weil ich schlechte Laune habe.
6. Ich singe, wenn ich glücklich bin.

Word Order in Questions

§4 Direct Questions

When a question forms the main clause (i.e., stands alone) it is called a *direct question*. In direct questions, the inflected verb is in first or second position. Direct questions may begin with a question word or the inflected verb.

Wann beginnt das Semester?   **Beginnt** das Semester im August?

   VERB   SUBJECT   VERB   SUBJECT

The inflected verb is in second position when the question begins with a question word, such as **wann** (*when*), **warum** (*why*), **wo** (*where*), or **wie viel** (*how much*). When there is no question word, the verb is in first position.

Note that there is no German equivalent for the English auxiliary verb *do* in questions.

> *Do you understand me?*   Verstehen Sie mich?

Übung 1-5

ANWENDEN Convert the following statements to questions.

A. Begin with the verb.

> MODEL: Britta hat keine Zeit.
>   Ja? Hat Britta wirklich keine Zeit?

Richard erklärt Max, was verschiedene Leute im Sommer machen. Max glaubt nicht, was Richard sagt und fragt nach.

1. Elke hat für den Sommer eine Arbeitsstelle.
2. Andreas arbeitet nicht.

3. Neumanns sind nächste Woche in Dresden.
4. Wir füttern ihre Katze.
5. Dimitri fährt im Juli nach Italien.
6. Nadja kauft ein Auto.

B. Begin with the indicated question word.

> MODEL: Es regnet heute. (warum)
>   <u>Warum regnet es heute?</u>

Nadja (5 Jahre alt) stellt ihrem Papa viele Fragen.

1. Mutti kommt nach Hause. (wann)
2. Wir spielen nicht draußen. (warum)
3. Du hast schlechte Laune, Papa! (warum)
4. Ich bekomme etwas Süßes. (wann)
5. Mein Teddybär hat nur ein Ohr. (warum)
6. Simone fährt Dreirad. (wo)

§5   Indirect Questions

A question that occurs in a dependent clause is called an *indirect question*. It depends on an introductory clause, such as **Ich weiß nicht**...(*I don't know*...) or **Ich möchte wissen**... (*I'd like to know*...). In an indirect question, the inflected verb stands last, and, just like in a direct question, an indirect question may begin with a question word or the inflected verb. Note how the following questions have been changed to indirect questions:

> Wann beginnt das Semester?
> Ich möchte wissen, wann das Semester beginnt.
> *I would like to know when the semester starts.*
>
> Beginnt das Semester im August?
> Ich möchte wissen, ob das Semester im August beginnt.
> *I'd like to know whether (if) the semester begins in August.*

In an indirect question, the question word functions as a subordinating conjunction, hence the dependent word order.

If the direct question has no question word, the subordinating conjunction **ob** (*whether, if*) introduces the indirect question.

Übung 1-6

ANWENDEN Convert the following direct questions to indirect questions, using the introductory clause of the model or another appropriate clause. Change the possessives as appropriate.

A. Direct questions with a question word

> MODEL: Wo ist deine Tasche?
> <u>Ich weiß nicht, wo meine Tasche ist.</u>

Nadjas Mutter stellt Fragen, aber Nadja (5 Jahre alt) kooperiert nicht.

1. Wo sind deine Schuhe?
2. Warum trägt die Puppe dein Kleid?
3. Wann isst du dein Frühstück?
4. Wie viele Becher hast du in deinem Zimmer?
5. Wo sind meine Schlüssel?
6. Warum ist das Radio so laut?

B. Direct questions without a question word

> MODEL: Hat Andreas eine Freundin?
> <u>Ich möchte wissen, ob Andreas eine Freundin hat.</u>

Sonja spricht mit ihrem Freund Lars am Telefon und muss alle Fragen wiederholen.

1. Hast du morgen abend Zeit?
2. Gehen wir vielleicht in einen Film?
3. Bist du irgendwie verärgert?
4. Bleibst du lieber zu Hause?
5. Sind Erik und Annette da?
6. Sehen wir uns dann am Wochenende?

The introductory clause may be a question, such as **Weißt du...?, Wissen Sie...?, Kannst du mir sagen...?, Können Sie mir sagen...?**

DIRECT QUESTION	INDIRECT QUESTION
Was ist das?	Weißt du, was das ist? *Do you know what that is?*
Sind die Schmidts zu Hause?	Wissen Sie, ob die Schmidts zu Hause sind? *Do you know whether the Schmidts are at home?*
Wo wohnen die Bergers?	Können Sie mir sagen, wo die Bergers wohnen? *Can you tell me where the Bergers live?*

Remember: An indirect question depends on an introductory clause (statement or question) and may be viewed as a "dependent question" requiring dependent word order.

Übung 1-7

ANWENDEN The following questions begin with or without a question word. Convert them to indirect questions, using the introductory clauses in parentheses.

MODEL: Wo ist der Bahnhof? (Können Sie mir sagen)
<u>Können Sie mir sagen, wo der Bahnhof ist?</u>

Stefanie ist bei der Touristeninformation in Aachen und versucht Auskunft zu bekommen.

1. Gibt es ein billiges Hotel im Zentrum? (Können Sie mir sagen)
2. Wann sind die Museen geöffnet? (Wissen Sie)
3. Wo ist ein italienisches Restaurant? (Wissen Sie)
4. Wie viel kostet eine Tageskarte für die U-Bahn? (Wissen Sie)
5. Fährt die U-Bahn auch spät am Abend? (Können Sie mir sagen)

Stefanie kommt mit einem jungen Mann ins Gespräch.

6. Ist der Bahnhof weit von hier? (Kannst du mir sagen)
7. Wo ist eine nette Kneipe für abends? (Kannst du mir sagen)
8. Hat Aachen ein schönes Schwimmbad? (Weißt du)
9. Wird das Wetter besser? (Weißt du)
10. Wandern Leute in der Nähe von Aachen? (Kannst du mir sagen)

§6   Summary

The following table illustrates the three word order patterns in German: subject–inflected verb, inverted, and dependent.

		INFLECTED VERB	
1. Subject– Inflected Verb	Die Studentin	liest	die Zeitung.
2. Inverted STATEMENT	Heute	liest	die Studentin die Zeitung.
DIRECT QUESTION WITH QUESTION WORD	Wann	liest	die Studentin die Zeitung?
WITHOUT QUESTION WORD		Liest	die Studentin die Zeitung?

The inflected verb is in second position except in direct questions that do not begin with a question word, in which case it is in first position.

			INFLECTED VERB
3. Dependent STATEMENT	Es ist möglich,	dass die Studentin die Zeitung	liest.
INDIRECT QUESTION	Ich weiß nicht,	wann die Studentin die Zeitung	liest.
	Ich weiß nicht,	ob die Studentin die Zeitung	liest.
	Weißt du,	wann sie die Zeitung	liest?

The inflected verb is in final position.

Übung 1-8

ZUSAMMENFASSUNG Word order of direct and indirect questions.
Form three kinds of questions from each statement, following the model.

MODEL: Monique: „Christine ist pünktlich."
Jens: „Ist sie pünktlich?
Hoffentlich ist sie pünktlich! Woher weißt du, ob sie
pünktlich ist!?"

*Jens hat eine Verabredung mit Christine und ist etwas nervös. Monique kennt Christine und
beschreibt sie für Jens.*

1. Christine hat gute Laune.
2. Sie geht gern ins Theater.
3. Sie ist tolerant.
4. Sie diskutiert gern.
5. Sie treibt viel Sport.
6. Und sie hat nette Eltern.

The Position of *nicht*

A distinction has to be made between normally accented negation and strong
negation of a particular element.

§7   Normally Accented Negation

Nicht follows the inflected verb, pronoun objects, and most noun objects.

INFLECTED VERB	Sein Bruder raucht **nicht.**
PRONOUN OBJECT	Ich kenne ihn **nicht.**
NOUN OBJECT	Ich kenne seinen Bruder **nicht.**

Nicht precedes most other elements, such as:

1. Predicate adjectives and predicate nouns (they follow the main verbs **sein,
   werden, heißen**)

   Ich bin **nicht** nervös.
   Sabine wird **nicht** Lehrerin.
   Er heißt **nicht** Martin.

2. Most adverbs

   Sie sprechen **nicht** laut genug.
   Wir fahren **nicht** zu schnell.

   But, **nicht** follows most adverbs of time.

   Er kommt heute **nicht.**
   Dieser Kassettenrecorder funktioniert manchmal **nicht.**

3. Most prepositional phrases

> Dieser Brief ist **nicht** für mich.
> Susanne wohnt **nicht** bei ihren Eltern.

If several of the above elements occur in a sentence, **nicht** usually precedes the first element.

> Sie ist **nicht** freundlich zu mir.
> Schmidts fliegen **nicht** mit uns nach Europa.

The position of **nicht** is the same in questions.

> Ist sie **nicht** freundlich zu dir?
> Warum fliegen Schmidts **nicht** mit uns nach Europa?

When negating dependent clauses, keep in mind that the inflected verb stands last. Compare:

> Frau Weber kennt meinen Vater **nicht**.
> Es ist möglich, dass Frau Weber meinen Vater **nicht** kennt.

Otherwise the position of **nicht** follows the same rules that are valid for main clauses. (For the position of **nicht** in sentences that contain verb complements, see Kap. 17 §4 [Note].)

§8   Strong Negation of a Particular Element

If one element is strongly negated, **nicht** precedes that particular element. Such an emphatic negation is often part of a contrast.

> Ulrich kauft **nicht diesen Wagen**; er kauft einen anderen.
> **Nicht Mathias** kauft diesen Wagen, sondern seine Schwester kauft ihn.

Übung 1-9

VERSTEHEN Explain the position of **nicht** in the following sentences.

> MODEL: Sie ist nicht nett zu mir.
> **Nicht** precedes the predicate adjective **nett**.

1. Helga ist nicht meine Freundin.
2. Klaus weiß, dass der Ring Annette nicht gefällt.
3. Ich verstehe die Hausaufgaben nicht.
4. Warum fragen Sie ihn nicht?
5. Ich möchte wissen, warum Sie ihn nicht fragen.
6. Das ist nicht mein Hobby.
7. Martin fliegt nicht mit seinen Eltern nach Florida.
8. Ich gehe mit Peter nicht ins Kino; wir gehen in die Disko.
9. Frau Schiller arbeitet nicht bei dieser Firma.
10. Warum glauben Sie mir nicht?
11. Schmidts besuchen uns morgen nicht.

Übung 1-10

ANWENDEN Negate the following sentences according to the rules for normally accented negation. (Do not negate the introductory clauses.)

> MODEL: Ich finde die Uni gut.
>   <u>Ich finde die Uni nicht gut.</u>

Martin hat schlechte Laune. Er reagiert negativ auf alles, was sein Freund Jochen sagt.

1. Der Kurs gefällt mir.
2. Ich kenne diesen Professor.
3. Ich denke, dass ich das Material verstehe.
4. Die anderen Studenten sind interessant.
5. Weißt du, ich finde Margot nett.

§9   Using *oder* and *oder nicht*

Du hast eine Schwester, **oder**?
You have a sister, don't you?

Du hast keinen Bruder, **oder**?
You don't have a brother, do you?

Hans und Margot haben geheiratet, **oder nicht**?
Hans and Margot got married, didn't they?

Du verstehst mich, **oder nicht**?
You understand me, don't you?

The German word **oder** (*or*) is used like English *don't you?, do you?, didn't they?, can't you?,* and similar phrases to seek confirmation of what was just said. **Oder nicht** cannot be used when the sentence contains a negative.

Themen und Vokabular

Feiern

der Geburtstag, -e	*birthday*
das Jubiläum, Jubileen	*anniversary*

Gewissheit

möglich	*possible*
sicher	*certain*
unwahrscheinlich	*unlikely*
wahrscheinlich	*likely*

In der Stadt

der Bahnhof, ¨e	*train station*
das Hotel, -s	*hotel*
das Kino, -s	*movie theatre*
die Kneipe, -n	*bar, pub*
das Museum, Museen	*museum*
das Restaurant, -s	*restaurant*
das Schwimmbad, ¨er	*swimming pool*
das Zentrum, Zentren	*city center, downtown*

Tägliche Aktivitäten

auf•stehen	*to get up*
jemanden (acc) besuchen	*to visit somebody*
diskutieren	*to discuss*

ein•kaufen (gehen)	*to shop, to go shopping*
zu Abend essen	*to have dinner*
zu Mittag essen	*to have lunch*
etwas erledigen	*to take care of something, run errands*
frühstücken	*to have breakfast*
kochen	*to cook*
gute/schlechte Laune haben	*to be in a good/bad mood*
Musik hören	*to listen to music*
schlafen (gehen)	*to sleep, to go to bed*
sich unterhalten	*to talk, converse*
spielen	*to play*

Eigenschaften

gesund	*healthy*
glücklich	*happy*
krank	*ill*
müde	*tired, fatigued*
zufrieden	*content*

2 Verbs in the Present Tense; The Imperative

Verbs in the Present Tense

§1 Basic Forms of the Present Tense

The infinitive is the form of the verb you will find in a German dictionary. It usually has the ending **-en**. A small group of verbs has the ending **-n**, such as **sammeln** (*to collect*), **bewundern** (*to admire*), and **tun** (*to do*). The verb stem or root may be obtained by dropping the ending **-en** or **-n**.

INFINITIVE		STEM		ENDING	
gehen			geh-		**-en**
studieren			studier-		**-en**
sammeln			sammel-		**-n**
bewundern			bewunder-		**-n**
tun			tu-		**-n**

The inflectional endings of the present tense are added to the stem. They are as follows:

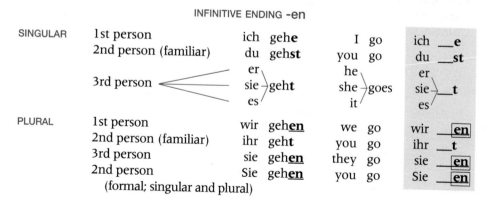

INFINITIVE ENDING -en

SINGULAR	1st person	ich geh**e**	I go	ich __**e**
	2nd person (familiar)	du geh**st**	you go	du __**st**
	3rd person	er \ sie ⟩geh**t** es /	he \ she ⟩goes it /	er \ sie ⟩__**t** es /
PLURAL	1st person	wir geh**en**	we go	wir __**en**
	2nd person (familiar)	ihr geh**t**	you go	ihr __**t**
	3rd person	sie geh**en**	they go	sie __**en**
	2nd person (formal; singular and plural)	Sie geh**en**	you go	Sie __**en**

Note that the three marked forms have the same endings as the infinitive.

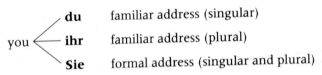

INFINITIVE ENDING **-n**

SINGULAR	1st person	ich samm(e)le*	ich bewund(e)re*	ich tue	ich ___e
	2nd person (familiar)	du sammelst	du bewunderst	du tust	du ___st
	3rd person	er\ sie⟩ sammelt es/	er\ sie⟩ bewundert es/	er\ sie⟩ tut es/	er\ sie⟩ ___t es/
PLURAL	1st person	wir sammeln	wir bewundern	wir tun	wir ___n
	2nd person (familiar)	ihr sammelt	ihr bewundert	ihr tut	ihr ___t
	3rd person	sie sammeln	sie bewundern	sie tun	sie ___n
	2nd person (formal; singular and plural)	Sie sammeln	Sie bewundern	Sie tun	Sie ___n

*Verbs ending in **-eln** or **-ern** often drop the **e** of the stem in the first-person singular.

The three marked forms add **-n** instead of **-en**, making them identical to the infinitive.

There are three German equivalents for the English *you*.

you ⟨
- **du**   familiar address (singular)
- **ihr**   familiar address (plural)
- **Sie**   formal address (singular and plural)

The familiar form **du** and its plural counterpart **ihr** are used when addressing relatives, close friends, children, teenagers up to about the age of 15, and pets. God is also addressed as **du**. Young people usually also say **du** to one another. Otherwise, **Sie** is used.

Übung 2-1

VERSTEHEN Indicate the subject of each sentence and the verb or verbs that agree with it.

MODEL: Am Wochenende schläft Ernst lange.   <u>Ernst; schläft</u>

Was machen Anke und Ernst am Wochenende?

1. Samstag Morgen gehen Anke und Ernst einkaufen.
2. Ihre Freundin Waltraud besuchen sie am Sonntag.
3. Am Sonntagabend trifft Erich seinen Bruder in einer Kneipe.
4. Anke holt ein Video und bleibt zu Hause.
5. Erichs Eltern ruft sie erst nächste Woche an.

Erichs Mutter spricht mit Anke über die Geburtstagsfeier zum 50. Geburtstag von Erichs Vater.

1. Am Freitagnachmittag kommen Christiane und Thomas aus Aachen.
2. Und Herrn und Frau Lieber holt ihr morgen am Bahnhof ab, oder?
3. Und stimmt es, dass du morgen Nachmittag zum Kuchenbacken kommst?
4. Die Getränke besorgt Erich am Donnerstag.
5. Und die Wurst- und Käseplatten bestelle ich morgen.

Übung 2-2

ANWENDEN A. Create short sentences using the verbs in parentheses. Maintain the subject of the original sentence.

> MODEL: Helga lernt viel. (studieren, arbeiten).
> <u>Helga studiert Physik. Helga arbeitet im Garten.</u>

1. Frank schreibt viel E-mail. (hören, erzählen)
2. Warum tust du das nicht? (lernen, studieren)
3. Das Kind weint abends. (lächeln, lachen, spielen)
4. Versteht ihr den Film? (erklären, organisieren)
5. Diese Professorin bewundere ich. (lieben, kritisieren)

B. Answer the following personalized questions.

1. Was studieren Sie? Was studieren Ihre Freunde?
2. Was sammeln Sie? Ein Bruder oder eine Schwester von Ihnen? Ihre Mutter oder Ihr Vater? Ein Freund oder eine Freundin von Ihnen?
3. Welchen Sport machen Sie/was spielen Sie? Was spielt Ihr bester Freund oder Ihre beste Freundin? Was spielen Ihre Geschwister und Ihre Eltern?
4. Wen bewundern Sie? Wen bewundern viele Teenager? Wen bewundert Ihr Vater oder Ihre Mutter?

Vokabulartip: studieren und lernen

Studieren is used

1. To refer to enrollment at a college or university

Klaus studiert an der Universität Bonn.	*Klaus goes to the University of Bonn.*
or: Klaus studiert in Bonn.	*Klaus is going to college in Bonn.*

2. To indicate a student's major

Anita studiert Chemie. (Meaning: *Anita's major is chemistry.*)	*Anita is studying chemistry.*

3. To mean *look over carefully*

Ich studiere den Fahrplan.	*I'm studying the timetable.*
Wir studieren die Speisekarte.	*We're really looking over the menu.*

Lernen means *to study* in the sense of studying for a test or an exam or of learning specific skills.

Ich lerne für eine Prüfung.	*I'm studying for an exam.*
Barbara lernt Deutsch und Spanisch.	*Barbara studies German and Spanish.*
(Meaning: *Barbara is taking German and Spanish courses.*)	
Jens lernt Bäcker.	*Jens is training to become a baker.*

§2   Verbs with Stems Ending in *-d, -t,* or Consonant Clusters

To facilitate pronunciation, an **e** is inserted between the stem and the endings of the third-person singulars, **er-sie-es**, and the **du-** and **ihr-** forms of

1. Verbs whose stems end in **-d** or **-t**, such as **antworten** (*to answer*), **arbeiten** (*to work*), **bedeuten** (*to mean*), **beneiden** (*to envy*), **finden** (*to find*), **heiraten** (*to marry*), **kosten** (*to cost*), **reden** (*to talk*), **warten** (*to wait*).

2. Verbs whose stems end in certain consonant combinations (consonant clusters), such as a single **m** or **n** that is preceded by a consonant other than **l** or **r**. Some typical examples are **atmen** (*to breathe*), **öffnen** (*to open*), **regnen** (*to rain*), **zeichnen** (*to draw*).

SINGULAR	1st person	ich rede	ich antworte	ich —**e**	
	2nd person (familiar)	du red**est**	du antwort**est**	du —**est**	**e** added
	3rd person	er\ sie ⟩red**et** es/	er\ sie ⟩antwort**et** es/	er\ sie ⟩—**et** es/	**e** added
PLURAL	1st person	wir red**en**	wir antwort**en**	wir —**en**	
	2nd (familiar)	ihr red**et**	ihr antwort**et**	ihr —**et**	**e** added
	3rd person	sie red**en**	sie antwort**en**	sie —**en**	
FORMAL	2nd person	Sie red**en**	Sie antwort**en**	Sie —**en**	

SINGULAR	1st person	ich öffne	ich —**e**	
	2nd person (familiar)	du öffn**est**	du —**est**	**e** added
	3rd person	er\ sie ⟩öffn**et** es/	er\ sie ⟩—**et** es/	**e** added
PLURAL	1st person	wir öffn**en**	wir —**en**	
	2nd (familiar)	ihr öffn**et**	ihr —**et**	**e** added
	3rd person	sie öffn**en**	sie —**en**	
FORMAL	2nd person	Sie öffn**en**	Sie —**en**	

(formal: singular and plural)   All endings begin with **e**.

Übung 2-3

ANWENDEN A. Supply the appropriate forms of the verbs in parentheses.

MODEL: Barbara _____. (reden, zeichnen)
<u>Barbara redet. Barbara zeichnet.</u>

1. Rainer _____ nicht gern. (arbeiten, antworten, warten)
2. _____ du mich? (beneiden, heiraten, bitten)
3. Warum _____ ihr nicht? (warten, antworten, reden, zeichnen)
4. _____ du den Brief nicht? (finden, öffnen)
5. Es _____ viel. (regnen, kosten, bedeuten)

B. Provide the correct form of a suitable verb in each blank.

1. Herr Kern ist jeden Tag von 7.00 Uhr morgens bis 19.00 Uhr abends im Büro. Er _arbeitet_ zu viel.
2. Es ist sehr heiß im Zimmer. Karin, _öffnet_ du bitte das Fenster?
3. Tut mir leid, dass es so spät ist. Wie lange _____ ihr schon?
4. Sie _____ zu viel! T u n Sie lieber etwas!
5. Hier sind Ihre Brötchen. Sie _kost_ 3 Mark 30.
6. Liest du *Der englische Patient*? Wie _findest_ du das Buch?
   /machst

C. *Studieren* oder *lernen*?

1. Birgit _lernet_ fleißig für ihr Examen.
2. Nächstes Jahr _studier_ Kurt in der Schweiz.
3. Diesen Sommer _lernen_ Doris und Peter Russisch. Sie fahren nach St. Petersburg. _studiert course catalog_
4. Gerda _lernt_studiert_ das Vorlesungsverzeichnis. Sie sucht ein interessantes Statistikseminar.
5. Ich _studiere_ Betriebswirtschaft. Ich arbeite nächstes Jahr für Bertelsmann.
6. Ist das dein erstes Semester in Mainz? Was _studierst_ du?

§3 Verbs with Stems Ending in -s, -ss, -ß, -tz, or -z

Verbs whose stems end in an **-s** sound add only **-t** to the stem of the **du-** form instead of the usual **-st** ending, thus the second- and third-person singular are identical.

Some verbs that belong to this group are **hassen** (*to hate*), **heißen** (*to be called*), **reisen** (*to travel*), **schließen** (*to close*), **schwänzen** (*to skip class*), **sitzen** (*to sit*), **tanzen** (*to dance*), **übersetzen** (*to translate*).

reisen	**hassen**	**heißen**	**sitzen**	**schwänzen**
ich reise	ich hasse	ich heiße*	ich sitze	ich schwänze
du reis**t**	du hass**t**	du heiß**t**	du sitz**t**	du schwänz**t**
er	er	er	er	er
sie → reis**t**	sie → hass**t**	sie → heiß**t**	sie → sitz**t**	sie → schwänz**t**
es	es	es	es	es

* **ss** becomes **ß** when following a long vowel or a diphthong, e.g., **ei, au**. (cf. Appendix §1)

Übung 2-4

ANWENDEN Formulate a question with **du** that follows logically from each statement given.

> MODEL: Ich schließe immer meinen Rucksack. Und du?
> <u>Schließt du immer deinen Rucksack?</u>

Marianne ist an einer neuen Schule und lernt eine Klassenkameradin kennen.

1. Ich heiße Marianne. Und du?
2. Ich sitze gern ganz vorne in der ersten Reihe. Und du?
3. Viele Schüler hier schwänzen oft. Und du?
4. Sport hasse ich. Und du?
5. Aber ich tanze gern. Und du?

§4   Verbs with Stem Vowel Changes

Many strong verbs (cf. Kap. 3 §4) change their stem vowels in the second- and third-person singular.

1. Stem vowels that change from **e** to **ie** or **i**

sehen (*to see*)		lesen (*to read*)		essen (*to eat*)		geben (*to give*)		nehmen (*to take*)	
ich	sehe	ich	lese	ich	esse	ich	gebe	ich	nehme
du	**siehst**	du	**liest**	du	**isst**	du	**gibst**	du	**nimmst**
er		er		er		er		er	
sie	→**sieht**	sie	→**liest**	sie	→**isst**	sie	→**gibt**	sie	→**nimmt**
es		es		es		es		es	
wir	sehen	wir	lesen	wir	essen	wir	geben	wir	nehmen
ihr	seht	ihr	lest	ihr	esst	ihr	gebt ·	ihr	nehmt
sie	sehen	sie	lesen	sie	essen	sie	geben	sie	nehmen
Sie	sehen	Sie	lesen	Sie	essen	Sie	geben	Sie	nehmen

The forms **du liest** and **du isst** add **-t**, rather than **-st**, because the stem ends in **s** or **ss**.

2. Stem vowels that change from **a, au, o** to **ä, äu, ö**

fahren (*to drive*)		schlafen (*to sleep*)		laufen (*to run*)		stoßen (*to push*)	
ich	fahre	ich	schlafe	ich	laufe	ich	stoße
du	**fährst**	du	**schläfst**	du	**läufst**	du	**stößt**
er		er		er		er	
sie	→**fährt**	sie	→**schläft**	sie	→**läuft**	sie	→**stößt**
es		es		es		es	
wir	fahren	wir	schlafen	wir	laufen	wir	stoßen
ihr	fahrt	ihr	schlaft	ihr	lauft	ihr	stoßt
sie	fahren	sie	schlafen	sie	laufen	sie	stoßen
Sie	fahren	Sie	schlafen	Sie	laufen	Sie	stoßen

3. Verbs whose stems end in **-d** or **-t** do not add the usual **e** in the second- and third-person singular (e.g., **er red<u>et</u>**) when the vowel changes.

laden (*to load*)		**halten** (*to hold, stop*)		**raten** (*to advise*)		**treten** (*to kick, step*)	
ich	lade	ich	halte	ich	rate	ich	trete
du	**lädst**	du	**hältst**	du	**rätst**	du	**trittst**
er sie → **lädt** es		er sie → **hält** es		er sie → **rät** es		er sie → **tritt** es	
wir	laden	wir	halten	wir	raten	wir	treten
ihr	ladet	ihr	haltet	ihr	ratet	ihr	tretet
sie	laden	sie	halten	sie	raten	sie	treten
Sie	laden	Sie	halten	Sie	raten	Sie	treten

Note that **halten** and **raten**, whose stems end in **-t**, do not add the **-t** ending in the third person singular.

Verbs with a stem change in the singular are listed in this book showing their third-person singular form as follows:

helfen (hilft)	*to help*
sprechen (spricht)	*to speak*
vergessen (vergisst)	*to forget*

§5   Irregular Conjugation of *haben, sein, werden,* and *wissen*

The high frequency verbs **haben, sein, werden,** and **wissen** have irregular conjugation patterns.

haben (*to have*)		**sein** (*to be*)		**werden** (*to become, get*)		**wissen** (*to know*)	
ich	habe	ich	bin	ich	werde	ich	weiß
du	hast	du	bist	du	wirst	du	weißt
er sie → hat es		er sie → ist es		er sie → wird es		er sie → weiß es	
wir	haben	wir	sind	wir	werden	wir	wissen
ihr	habt	ihr	seid	ihr	werdet	ihr	wisst
sie	haben	sie	sind	sie	werden	sie	wissen
Sie	haben	Sie	sind	Sie	werden	Sie	wissen

Vokabulartip: **wissen** *und* **kennen**

The verb **wissen** is used to state knowledge of something as a fact. It is never used to refer to persons.

Ich **weiß** die Adresse von Gerd nicht.	*I don't know Gerd's address.*
Weißt du, wo er wohnt?	*Do you know where he lives?*

Kennen indicates familiarity with something or somebody.

Kennst du diesen Film?	*Do you know this movie?*
Ich **kenne** Berlin gut. Meine Eltern wohnen dort.	*I know Berlin well. My parents live there.*
Mein Bruder **kennt** Erichs Freundin.	*My brother knows Erik's girlfriend.*

Wissen is frequently used to form an introductory clause (**Wissen Sie,...?, Ich weiß,...**). **Kennen** takes only nouns as objects.

Ich **weiß**, dass du Hanna **kennst**.	*I know that you know Hanna.*

Übung 2-5

VERSTEHEN Insert the correct form of **wissen** or **kennen**.

Richard und Walter unterhalten sich über Dagmar. Walter erinnert sich nicht an sie.

1. Richard: _____ du, wo Dagmar wohnt?
   Walter: Dagmar? Ich _____ niemanden mit dem Namen „Dagmar." Wer ist sie?
2. Richard: Ich _____, dass du sie letztes Wochenende kennengelernt hast. Auf Rolands Party.
   Walter: Da waren so viele Leute. Ich kann unmöglich die Namen von allen _____. Frag doch Roland! Er _____ bestimmt alle Leute, die auf seiner Party waren. Vielleicht _____ er die Adresse von dieser Dagmar.
3. Richard: _____ wir nicht Dagmars Zimmerkollegin, Anika? Ich sehe sie oft in der Mensa. Vielleicht frage ich sie einfach.
   Walter: Na, hoffentlich _____ du, was du tust!

Übung 2-6

ANWENDEN Use each of the following verbs to formulate questions and statements that logically follow each other. Be creative!

MODEL: sprechen   →   Sprichst du jede Woche mit deinen Eltern?

Anita möchte wissen, wie ein typischer Tag für ihre Kollegin Hannelore aussieht. Was fragt Anita vielleicht?

1. sein	3. laufen	5. fahren	7. lesen	9. nehmen (Bus, Auto, Fahrrad)
2. haben	4. essen	6. schlafen	8. tragen	

Anita mag ihr Englischseminar nicht. Was sagt sie vielleicht über den Professor, die Studenten und sich selbst?

1. sein	3. schlafen	5. helfen	7. sehen	9. werden
2. sprechen	4. nehmen	6. vergessen	8. haben	10. wissen

§6   Uses of the Present Tense

1. Present time

English has various ways to refer to something that occurs in the present time: the present-tense form, the progressive form, and the emphatic form. German has neither a progressive nor an emphatic form; a single present-tense form in German may therefore have any of three English equivalents.

Sie raucht. — *She smokes.*
She is smoking. (progressive form)
She does smoke. (emphatic form)

The context generally indicates which meaning is applicable. To make clear in German that an action is in progress, an adverb (e.g., **gerade**) may be added, a verb construction with **am** + verb may be used, or the sentence may be introduced with a particular phrase (**Ich bin gerade dabei,...**).

Er kommt **gerade**.	*He is coming this very moment.*
Ich bin **am** Telefonieren.	*I am talking on the phone right now.*
Ich bin gerade dabei einen Brief zu schreiben.	*I am in the process of writing a letter.*

Emphasis may be expressed by intonation or by adding the flavoring particle **doch** (cf. Appendix §4).

Er weiß das **doch**.	*He does know that.*

2. Future time

The present tense often has future meaning. Often, adverbs of time, such as **morgen** (*tomorrow*), **nächste Woche** (*next week*), or **bald** (*soon*), make the future reference clear.

Morgen gehe ich ins Kino.	*Tomorrow I'm going to the movies.*

3. Duration from past to present

The present tense is also used to express a length of time that began in the past and continues into the present. If the duration of time is considered short, the expression **erst** or **erst seit** (*only, just*) is used instead of **schon** or **schon seit** (*already*).

Wie lange lernen Sie **schon** Deutsch?	*How long have you been studying German?*
Schon vier Jahre.	*For four years.*
Wie lange kennen Sie **schon** Herrn Berger?	*How long have you known Mr. Berger?*
Ich kenne ihn **erst** zwei Monate.	*I have only known him for two months.*

Note that, in German, the time element generally precedes the place element.

Wir wohnen schon fünf Jahre in Hamburg.	*We have been living in Hamburg for five years.*
Ich arbeite erst seit April bei Siemens.	*I've only been working at Siemens since April.*

4. Past-time narrative

The present tense may also be used in narratives about events that occurred in the past to achieve a more immediate effect for the listener or reader. This use of the present tense is sometimes referred to as the historical present.

Ich muss dir erzählen, was gestern passiert ist: Kurt **setzt** sich in sein Auto, **fährt** los und **kommt** an die Ampel. Plötzlich **hört** er einen lauten Krach.	*I have to tell you what happened yesterday: Kurt gets in his car, starts driving, and gets to the light. Suddenly he hears a loud bang.*

Übung 2-7

VERSTEHEN Determine whether the sentences refer to the present time, duration from past to present, future time, or past time.

Karin Petri beginnt heute ihre neue Arbeitsstelle in Stuttgart. Beim Mittagessen kommentieren ihre Arbeitskollegen Karins ersten Tag und stellen ihr ein paar Fragen.

1. Und wie läuft Ihr erster Tag?
2. Also, heute Morgen kommt Frau Petri ins Büro, geht zu ihrem Schreibtisch und hat einen wunderschönen Blumenstrauß!
3. Ah, die Blumen sind von Ihrem Mann? Wie lange sind Sie schon verheiratet?
4. Und seit wann wohnen Sie schon in Stuttgart?
5. Liegt Ihre Wohnung in der Innenstadt oder außerhalb?
6. Ach, Sie haben die Wohnung erst seit einem Monat.
7. Kommen Sie am Freitagabend auf die Betriebsfeier?
8. Sie brauchen nach der ersten Woche hier sicher ein freies Wochenende!

Übung 2-8

ZUSAMMENFASSUNG   Uses of the present tense.

A. Express the following note in German. Make sure that the form of address (second-person pronoun) in the note corresponds to the use of the last name.

Susanne Kramers Haushaltshilfe, Frau Wacker, schreibt einen Zettel, bevor sie nach Hause geht.

> *Dear Ms. Kramer,*
>
> *The kids are playing at (**bei**) Marc's and will eat dinner there. I won't come tomorrow. My friend Britta (you know her) is visiting me this week, and we are going for a hike.*
>
> *I am taking the bus home and am leaving the car here. No gas!*
>
> *I'll see you on Thursday. Will you work late?*
>
> *Bye!*
>
> *P.S. You need milk and bread.*

B. State how long you have been doing things. Use **schon** if you think it has been a long time and **erst** if you think it has been a relatively short time.

> MODEL: Auto fahren   →   Ich fahre schon zehn Jahre Auto.

1. in _____ studieren
2. eigene Wohnung oder eigenes Apartment haben
3. einer Sportart nachgehen (Tennis, Fußball, Squash, Volleyball spielen)
4. ein Instrument spielen
5. ein Haustier haben
6. Familie in _____ wohnen
7. Eltern verheiratet sein
8. Auto (Motorrad, Fahrrad) fahren (Bruder, Schwester, Freund)

C. State ten things that you, your friends, and your family members will do in the next few days. Use the present tense with future time expressions.

> MODEL: Morgen mache ich eine Radtour.
> Meine Eltern besuchen am Wochenende Freunde.

Verbs with Prefixes

There are two basic types of verb prefixes: inseparable and separable. As a rule, inseparable prefixes (e.g., **be-**, **ent-**, **ver-**) cannot stand alone and only occur attached to a verb. Separable prefixes can stand alone, often as prepositions (e.g., **aus, an, über**).

§7 Verbs with Inseparable Prefixes

The following prefixes always remain attached to the verb:

be-	bekommen	*to get, receive*
emp-	empfehlen (empfiehlt)	*to recommend*
ent-	entlassen (entlässt)	*to dismiss, fire*
er-	erklären	*to explain*
ge-	gewinnen	*to win*
miss-	missverstehen	*to misunderstand*
ver-	verkaufen	*to sell*
zer-	zerreißen	*to tear up*

These prefixes remain unstressed with the exception of **miss-**, in which the stress varies. It carries the stress in **miss**verstehen, whereas the verb **missachten** (*to disregard*) may be pronounced **miss**achten or **miss**achten.

Vokabulartip: bekommen *und* werden

To express *to get* in the sense of *to receive*, the verb **bekommen** is used.

Martin **bekommt** zum Geburstag einen CD-Spieler.

Martin will get a CD player for his birthday.

To get in the sense of *to become* is rendered with the irregular verb **werden**.

Wir **werden** nicht jünger!

We are not getting younger!

Werden may also be used as an auxiliary verb which, combined with a main verb, expresses future time (cf. Kap. 3, 11).

Übung 2-9

VERSTEHEN Determine which prefixes are most likely separable and which are most likely inseparable. Put them in separate lists.

verlegen, bestehen, einstellen, überarbeiten, vorstellen, zergehen, gestehen, erlauben, empfinden, ausbeuten, vergessen, hervorheben, entführen, berichten, nachdenken, zusammenfassen, erzählen, umstellen, herausfinden

Übung 2-10

ANWENDEN A. Supply the appropriate forms of the verbs given in parentheses.

Karola hat Probleme bei ihrer Arbeit.

1. Mein Chef _____ jede Woche jemanden. (entlassen)
2. Sein Assistent _____ nie, was er erwartet. (erklären)
3. Die Sekretärin _____ mich. (missverstehen)
4. Und dann _____ sie vor meinen Augen ihre Notizen! (zerreißen)
5. Meine Kollegen _____ oft meine Ratschläge. (missachten)
6. Und ich _____ viel zu wenig Geld. (bekommen)
7. Ich _____ echt deprimiert! (werden)

B. Insert the correct form of **bekommen** or **werden**.

Sandra und ihr Freund besprechen einige Dinge, die ihnen Sorgen machen.

1. Warum _____ ich so dick?
2. Ich _____ nie Post von Freunden.
3. Und du _____ viel zu viele Telefonanrufe!
4. Wann _____ das Wetter endlich besser?
5. Und wann _____ eine Frau die Präsidentin der USA?

§8   Verbs with Separable Prefixes

In English, there are a number of verbs that complete or extend their meanings by using additional words, called *complements*.

to give: to give up, give in
to turn: to turn on, turn off, turn down, turn in, turn out

The position of these complements may vary.

    They turned down our offer.
or: They turned our offer down.

In German, such a complement is attached to the front of the infinitive.

nach•geben   *to give in, yield*
auf•geben   *to give up*
an•geben   *to show off, brag*

These complements are called *separable prefixes* because they are separated from the verb under certain conditions. (The dot is not part of the spelling of the infinitive; it is used in this book to identify separable prefixes.) The separable prefix is always accented: <u>nach</u>•geben, <u>auf</u>•geben, <u>an</u>•geben.

§9   Use of Verbs with Separable Prefixes in Main Clauses

The prefix stands last in statements.

a. Peter gibt **an**.   *Peter is showing off.*

b. Peter gibt an.   *Peter is showing off today.*
   heute

c. Peter gibt **an**.   *Peter is showing off today with his new*
                                         *   motorcycle.*
heute mit seinem neuen Motorrad

Sentence a. contains the minimum number of words. The additions in sentences b. and c. are inserted between the verb and the prefix.

The placement of the prefix also applies to questions.

Warum gibt Peter heute so **an**?

The meaning of the separable-prefix verbs is often transparent. The separable prefix, which may also occur as a preposition, narrows the broader meaning of the verb to which it is attached. Note that verbs with prefixes have the same stem changes as their forms without prefixes. Here are some of the common separable-prefix verbs and their meanings:

ab•holen	*to pick up*
ab•nehmen (nimmt ab)	*to decrease; lose weight*
an•fangen (fängt an)	*to begin, start*
an•geben (gibt an)	*to show off, brag; indicate*
an•nehmen (nimmt an)	*to accept, assume*
an•rufen	*to phone, call up*
auf•geben (gibt auf)	*to give up*
auf•hören	*to stop, end, cease*
auf•machen	*to open*
auf•passen	*to pay attention, watch out, keep an eye on*
aus•gehen	*to go out*
aus•sehen (sieht aus)	*to appear, look*
ein•laden (lädt ein)	*to invite*
mit•bringen	*to bring along*
mit•kommen	*to come along*
mit•nehmen (nimmt mit)	*to take along*
nach•geben (gibt nach)	*to give in, yield*
übel•nehmen	*to take offense*
vor•haben	*to plan, have plans*
weiter•lesen (liest weiter)	*to continue reading, go on reading*
weiter•machen	*to continue (doing something)*
weiter•sprechen (spricht weiter)	*to continue talking, go on talking*
zu•hören	*to listen*
zu•machen	*to close*

zu•nehmen (nimmt zu)	*to increase; gain weight*
zurück•bringen	*to bring back*
zurück•fahren (fährt zurück)	*to drive back, return*
zurück•geben (gibt zurück)	*to give back, return*
zurück•gehen	*to go back, return*

Übung 2-11

ANWENDEN A. Insert the correct forms of the separable prefix verbs given in parentheses.

Nikki und Harald besprechen ihre Pläne für eine Feier mit Freunden.

1. Wann _____ die Feier _____? (anfangen)
2. Und _____ wir gegen Mitternacht _____? (aufhören)
3. Wie viele Leute _____ wir _____? (einladen)
4. Hoffentlich _____ Jens ein paar CDs _____! (mitbringen)
5. Klaus _____ es uns bestimmt _____, wenn wir ihn nicht einladen. (übelnehmen)
6. Nikki, ich _____ schnell Anke _____. (anrufen)
7. Anke, _____ du auf unsere Kinder _____? (aufpassen)
8. Wir _____ dich um 18.00 Uhr _____. (abholen)
9. Nikki, wann _____ wir Anke _____? (zurückbringen)
10. Harald, wie _____ mein neues Kleid _____? (aussehen)

B. Guess the meaning of the following prefix verbs. Remember that the prefix often narrows the meaning of the verb or makes its meaning more specific.

1. aufgehen (Sonne), auflegen, aufsetzen
2. ausgraben (graben = *to dig*), austrinken, ausschlafen
3. mitfahren, mitgehen, mitlesen, mitreden
4. vorfahren, vormachen, vorsprechen
5. weiteressen, weiterfahren, weiterspielen
6. zurücklegen, zurückspulen (spulen = *to wind*)

C. Now pick five of the verbs in Übung 2-11 B and make up one sentence with each. Try to insert at least one element between the verb and the prefix.

MODEL: aufsetzen   →   <u>Konrad setzt seinen Hut auf und geht.</u>

§10   Verbs with Separable Prefixes in Dependent Clauses

Compare these two sentences.

Karin **kommt** nicht **mit**.

Es ist schade, dass Karin nicht **mitkommt**.

In dependent clauses, the verb and its prefix (**mitkommen**) stay together and are not separated.

Übung 2-12

ANWENDEN Restate the following sentences, using the given introductory clauses. Instead of repeating the subject in the second sentence, use a pronoun.

> MODEL: Gerd: Markus ruft uns heute Abend an.
> Emma: <u>Ja, es ist möglich, dass er heute Abend anruft.</u>

Gerd und Emma telefonieren miteinander. Emma kommentiert Gerds Mitteilungen. (Nicht immer positiv!)

1. Elke bringt morgen Abend ihren Freund mit.
   Ich glaube nicht, dass...
2. Was meinst du? Gibt Annette mir morgen endlich meine zwanzig Mark zurück?
   Ich hoffe, dass...
3. Hans lädt uns zu seiner Geburtstagsfeier ein.
   Ja, es ist möglich, dass...
4. Margot kommt nicht zum Abendessen. Sie hat heute Abend etwas vor.
   Das ist aber schade, dass...
5. Die Bank macht erst um 18.00 Uhr zu.
   Also, ich weiß nicht, ob...
6. Dieter nimmt alle kritischen Kommentare sehr übel.
   Also, ich verstehe, dass...
7. Aber ich lade Dieter trotzdem zum Abendessen ein!
   Ja? Ich finde es gut, dass...

§11   The Use of *her* and *hin* as Separable Prefixes

To express different directions of motion, the prefixes **her** and **hin** may be used with verbs that suggest motion, e.g., **kommen, gehen, fahren,** and **laufen. Her** suggests motion toward the speaker (*this way, here*), and **hin** suggests motion away from the speaker (*that way, there*).

her•kommen *to come here*

Anke sieht mich. Sie kommt her.

hin•gehen *to go there*

Ich sehe Anke da drüben. Ich gehe hin.

Her most commonly attaches to **kommen; hin** often combines with **gehen, laufen,** and **fahren.** Note how this is illustrated in common questions with **woher** and **wohin.**

Woher kommst du?

Ich komme aus Bern.

Wohin geht ihr heute Abend?

Wir gehen zuerst in die Oper und dann zum Essen.

Her and **hin** may also be combined with other adverbs and prepositions.

herauf•kommen *to come up (here)*
Sie kommt die Treppe herauf.

hinunter•gehen *to go down (there)*
Sie geht die Treppe hinunter.

herein•kommen *to come in (here)*
Warum kommen Sie nicht herein?

hinein•gehen *to go in (there)*
Warum gehen Sie nicht hinein?

Idiom: **Herein!** *Come in.*

In spoken German, however, the rather common abbreviation of these combinations eliminates the contrast between **hin** and **her**.

Die Katze läuft schnell die Treppe 'rauf.
  (herauf)

Max fährt den Berg 'runter.
  (hinunter)

Warum kommt ihr nicht 'rein?
  (herein)

Die Gäste gehen später 'rein.
  (hinein)

Wo...hin? wo...her?

In spoken German, the question words **wohin** and **woher** are often separated: **wo** is placed at the start of the question, while **hin** and **her** are treated as separable prefixes.

Wohin geht Renate?
or: **Wo** geht Renate **hin**? — *Where is Renate going?*

Ich weiß nicht, **wohin** Renate geht.
or: Ich weiß nicht, **wo** Renate **hin**geht. — *I don't know where Renate is going.*

Woher kommt Andreas?
or: **Wo** kommt Andreas **her**? — *Where does Andreas come from?*

Ich weiß nicht, **woher** Andreas kommt.
or: Ich weiß nicht, **wo** Andreas **her**kommt. — *I don't know where Andreas comes from.*

Übung 2-13

ANWENDEN Formulate questions with **woher** and **wohin**.

MODEL: Die Familie Golub kommt aus Usbekistan.
          <u>Wie bitte? **Woher** kommt sie?</u>

Irmgard versteht nicht genau, was ihr Mann Kurt sagt und muss nachfragen.

1. Annette fährt dieses Wochenende nach Amsterdam.
2. Und Erika und ihr Mann Phillip fliegen im August nach Florida.
3. Phillip kommt aus den USA, aus Charleston, glaube ich.
4. Ich gehe noch schnell zum Einkaufen.
5. Und heute Abend gehen wir ins Theater, oder?

§12   Prefixes That Are Used Separably and Inseparably

Some prefixes, such as **durch-**, **über-**, **um-**, and **wieder-**, are used both separably and inseparably with different meanings. The verb with the separable prefix is usually used in its literal sense, whereas its inseparable counterpart often has a figurative meaning.

SEPARABLE	INSEPARABLE

durch-

durch•fahren *to go nonstop*

Der Zug **fährt** bis Hamburg **durch**.
The train runs nonstop through to Hamburg.

durchfahren *to run through, go through*

Ein großer Schreck **durchfährt** die Menge.
A (feeling of) great horror is running through the crowd.

über-

über•setzen *to ferry across*

Hier ist keine Brücke. Ein Boot **setzt** die Leute **hinüber**.
There is no bridge here. A boat ferries the people across.

übersetzen *to translate*

Wie **übersetzt** man das?
How does one translate that?

um-

um•gehen *to go around, circulate*

Dumme Gerüchte **gehen um**.
Silly rumors are circulating.

umgehen *to circumvent, dodge, evade, bypass*

Sie **umgehen** meine Frage.
You are dodging my question.

wieder-

wieder•holen *to (go and) get (something or someone) back, to retrieve*

Die Zeitung ist im Mülleimer. Ich **hole** sie **wieder**.
The newspaper is in the garbage can. I'll (go and) get it back.

wiederholen *to repeat, to review*

Ich **wiederhole** meine Frage.
I repeat my question.
Wir **wiederholen** die Grammatik.
We are reviewing the grammar.

Übung 2-14

ZUSAMMENFASSUNG Separable and inseparable prefix verbs.

A. Supply the appropriate form of each verb in parentheses. Note that only one blank appears whether the prefix is separable or inseparable, although a separable prefix should still be placed at the end of the sentence.

Annette, Fred, und Gabriele sind mit dem Auto unterwegs. Sie werden das Wochenende in Wien verbringen.

1. Annette: Gabi, _____ du an der nächsten Tankstelle? (anhalten)
   Gabriele: Du, wir haben noch genug Benzin. _____ wir bis Wien! (durchfahren)
2. Fred: Gabi, du _____ ganz schön müde. (aussehen). _____ beim Fahren nicht! (einschlafen)
   Annette: Fred, _____ du ein Stück zu fahren? Ich _____ mein Buch. (vorhaben, weiterlesen)
3. Gabi: _____ du immer etwas zum Lesen im Auto? (mitnehmen). Ich _____ das oft. (vergessen)
4. Fred: Gabi, ich _____ dich gerne. (ablösen)
   Gabi: Super! Dein Angebot _____ ich gerne! (annehmen)
5. Annette: Also, wenn wir halten, _____ ich schnell meine Mutti. (anrufen) _____ ihr in die Raststätte? (mitkommen) Ich möchte etwas trinken.
6. Fred: Annette, _____ du für die Getränke? (bezahlen) Ich _____ dir das Geld, (zurückgeben) wenn ich Schillinge _____. (bekommen)

The Imperative

Imperatives express commands, requests, or directives. German has three imperative forms corresponding to the three words **Sie**, **du**, and **ihr** for the second-person pronoun *you*.

Sie-address	Bitte kommen Sie.	
du-address	Komm bitte!	*Please come.*
ihr-address	Bitte kommt.	

Imperative sentences end with a period or an exclamation mark, depending on how strong the emphasis is.

The position of bitte

Bitte may be placed at the beginning or end of an imperative. When at the end, **bitte** is set off by a comma except where the sentence is very short.

Bitte rufen Sie mich an.
Rufen Sie mich an, **bitte**.
Warten Sie **bitte**. Warte **bitte**.

Bitte may also be placed in the middle of a sentence. It generally follows pronoun objects but precedes all other elements.

Rufen Sie mich **bitte** an.
Rufen Sie **bitte** Frau Krause morgen Abend an.

§13   Basic Pattern of the Imperative

1. The formal (**Sie**-address) imperative verb form is identical to the present tense **Sie**-form and uses the same word order as questions. Intonation (and context) distinguish between an imperative and a question. The intonation rises at the end of a question, but not at the end of an imperative.

PRESENT TENSE	IMPERATIVE	
Sie stören	**Stören Sie** mich bitte nicht.	*Don't disturb me, please.*
Sie tun	**Tun Sie** das nicht!	*Don't do that!*
Sie haben	**Haben Sie** keine Angst.	*Don't be afraid.*
Sie rufen an	**Rufen Sie** Herrn Köhler an.	*Call Mr. Köhler.*

2. The familiar singular (**du**-address) imperative consists of the stem of the verb. The pronoun **du** is omitted.

Stör mich nicht, bitte.
Tu das nicht!
Hab keine Angst.
Ruf Herrn Köhler an.

An **-e** is added to stems ending in

a. **-d**, **-t**, or certain consonant clusters (cf. §2)

Bade nicht zu lange!
Arbeite schneller!
Öffne die Tür!

b. **-ig**, as in **erledigen** (*to take care of, settle*) and **beleidigen** (*to insult*).

Erledige das sofort!   *Take care of that immediately.*

Beleidige mich nicht!   *Don't insult me.*

3. The familiar plural (**ihr**-address) imperative is identical to the **ihr**-form of the present tense, except that **ihr** is omitted.

PRESENT TENSE	IMPERATIVE
ihr stört	**Stört** mich nicht!
ihr tut	**Tut** das nicht.
ihr habt	**Habt** keine Angst!
ihr ruft an	**Ruft** Herrn Köhler an!

Übung 2-15

ANWENDEN Supply an appropriate imperative form from the information given.

Frau Wagner passt tagsüber auf die Kinder von Susanne Kramer auf. Sie sagt den Kindern, was sie tun müssen, während sie in der Küche sind. Dabei ruft Frau Kramer von ihrer Arbeit an.

1. Andreas und Matthias, _____. (zum Essen kommen)
2. Andreas, _____! (den Apfel essen)
3. Matthias, _____! (die Milch trinken)
4. Matthias und Andreas, _____. (bitte noch nicht draußen spielen)
5. _____! (zuerst eure Hausaufgaben machen)
6. Hallo, Frau Kramer! _____. (bitte etwas früher nach Hause kommen)
7. Und _____. (bitte Milch und Brot mitbringen)
8. Matthias, _____! (dein Mathematikbuch holen)
9. Andreas, _____! (deinen Schreibblock suchen)
10. Andreas und Matthias, _____! (hier in der Küche bleiben)

§14   The German Equivalent of the English *Let's ...*

Another command form is the **wir**-command, which is used the same way as the English *let's*. The word order is the same as in questions, just like for the **Sie**-command.

Gehen wir nach Hause.	*Let's go home.*
Fangen wir an.	*Let's begin.*
Hören wir auf.	*Let's stop (come to an end).*
or: **Machen wir** Schluss.	
Seien wir doch fair.	*Let's be fair.*

Übung 2-16

ANWENDEN Form appropriate **wir**-commands from the questions that are given.

> MODEL: Wollen wir eine Radtour machen?
> <u>O.K., machen wir morgen eine Radtour.</u>

Angelika und Franziska machen Pläne fürs Wochenende. Angelika macht mehrere Vorschläge.

1. Wollen wir Samstagabend in die Disko gehen?
2. Wollen wir vielleicht Sonja anrufen?
3. Und wollen wir vielleicht Sonntagmorgen irgendwo frühstücken gehen?
4. Wollen wir heute einfach faul sein?
5. Wollen wir heute Abend gemütlich zu Hause bleiben?
6. Wollen wir etwas zusammen kochen?
7. Und wollen wir vielleicht ein Video anschauen?
8. Oder sollen wir jemanden einladen?

The use of doch *or* doch mal *in imperatives*

Doch adds a sense of urgency.

> Ruf **doch** an! Iss **doch** etwas.   *Do call. Do eat something.*

When **doch** is followed by **mal**, the tone is a bit more casual.

> Ruf **doch mal** an!   *Go ahead and call.*

Mal alone adds a sense of impatience.

> Iss **mal**!   *Come on and eat.*

§15   Variations and Irregularities in Imperative Forms

1. The familiar singular form of the imperative has the same stem changes that occur in the present tense singular. Note the imperative forms of verbs with a vowel change from **e** to **i** or **ie**.

helfen (hilft)	Helfen Sie mir!	
	Hilf mir!	*Help me.*
	Helft mir!	
essen (isst)	Essen Sie das nicht!	
	Iss das nicht!	*Don't eat that.*
	Esst das nicht!	
übel•nehmen	Nehmen Sie es nicht übel!	
(nimmt übel)	**Nimm** es nicht übel!	*Don't take offense.*
	Nehmt es nicht übel!	

EXCEPTION

werden (wird)	Werden Sie nicht krank!
	Werde nicht krank! ———> *Don't get sick.*
	Werdet nicht krank!

In this case, the familiar singular form has no vowel change and adds the ending **-e**.

The usual changes in the present tense from a to ä, au to äu, and o to ö do not occur in the imperative.

schlafen (schläft)	**Schlaf** gut.
ein•laden (lädt ein)	**Lade** auch Margot **ein**.
laufen (läuft)	**Lauf** doch nicht so schnell!
stoßen (stößt)	**Stoß** mich doch nicht so!

2. The imperative forms of **sein** (*to be*)

formal	**Seien** Sie still!
familiar singular	**Sei** still! ———> *Be quiet.*
familiar plural	**Seid** still!

In the formal address, the ending **-en** is added to the stem **sei-**.

The familiar plural address ends in **-d**; it is identical to the **ihr-** form of the present tense: **ihr seid**.

Übung 2-17

ANWENDEN A. Formulate familiar imperative forms. Use singular when Daniela appears in parentheses and plural otherwise.

Daniela und ihre Freunde (16 und 17 Jahre alt) machen zusammen eine Wochenendreise nach Berlin. Danielas Eltern geben den Teenagern ein paar Ratschläge.

1. nicht den Führerschein vergessen (Daniela)
2. und nicht zu schnell fahren (Daniela)
3. regelmäßig essen
4. abends nicht zu viel trinken
5. ein bisschen laufen oder wandern
6. uns eine Telefonnummer in Berlin geben (Daniela)
7. vorsichtig sein
8. nicht zu unabhängig werden

B. Supply formal imperative forms.

Der Leiter eines Bekleidungsgeschäfts erklärt einem neuen Angestellten, wie er mit Kunden umgehen soll.

1. immer freundlich sein
2. den Kunden schnell helfen
3. nicht zu viel reden
4. nie ungeduldig werden
5. nur hier stehen und bitte nie sitzen

§16   Using Infinitives

Using an infinitive form without a personal pronoun makes a command less direct. Commonly, but not exclusively, this form occurs in directives to the public. The infinitive is usually placed in the final position of the sentence. However, **bitte** may follow it.

Bitte **weitergehen**!	*Please keep moving.*
(instead of: Bitte gehen Sie weiter!)	
Alle **einsteigen**!	*All aboard!*
(instead of: Bitte steigen Sie ein!)	
Eure Milch **trinken**, bitte!	*Drink your milk, please.*
(instead of: Trinkt bitte eure Milch.)	

Übung 2-18

ZUSAMMENFASSUNG   Imperative forms.

A. Change the following commands to directives using the infinitive.

> MODEL: Schließen Sie bitte die Türen!
> <u>Bitte die Türen schließen!</u>

1. Öffnen Sie bitte nicht die Fenster!
2. Stell bitte den Motor ab!
3. Rufen Sie bitte nicht nach 22 Uhr an!
4. Wascht euch vor dem Essen (die) Hände!
5. Pflückt bitte nicht die Blumen!

B. Supply an appropriate imperative form (singular/plural formal, singular/plural familiar, **wir**-command) for the following situations.

MODEL: Zwei Studenten in Ihrem Kurs kommen immer zu spät.
<u>Kommt bitte pünktlich!</u>
or: <u>Stört nicht immer den Unterricht!</u>

1. Ihre Lehrerin spricht zu leise.
2. Ihr Vater fährt immer zu schnell.
3. Eine Freundin von Ihnen wird sehr schnell ungeduldig.
4. Sie möchten mit Ihrer Mutter einkaufen gehen.
5. Zwei Kinder machen furchtbar viel Lärm.
6. Sie haben eine Autopanne und bitten zwei Fremde um Hilfe.
7. Sie sehen, wie ein Junge einen Hund mit den Füßen tritt.

C. Write five commands a babysitter might give children. Use both singular and plural familiar forms of address.

Themen und Vokabular

Einkaufen, Essen und Getränke

der Geburtstag, -e	birthday
die Geburtstagsfeier, -n	birthday party
das Getränk, -e	beverage, drink
der Käse	cheese
ein•kaufen	to go shopping, to go to the store
der Kuchen, -	cake
die Wurst, ̈e	sausage, cold cuts
die Wurstplatte, -n	cold cut platter

An der Universität

die Betriebswirtschaft	business administration (university subject)
das Examen, -	comprehensive exam
schwänzen	to skip class
das Seminar, -e	seminar, class
der Studienkollege, -n	fellow student (m.)
die Studienkollegin, -nen	fellow student (f.)
das Vorlesungsverzeichnis, -se	course catalog, schedule

Bei der Arbeit

die Arbeitsstelle, -n	job, position
der Betrieb, -e	company, business
die Betriebsfeier, -n	company party

Auf Reisen

das Benzin	gasoline
der Führerschein, -e	driver's license
die Raststätte, -n	highway stop, restaurant
der Schilling, -e	shilling (Austrian currency)
die Tankstelle, -n	gas station

Eigenschaften

freundlich	friendly
unabhängig	independent
ungeduldig	impatient

3 Verbs in the Past and Future Tenses

Introduction

There are six tenses in English.

Present tense	*she sings (is singing, does sing)*

Three past tenses ⟨ Simple past — *she sang (was singing, did sing)*
Present perfect — *she has sung (has been singing)*
Past perfect — *she had sung (had been singing)*

Two future tenses ⟨ Future — *she will sing (will be singing)*
Future perfect — *she will have sung (will have been singing)*

Note that only the present tense (*he asks*) and the simple past tense (*he asked*) are "one-verb" forms. All other tenses involve additional verbal elements, namely the auxiliaries *have* and *will*.

The tenses can be derived from three basic verb forms, the *principal parts* of a verb.

	INFINITIVE	PAST	PAST PARTICIPLE
REGULAR VERB	to ask	asked	has asked
IRREGULAR VERB	to sing	sang	has sung

Ordinarily, the principal parts are stated only for irregular verbs, because the forms of regular verbs are predictable, adding the ending **-ed** in all past tenses (e.g. to play-played-has played) and need not be learned.

As in English, there are six verb tenses in German, but unlike English, German has no progressive or emphatic forms (cf. Kap. 2 §6, 1). German distinguishes between *weak verbs* (corresponding to English regular verbs) and *strong verbs* (corresponding to English irregular verbs). In addition, there is a third group of verbs that fits neither pattern; they are referred to as *irregular verbs*.

The Simple Past and Present Perfect of Weak Verbs

§1   The Simple Past Tense

Formation

To form the simple past tense, personal endings are added to the stem as shown here:

Infinitive: **lachen**	ich	lach**te**	*I*	*laughed*	ich	__**te**
	du	lach**test**	*you*	*laughed*	du	__**test**
	er		*he*		er	
	sie →	lach**te**	*she* →	*laughed*	sie →	__**te**
	es		*it*		es	
	wir	lach**ten**	*we*	*laughed*	wir	__**ten**
	ihr	lach**tet**	*you*	*laughed*	ihr	__**tet**
	sie	lach**ten**	*they*	*laughed*	sie	__**ten**
	Sie	lach**ten**	*you*	*laughed*	Sie	__**ten**

Übung 3-1

VERSTEHEN Indicate which sentences refer to an event in the past and which to an event in the present.

> MODEL: Markus holte seine Freundin ab.   <u>past</u>

1. Klaus glaubt seiner Mutter nicht.
2. Wem erklärte er, wie man das Videogerät bedient?
3. Was sagten Karin und Brigitte über den Kurs?
4. Arbeiten alle Studenten in den Ferien?
5. Fragt ihr, wann das Konzert beginnt?
6. Ich fragte nach dem Weg.

Verbs with stems ending in **-d**, **-t**, or certain consonant clusters (cf. Kap. 2 §2) insert an **e** between the stem and the personal endings.

Infinitive: **antworten**	ich	antwort**ete**	*I*	*answered*	ich	__**ete**
	du	antwort**etest**	*you*	*answered*	du	__**etest**
	er		*he*		er	
	sie →	antwort**ete**	*she* →	*answered*	sie →	__**ete**
	es		*it*		es	
	wir	antwort**eten**	*we*	*answered*	wir	__**eten**
	ihr	antwort**etet**	*you*	*answered*	ihr	__**etet**
	sie	antwort**eten**	*they*	*answered*	sie	__**eten**
	Sie	antwort**eten**	*you*	*answered*	Sie	__**eten**

Übung 3-2

ANWENDEN Insert the simple past tense form of each verb given in parentheses.

Annette schreibt einen Bericht für ihren Chef. Sie hatte mit Arbeitskollegen eine Besprechung über ein Projekt.

1. Wir _____ über das Projekt von 8.00 Uhr bis 15.00 Uhr. (reden)
2. Viele der Anwesenden _____, wie viel es kosten wird. (fragen)
3. Sie _____, das letzte _____ Projekt zu viel. (sagen, kosten)
4. Ich _____, dass einige Kollegen ungeduldig wurden. (merken)
5. Sie _____ auf meine Erklärung. (warten)
6. Ich _____ auf ihre Fragen. (antworten)

Use of the simple past

In German, the simple past tense commonly expresses connected past actions. It is used mainly in written descriptions and narratives and is therefore also called *narrative past*. Thus we might read the following in a report of a meeting:

> "Der Redner **merkte** nicht, dass die Zuhörer **gähnten**. Er **redete** und **redete**. Als er endlich **aufhörte**, **applaudierten** nur seine höflichen Freunde."

> *"The speaker did not notice that the audience was yawning. He talked and talked. When he finally stopped, only his polite friends applauded."*

§2   The Present Perfect Tense

The basic difference between the English and German use of the present perfect

Compare the following two sentences.

> I **paid** the bill yesterday.

> I **haven't paid** the bill yet.

The first sentence expresses an act completed at a point in time in the past, i.e., yesterday. There is no relation to the present; the simple past is used. The second sentence relates to the present and is expressed in the present perfect.

The German equivalents of the two sentences above are:

> Ich **habe** die Rechnung gestern **bezahlt**.

> Ich **habe** die Rechnung noch nicht **bezahlt**.

In contrast to its English equivalent, the first sentence is in the present perfect tense. As mentioned in §1, in German the simple past is also called *narrative past*, because it mainly occurs in written descriptions and narratives. Not being part of a narrative, the sentence is expressed in the *conversational past*, i.e., the present perfect, which is commonly used in spoken German and informal writing, such as in notes, personal letters, and diaries.

As the following examples illustrate, sentences in the present perfect used as conversational past are rendered into English by the simple past tense.

Was **hast** du gestern **gemacht**?
*What **did** you **do** yesterday?*

Ich **habe** Tennis **gespielt**.
*I **played** tennis.*

Am Samstag **hat** mich mein Freund **abgeholt**. Wir **haben** Geschenke für den Muttertag **gekauft**. Dann **haben** wir einen lustigen Film in einem kleinen Kino **gesehen**.

*On Saturday, my friend **picked** me up. We **bought** presents for Mother's Day. Then we **saw** a funny film in a small movie house.*

Formation of the present perfect

The present perfect is formed with an auxiliary verb (in most cases, **haben**; otherwise, **sein**) and the past participle of the main verb.

Infinitive: **fragen**   Conjugation:

ich	**habe** gefragt
du	**hast** gefragt
er sie	**hat** gefragt
es	
wir	**haben** gefragt
ihr	**habt** gefragt
sie	**haben** gefragt
Sie	**haben** gefragt

The auxiliary verb **haben** is always in agreement with its subject. **Haben** is used with any verb that is *transitive*, meaning that it can take a direct object. The past participle **gefragt** remains unchanged, positioned at the end of the sentence. It is formed as follows:

1. The prefix **ge-** and the ending **-t** are added to the stem of the verb.

lernen	**hat gelernt**	fragen	**hat gefragt**
lachen	**hat gelacht**	lächeln	**hat gelächelt**

2. With past participles, verbs whose stems end in **-d**, **-t**, or certain consonant clusters add **-et** to the stem.

antworten	**hat geantwortet**	öffnen	**hat geöffnet**
kosten	**hat gekostet**	reden	**hat geredet**

3. No **ge-** is added to

a. Verbs that end in **-ieren**

studieren	**hat studiert**	telefonieren	**hat telefoniert**

b. Verbs with inseparable prefixes (cf. Kap. 2 §7)

versuchen	**hat versucht**	beleidigen	**hat beleidigt**

4. Verbs with separable prefixes insert **ge-** between the prefix and stem.

auf•räumen	**hat aufgeräumt**
aus•lachen	**hat ausgelacht**
zu•hören	**hat zugehört**

Übung 3-3

VERSTEHEN State the past participles of the following verbs.

1. lachen	9. antworten	17. versuchen	25. auf•räumen
2. aus•lachen	10. arbeiten	18. verdienen	26. irritieren
3. machen	11. mieten	19. kaufen	27. lächeln
4. auf•machen	12. heiraten	20. verkaufen	28. auf•hören
5. zu•machen	13. studieren	21. schenken	29. bewundern
6. hören	14. studieren	22. schneien	30. beneiden
7. zu•hören	15. ignorieren	23. reden	31. gähnen → to yawn
8. holen	16. beleidigen	24. regnen	32. stören

Word order in main clauses

In main clauses, **haben** occupies the position of the inflected verb; the past participle is in final position.

STATEMENT:	SUBJECT-VERB ORDER	Du glaubst das nicht.
		Du **hast** das nicht **geglaubt**.
	INVERTED WORD ORDER	Natürlich glaubst du das nicht.
		Natürlich **hast** du das nicht **geglaubt**.
QUESTION:	WITHOUT A QUESTION WORD	Glaubst du das nicht?
		Hast du das nicht **geglaubt**?
	WITH A QUESTION WORD	Warum glaubst du das nicht?
		Warum **hast** du das nicht **geglaubt**?

Vokabulartip: Begriffe für Gegenwart und Vergangenheit

Time expressions, along with contextual clues, help situate an event in the present, past, or future (cf. §11).

Following are some common present and past time expressions:

heute	*today*	schon	*already*
gestern / vorgestern	*yesterday / the day before yesterday*	gerade	*just*
früher	*in the past*	vorher	*earlier, before*
heute / gestern Morgen	*this / yesterday morning*	diese / letzte Woche	*this / last week*

heute / gestern	*this / yesterday*	dieses / letztes	*this / last year*
Nachmittag	*afternoon*	Jahr	

Übung 3-4

ANWENDEN A. Form sentences with subject-verb order and with inverted word order in the present perfect. Start each sentence with the words given for first position.

Erich spricht mit seiner Kollegin, Angelika, und seiner Chefin, Frau Kern, im Büro.

> MODEL: Erich: Frau Arendt / heute Morgen / anrufen
> <u>Frau Arendt hat heute Morgen angerufen.</u>
>
> Frau Kern: Gestern / sie / mit mir / telefonieren
> <u>Gestern hat sie mit mir telefoniert.</u>

1. Erich: ich / Frau Arendts Kommentare / ignorieren
   Angelika: wahrscheinlich / du / Frau Arendt / beleidigen
2. Frau Kern: Herr Roth / auf meine E-mail / nicht / antworten
   Erich: leider / er / die Aktien / schon / verkaufen
3. Frau Kern: wir / wenig / dabei / verdienen
   Erich: natürlich / er / eine Menge Geld / machen
4. Angelika: Frau Kern, Sie / gestern / mit Herrn Lenk / reden
   Frau Kern: hoffentlich / meine Ratschläge / nicht / ignorieren
5. Erich: Ich / die Rechnungen / heute Morgen / bezahlen
   Angelika: gestern / Herr Zimmer / seinen Scheck / abholen

B. Form two questions in the present perfect tense, the first, a general question, the second, a specific question using the question word indicated in parentheses. Address the questions to the persons indicated in parentheses.

Daniela ist furchtbar vergesslich. Sie fragt verschiedene Leute, ob sie bestimmte Dinge schon gemacht haben.

> MODEL: ihr / für die Prüfung / lernen? (Nina und Franz; wann)
> <u>Nina und Franz, habt ihr für die Prüfung gelernt?</u>
> <u>Und wann habt ihr für die Prüfung gelernt?</u>

1. du / Margot / abholen? (Erika; wo)
2. es / gestern / regnen? (Sabine; wie lange)
3. ihr / den Strafzettel / bezahlen? (Mutti und Papi; wie viel)
4. wir / Margot / ein Geburtstagsgeschenk kaufen? (Daniela und Sabine; wo)
5. ich / dich / letzte Woche / anrufen? (Ingo; warum)

Use of the auxiliary **sein** *instead of* **haben**

Sabine **ist** durch ganz Europa **gereist**.
Sabine has traveled through all of Europe.
or: *Sabine traveled through all of Europe.*

Intransitive verbs, namely, verbs that do not take an accusative object, use the auxiliary **sein** instead of **haben**. Often these are verbs of motion.

gehen / **ist gegangen**	laufen / **ist gelaufen**	folgen / **ist gefolgt**
fahren / **ist gefahren**	rennen / **ist gerannt**	kommen / **ist gekommen**
fliegen / **ist geflogen**	wandern / **ist gewandert**	schwimmen / **ist geschwommen**
starten / **ist gestartet**	reisen / **ist gereist**	segeln / **ist gesegelt**
landen / **ist gelandet**	passieren / **ist passiert**	

The weak verbs, which are underlined, are conjugated like **reisen**, the example below. The other verbs listed are strong verbs. Their conjugation will be shown in §4.

ich	**bin** gereist	*I have traveled*	wir	**sind** gereist	*we have traveled*
du	**bist** gereist	*you have traveled*	ihr	**seid** gereist	*you have traveled*
er		*he*	sie	**sind** gereist	*they have traveled*
sie →	**ist** gereist	*she → has traveled*	Sie	**sind** gereist	*you have traveled*
es		*it*			

Some of the verbs may also be used transitively, i.e., with a direct object. They then use **haben** instead of **sein** to form the present perfect.

Der Pilot **hat** das Flugzeug sicher **gelandet**.   *The pilot landed the plane safely.*

Übung 3-5

VERSTEHEN Determine which sentences are transitive and which are intransitive.

1. Gerd hat seiner Mutter ein Buch gekauft.
2. Sind Sabine und Frank viel gereist?
3. Meine Familie hat in Rostock gewohnt.
4. Hat Kurt seinen Wagen immer so schnell gefahren?
5. Das Flugzeug ist um 17 Uhr 20 gelandet.
6. Hast du meinen Freund da drüben gesehen?
7. Wann ist Helga nach Hause gekommen?

Übung 3-6

ANWENDEN Form sentences in the present perfect.

MODEL: das Flugzeug / in Düsseldorf / starten
          Das Flugzeug ist in Düsseldorf gestartet.

Angela erzählt ihren Freunden von ihrer Reise.

1. das Flugzeug / in Zürich / landen
2. dann / ich / durch die Schweiz / reisen
3. meine Eltern / später / folgen
4. wir / zusammen / in Österreich / wandern
5. zu Hause / nichts Besonderes / passieren

Dependent word order

Compare these two sentences.

> Sie **hat** die Wahrheit **gesagt**.

> Ich nehme an, dass sie die Wahrheit **gesagt hat**.

As the inflected verb, the auxiliary is in last position in the dependent clause. It is preceded by the past participle.

Übung 3-7

ANWENDEN Restate the sentences, using the introductory clauses provided.

1. Sind die Baumanns durch ganz Europa gereist?
   Ja, ich glaube, dass...
2. Haben sie ein Auto gemietet?
   Ich bin sicher, dass...
3. Ist etwas bei der Autofahrt passiert?
   Ich habe keine Ahnung, ob…
4. Haben sie viel für das Hotel bezahlt?
   Ja, ich bin überzeugt, dass…
5. Hat die Tochter von Baumanns Geschenke gekauft?
   Ich weiß nicht, ob...
6. Hat es während der Reise geregnet?
   Ich hoffe, dass... (nicht)

§3 Patterns for Word Order in the Present Perfect Tense

The patterns stated in Kapitel 1 §6, may be applied to sentences in the present perfect tense.

		INFLECTED VERB		UNINFLECTED VERB
a. Subject-Verb Order	Helga	ist	nach Italien	gefahren.
b. Inverted Word Order				
STATEMENT	Heute	ist	Helga nach Italien	gefahren.
DIRECT QUESTION				
WITH QUESTION WORD	Wann	ist	Helga nach Italien	gefahren?
WITHOUT QUESTION WORD		Ist	Helga nach Italien	gefahren?

The inflected verb is in the second position in a statement and in the first position in a question. The uninflected verb (past participle) is always in final position.

c. Dependent Word Order

		UNINFLECTED VERB	INFLECTED VERB
STATEMENT	Es ist schön, dass Helga nach Italien	gefahren	ist.
INDIRECT QUESTION	Ich weiß nicht, wann Helga nach Italien	gefahren	ist.
DIRECT QUESTION	Weißt du, ob Helga nach Italien	gefahren	ist?

The inflected verb is in last position; it is directly preceded by the uninflected verb.

The Simple Past and Present Perfect of Strong Verbs

§4   The Principal Parts of Strong Verbs

As in English, all tenses can be derived from three basic verb forms called "principal parts." They are the infinitive, the simple past, and the past participle.

Compare the following sentences.

	WEAK VERBS	STRONG VERBS
PRESENT	Barbara **lernt** Deutsch.	Der Tenor **singt** gut.
SIMPLE PAST	Barbara **lernte** Deutsch.	Der Tenor **sang** gut.
PAST PARTICIPLE	Barbara **hat** Deutsch **gelernt**.	Der Tenor **hat** gut **gesungen**.

PRINCIPAL PARTS

lernen	**lernte**	**gelernt**
	-**te** ENDING	-**t** ENDING

The verb stem remains unchanged.

PRINCIPAL PARTS

singen	**sang**	**gesungen**
	NO ENDING	-**en** ENDING

The stem vowel changes.

The principal parts of strong verbs are not predictable. They have to be learned. The strong verbs are divided into seven classes according to their vowel changes. It is helpful to learn the principal parts of strong verbs together with other verbs of the same class. The following table lists some common examples of each class. A more complete listing (in alphabetical order) appears in Appendix §2. **Ist** before a past participle indicates that the auxiliary **sein** is required; **hat** indicates that the auxiliary **haben** is required.

CLASS	STEM VOWELS	INFINITIVE	SIMPLE PAST	PAST PARTICIPLE	MEANING
I	ei – ie – ie	bleiben	blieb	ist geblieben	*to stay, remain*
		schreiben	schrieb	hat geschrieben	*to write*
		steigen	stieg	ist gestiegen	*to climb, go up*
		ein•steigen	stieg ein	ist eingestiegen	*to climb in, get on, get aboard*

CLASS	STEM VOWELS	INFINITIVE	SIMPLE PAST	PAST PARTICIPLE	MEANING
		aus•steigen	stieg aus	ist ausgestiegen	*to get off, exit a vehicle*
	ei – i – i	reiten	ritt	ist geritten	*to ride, go on horseback*
II	ie – o – o	fliegen	flog	ist geflogen	*to fly*
		verlieren	verlor	hat verloren	*to lose*
	e – o – o	heben	hob	hat gehoben	*to raise, lift*
III	i – a – u	finden	fand	hat gefunden	*to find*
		singen	sang	hat gesungen	*to sing*
		trinken	trank	hat getrunken	*to drink*
	i – a – o	beginnen	begann	hat begonnen	*to begin*
		gewinnen	gewann	hat gewonnen	*to win*
IV	e – a – o	brechen (bricht)	brach	hat gebrochen	*to break*
		unterbrechen (unterbricht)	unterbrach	hat unterbrochen	*to interrupt*
		helfen (hilft)	half	hat geholfen	*to help*
		nehmen (nimmt)	nahm	hat genommen	*to take*
		ab•nehmen (nimmt ab)	nahm ab	hat abgenommen	*to decrease; lose weight*
		zu•nehmen (nimmt zu)	nahm zu	hat zugenommen	*to increase; gain weight*
		übel•nehmen (nimmt übel)	nahm übel	hat übelgenommen	*to take amiss, take offense, resent*
		sprechen (spricht)	sprach	hat gesprochen	*to speak*
		versprechen (verspricht)	versprach	hat versprochen	*to promise*
		sterben (stirbt)	starb	ist gestorben	*to die*
V	e – a – e	essen (isst)	aß	hat gegessen	*to eat*
		vergessen (vergisst)	vergaß	hat vergessen	*to forget*
		geben (gibt)	gab	hat gegeben	*to give*
		auf•geben (gibt auf)	gab auf	hat aufgegeben	*to give up*
		nach•geben (gibt nach)	gab nach	hat nachgegeben	*to give in*
		lesen (liest)	las	hat gelesen	*to read*
		vor•lesen (liest vor)	las vor	hat vorgelesen	*to read aloud*
		sehen (sieht)	sah	hat gesehen	*to see*
	i – a – e	bitten	bat	hat gebeten	*to ask for, request*
		sitzen	saß	hat gesessen	*to sit*
	ie – a – e	liegen	lag	hat gelegen	*to lie, be situated*
VI	a – u – a	fahren (fährt)	fuhr	ist gefahren	*to drive, go (by locomotion)*
		mit•fahren (fährt mit)	fuhr mit	ist mitgefahren	*to ride with (someone)*

CLASS	STEM VOWELS	INFINITIVE	SIMPLE PAST	PAST PARTICIPLE	MEANING
		laden (lädt)	lud	hat geladen	*to load*
		ein•laden (lädt ein)	lud ein	hat eingeladen	*to invite*
		tragen (trägt)	trug	hat getragen	*to carry*
VII	a – ie –a	fallen (fällt)	fiel	ist gefallen	*to fall*
		durch•fallen (fällt durch)	fiel durch	ist durchgefallen	*to fall through, flunk (exam)*
		gefallen (gefällt)	gefiel	hat gefallen	*to please, like*
		halten (hält)	hielt	hat gehalten	*to hold, stop*
		lassen (lässt)	ließ	hat gelassen	*to let, leave*
		schlafen (schläft)	schlief	hat geschlafen	*to sleep*
		ein•schlafen (schläft ein)	schlief ein	ist eingeschlafen	*to fall asleep*
	au – ie – au	laufen (läuft)	lief	ist gelaufen	*to run, walk*
	ei – ie – ei	heißen	hieß	hat geheißen	*to be named*
	u – ie – u	rufen	rief	hat gerufen	*to call, shout*
		an•rufen	rief an	hat angerufen	*to phone*
	o – ie – o	stoßen (stößt)	stieß	hat gestoßen	*to push*
	a – i – a	fangen (fängt)	fing	hat gefangen	*to catch*
		an•fangen (fängt an)	fing an	hat angefangen	*to begin, start*

All verbs in this class change the stem vowel to **ie** or **i** in the simple past. The past participle retains the stem vowel.

Some common verbs that do not fit into any of the seven classes are:

INFINITIVE	SIMPLE PAST	PAST PARTICIPLE	MEANING
tun	tat	hat getan	*to do*
stehen	stand	hat gestanden	*to stand*
auf•stehen	stand auf	ist aufgestanden	*to rise, get up*
bestehen	bestand	hat bestanden	*to pass (exam)*
verstehen	verstand	hat verstanden	*to understand*
gehen	ging	ist gegangen	*to go*
spazieren gehen	ging spazieren	ist spazierengegangen	*to go for a walk*
kommen	kam	ist gekommen	*to come*
mit•kommen	kam mit	ist mitgekommen	*to come along, join*
bekommen	bekam	hat bekommen	*to receive, get*

§5 Verbs Requiring the Auxiliary *sein*

Verbs requiring the auxiliary **sein** are *intransitive*, they do not take an accusative object, and denote a change of location (**gehen, fahren, kommen, reisen, wandern**) or a condition (**ein•schlafen, sterben, explodieren, platzen** [*to burst*]). There are exceptions to this, the most common of which are **bleiben** (*to stay, remain*) and **sein** (*to be* [cf. §9b]), which take the auxiliary **sein** despite their meanings.

§6 The Simple Past Tense of Strong Verbs

Personal endings are added to the stem of the simple past (the second principal part).

sprechen (spricht) - sprach - hat gesprochen

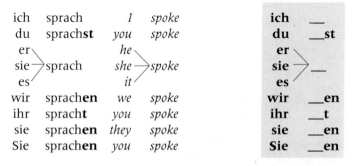

ich	sprach	*I*	*spoke*		ich	__
du	sprach**st**	*you*	*spoke*		du	__st
er		*he*			er	
sie	sprach	*she*	spoke		sie	__
es		*it*			es	
wir	sprach**en**	*we*	*spoke*		wir	__en
ihr	sprach**t**	*you*	*spoke*		ihr	__t
sie	sprach**en**	*they*	*spoke*		sie	__en
Sie	sprach**en**	*you*	*spoke*		Sie	__en

Note that the first- and third-person singular have no personal endings. When the stem ends in **d, t, s, ss**, or **ß**, an **e** is inserted in the **du** and **ihr** forms.

ich fand	ich hielt	ich ließ
du fand**est**	du hielt**est**	du ließ**est**
ihr fand**et**	ihr hielt**et**	ihr ließ**et**
		or: ließt (**e** is usually omitted in the **ihr**-form after **ß/s**)

§7 The Present Perfect Tense of Strong Verbs

The auxiliaries **haben** and **sein** are conjugated; the past participle does not change.

ich	**habe** gesprochen		ich	**bin** gefahren
du	**hast** gesprochen		du	**bist** gefahren
er			er	
sie	**hat** gesprochen		sie	**ist** gefahren
es			es	
wir	**haben** gesprochen		wir	**sind** gefahren
ihr	**habt** gesprochen		ihr	**seid** gefahren
sie	**haben** gesprochen		sie	**sind** gefahren
Sie	**haben** gesprochen		Sie	**sind** gefahren

Übung 3-8

VERSTEHEN A. First, study the simple past tense forms of the verbs in classes I, II, III, and IV; then, give the infinitive form of each underlined verb.

>MODEL: Mein Nachbar <u>half</u> mir die Tür zu öffnen.   <u>helfen</u>

1. Der Redner <u>sprach</u> zu schnell.
2. Ein Student <u>unterbrach</u> den Redner.
3. Sabine <u>blieb</u> zu Hause.
4. Das Konzert <u>begann</u> um 20 Uhr.
5. Ich <u>fand</u> den Film todlangweilig.
6. Warum <u>hob</u> Dieter die Hand?
7. Er <u>schrieb</u> keinen einzigen Brief aus Venedig.
8. Er <u>sang</u> ein Lied für die Kinder.
9. Wir <u>ritten</u> jeden Sonntag durch den Wald.
10. Familie Baumann <u>flog</u> nach Rom.
11. Corinna <u>stieg</u> schnell in den Bus.
12. Anke <u>nahm</u> in den Ferien zehn Kilo <u>zu</u>.
13. Bayern München <u>gewann</u> das Spiel.
14. Ajax Asterdam <u>verlor</u> das Spiel.

B. Now, give the past participle of each underlined verb in the sentences you have just read.

Übung 3-9

VERSTEHEN A. First, study the simple past tense forms of the verbs in classes V, VI, and VII, and of the verbs that do not fit in the seven classes; then, give the infinitive form of each underlined verb.

1. Ich <u>ging</u> immer zu Fuß zur Uni.
2. Mein Bruder <u>kam</u> nie <u>mit</u>.
3. Monika <u>bekam</u> eine Postkarte.
4. Niemand <u>verstand</u> die Vorlesung.
5. Das <u>tat</u> mir leid.
6. Klaus <u>stand</u> am Fenster.
7. Der Film <u>gefiel</u> meinen Eltern nicht.
8. Das Baby <u>schlief</u> bald <u>ein</u>.
9. Das Fußballspiel <u>fing</u> um 15 Uhr <u>an</u>.
10. Klaus <u>rief</u> seine Freundin <u>an</u>.
11. Wir <u>ließen</u> das Gepäck im Auto.
12. <u>Lief</u> er zur Uni?
13. Der Bus <u>hielt</u> an der Ecke.
14. Er <u>aß</u> alles.
15. Helga <u>fuhr</u> <u>mit</u>.

B. Now give the past participle of each underlined verb in the sentences you have just read.

Übung 3-10

ANWENDEN Formulate a statement or question with the introductory clause indicated in parentheses and the dependent clause in the present perfect.

> MODEL: ich / Prüfung / nicht bestehen   (ich fürchte, dass)
> <u>Ich fürchte, dass ich die Prüfung nicht bestanden habe.</u>

Anke und ihr Freund, Kurt, sprechen über die vergangene Woche. Anke kommentiert und stellt Fragen.

1. ich / meinen Schlüssel / verlieren   (weißt du, dass)
2. wir / letzte Woche / Auto waschen   (weißt du noch, ob)
3. mein Vater / uns / helfen   (es ist toll, dass)
4. Brigitte und Roland / einen Brief / schreiben   (denkst du, dass)
5. Annette / so viel / zunehmen   (schade, dass)
6. ich / Professor Goetz / im Kino / sehen   (ich bin sicher, dass)
7. Erich / einen Job / finden   (weißt du, ob)
8. Natalie / uns / nicht / einladen   (verstehst du, warum)
9. Rosi / heute morgen / anrufen   (kannst du mir sagen, ob)
10. du / unsere Verabredung / vergessen   (ich finde es nicht gut, dass)

The Simple Past and Present Perfect of Irregular Verbs

§8   Mixed Verbs

A small group of verbs have the endings of weak verbs but the vowel change of strong verbs. They are, therefore, often referred to as *mixed verbs*. Their principal parts are listed below.

INFINITIVE	SIMPLE PAST	PAST PARTICIPLE	MEANING
brennen	brannte	hat gebrannt	*to burn, be on fire*
bringen	bra<u>ch</u>te	hat gebra<u>ch</u>t	*to bring*
denken	da<u>ch</u>te	hat geda<u>ch</u>t	*to think*
kennen	kannte	hat gekannt	*to know, be familiar with*
nennen	nannte	hat genannt	*to call, name*
rennen	rannte	ist gerannt	*to run*
senden	sandte	hat gesandt	*to send*
(rarely used)	sendete	hat gesendet	
wenden	wandte	hat gewandt	*to turn*
(rarely used)	wendete	hat gewendet	
wissen (weiß)	wusste	hat gewußt	*to know (a fact)*

Note that **bringen** and **denken** also change consonants in the simple past and past participle.

§9   Irregular Forms of *haben, sein,* and *werden*

1. The principal parts of **haben** are **haben - hatte - hat gehabt**.

Note the slight irregularity in the simple past tense.

PRESENT				SIMPLE PAST				PRESENT PERFECT			
ich	habe	*I*	*have*	ich	hatte	*I*	*had*	ich	habe gehabt	*I*	*have had*
du	hast	*you*	*have*	du	hattest	*you*	*had*	du	hast gehabt	*you*	*have had*
er		*he*		er		*he*		er		*he*	
sie	hat	*she*	*has*	sie	hatte	*she*	*had*	sie	hat gehabt	*she*	*has had*
es		*it*		es		*it*		es		*it*	
wir	haben	*we*	*have*	wir	hatten	*we*	*had*	wir	haben gehabt	*we*	*have had*
ihr	habt	*you*	*have*	ihr	hattet	*you*	*had*	ihr	habt gehabt	*you*	*have had*
sie	haben	*they*	*have*	sie	hatten	*they*	*had*	sie	haben gehabt	*they*	*have had*
Sie	haben	*you*	*have*	Sie	hatten	*you*	*had*	Sie	haben gehabt	*you*	*have had*

Remember: er **hat**   *he has*   er **hatte**   *he had*

2. The principal parts of **sein** are **sein - war - ist gewesen**.

Sein is a highly irregular verb.

PRESENT				SIMPLE PAST				PRESENT PERFECT			
ich	bin	*I*	*am*	ich	war	*I*	*was*	ich	bin gewesen	*I*	*have been*
du	bist	*you*	*are*	du	warst	*you*	*were*	du	bist gewesen	*you*	*have been*
er		*he*	*is*	er		*he*		er		*he*	
sie	ist	*she*	*is*	sie	war	*she*	*was*	sie	ist gewesen	*she*	*has been*
es		*it*	*is*	es		*it*		es		*it*	
wir	sind	*we*	*are*	wir	waren	*we*	*were*	wir	sind gewesen	*we*	*have been*
ihr	seid	*you*	*are*	ihr	wart	*you*	*were*	ihr	seid gewesen	*you*	*have been*
sie	sind	*they*	*are*	sie	waren	*they*	*were*	sie	sind gewesen	*they*	*have been*
Sie	sind	*you*	*are*	Sie	waren	*you*	*were*	Sie	sind gewesen	*you*	*have been*

3. The principal parts of **werden** are **werden (wird) - wurde - ist geworden**.

Note that **werden** has an **-e** ending in the first-person and third-person singular of the simple past.

PRESENT				SIMPLE PAST				PRESENT PERFECT			
ich	werde	*I*	*become*	ich	wurde	*I*	*became*	ich	bin geworden	*I*	*have become*
du	wirst	*you*	*become*	du	wurdest	*you*	*became*	du	bist geworden	*you*	*have become*
er		*he*		er		*he*		er		*he*	
sie	wird	*she*	*becomes*	sie	wurde	*she*	*became*	sie	ist geworden	*she*	*has become*
es		*it*		es		*it*		es		*it*	
wir	werden	*we*	*become*	wir	wurden	*we*	*became*	wir	sind geworden	*we*	*have become*
ihr	werdet	*you*	*become*	ihr	wurdet	*you*	*became*	ihr	seid geworden	*you*	*have become*
sie	werden	*they*	*become*	sie	wurden	*they*	*became*	sie	sind geworden	*they*	*have become*
Sie	werden	*you*	*become*	Sie	wurden	*you*	*became*	Sie	sind geworden	*you*	*have become*

Übung 3-11

VERSTEHEN Indicate which sentences are in the present and which are in the past tense.

1. Ich wurde schnell müde.
2. Frank hatte immer recht.
3. Wir haben keine Zeit.
4. Ich dachte an alles.
5. Wusstest du seinen Namen?
6. Er rannte ins Haus.
7. Das Licht brennt den ganzen Tag.
8. Sie kannten die Stadt nicht.

Übung 3-12

ANWENDEN Provide an appropriate verb in the simple past tense form for each blank in the letter below. Use each verb from the list only once.

Frau Rütli schreibt einen Brief an ihre Enkeltochter Konstanze. Konstanze studiert dieses Jahr in den USA.

bekommen, freuen, haben, lesen, kennen, kommen, sein, sitzen, denken, sagen, bleiben, fahren

Bern, den 25. September 1998

Liebe Konstanze!

Ich _____ mich so sehr, als ich gestern deinen Brief aus Berkeley 2_____. Wir alle _3_ sehr neugierig und wollten hören, wie deine erste Woche in Berkeley verlaufen ist. Am Abend ___4___ ich dann gemütlich auf meiner Couch und ___5___ deinen Brief ganz in Ruhe. Schön, dass du schon ein paar nette Leute kennengelernt hast! ___6___ du einige schon von der Uni in Bremen?

Gestern ___7___ deine Mutter zu mir und sie _____ mir, dass sie dich im Frühjahr besuchen kommt. Finde ich ganz wunderbar! Ich ___9___ mir schon, dass sie dich unbedingt sehen möchte. Weißt du, früher ___10___ deine Eltern oft zusammen ins Ausland, während ich zu Hause bei den Enkelkindern ___11___. Wir ___12___ immer viel Spaß zusammen!

Schreib mir, wenn du Zeit hast, und weiterhin viel Erfolg!

Ganz liebe Grüße und eine feste Umarmung,

deine Oma

The use of the simple past tense of strong and irregular verbs

In conversational German, contrary to the general practice of using the present perfect to refer to past events, a few strong verbs also occur in the simple past more frequently. They are **geben** (**gab**), **gehen** (**ging**), (**mit- / zurück- / an-**)**kommen** (**kam**), **bekommen** (**bekam**), **finden** (**fand**), **liegen** (**lag**), **denken** (**dachte**), and **wissen** (**wusste**).

Similarly, sentences with **sein** or **haben** as the main verb frequently use the simple past.

Habt ihr gestern Karten gespielt?	Nein, wir waren im Kino.
Ist Rainer auch mitgekommen?	Nein, er hatte keine Zeit.

Übung 3-13

ANWENDEN This exercise provides practice in using the verbs that most commonly occur in the simple past tense in spoken German. Insert the simple past tense form of the verb given in parentheses.

Susanne fragt ihre Großmutter über Ereignisse in der Vergangenheit.

1. Wann _____ der Opa nach Russland? (gehen)
2. Weißt du, wann er wieder _____? (zurückkommen)
3. Und wann _____ Papa seine Arbeit in Berlin? (bekommen)
4. _____ es da schon die Mauer? (geben)
5. Wo _____ eure Wohnung in Berlin? (liegen)
6. _____ ihr die Stadt schön? (finden)
7. Das _____ ich überhapt nicht. (wissen)

Übung 3-14

ANWENDEN Give an appropriate response to each question. Use the simple past tense when the verb is underlined and the present perfect otherwise. Include the time expressions given in parentheses.

MODEL: Kommt Sabine heute zurück?   (gestern)
         Nein, sie ist gestern zurückgekommen.
         Sind die Ritters jetzt beim Arzt?   (vorher)
         Nein, sie waren vorher beim Arzt.

Thomas (5 Jahre alt) hat vergessen, welche Ereignisse schon stattgefunden haben. Seine Mutter beantwortet seine Fragen.

1. Fangen die Sommerferien nächsten Montag an?   (letzten Montag)
2. Fliegen wir diesen Sommer in die USA?   (letzten Sommer)
3. Trinkst du einen Kaffee?   (heute Morgen)
4. Schläfst du ein bisschen?   (schon)
5. Rufst du den Papa heute Abend an?   (gestern Abend)
6. Essen wir ein paar Kekse?   (gerade)
7. Haben Oma und Opa diese Woche Besuch?   (letzte Woche)
8. Kommt heute Nachmittag „Der König der Löwen"
   im Fernsehen?   (gestern Nachmittag)
9. Verliert Michael oft sein Basketballspiel?   (nur letzten Sonntag)
10. Nimmst du zehn Kilo zu?   (abnehmen!)

The Past Perfect, Future, and Future Perfect of Weak, Strong, and Irregular Verbs

§10   The Past Perfect Tense

The past perfect expresses a past event that occurred prior to some other past event. It corresponds to the same tense in English.

PAST

Ein Polizist **gab** Klaus einen Strafzettel, weil er den
Wagen auf der falschen Straßenseite **geparkt hatte**.

PAST PERFECT

*A policeman **gave** Klaus a ticket because he **had parked***
the car on the wrong side of the street.

In this sentence, two past events are expressed that did not occur simultaneously. First, Klaus parked on the wrong side of the street; then, the policeman gave him a ticket. The first event is in the past perfect tense, the other is in the simple past tense. Note, however, that the first event may be merely implied.

Ich **hatte** das Essen schon **gekocht**.   (... als alle nach Hause kamen)

The forms of the past perfect differ from the present perfect only in that the auxiliary verb **haben** or **sein** is in the simple past tense rather than in the present tense.

Compare:

PRESENT PERFECT	PAST PERFECT
Sie **hat** mich nicht **angerufen**.	Sie **hatte** mich nicht angerufen.
She didn't call me.	*She had not called me.*
Wir **sind** nach Hause gefahren.	Wir **waren** nach **Hause** gefahren.
We went home.	*We had gone home.*

Use of the past perfect tense

In conversational German, the past perfect tense occurs infrequently. Often lexical items such as **bevor** and **vorher** (*before*), rather than tense forms, mark the sequence of events. The present perfect is then used for both events.

Wir **haben** Anne **besucht**, <u>bevor</u> wir ins Kino **gegangen sind**.
We visited Anne before we went to the movies.

Er **ist** um zwölf Uhr ins Bett **gegangen** und <u>vorher</u> **hat** er die Zeitung **gelesen**.
He went to bed at midnight and before that he read the newspaper.

Übung 3-15

VERSTEHEN Put the event that logically precedes the other in the past perfect tense.

> MODEL: Anita ist einkaufen gegangen. Sie hat eine Liste gemacht.
> <u>Sie hatte eine Liste gemacht.</u>

1. Ich habe die Frage nicht verstanden. Professor Wildner hat die Frage wiederholt.
2. Die Kinder sind lange draußen geblieben. Sie sind spät schlafen gegangen.
3. Es hat plötzlich zu regnen begonnen. Die Sonne hat den ganzen Tag geschienen.
4. Helga hat sich entschuldigt. Helga hat meinen Geburtstag vergessen.
5. Es ist kälter geworden. Ich habe etwas Warmes angezogen.

Word order in dependent clauses

The inflected verb is in last position.

> Wir gingen spazieren, nachdem wir gegessen **hatten**.
> *We went for a walk after we had eaten.*

§11   The Future Tense

Formation

The future tense is formed with the present tense of the auxiliary **werden** and the infinitive of the main verb.

PRESENT	Barbara hilft mir bei den Hausaufgaben.
FUTURE	Barbara **wird** mir bei den Hausaufgaben **helfen**.
	Barbara will help me with the homework.

ich	**werde** helfen	*I*	*will help*
du	**wirst** helfen	*you*	*will help*
er		*he*	
sie →	**wird** helfen	*she* →	*will help*
es		*it*	
wir	**werden** helfen	*we*	*will help*
ihr	**werdet** helfen	*you*	*will help*
sie	**werden** helfen	*they*	*will help*
Sie	**werden** helfen	*you*	*will help*

werden + infinitive	*will* + infinitive

In main clauses and questions, **werden** takes the position of the inflected verb; the infinitive is in last position. Compare these present- and future-tense sentences.

Sie fährt nach Hause.   Fährt sie nach Hause?

Sie **wird** nach Hause **fahren**.   **Wird** sie nach Hause **fahren**?

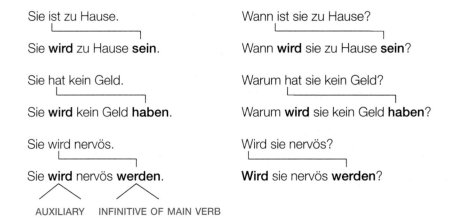

Sie ist zu Hause.

Sie **wird** zu Hause **sein**.

Wann ist sie zu Hause?

Wann **wird** sie zu Hause **sein**?

Sie hat kein Geld.

Sie **wird** kein Geld **haben**.

Warum hat sie kein Geld?

Warum **wird** sie kein Geld **haben**?

Sie wird nervös.

Sie **wird** nervös **werden**.

Wird sie nervös?

Wird sie nervös **werden**?

AUXILIARY   INFINITIVE OF MAIN VERB

Note that **werden** is used to form the future tense but can also stand alone. When it is used alone it means *become* or *to get*, as in „**Sie *wird* nervös**" (*She is getting nervous*) and „**Sie *wird* nervös werden**" (future tense: *She will be getting nervous*).

When the infinitive has a separable prefix, it is attached to the verb.

Sie ruft ihn an.

Sie wird ihn **anrufen**.

Ruft sie ihn an?

Wird sie ihn **anrufen**?

Vokabulartip: Begriffe für Zukunft

Note these common future time expressions.

morgen	*tomorrow*	bald	*soon*
übermorgen	*the day after tomorrow*	in Zukunft	*in the future*
morgen früh	*tomorrow morning*	nächste Woche	*next week*
morgen Nachmittag	*tomorrow afternoon*	nächsten Monat	*next month*
morgen Abend	*tomorrow evening*	nächstes Jahr	*next year*

Übung 3-16

ANWENDEN A. Formulate questions and statements in the future tense from the elements that are given.

Gute Vorsätze! Freunde auf einer Silvesterparty (31. Dezember) fassen gute Vorsätze fürs neue Jahr.

1. Rudolf: Ich / nie wieder / zu schnell / fahren
2. Sandra: Kurt, / du / im nächsten Jahr / mit dem Rauchen / aufhören?
3. Brigitte und Ernst: Wir / uns / mehr / um unsere Großeltern / kümmern
4. Rudolf: Brigitte und Ernst, / wann / euren alten VW / verkaufen?
5. Tanja: Also, / ich / meine Ausbildung / abschließen
6. Iris: Tanja, / dann / eine Arbeitsstelle / suchen?
7. Veronika und Lars: Wir / jeden Tag / laufen / und / wir / fit werden

B. Give creative answers to the questions. Use future tense forms.

> MODEL: Bleibst du hier in Regensburg?
> <u>Aber nein! Ich werde in Paris wohnen.</u>

Oliver und Sven sind mit der Schule fertig (sie haben ihr Abitur gemacht). Oliver fragt seinen Freund Sven über die Zukunft. Sven ist sehr ehrgeizig und hat ziemlich großspurige Pläne für die Zukunft.

1. Mietest du vielleicht eine Wohnung?
2. Besuchen dich deine Freunde dann einmal im Jahr?
3. Isst du abends zu Hause?
4. Nimmst du den Bus oder die Straßenbahn zur Arbeit?
5. Fährst du im Urlaub vielleicht nach Bayern?
6. Gehen wir heute Abend ein Bier trinken?
7. Bleiben wir Freunde?

Word order in dependent clauses

In dependent clauses, the inflected auxiliary **werden** is in last position; it is preceded by the infinitive of the main verb.

> Er **wird** es mir nicht **sagen**.

> Ich bin überzeugt, dass er es mir nicht **sagen wird**.

> *I am convinced that he won't tell me.*

Übung 3-17

VERSTEHEN Give logical and creative responses to the statements, using the future tense.

> MODEL: Anton: Die meisten Leute sind bestimmt nett.
> Annemarie: <u>Ich bin überzeugt, dass die meisten Leute langweilig
> sein werden.</u>

Anton und Annemarie sind zum Abendessen eingeladen. Annemarie sieht der Einladung sehr negativ entgegen und glaubt nicht, was ihr Mann sagt.

1. Das Essen ist bestimmt gut.
2. Und sie haben bestimmt genug Getränke.
3. Die Kinder schlafen sicher schon.
4. Und der Hund ist bestimmt in der Küche.
5. Herr Dorn redet bestimmt ziemlich wenig.
6. Und Frau Kaiser trägt bestimmt nur ein bisschen Parfüm.
7. Du lernst sicher ein paar nette Leute kennen.
8. Wir haben bestimmt viel Spaß.

Use of the future tense

The present tense is often used to express future time if an adverb or the context already indicates that the future is referred to (cf. Kap. 2 §6, 2).

Ich rufe dich morgen an.	*I'll call you tomorrow.*
Ich rufe dich bestimmt an.	*I'll certainly call you.*

The future tense has to be used if the future is not otherwise indicated. Compare these sentences:

Sie **unterstützt** ihre Eltern.	*She supports her parents.*
Sie **wird** ihre Eltern **unterstützen**.	*She will support her parents.*

The future tense is also used to express assumptions. Adverbs such as **wohl** (*in all likelihood*), **wahrscheinlich** (*probably*), and **vielleicht** (*perhaps*), often enhance this notion. Compare:

Klaus ist wahrscheinlich krank.	*Klaus is probably ill.*
Klaus **wird wohl** (wahrscheinlich) krank **sein**.	

Helga kommt wahrscheinlich nicht mit.	*Helga is probably not coming along.*
Helga **wird wohl** (wahrscheinlich) nicht **mitkommen**.	

Übung 3-18

VERSTEHEN Restate the following sentences expressing an assumption by using the future tense and **wohl**.

MODEL: Hannelore erkennt mich wahrscheinlich nicht.
          Hannelore wird mich wohl nicht erkennen.

Kerstin Decker trifft sich mit einer Schulkameradin, die sie lange nicht gesehen hat. Sie überlegt, wie das Treffen verlaufen wird.

1. Ich erkenne Hannelore vielleicht nicht.
2. Hannelore erzählt wahrscheinlich von ihrer Familie.
3. Hannelores Kinder sind wahrscheinlich erwachsen.
4. Sie hat bestimmt Fotos von ihnen.
5. Wir sprechen bestimmt über alte Zeiten.
6. Wir verbringen sicher den ganzen Tag miteinander.

§12   The Future Perfect Tense

The future perfect tense expresses a supposition or probability referring to a past event.

PRESENT PERFECT	Sie **haben** wahrscheinlich Tennis **gespielt**.	*They probably played tennis.*
FUTURE PERFECT	Sie **werden** wohl Tennis **gespielt haben**.	

The future perfect is formed with the auxiliary **werden** + the perfect infinitive **gespielt haben**. Compare the future and the future perfect.

FUTURE	FUTURE	FUTURE PERFECT	FUTURE PERFECT
er wird bezahlen	*he will pay*	er wird **bezahlt haben**	*he will have paid*
er wird gehen	*he will go*	er wird **gegangen sein**	*he will have gone*
er wird haben	*he will have*	er wird **gehabt haben**	*he will have had*
er wird sein	*he will be*	er wird **gewesen sein**	*he will have been*
er wird werden	*he will become*	er wird **geworden sein**	*he will have become*
werden + infinitive	*will* + infinitive	**werden** + perfect infinitive	*will* + perfect infinitive

In German, the perfect infinitive consists of the past participle followed by the infinitive of the auxiliary **haben** or **sein**, depending on the past participle. In English, the auxiliary *have* precedes the past participle.

The future perfect tense may also express the anticipated conclusion of an action by a certain time in the future. This use is typically marked by a time expression preceded by **bis** (*by*), as in **bis Ende des Sommers** (*by the end of the summer*), or as in a clear future time expression, e.g., **nächste Woche**.

FUTURE	Wir **werden** unser Haus im Sommer **verkaufen**.	*We will sell our house in the summer.*
FUTURE PERFECT	Wir **werden** es hoffentlich bis Ende des Sommers **verkauft haben**.	*Hopefully, we will have sold it by the end of the summer.*

Übung 3-19

VERSTEHEN Determine whether the sentences refer to the probability of a past event or to the conclusion of an event in the future.

1. Der Lärm wird meine Nachbarn gestört haben.
2. Anita wird bis Sonntag zum Arzt gegangen sein.
3. Der Chef wird wohl nervös geworden sein.
4. Es wird in der Nacht geregnet haben.
5. Ich werde das Projekt nächsten Monat erledigt haben.
6. Im Dezember wird Frau Sommer 25 Jahre bei der Firma gearbeitet haben.

§13   Reference Chart: Synopsis of the Tenses

The following verbs have been selected as examples:

fragen	weak verb
mit•kommen	strong verb with separable prefix, using **sein**
haben	
sein	functioning as main verbs
werden	

MAIN CLAUSES	DEPENDENT CLAUSES
PRESENT	
Er **fragt** (nicht).	dass er (nicht) **fragt**.
Er **kommt** (nicht) **mit**.	dass er (nicht) **mitkommt**.
Er **hat** (kein) Geld.	dass er (kein) Geld **hat**.
Er **ist** (nicht) nervös.	dass er (nicht) nervös **ist**.
Er **wird** (nicht) nervös.	dass er (nicht) nervös **wird**.
PAST	
Er **fragte** (nicht).	dass er (nicht) **fragte**.
Er **kam** (nicht) mit.	dass er (nicht) **mitkam**.
Er **hatte** (kein) Geld.	dass er (kein) Geld **hatte**.
Er **war** (nicht) nervös.	dass er (nicht) nervös **war**.
Er **wurde** (nicht) nervös.	dass er (nicht) nervös **wurde**.
PRESENT PERFECT	
Er **hat** (nicht) **gefragt**.	dass er (nicht) **gefragt hat**.
Er **ist** (nicht) **mitgekommen**.	dass er (nicht) **mitgekommen ist**.
Er **hat** (kein) Geld **gehabt**.	dass er (kein) Geld **gehabt hat**.
Er **ist** (nicht) nervös **gewesen**.	dass er (nicht) nervös **gewesen ist**.
Er **ist** (nicht) nervös **geworden**.	dass er (nicht) nervös **geworden ist**.
PAST PERFECT	
Er **hatte** (nicht) **gefragt**.	dass er (nicht) **gefragt hatte**.
Er **war** (nicht) **mitgekommen**.	dass er (nicht) **mitgekommen war**.
Er **hatte** (kein) Geld **gehabt**.	dass er (kein) Geld **gehabt hatte**.
Er **war** (nicht) nervös **gewesen**.	dass er (nicht) nervös **gewesen war**.
Er **war** (nicht) nervös **geworden**.	dass er (nicht) nervös **geworden war**.

FUTURE

Er **wird** (nicht) **fragen**.	dass er (nicht) **fragen wird**.
Er **wird** (nicht) **mitkommen**.	dass er (nicht) **mitkommen wird**.
Er **wird** (kein) Geld **haben**.	dass er (kein) Geld **haben wird**.
Er **wird** (nicht) nervös **sein**.	dass er (nicht) nervös **sein wird**.
Er **wird** (nicht) nervös **werden**.	dass er (nicht) nervös **werden wird**.

FUTURE PERFECT

Er **wird** (nicht) **gefragt haben**.	dass er (nicht) **gefragt haben wird**.*
Er **wird** (nicht) **mitgekommen sein**.	dass er (nicht) **mitgekommen sein wird**.
Er **wird** (kein) Geld **gehabt haben**.	dass er (kein) Geld **gehabt haben wird**.
Er **wird** (nicht) nervös **gewesen sein**.	dass er (nicht) nervös **gewesen sein wird**.
Er **wird** (nicht) nervös **geworden sein**.	dass er (nicht) nervös **geworden sein wird**.

*The future perfect very rarely occurs in dependent clauses.

The present and the simple past are formed without an auxiliary; they are *simple tenses*. The other four tenses are formed with the auxiliary **haben, sein,** or **werden;** they are *compound tenses*.

§14   The Position of Separable Prefixes

The separable prefix is separated when the verb to which it belongs is in first or second position. This occurs in the following instances:

	MAIN CLAUSE	DIRECT QUESTION	IMPERATIVE
PRESENT	Sie kommt **mit**.	Kommt sie **mit**?	Komm **mit**!
PAST	Sie kam **mit**.	Wer kam **mit**?	

In all other instances, the prefix is attached to the verb, i.e., in infinitives, past participles, and in dependent clauses (including indirect questions).

Sie wird nicht **mitkommen**.

Sie ist nicht **mitgekommen**.

Schade, dass sie nicht **mitkommt**.

Ich möchte wissen, warum sie nicht **mitkommt**.

Übung 3-20

ZUSAMMENFASSUNG Simple past, present perfect, past perfect, and future tenses.

A. Form questions from the elements given. Address the people in parentheses directly when the second person pronoun is given. Otherwise, use third person forms.

> MODEL: im Winter / Ski fahren (Thomas und Gerd / ihr; future)
> <u>Werdet ihr im Winter Ski fahren?</u>
> or: <u>Thomas und Gerd, werdet ihr im Winter Ski fahren?</u>

Bei einem Familientreffen unterhalten Sie sich mit vielen Leuten, und über verschiedene Leute.

1. letztes Jahr / Urlaub im Ausland / machen   (Tante Marlies / du; present perfect)
2. wohin / fahren   (Tante Marlies und Onkel Heinz / ihr; present perfect)
3. Weißt du, ob / dieses Jahr / heiraten   (meine Kusine Franziska; future)
4. Wann / gestern / ankommen   (die Frommers; simple past)
5. die Frommers / letztes Jahr / kennenlernen   (ihr; past perfect)
6. heute Morgen / im Stadtpark / spazieren gehen   (ich; present perfect)
7. davor / mit meiner Freundin / in Brüssel / sprechen   (ich; past perfect)
8. Was / zum Mittagessen / geben   (es; simple past)
9. Wann / zu Abend / essen   (wir; future)

B. Write down your own New Year's resolutions and those of five different people in the future tense.

C. Write a paragraph in which you describe events chronologically from the current year in the past, present, and future tenses. Use a variety of verbs and include time expressions.

Themen und Vokabular

Bei der Arbeit

der/die Angestellte, -n	*employee*
die Anwesenden	*attendees*
die Ausbildung	*training, apprenticeship*
der Bericht, -e	*report*
die Besprechung, -en	*meeting, conference*
der Chef, -s	*boss (m.)*
die Chefin, -nen	*boss (f.)*
die Erklärung, -en	*explanation*

Zeit

bald	*soon*
diese/letzte/nächste Woche	*this/last/next week*
diesen/letzten/ nächsten Monat	*this/last/next month*
dieses/letztes/ nächstes Jahr	*this/last/next year*
früher	*in earlier times*
die Gegenwart	*present*
gerade	*just*
gestern/vorgestern	*yesterday/the day before yesterday*
heute	*today*
heute/gestern Morgen	*this/yesterday morning*
heute/gestern/ morgen Abend	*this/yesterday/ tomorrow evening*
heute/gestern/ morgen Nachmittag	*this/yesterday/ tomorrow afternoon*
morgen	*tomorrow*
morgen früh	*tomorrow morning*
schon	*already*
übermorgen	*the day after tomorrow*
die Vergangenheit	*past*
vorher	*earlier*

der Vorsatz	*resolution, plan*
gute Vorsätze fürs neue Jahr fassen	*make New Year's resolutions*
die Zukunft	*future*
in Zukunft	*in the future*

In Bewegung

fahren, fuhr, ist gefahren	*to ride, drive*
fliegen, flog, ist geflogen	*to fly*
folgen	*to follow*
gehen, ging, ist gegangen	*to go*
kommen, kam, ist gekommen	*to come*
landen	*to land*
laufen, lief, ist gelaufen	*to walk, jog*
marschieren	*to march*
passieren	*to happen*
reisen	*to travel*
rennen, rannte, ist gerannt	*to run*
schwimmen, schwamm, ist geschwommen	*to swim*
segeln	*to sail*
starten	*to take off, start*
wandern	*to hike, wander*

Transportmittel

das Auto, -s	*car, automobile*
die Bahn	*rail, train*
die Fähre, -n	*ferry*
das Fahrrad, ¨-er	*bicycle*
das Flugzeug, -e	*airplane, plane*
das Schiff, -e	*ship*
die Straßenbahn	*trolley*
die U-Bahn, -en	*subway*
der Wagen, -	*car*
der Zug, ¨-e	*train*

4 Modal Auxiliaries

Introduction

Compare sentence a. with the modified sentences in b.

a. Ich **helfe** Inge bei den Hausaufgaben.   *I am helping Inge with the homework.*

b. Ich **kann** Inge bei den Hausaufgaben **helfen**.   *I can help Inge ...*

Ich **muss** Inge bei den Hausaufgaben **helfen**.   *I must help Inge ...*

Ich **soll** Inge bei den Hausaufgaben **helfen**.   *I am supposed to help Inge ...*

Sentence a. simply states the act of helping. The act is then modified in each of the three following sentences by the use of **können**, **müssen**, or **sollen**. These modal auxiliaries, commonly called *modals*, are inflected, whereas the accompanying verb **helfen** is in the infinitive, positioned as the final element in the sentence. This accompanying verb is referred to as a *dependent infinitive*.

In German, there are six modals.

dürfen	*may* *to be allowed to* *to be permitted to*	expression of: permission, politeness
können	*can* *to be able to*	ability, possibility
mögen/möchten	*to like to/would like to* *to want to* *to care to*	liking, wish
müssen	*must* *to have to*	necessity, probability
sollen	*should* *to be expected to* *to be supposed to*	obligation, expectation
wollen	*to want to* *to intend to*	wish, desire, intention

Vokabulartip: **wollen** *und* **möchten**

Both **wollen** and **möchten** can express a wish or desire. However, **möchten** (*would like to*) may be considered more polite, while **wollen** (*want to*) may be perceived as more direct, even blunt.

Was **möchtet** ihr trinken?	*What would you like to drink?*
Was **wollt** ihr trinken?	*What do you want to drink?*

All German modals take the dependent infinitive without **zu**.

Wir dürfen hier parken.	*We may park here.* *We are allowed to park here.*
Wir können das nicht bezahlen.	*We cannot pay that.* *We are not able to pay that.*
Wir möchten jetzt nicht Tennis spielen.	*We don't care to play tennis now.*
Ich möchte euch einladen.	*I want to invite you.*
Wir müssen auf Barbara warten.	*We must wait for Barbara.* *We have to wait for Barbara.*
Dieses Haus muss sehr teuer sein.	*This house must be very expensive.*
Wir sollen den Fall der Polizei melden.	*We are expected to report the case to the police.* *We should report the case to the police.*
Morgen soll es wieder regnen.	*It is supposed to rain again tomorrow.*
Wir wollen ein Haus kaufen.	*We want to buy a house.* *We intend to buy a house.*

The Modals in the Simple Tenses

§1   The Present Tense

Formation

dürfen	können	mögen	möchten	müssen	sollen	wollen
ich darf	ich kann	ich mag	ich möchte	ich muss	ich soll	ich will
I may,	*I can,*	*I like to,*	*I would like to,*	*I must,*	*I am expected to,*	*I want to,*
I am	*I am able to,*	*I care to,*	*I want to,*	*I have to,*	*I should, I am*	*I intend to,*
allowed	*etc.*	*etc.*	*etc.*	*etc.*	*supposed to,*	*etc.*
to, etc.					*etc.*	
du darfst	du kannst	du magst	du möchtest	du musst	du sollst	du willst
er ⟍	er ⟍	er ⟍	er ⟍	er ⟍	er ⟍	er ⟍
sie ⟩darf	sie ⟩kann	sie ⟩mag	sie ⟩möchte	sie ⟩muss	sie ⟩soll	sie ⟩will
es ⟋	es ⟋	es ⟋	es ⟋	es ⟋	es ⟋	es ⟋
wir dürfen	wir können	wir mögen	wir möchten	wir müssen	wir sollen	wir wollen
ihr dürft	ihr könnt	ihr mögt	ihr möchtet	ihr müsst	ihr sollt	ihr wollt
sie dürfen	sie können	sie mögen	sie möchten	sie müssen	sie sollen	sie wollen
Sie dürfen	Sie können	Sie mögen	Sie möchten	Sie müssen	Sie sollen	Sie wollen

Note: a. The first and third person singular forms are identical, and the first and third
person plural forms are identical to the infinitive.

    b. The vowel change occurs throughout the singular but never in the plural;
sollen, however, has no vowel change.

    c. The modal **mögen** is mostly used in the subjunctive form **möchten**.
Möchten has no vowel change. **Mögen** usually occurs with noun objects
rather than a dependent infinitive. For a more detailed discussion of **mögen**
and **möchten**, see §14 in this Kapitel.

Übung 4-1

VERSTEHEN Indicate what the sentences express: permission, ability or possibility,
liking, necessity or probability, obligation or expectation, wish or desire, or intention.

    MODEL: Kannst du morgen vorbeikommen?   <u>ability</u>

    1. Das Wetter kann gut werden.
    2. Musst du Joschka helfen?
    3. Wollen wir morgen abend ausgehen?
    4. Wir sollen bald nach Hause gehen.
    5. Kannst du gut singen?
    6. Dürft ihr schon Auto fahren?
    7. Magst du Fisch?
    8. Möchtest du morgen wandern gehen?
    9. Die Reise muss sehr schön gewesen sein.

Übung 4-2

ANWENDEN Express the following sentences in English.

Corinna schreibt einen Zettel mit Informationen für ihre Zimmerkollegin.

1. Maria kann heute nicht vorbeikommen und Andreas will morgen nicht mitkommen.
2. Du musst heute deine Mutti anrufen.
3. Gerd hat gefragt, ob er dich zu einer Tasse Kaffee einladen darf.
4. Morgen soll das Wetter schön werden. Wollen wir eine Radtour machen?

Modals in main clauses

When modals are introduced, the following changes occur in the structure of main clauses:

1. Statements

The inflected verb becomes the dependent infinitive and goes to the end of the sentence, while the modal becomes the inflected verb and thus occupies the second position.

Ich **glaube** das nicht.
Ich **kann** das nicht **glauben**.

Note the use of **haben**, **sein**, and **werden** as dependent infinitives.

Ich bin still.   Sie hat viel Zeit.   Er wird reich.
Ich **soll** still **sein**.   Sie **muss** viel Zeit **haben**.   Er **will** reich **werden**.

When verbs with a separable prefix are dependent infinitives, the separable prefix remains attached.

Hans ruft mich heute nicht an.
Hans **kann** mich heute nicht **anrufen**.

Warum **kann** er dich heute nicht **anrufen**?

Kann er dich heute nicht **anrufen**?

2. Questions

For questions beginning with a question word, the modal is in second position.

Warum **glaubst** du das nicht?
Warum **kannst** du das nicht **glauben**?

For questions without a question word, the modal is in first position.

Glaubst du das nicht?
Kannst du das nicht **glauben**?

Übung 4-3

ANWENDEN A. Formulate statements and questions using the appropriate forms of the modals given in parentheses.

Martina macht ihrer Freundin Kirstin ein paar Vorschläge. Kirstin ist zur Zeit mit allem unzufrieden.

> MODEL: heute/du/dein Seminar/schwänzen (dürfen)
> <u>Heute darfst du dein Seminar schwänzen.</u>

1. du / ein paar Tage / frei nehmen? (können)
2. vielleicht / deine Freunde / mit dir / sprechen (sollen)
3. du / nicht / jedes Wochenende / nicht / arbeiten (müssen)
4. wir / heute abend / einen Spaziergang machen? (können)
5. oder / den Abend / alleine / verbringen? (möchten)

B. Formulate questions using an appropriate modal and the personal pronouns in parentheses. The questions should contain the phrases provided.

> MODEL: gut kochen (deine Eltern, deine Freundin, du)
> <u>Können deine Eltern gut kochen? Kann deine Freundin gut kochen?</u>
> <u>Kannst du gut kochen?</u>

Andreas fragt einen Klassenkameraden, Fred, über Hobbies, Interessen und Verpflichtungen zu Hause.

1. ein Instrument spielen (ihr; du; deine Eltern)
2. abends lange ausgehen (du; dein Bruder)
3. Obst und Gemüse (deine Familie; deine Freunde, du)
4. viel zu Hause helfen (du; ihr [Fred und seine Geschwister])
5. eine Fremdsprache lernen (deine Freunde; du; deine Freundin)
6. Fußball spielen (wir; die ganze Klasse; dein Vater mit uns)

Vokabulartip: werden *und* wollen

Do not confuse the verbs **wollen**(*want to*) and **werden** (*will* [future tense]).

> Sie **will** eine Radtour machen.   *She wants to go on a bike ride.*
> Er **wird** eine Radtour machen.   *He will go on a bike ride.*

Modals in dependent clauses

In dependent clauses, the conjugated modal is in last position; the dependent infinitive precedes it.

> **MAIN CLAUSE**   Barbara **kann** nicht **mitkommen.**
>
> DEPENDENT CLAUSE   Ich weiß, dass Barbara nicht **mitkommen kann.**

Übung 4-4

ANWENDEN   Restate the following sentences, using the indicated introductory clauses.

> MODEL: Können Thomas und Gerd Getränke bringen?
> <u>Ich bin nicht sicher, ob Thomas und Gerd Getränke bringen können.</u>

Partyplanung: Sabine fragt Ruth über einige Details für ihre Sommerparty.

1. Will Manfred seine Freundin mitbringen?
   Ich weiß nicht, ob...
2. Sollen wir unsere Eltern einladen?
   Ich glaube nicht, dass...
3. Musst du alle Getränke kalt stellen?
   Ich glaube schon, dass...
4. Müssen wir noch etwas einkaufen?
   Ich weiß nicht, ob...
5. Sollen die Gäste vorher anrufen?
   Du weißt doch, dass...
6. Dürfen die Gäste laut singen?
   Ich hoffe, dass...

Use of modals without a dependent infinitive

Kannst du mir **helfen**?	Nein, ich **kann** nicht.	*No, I can't.*
	Nein, ich **kann** es nicht.	*No, I can't do it.*
	Nein, ich **kann** das nicht.	*No, I can't do that.*

Dependent infinitives need not be repeated in such sequences. They may be omitted completely or replaced by **es** or **das**.

Verbs such as **fahren**, **gehen**, **machen**, and **tun** are often omitted because they are clearly understood from the context.

Ich **muss** in die Bibliothek.	*I've got to go to the library.*
Wo **willst** du hin?	*Where do you want to go?*
Was **soll** ich mit diesen Sachen?	*What am I supposed to do with these things?*

Übung 4-5

VERSTEHEN   Supply the implied verb that would occur as the dependent infinitive.

> MODEL: Was soll ich mit der Zeitung?   <u>machen</u>

1. Müsst ihr wirklich schon nach Hause?
2. Du hast Spinat gekauft? Ich will ihn nicht.
3. Wollt ihr mit dem Auto in die Stadt?
4. Was soll er mit dem Aspirin?
5. Möchtest du ein Glas Orangensaft?

Übung 4-6

ZUSAMMENFASSUNG Modals in the present tense in main and dependent clauses.

A. Make up questions from the elements given using the appropriate forms of the personal pronouns (**ich, wir, du, ihr, Sie**).

> MODEL: Herr Pfister: nicht mitkommen (du; wollen)
> <u>Willst du wirklich nicht mitkommen?</u>

Herr Pfister und viele seiner Kollegen haben sich zu einer Geburtstagsfeier in einem Restaurant getroffen. Herr Pfister bittet um verschiedene Dinge und organisiert alles.

1. Frau Beck und Frau Conrad: etwas trinken (wir; wollen)
2. Herr Pfister: die Speisekarte bringen (Sie; können)
3. Herr Pfister: eine Flasche Wein bestellen (wir; wollen)
4. Dorle Pfister: auf Marlene warten (ich; sollen)
5. Hans Zimmer: sie schnell anrufen (du; können)

B. Form sentences in German according to the directions given in English.

Sie und Ihre Freunde machen Pläne für eine Radtour am Wochenende. Sie wollen, dass alles perfekt ist!

1. You ask your friends if all of you (**wir**) should meet Saturday morning.
2. You say that you can get up at 7:00 A.M.
3. And you ask your friends if they want to get up early, too.
4. You ask Jürgen if he has to repair his bike first.
5. You say that Anke will pick up her bike tomorrow.
6. You ask Anke (she is only 16) if she is allowed to spend the whole weekend with all of you . . .
7. or if you should ask her parents first . . .
8. You say you will ask Sandra if all of you can stay overnight at her house (**bei ihr übernachten**).
9. You wonder if some people should reserve a hotel room.
10. You tell your friends that you think they should prepare everything Friday night.

C. Answer the personalized questions.

1. Was müssen Sie jeden Tag erledigen?
2. Was soll Ihr Freund (Ihr Mann/Ihre Frau, Ihr Partner, ein Freund oder eine Freundin) für Sie tun?
3. Was möchten Sie in den nächsten Ferien machen?
4. Was können Sie besonders gut (machen)? Was kann jemand in Ihrer Familie besonders gut (machen)?
5. Was darf man als Teenager nicht tun?

§2   The Simple Past Tense

Formation

dürfen	können	mögen/möchten	müssen	sollen	wollen
ich durfte	ich konnte	ich mochte	ich musste	ich sollte	ich wollte
I was allowed to	*I could, I was able to, etc.*	*I liked to, etc.*	*I had to, etc.*	*I was expected to, I was supposed to, etc.*	*I wanted to, I intended to, etc.*
du durftest	du konntest	du mochtest	du musstest	du solltest	du wolltest
er⎫ sie⎬durfte es⎭	er⎫ sie⎬konnte es⎭	er⎫ sie⎬mochte es⎭	er⎫ sie⎬musste es⎭	er⎫ sie⎬sollte es⎭	er⎫ sie⎬wollte es⎭
wir durften	wir konnten	wir mochten	wir mussten	wir sollten	wir wollten
ihr durftet	ihr konntet	ihr mochtet	ihr musstet	ihr solltet	ihr wolltet
sie durften	sie konnten	sie mochten	sie mussten	sie sollten	sie wollten
Sie durften	Sie konnten	Sie mochten	Sie mussten	Sie sollten	Sie wollten

Note: a. Modals take the same endings in the simple past as weak verbs.
   b. Modals have no umlaut in the past.
   c. The modal **mögen** has a change of consonants: **mögen > mochten**

The use of modals in the simple past tense

To express past time, modals generally use the simple past tense even in conversational German, where most other verbs are used in the present perfect tense (cf. Kap. 3 §2). This parallels the English use of the simple past tense.

X: Warum sind Sie nur zwei Tage in München geblieben?
   Why did you stay only two days in Munich?

Y: Mein Freund konnte nicht länger bleiben.
   My friend could not stay any longer.

Übung 4-7

ANWENDEN Formulate questions in the past tense from the elements given. Use the modals given in parentheses.

MODEL: ihr in der Stadt / wohnen? (wollen)
        <u>Wolltet ihr in der Stadt wohnen?</u>

Gabriele fragt ihre Großmutter über ihre Vergangenheit.

1. viele Leute / früher / Reisen machen? (können)
2. die Kinder / viel / zu Hause / helfen? (müssen)
3. ich / als Kind / früh / sprechen (können)

4. meine Mutter / abends / ausgehen? (dürfen)
5. du / den Opa / schon / als Student? (mögen)
6. ihr / miteinander / ausgehen? (dürfen)
7. du / ihn / heiraten? (wollen)
8. ich / nicht / so viele Fragen / stellen!? (sollen)

The Modals in Compound Tenses

§3   The Present Perfect Tense

Formation

A distinction must be made between the form of modals with and without an
accompanying infinitive.

WITHOUT ACCOMPANYING INFINITIVE	WITH ACCOMPANYING INFINITIVE
Ich habe (es) nicht **gekonnt.** **gedurft.** **gemusst.** **gewollt.** **gemocht.**	Ich habe nicht **mitfahren können.** **mitfahren dürfen.** **mitfahren müssen.** **mitfahren wollen.** **mitfahren mögen.**

The past participle of the modal follows the pattern of weak verbs. It has no umlaut. **Mögen** has a change of consonants: **gemocht.**

When an accompanying infinitive is present, the modal verbs form the present perfect with the infinitive instead of the past participle. It stands at the end of the clause. This produces the *double infinitive* construction.

Modals always use the auxiliary **haben** as the conjugated verb in present perfect
sentences.

Er **ist** noch nie **mitgefahren.**
but: Er **hat** noch nie **mitfahren können.**

The use of modals in the present perfect tense

The present perfect tense of the modals tends to be used in contexts where English
would also use the present perfect rather than the simple past. This occurs, for
example, with the open time expressions **noch nie** (*never*), **schon oft** (*often*), **schon
immer** (*always*).

Frau Berger **hat** das noch nie zugeben **wollen.**
Ms Berger has never wanted to admit that.

Ich **habe** ihm schon oft bei den Hausaufgaben **helfen müssen.**
I've often had to help him with the homework.

Wir **haben** <u>schon immer</u> hier **parken dürfen**.
We've always been allowed to park here.

Note the position of these time expressions: they normally follow pronoun objects but precede all other elements.

Übung 4-8

ANWENDEN Formulate statements with the modal in the present perfect tense. Use the time expression given in parentheses.

MODEL: Frau Sorge: Ich muss jeden Morgen meinen Sohn wecken. (schon immer)

Frau Jammer: <u>Wem sagen Sie das? Ich habe meinen Sohn schon immer wecken müssen.</u>

Frau Sorge und Frau Jammer beklagen sich über alles.

1. Ich muss mein Auto selbst in die Werkstatt bringen. (schon oft)
2. Ich muss alle Einkäufe selbst erledigen. (schon immer)
3. Und ich kann das nicht. (noch nie)
4. Mein Mann kann mich nicht verstehen. (noch nie)
5. Meine Tocher will von zu Hause weggehen. (schon oft)
6. Meine Kinder mögen kein Obst oder Gemüse. (noch nie)

§4   The Past Perfect Tense

The past perfect tense of modals is identical to the present perfect, except that the simple past tense of **haben** is used as the auxiliary.

Ich **hatte** (es) nicht **gekonnt**.   Ich **hatte** nicht **mitfahren können**.
I had not been able to do it.   *I had not been able to come along.*

§5   The Future Tense

Compare: PRESENT   Er **kann** es nicht.   Er **kann** nicht **mitkommen**.

FUTURE   Er **wird** es nicht **können**.   Er **wird** nicht **mitkommen können**.
He will not be able to.   *He will not be able to come along.*

The future tense is formed with the auxiliary **werden**; the modal appears as an infinitive at the end of a clause. If there is an accompanying infinitive, it precedes the modal (another instance of a double infinitive construction).

If the future is used to express supposition or probability, adverbs such as **wohl**, **wahrscheinlich**, or **vielleicht** are usually added (cf. Kap. 3 §11).

Sie werden mir **wohl** nicht helfen können.
I suppose you won't be able to help me.

Übung 4-9

ANWENDEN Formulate sentences in the future tense. Use the sentences and the elements given in parentheses to formulate sentences in the future tense and with the adverb **wohl**.

> MODEL: Frank ist furchtbar müde. (nicht zur Party gehen / wollen)
> <u>Frank wird wohl nicht zu der Party gehen wollen.</u>

1. Der Kaffee ist zu dünn. (niemand / trinken / wollen)
2. Das Chili ist wahnsinnig scharf. (du / nicht essen / können)
3. Annette ist verreist. (wir / nicht einladen / müssen)
4. Erika hat ihr Haus verkauft. (sie / bei ihren Eltern wohnen / dürfen)

§6   The Future Perfect Tense

Modals with a dependent infinitive very rarely appear in the future perfect tense. Modals without a dependent infinitive are used occasionally in the future perfect to express a past supposition or probability (cf. Kap. 3 §12).

> Er **wird** das Essen wohl nicht **gemocht haben.**   *He probably did not like the food.*
> PERFECT INFINITIVE

§7   Dependent Word Order in Compound Tenses

WITHOUT DEPENDENT INFINITIVE

Ich weiß,
   dass er es nicht **gekonnt hat.**
   dass er es nicht **gekonnt hatte.**
   dass er es nicht **können wird.**

WITH DEPENDENT INFINITIVE

Ich weiß,
   dass er nicht **hat mitkommen können.**
   dass er nicht **hatte mitkommen können.**
   dass er nicht **wird mitkommen können.**

The inflected auxiliary is positioned last in accordance with the general rule for dependent word order.

A double infinitive is always in the final position in its clause.

Übung 4-10

ANWENDEN Restate each of the following sentences, using the indicated introductory clause.

> MODEL: Er hat das nicht gekonnt. Warum denken Sie, dass...
> <u>Warum denken Sie, dass er das nicht gekonnt hat?</u>

1. Sie hat es nicht gedurft. Warum denkst du, dass...
2. Sie hatte es nicht gewollt. Es ist möglich, dass...
3. Er wird das können. Ich nehme an, dass...
4. Wir konnten so etwas nicht voraussehen. Sie verstehen, dass...
5. Die Leute haben das Problem nicht erledigen können. Ich habe gehört, dass...

§8 Reference Chart: Synopsis of the Tenses of Modals and Their Basic Meanings

Keep in mind: With modals, the use of the simple past and present perfect in German parallels the English use of these tenses (§2 and §3).

DÜRFEN

PRESENT	ich darf es	ich darf anrufen	*I may, I am allowed to*
PAST	ich durfte es	ich durfte anrufen	*I was allowed to*
PRESENT PERFECT	ich habe es gedurft	ich habe anrufen dürfen	*I have been allowed to*
PAST PERFECT	ich hatte es gedurft	ich hatte anrufen dürfen	*I had been allowed to*
FUTURE	ich werde es dürfen	ich werde anrufen dürfen	*I will be allowed to*

KÖNNEN

PRESENT	ich kann es	ich kann anrufen	*I can, I am able to*
PAST	ich konnte es	ich konnte anrufen	*I could, I was able to*
PRESENT PERFECT	ich habe es gekonnt	ich habe anrufen können	*I have been able to*
PAST PERFECT	ich hatte es gekonnt	ich hatte anrufen können	*I had been able to*
FUTURE	ich werde es können	ich werde anrufen können	*I will be able to*

MÖGEN/MÖCHTEN

PRESENT	ich mag/möchte es nicht	ich mag/möchte nicht anrufen	*I do not/would not/ like to*
PAST	ich mochte es nicht	ich mochte nicht anrufen	*I did not like to*
PRESENT PERFECT	ich habe es nicht gemocht	ich habe nicht anrufen mögen	*I have not liked to*
PAST PERFECT	ich hatte es nicht gemocht	ich hatte nicht anrufen mögen	*I had not liked to*
FUTURE	ich werde es nicht mögen	ich werde nicht anrufen mögen	*I will not like to*

MÜSSEN

PRESENT	ich muss es	ich muss anrufen	*I must, I have to*
PAST	ich musste es	ich musste anrufen	*I had to*
PRESENT PERFECT	ich habe es gemusst	ich habe anrufen müssen	*I have had to*
PAST PERFECT	ich hatte es gemusst	ich hatte anrufen müssen	*I had had to*
FUTURE	ich werde es müssen	ich werde anrufen müssen	*I will have to*

SOLLEN

PRESENT	ich soll es	ich soll anrufen	*I am expected to, I should*
PAST	ich sollte es	ich sollte anrufen	*I was expected to*
PRESENT PERFECT	ich habe es gesollt	ich habe anrufen sollen	*I have been expected to*
PAST PERFECT	ich hatte es gesollt	ich hatte anrufen sollen	*I had been expected to*
FUTURE	ich werde es sollen	ich werde anrufen sollen	*I will be expected to*

WOLLEN

PRESENT	ich will es	ich will anrufen	*I want to*
PAST	ich wollte es	ich wollte anrufen	*I wanted to*
PRESENT PERFECT	ich habe es gewollt	ich habe anrufen wollen	*I have wanted to*
PAST PERFECT	ich hatte es gewollt	ich hatte anrufen wollen	*I had wanted to*
FUTURE	ich werde es wollen	ich werde anrufen wollen	*I will want to*

Note that the constructions that result in three verbal elements at the end of the clause occur quite rarely.

§9   Summary of Word Order in Dependent Clauses

WITHOUT DEPENDENT INFINITIVE	WITH DEPENDENT INFINITIVE
Ich weiß,	Ich weiß,
dass er es nicht **kann**.	dass er nicht **anrufen kann**.
dass er es nicht **konnte**.	dass er nicht **anrufen konnte**.
dass er es nicht **gekonnt hat**.	dass er nicht **hat anrufen können**.
dass er es nicht **gekonnt hatte**.	dass er nicht **hatte anrufen können**.
dass er es nicht **können wird**.	dass er nicht **wird anrufen können**.

Übung 4-11

ZUSAMMENFASSUNG   Modals in the past, present and past perfect, and future tenses.

A. Respond to the questions in the past perfect tense, using the phrases provided.

MODEL: Wolltest du früher Arzt werden?
..., bevor ich in die Schule kam.
Ich hatte Arzt werden wollen, bevor ich in die Schule kam.

1. Durftest du Auto fahren?
..., bevor ich einen Unfall hatte.
2. Konnten deine Freunde dich zu Hause besuchen?
..., bevor sie das Fenster kaputt machten.
3. Musstest du immer früh zu Hause sein?
..., bevor ich 18 wurde.

B. Supply a logical follow-up in the future tense to the sentence. You may maintain the modal from the given statement or supply a different one.

MODEL: Diese Woche darf ich keinen Sport machen.
Vielleicht werde ich nächste Woche joggen oder Rad fahren dürfen.

1. Dieses Jahr muss ich ein Apartment mieten.
2. Heute darfst du nicht fernsehen.
3. Diesen Sommer können wir keinen Urlaub machen.
4. Diese Woche wollt ihr eure Großeltern besuchen.

C. Respond to the following personalized questions in the simple past and present perfect.

1. Was konnten Sie als Kind gut (machen)? Was konnten Sie früher nicht (aber können es jetzt)?
2. Was wollten Sie als Kind oder Teenager (von Beruf) werden?
3. Welches Essen haben Sie früher nicht gemocht?
4. Was durften Sie als Teenager nicht machen?
5. Beschreiben Sie, wie Sie (oder Sie und Ihre Geschwister) zu Hause helfen mussten.
6. Was haben Sie letzte Woche machen sollen? Wollten Sie das machen?

7. Was haben Sie noch nie machen wollen?
8. Welches Buch haben Sie schon immer lesen wollen?
9. Welchen Film schon immer sehen wollen? Welche Person haben Sie schon immer kennenlernen wollen?

Additional Meanings and Uses of Modal Auxiliaries

Modal auxiliaries may express various shades of meaning, depending mostly on the context in which they occur. The preceding section focused on the basic meanings of modals. Here are some additional connotations.

§10   *Nicht dürfen*

Sie **müssen** das tun. ———— *You have to do that.*
                        ———— *You must do that.*

Both English sentences express the same thing as does their German counterpart, i.e., the necessity of doing something. But notice the difference in meaning of the respective negative forms of the following two English sentences:

You don't have to do that.   no obligation
You mustn't do that.   strong warning or prohibition

This distinction is expressed in German by **nicht müssen** and **nicht dürfen**.

You don't have to do that.   Sie **müssen** das **nicht** tun.
You mustn't do that.   Sie **dürfen** das **nicht** tun.

Remember: *must not* = **nicht dürfen**

§11   *Können*

1. Just as English speakers often use *can* instead of *may*, Germans often use **können** instead of **dürfen**.

   Du **kannst** das Geld behalten.   *You can keep the money.*
                 instead of:
   Du **darfst** das Geld behalten.   *You may keep the money.*

2. Another meaning of **können** is to know how to do something.

   Kannst du schwimmen?   *Do you know how to swim?*
   Können Sie Deutsch?   *Do you know German?*
                                    Do you speak German?

   Sie **kann** kein Englisch.   *She doesn't know English.*
                                    She doesn't speak English.

3. Können is used in the idiomatic expression.

Ich **kann** nicht anders.	*I can't help it.*
Ich **konnte** nicht anders, ich musste lachen.	*I couldn't help it, I had to laugh. (I couldn't help laughing.)*

§12   *Sollen*

Sollen may have the meaning of *may*, principally in questions expressing a suggestion.

Soll ich Ihnen einen Stuhl bringen?	***May** I bring you a chair?*

§13   *Wollte gerade* or *wollte eben*

In conversational German, **wollte gerade** or **wollte eben** is frequently used in the sense of *was (just) about to*.

Ich **wollte** Sie **gerade** anrufen.	*I wanted (was about) to call you.*
Wir **wollten eben** wegfahren.	*We were (just) about to leave.*

§14   *Mögen*

Mögen is typically used as a main verb in questions about food, drink, persons, and places.

Mögen Sie Fisch?	*Do you like fish?*
Magst du diesen Tee?	*Do you like this tea?*
Mögt ihr eure Nachbarn?	*Do you like your neighbors?*
Mögen Ihre Kinder die neue Schule?	*Do your children like the new school?*

The subjunctive form **möchte** (*would like*) is used both with a dependent infinitive and as a main verb.

Ich **möchte** ihn **anrufen**.	*I would like to call him.*
Was **möchtest** du?	*What would you like?*
Ich **möchte** eine Tasse Kaffee.	*I would like a cup of coffee.*

§15   The Use of *nicht brauchen zu* instead of *nicht müssen*

Sie **müssen** es mir **nicht** sagen.	*You don't have to tell me.*
Sie **brauchen** es mir **nicht zu** sagen.	

Nicht müssen, meaning *don't / doesn't have to*, is frequently expressed by **nicht brauchen zu** (literally *need not to*). It takes a dependent infinitive preceded by **zu** positioned at the end of the sentence. This is in contrast to the modal auxiliaries, which never include **zu**.

Zu is inserted between the prefix and the verb for verbs with separable prefixes.

Sie **brauchen** das Buch nicht zurück**zu**geben.	*You don't have to return the book.*

Wit inseparable prefix verbs, **zu** is positioned before the dependent infinitive.

Du **brauchst** ihr Foto nicht **zu** behalten.	*You don't need to keep her picture.*

Übung 4-12

ANWENDEN Respond to each statement using **nicht brauchen zu** instead of **nicht müssen**.

MODEL: Nikolas muss mir nicht in der Küche helfen.
<u>Wirklich? Er braucht dir nicht zu helfen?</u>

Irmgard spricht mit ihren Geschwistern. Es gibt weniger zu erledigen als Irmgard gedacht hat.

1. Ich bin so froh! Ich muss heute nicht arbeiten.
2. Und Mutti und Papi müssen nächstes Wochenende nicht das Auto reparieren.
3. Christof, du musst das Geschenk nicht heute Nachmittag besorgen.
4. Und für morgen müssen wir nichts einkaufen.
5. Und...heute Abend müsst ihr nicht so früh ins Bett!

The following illustrate the use of **nicht brauchen zu** in the simple past and present perfect.

Wir **brauchten** das nicht **zu übersetzen.**	*We didn't have to translate that.*
Wir **haben** das nicht **zu übersetzen brauchen.**	
INFINITIVE INFINITIVE	

Sie **brauchten** mein Angebot nicht **anzunehmen.**	*You didn't have to accept my offer.*
Sie **haben** mein Angebot nicht **anzunehmen brauchen.**	
INFINITIVE INFINITIVE	

In compound tenses, a double infinitive with **zu** is used.

Übung 4-13

ZUSAMMENFASSUNG Special meanings of modals.

A. Change the direct commands to more polite suggestions with **können** or **sollen**.

MODEL: Mach die Tür auf!   <u>Kannst du die Tür aufmachen?</u>
Machen wir einen Spaziergang!   <u>Sollen wir einen Spaziergang machen?</u>

1. Gehen wir heute Abend aus!
2. Ruf mich heute Nachmittag an!
3. Leih mir dein Auto!
4. Bleibt sitzen!
5. Seien Sie ruhig!
6. Bleiben wir zu Hause!

B. Formulate questions with **möchten**, both with and without dependent infinitives. Use the appropriate personal pronoun (**du, ihr, Sie, sie, er/sie**) for each question.

MODEL: ein Glas Saft (Sabine)   <u>Sabine, möchtest du ein Glas Saft?</u>

Sie haben Gäste und fragen, welche Wünsche sie haben. Einige der Gäste sind gute Freunde (Vornamen), andere sind Arbeitskollegen (Nachnamen).

1. ein Glas Wein (Herr Vogt)
2. sich ausruhen (Anneliese)
3. etwas essen (Kurt und Max)
4. ein Sandwich oder einen Jogurt (die Kinder)
5. ein Buch oder eine Zeitschrift lesen (Gerda)
6. die Nachrichten anhören (Herr und Frau Winkler)

C. Using **mögen**, formulate five questions asking different people about foods they like. Use the appropriate personal pronoun.

MODEL: Ihr Neffe   →   <u>Magst du Obst? Magst du Jogurt?</u>

Ihre Familie hat eine Menge Gäste (Verwandte, Freunde, Kollegen) im Haus. Sie versuchen herauszufinden, was alle mögen (welches Essen, welche Getränke).

1. zwei Freunde
2. Nachbarn von Ihren Eltern (Sie kennen die Leute nicht)
3. ein Freund
4. Ihre Großeltern
5. eine Kollegin Ihrer Mutter

D. Use the verbs **nicht brauchen zu** and **nicht dürfen** to deny these children their requests.

MODEL: Mutti, können wir ein Video sehen?   Nein,...
          <u>Nein, ihr dürft kein Video sehen.</u>

1. Vati, muss ich mit dem Hund spazierengehen?   Nein,...
2. Mutti, kann Renate bei mir übernachten?   Nein,...
3. Vati, wollen wir uns ein Pizza bestellen?   Nein,...
4. Mutti, kann ich mir dein Fahrrad ausleihen?   Nein,...
5. Vati, sollst du die Babysitter anrufen?   Nein,...

Themen und Vokabular

Einladungen

an•rufen	*to call on the phone*
die Einladung, -en	*invitation*
feiern	*to celebrate*
das Fest, -e	*party, fest*
der Gast, ⸚e	*guest*
die Gesellschaft	*company*
Gesellschaft haben	*to have company*
die Party, -s	*party*

Essen

der Braten	*roast*
das Brot, -e	*bread*
das Brötchen, -	*roll*
die Butter	*butter*
das Essen	*meal, food*
der Fisch	*fish*
das Gemüse (pl. die Gemüsesorten)	*vegetable*
das Getränk, -e	*drink, beverage*
das Huhn	*chicken*
der Jogurt, -s	*yogurt*
die Nudel, -n	*noodle, pasta*
das Obst (pl. die Obstsorten)	*fruit*

der Salat, -e	*salad (also: lettuce)*
das Sandwich	*sandwich*

Getränke

das Bier	*beer*
der Kaffee	*coffee*
die Limo	*soft drink*
die Milch	*milk*
der Saft, ⸚e	*juice*
der Sprudel (das Mineralwasser)	*sparkling water, club soda*
der Tee	*tea*
der Wein	*wine*

Erinnerungen und Zukunftspläne

von Beruf (sein, werden)	*as an occupation*
die Fähigkeit, -en	*ability, skill*
die Fremdsprache, -n	*foreign language*
die Gegenwart	*present*
als Kind	*as a child*
als Teenager	*as a teenager*
die Vergangenheit	*past*
die Zukunft	*future*

5 The Nouns

Gender and Plural

§1 Gender

The definite article indicates the gender of the noun that follows it.

der (masculine) der Vater
die (feminine) die Mutter
das (neuter) das Kind

In English, nouns referring to inanimate objects and abstract ideas are neuter.
In German, however, the *grammatical gender* of such nouns is masculine, feminine, or neuter. It is imperative to learn each German noun with its corresponding definite article, since the gender of a noun is often the most important clue to the function of the noun in a sentence.

Here are a few useful guidelines for determining the gender of a noun.

Masculine

1. Nouns referring to male persons, their professions, and their nationalities

> der Vater, der Bruder, der Junge, der Freund, der Lehrer, der Professor,
> der Arzt (*doctor*), der Chef (*boss*), der Polizist, der Verkäufer (*salesman*),
> der Komponist (*composer*), der Präsident, der Engländer, der Amerikaner,
> der Franzose, der Deutsche, der Ausländer (*foreigner*)

2. Names of all seasons, months, days of the week, and most times of the day.

> der Frühling, der Sommer, der Herbst, der Winter
> der Januar, der Februar, der März, etc.
> der Montag, der Dienstag, der Mittwoch, etc.
> der Morgen, der Vormittag, der Mittag, der Nachmittag, der Abend

3. Most nouns ending in **-en**

> der Wagen, der Regen, der Garten, der Süden, der Norden, der Osten,
> der Westen

Feminine

1. Nouns referring to female persons

   die Mutter, die Frau, die Tante, etc.

   Many feminine nouns referring to professions and nationalities are formed from masculine nouns by adding the suffix **-in**.

   die Freundin, die Lehrerin, die Professorin, die Assistentin, die Ärztin, die Sekretärin, die Amerikanerin, die Ausländerin

   A fairly recent convention (among progressive and younger Germans) is to capitalize the **-in** ending of the feminine nouns that are formed from masculine nouns.

   die ÄrztIn, die AmerikanerIn, die SekretärIn

2. Most nouns ending in unstressed **-e**

   die Liebe, die Frage, die Straße, die Karte, die Reise, die Schule

   Common exceptions

   der Name, der Käse, das Ende, das Auge

3. All nouns ending in **-ei**, **-ie**, **-ik**, **-ion**, **-heit**, **-keit**, **-schaft**, **-tät**, **-ung**

   die Bäckerei (*bakery*), die Polizei (*police*), die Philosophie, die Musik, die Religion, die Freiheit (*freedom, liberty*), die Möglichkeit (*possibility*), die Freundschaft (*friendship*), die Universität, die Meinung (*opinion*)

Neuter

1. Nouns referring to the young of animals and human beings

   das Kalb (*calf*), das Fohlen (*foal, colt, filly*), das Lamm, das Kind, das Baby

2. Nouns with the diminutive suffixes **-chen** or **-lein**

   das Mädchen, das Brötchen, das Kätzlein

   All nouns become neuter and usually add an umlaut (if possible) when they take on the diminutive form.

die Stadt (*town, city*)	das Städtchen (*small town*)
der Hund (*dog*)	das Hündchen (*small dog, puppy*)
die Katze (*cat*)	das Kätzlein (*kitten*)

   The diminutive of names is sometimes used for children or simply for endearment.

   Hans—Hänschen

   The ending **-chen** is more common than **-lein**.

3. Most metals

> das Gold, das Silber, das Eisen (*iron*), das Blei (*lead*), das Kupfer, das Metall (but: die Bronze)

4. Infinitives used as nouns

> das Rauchen (*smoking*), das Trinken (*drinking*), das Essen (*meal*)

5. Letters used as nouns

> das A, das B, das C

Übung 5-1

VERSTEHEN   In each group, identify which noun has a gender that is different from all the others.

1. Wahnsinn, Brüderlichkeit, Einheit, Verfolgung, Dummheit
2. Tante, Mutter, Kind, Schwester, Kusine, Oma
3. Gold, Laufen, Lachen, Essen, Kupfer, Sommer, Trinken
4. Afrikaner, Engländer, Araber, Schweizerin, Franzose
5. Kätzchen, Kälbchen, Vogel, Pferdchen, Mäuslein

Übung 5-2

ANWENDEN   A. Supply the definite article for the following fifty nouns.

1. _____ Frage		22. _____ Musik
2. _____ Platte		23. _____ Grammatik
3. _____ Lüge (*lie*)		24. _____ Fabrik (*factory*)
4. _____ Rauchen		25. _____ Republik
5. _____ Essen		26. _____ Winter
6. _____ A		27. _____ Sonntag
7. _____ F		28. _____ Schwester
8. _____ Arzt		29. _____ Schwesterchen
9. _____ Ärztin		30. _____ Wagen
10. _____ Verkäufer		31. _____ Garten
11. _____ Verkäuferin		32. _____ Osten
12. _____ Polizist		33. _____ Kind
13. _____ Polizistin		34. _____ Baby
14. _____ Polizei		35. _____ Universität
15. _____ Konditorei (*pastry shop*)		36. _____ Spezialität
16. _____ Religion		37. _____ Gold
17. _____ Operation		38. _____ Silber
18. _____ Million		39. _____ Freiheit
19. _____ Vorlesung		40. _____ Krankheit
20. _____ Warnung		41. _____ Möglichkeit
21. _____ Erkältung (*cold*)		42. _____ Freundlichkeit

43. _____ Held (*hero*)   47. _____ Information
44. _____ Heldin   48. _____ Meinung
45. _____ C   49. _____ Bruder
46. _____ Liebe   50. _____ Brüderchen

B. For each noun given, provide three additional nouns that you associate with it. Supply the correct articles.

MODEL: das Haus → <u>das Fenster, die Tür, der Garten</u>

1. die Musik   6. das Essen
2. das Buch   7. der Computer
3. das Frühstück   8. der Sommer
4. die Ferien   9. die Wanderung
5. die Familie   10. das Auto

Gender of compound nouns

Compound nouns combine two or more nouns into one. They are written as one word in German and take the gender of the last noun in the compound. (For information on the spelling of compound nouns, see Appendix §1.)

das Semester
die Arbeit   **die** Semesterarbeit

Übung 5-3

ANWENDEN Provide the definite article for the following noun compounds.

1. Tageszeitung   5. Kinderärztin   9. Touristeninformation
2. Wonnemonat   6. Hausfreund   10. Faschingsdienstag
3. Türklinke   7. Straßenführer   11. Winterkleidung
4. Schnellkochplatte 8. Baletttruppe   12. Musiklehrer

§2 The Plural

The plural of the definite article is the same for all genders: **die**.

die Väter, **die** Mütter, **die** Kinder

English ordinarily adds an **-s** or **-es** to the singular of a noun to form the plural. There are a few irregular noun plurals, such as *child - children, foot - feet, man - men*, etc.

In German, nouns form their plurals in several different ways.

Some nouns add an ending: **-e**, **-er**, **-en**, **-n**, or **-s**.

SINGULAR	PLURAL	DICTIONARY INDICATION OF PLURAL FORM
der Tag	die Tage	der Tag, **-e**
das Lied	die Lieder	das Lied, **-er**
die Nation	die Nationen	die Nation, **-en**
die Frage	die Fragen	die Frage, **-n**
das Hotel	die Hotels	das Hotel, **-s**

Some nouns add no ending to form the plural.

der Lehrer	die Lehrer	der Lehrer, **-**

Some nouns umlaut the stem vowel to form the plural.

der Gast	die Gäste	der Gast, **⸚e**

Because of the many ways German plurals are formed, it is very important to learn the plural form (along with the gender) of each noun when you learn the noun's meaning. You may find it helpful to study the following charts, which provide an overview of the most common patterns of German plural formation. There are many exceptions to these patterns, however, and while these charts can help you guess a plural, they are no substitute for learning the individual plural forms.

§3   Monosyllabics (nouns of one syllable)

Most monosyllabic masculine and feminine nouns add **-e**; neuter nouns add **-er** and less frequently **-e**.

MASCULINE		FEMININE		NEUTER	
add **-e** some also add umlaut		add **-e** and umlaut if possible		add **-er** or **-e** and umlaut if possible	
der Punkt	die Punkte	die Nacht	die Nächte	das Buch	die Bücher
der Hund	die Hunde	die Stadt	die Städte	das Haus	die Häuser
der Satz	die Sätze	die Hand	die Hände	das Licht	die Lichter
der Baum	die Bäume	die Wurst	die Würste	das Rad	die Räder
der Saal	die Säle	but: die Frau	die Frauen	das Ding	die Dinge
but: der Mann	die Männer	die Tür	die Türen	das Jahr	die Jahre
der Wald	die Wälder			das Stück	die Stücke

Keep in mind: **a, o, u**, and **au** with an umlaut become **ä, ö, ü**, and **äu**; **aa** becomes **ä**.

§4   Polysyllabics (nouns of more than one syllable)

MASCULINE AND NEUTER	FEMININE

add no ending to nouns that end in **-el**, **-en**, **-er**, **-chen**, **-lein**; some masculine nouns take an umlaut

der Mantel	die Mäntel		
der Wagen	die Wägen		
der Lehrer	die Lehrer		
das Mädchen	die Mädchen		
das Kätzlein	die Kätzlein		

ending **-e** added to most other nouns; some masculine nouns also add an umlaut

der Anzug	die Anzüge
der Versuch	die Versuche
der Vertrag	die Verträge
das Paket	die Pakete
das Problem	die Probleme
der Bus	die Busse

Note: Nouns with the ending **-nis** and **-us** double the **-s** when a declensional ending is added.

add **-n** to nouns ending in **-e**, **-el**, **-er**; add **-en** to all others

die Familie	die Familien
die Stunde	die Stunden
die Vokabel	die Vokabeln
die Schwester	die Schwestern
die Antwort	die Antworten
die Arbeit	die Arbeiten
die Nation	die Nationen
die Universität	die Universitäten
die Rechnung	die Rechnungen
die Studentin	die Studentinnen

Note: Feminine nouns with the ending **-in** have double **-n** in the plural.

Mutter and **Tochter** do not add a plural ending; they umlaut the stem vowel.

die Mutter	**die Mütter**
die Tochter	**die Töchter**

For masculine nouns ending **-(e)n**, see Special Declensions of Nouns in this Kapitel §7, 1. For foreign nouns that add the plural ending **-s**, see Special Declensions of Nouns in this Kapitel §5, 3.

Übung 5-4

ANWENDEN The following nouns, organized by theme, form the plural in accordance with the guidelines just given. State the plural forms of these nouns and add an umlaut where indicated.

MODELS:	der Freund	die Freunde
	das Glas (umlaut)	die Gläser
	der Koffer	die Koffer
	das Programm	die Programme
	die Straße	die Straßen

1. der Stuhl (umlaut)
2. der Tisch
3. der Schrank (umlaut)
4. der Fernseher

5. das Regal
6. die Kommode (*chest of drawers*)
7. der Sessel
8. das Bild

 9. das Kleid
10. der Hut (umlaut)
11. der Mantel (umlaut)
12. der Anzug (umlaut)
13. die Jacke
14. der Rock (umlaut)
15. der Strumpf (umlaut)
16. der Schuh

17. das Flugzeug (~~umlaut~~) *falsch*
18. der Zug (umlaut)
19. der Bus
20. das Schiff
21. das Boot
22. das Rad (umlaut)

23. die Frage
24. das Problem
25. die Prüfung
26. die Erfindung
27. das Experiment

28. die Studentin
29. die Sekretärin
30. der Assistent
31. der Professor
32. die Universität
33. die Arbeit
34. der Saal (umlaut)
35. das Zimmer

36. die Stunde
37. der Zeiger (*hand on a watch*)
38. der Monat
39. das Jahr
40. die Zeit
41. die Minute
42. der Wecker (*alarm clock*)
43. die Sekunde

44. das Glas (umlaut)
45. der Teller
46. die Tasse
47. die Gabel
48. die Serviette (*napkin*)
49. der Topf (umlaut)

50. das Telefon
51. der Anruf
52. die Karte
53. der Brief
54. das Paket

Compound nouns in the plural

The last noun element in a compound noun, which determines its gender, also determines its plural form. The other elements remain unchanged.

	SINGULAR	PLURAL
der Motor das Rad	das Motorrad	die Motorräder

Übung 5-5

ANWENDEN Supply the plurals of the following compound nouns.

 1. der Geburtstag
 2. die Mathematikprüfung
 3. die Telefonnummer
 4. der Fußballtrainer
 5. das Sommerkleid
 6. der Handschuh
 7. das Weinglas
 8. die Semesterarbeit
 9. der Konzertsaal
10. der Wintermantel

The Cases

§5   General Pattern for Declining German Nouns

There are four cases in German: nominative, accusative, dative, and genitive. The following paradigm shows typical masculine, neuter, and feminine nouns along with all their singular and plural forms.

		MASCULINE	FEMININE	NEUTER
SINGULAR	NOMINATIVE	der Freund	die Stadt	das Kleid
	ACCUSATIVE	den Freund	die Stadt	das Kleid
	DATIVE	dem Freund	der Stadt	dem Kleid
	GENITIVE	des Freundes	der Stadt	des Kleid(e)s
PLURAL	NOMINATIVE	die Freunde	die Städte	die Kleider
	ACCUSATIVE	die Freunde	die Städte	die Kleider
	DATIVE	den Freunden	den Städten	den Kleidern
	GENITIVE	der Freunde	der Städte	der Kleider

Note: a. The nominative and accusative cases are identical in form, except for the article in the masculine accusative singular.

b. Some fixed expressions have maintained the dative **-e** that used to be common for masculine and neuter of monosyllabics.

nach (zu) Hause, auf dem Lande (*in the country*), **im Jahre** (*in the year of*)

In colloquial speech, the **-e** may be omitted in these expressions also.

c. The dative plural adds **-n** to all nouns unless the plural ends in **-n** or **-s**.

d. The genitive masculine and neuter may add **-es** or **-s**.
   1. **-es** is usually added to monosyllabics (**des Buches, des Tisches**), although in colloquial speech only the **-s** may be added.
   2. The **-es** ending is mandatory with all nouns that end in **-s, -ss, -ß, -z**, and **-x** (des Glas**es**, Gruß**es**, Gesetz**es**, Reflex**es**).
   3. **-s** is added in all other instances.

e. Feminine nouns never take an ending in the singular.

Note the summary of the declension of German nouns.

	MASCULINE	FEMININE	NEUTER	PLURAL
NOMINATIVE	der ___	die ___	das ___	die ___
ACCUSATIVE	den ___	die ___	das ___	die ___
DATIVE	dem ___(e)	der ___	dem ___(e)	den ___n
GENITIVE	des ___(e)s	der ___	des ___(e)s	der ___

§6   The Main Uses of the Cases

1. The nominative

a. The nominative is the case of the *subject* of the sentence, the noun (person or thing) that performs the action described by the verb.

> **Der Katalog** liegt auf meinem Schreibtisch.
> **Die Studentin** heißt Margot Bauer.
> Das glauben **die Leute** nicht.*
> **Das Mädchen** kennt mich vielleicht nicht.

> *Remember that many elements other than the subject may precede the verb. The subject, however, is the element that the verb agrees with in person and number, whether it precedes or follows the verb.

b. The nominative is the case of the predicate noun, also called *predicate nominative*. It is a noun that completes the meaning of the verbs **sein, werden, bleiben** (*to remain*), and **heißen**.

> Die Feier ist **der Höhepunkt** seines Lebens.
> Das wird **der Höhepunkt** seines Lebens.
> Das bleibt **der Höhepunkt** seines Lebens.
> Der Direktor heißt **Herr Bachmann**.

2. The accusative

The accusative is the case of the direct object of the verb. The direct object is the noun (or pronoun) that receives the direct action implied in the meaning of the verb.

> Bitte fragen Sie **den Chef**!
> **Den Musiklehrer** kenne ich nicht.

Note that the object may be placed before the verb. In German, it is not the position of a noun, but its case (e.g., accusative) and meaning that indicate the noun's function in a sentence.

Do not confuse:
> Inge hat **den Katalog**. (direct object)
> Das ist **der Katalog**. (predicate nominative)

The accusative is also used with a group of prepositions (cf. Kap. 7) and time phrases (cf. Kap. 11) discussed later in this book.

Übung 5-6

ANWENDEN For each blank, provide the appropriate form of each noun in parentheses. Adjust the verb (singular/plural) when necessary.

1. Das ist _____ für Renate. (der Scheck, das Paket, die Zeitung)
2. Holst du bitte _____ für Renate? (der Scheck, das Paket, die Zeitung)

3. Das ist _____ von Sabine. (die Kamera, der Fernseher, das Bild, die CDs)
4. Bringst du bitte _____ ? (die Kamera, der Fernseher, das Bild, die CDs)
5. Das ist _____ von Karen Clausen. (das Kleid, die Kleider, das Kostüm, die Bluse, die Blusen)
6. Wäschst du bitte _____ ? (das Kleid, die Kleider, das Kostüm, die Bluse, die Blusen)

3. The dative

The dative is the case of the *indirect* object, namely, the person (or thing) to whom something is given or said, or for whom something is done. In a sentence with two objects, the dative object is typically the one that is *animate*, a person or other living being.

Frau Korb	**dem Chef die Post.**	*Ms. Korb is giving the boss the mail.* (or: *Ms. Korb is giving the mail to the boss.*)
Gib	**der Katze das Futter.**	*Give the cat the food* (or: *Give the food to the cat.*)
	INDIRECT DIRECT	
	OBJECT OBJECT	

When both objects are nouns, the indirect object (usually animate) normally precedes the direct object (usually a thing). However, if the indirect object is supposed to be stressed, it can follow the direct object since function and case are indicated by the articles rather than by position alone (cf. Kap. 17 §5, 2).

Vokabulartip: **schenken** *und* **geben**

In German, the verb **schenken** means *to give as a gift*. The verb **geben** is not used in this sense, but rather in the sense of *to give, to hand*.

Ich **gebe** dem Chef die Post.	*I am **giving (handing)** the boss the mail.*
Ich **schenke** der Chefin das Buch.	*I am **giving** the boss a book [as a present].*

The dative is also used with a large group of prepositions (cf. Kap. 7) and time phrases (cf. Kap. 11) discussed later in this book.

Übung 5-7

ANWENDEN Insert the appropriate forms of the direct and indirect objects.

Frau Sommer fragt, ob ihre Kinder verschiedene Sachen erledigt haben.

1. Peter, hast du _____ _____ gebacken?
   (die Oma) (der Kuchen)
2. Habt ihr _____ _____ gebracht?
   (der Opa) (die Zeitschrift)
3. Wer hat _____ _____ gekauft?
   (die Kinder) (die Süßigkeiten)

4. Hat Christian _____ _____ gebracht?
      (die Nachbarin) (das Mittagessen)
5. Habt ihr _____ _____ geschrieben?
      (die Verwandten) (die Briefe)

Some verbs have only a dative object without an accusative object. These include:

antworten	*to answer*
danken	*to thank*
folgen	*to follow*
gefallen (gefällt), gefiel, hat gefallen	*to please, like*
gehören	*to belong to*
gratulieren	*to congratulate*
helfen (hilft), half, hat geholfen	*to help*
trauen	*to trust*
widersprechen (widerspricht), widersprach, hat widersprochen	*to contradict*

Übung 5-8

ANWENDEN For each blank, provide the dative forms of the nouns in parentheses.

Matthias hat Probleme in der Schule. Sein Schulleiter (principal) spricht mit ihm.

1. Schüler sollen _____ nicht widersprechen. (die Assistentin, der Schulleiter)
2. Warum antwortest du _____ nicht? (die Lehrerin, der Lehrer)
3. Warum hilfst du _____ nicht? (die Leute, die Schülerinnen)
4. Du kannst _____ für ihre Hilfe danken. (die Eltern, der Lehrer)
5. Warum traust du _____ nicht? (die Schule)

Vokabulartip: gefallen

Although **gefallen** functions grammatically like the other dative verbs listed above, note how the use of **gefallen** is different from the uses of its English equivalent.

Der Protest **gefällt** dem Bürgermeister nicht.	literally: *The protest does not please the mayor.*
	idiom: *The mayor does not like the protest.*

In German, the person or thing liked or disliked is the subject of the sentence and thus agrees in person and number with the verb **gefallen**.

Der Protest *(third-person singular)* **gefällt** dem Bürgermeister nicht.

The person who does the liking or disliking is the dative object of the verb (**dem Bürgermeister**).

Frequently, the dative is in first position.

> **Dem Bürgermeister** hat der Protest nicht gefallen.
> *The mayor did not like the protest.*

The verb **gefallen** is used almost exclusively in the third person singular and plural. Rarely, it is used with the first or second person.

> **Du gefällst** mir!   *I like you!*

Übung 5-9

VERSTEHEN For each sentence, first state who is doing the liking or disliking, then who or what is being liked or disliked.

> MODEL: Dem Engländer gefallen die Krawatten nicht.
>   <u>Der Engländer; die Krawatten</u>

1. Das Kleid gefällt der Dame nicht.
2. Dem Mädchen gefiel der Junge nicht.
3. Der Familie hat das Haus sehr gefallen.
4. Die Gemälde gefallen der Großmutter.
5. Den Kindern hat das Buch nicht gefallen.

Übung 5-10

ANWENDEN Express the following sentences in German. Begin sentences **1.** and **2.** with the item being liked or disliked. Begin sentences **3.** through **5.** with the person doing the liking or disliking.

1. The customer (*f.*) likes the dresses.
2. The man likes the suits.
3. The boy likes the earring.
4. The girl likes the hat.
5. The teenagers like the T-shirts.

4. The genitive

The genitive case indicates a possessive relationship or a relationship of belonging together. In English, it is expressed by *of* or *'s,* as seen in the following examples:

> Das ist der Vorname **des Vaters**.   *That is the first name **of the father**.*
>   or: *That is **the father's** first name.*

> Das ist die Verantwortung **der Mutter**.   *That is the responsibility **of the mother**.*
>   or: *That is **the mother's** responsibility.*

Ich repariere das Spielzeug **des Kindes**. *I'm fixing the toy **of the child**.*
or: *I'm fixing **the child's** toy.*

Das ist die Pflicht **der Eltern**.   *That is the duty **of the parents**.*
or: *That is **the parents'** duty.*

In spoken German, **von** + dative is often used instead of the genitive.

Das ist die Verantwortung **von der Mutter**.
Das ist der Vorname **von dem Kind**.

The use of the genitive with proper names:

Ich liebe **Barbaras Hund**.   *I love **Barbara's** dog.*

but: Den Hund **des Hausmeisters** mag ich nicht. *I don't like the **janitor's** dog.*

The genitive **-s** is added to a *proper noun*, namely, a person's given name,
regardless of gender; it is not separated from the name by an apostrophe. This
form is commonly used with proper names but seldom with other nouns. When
the proper name ends in an **s** sound (**-s**, **-ss**, **-ß**, **-z**, **-tz**), **-s** is not added to the
name. The omission is indicated by an apostrophe.

Das ist **Thomas'** Wagen.

However, in these instances the construction with **von** is generally preferred.

Das ist der Wagen **von Thomas**.

The genitive is also used with a set of prepositions (cf. Kap. 7) and time phrases
(cf. Kap. 11) discussed later in this book.

Übung 5-11

ANWENDEN Match each item logically with a person and provide a sentence
expressing possession with the genitive case.

MODEL: der Hut   die Dame   <u>Meine Tochter trägt den Hut der Dame.</u>

das Buch	der Schweizer
das Gemälde	die Kinder
der Rucksack	die Eltern
die Spielsachen	das Mädchen
der Walkman	die Studentin
die Autos	die Professorin
das Fahrrad	der Österreicher
das Haus	der Künstler

§7   Special Declensions of Nouns

1. Some masculine nouns add **-(e)n** in all cases except in the nominative singular. They are usually referred to as weak nouns.

SINGULAR	NOMINATIVE	der Student	der Junge	der Herr
	ACCUSATIVE	den Studenten	den Jungen	den Herrn
	DATIVE	dem Studenten	dem Jungen	dem Herrn
	GENITIVE	des Studenten	des Jungen	des Herrn
PLURAL	NOMINATIVE	die Studenten	die Jungen	die Herren
	ACCUSATIVE	die Studenten	die Jungen	die Herren
	DATIVE	den Studenten	den Jungen	den Herren
	GENITIVE	der Studenten	der Jungen	der Herren

These nouns do not take the customary **-s** in the genitive singular. Note that **Herr** adds **-n** in the singular and **-en** in the plural. When used with a name, **Herr** is declined in accordance with its function in the sentence.

> Wo ist Herr Berger?
> Haben Sie **Herrn** Berger gesehen?

This group of nouns includes:

a. many nouns of foreign origin that are accented on the last syllable, such as **der Assistent, der Demokrat, der Komponist, der Philosoph, der Polizist, der Präsident, der Student, der Tourist**;

b. masculine nouns that end in an unstressed **-e**, such as **der Jude** (*Jew*), **der Junge, der Kunde** (*customer*), **der Löwe**

c. a few monosyllabic nouns, such as **der Mensch, der Christ, der Held, der Herr**

2. A very few masculine nouns, such as **der Buchstabe** (*letter of the alphabet*), **der Friede** (*peace*), **der Gedanke** (*thought*), **der Glaube** (*faith*), **der Name**, and **der Wille**, have the endings of the weak noun declension and an additional **-s** in the genitive (**des Namens, des Willens**).

One neuter noun, **das Herz**, does not add the weak noun ending in the accusative singular. Compare the declensions of **der Name** and **das Herz**.

SINGULAR	der Name	das Herz
	den Namen	das Herz
	dem Namen	dem Herzen
	des Namens	des Herzens
PLURAL	die Namen	die Herzen
	die Namen	die Herzen
	den Namen	den Herzen
	der Namen	der Herzen

3. Nouns of foreign origin that form the plural by adding **-s** have the ending **-s** in all cases of the plural.

		MASCULINE	FEMININE	NEUTER
SINGULAR	NOMINATIVE	der Scheck	die Party	das Auto
	ACCUSATIVE	den Scheck	die Party	das Auto
	DATIVE	dem Scheck	der Party	dem Auto
	GENITIVE	des Schecks	der Party	des Autos
PLURAL	NOMINATIVE	die Schecks	die Partys	die Autos
	ACCUSATIVE	die Schecks	die Partys	die Autos
	DATIVE	den Schecks	den Partys	den Autos
	GENITIVE	der Schecks	der Partys	der Autos

Other common nouns of this group are: **das Baby, -s; der Chef, -s; das Hobby, -s; das Hotel, -s; die Kamera, -s; das Kino, -s; das Restaurant,-s; der Tip,-s; das Radio, -s.**

Keep in mind: Only with nouns of foreign origin may the declensional ending **-s** be a plural form; otherwise, it signals the genitive singular case.

4. Some nouns of foreign origin have special plurals.

SINGULAR	NOMINATIVE	das Thema	das Drama	das Datum	das Museum	das Stipendium
	ACCUSATIVE	das Thema				
	DATIVE	dem Thema				
	GENITIVE	des Themas				
PLURAL	NOMINATIVE	die Themen	die Dram**en**	die Dat**en**	die Mus**een**	die Stipendi**en**
	ACCUSATIVE	die Themen				
	DATIVE	den Themen				
	GENITIVE	der Themen				

Übung 5-12

ZUSAMMENFASSUNG Nouns, direct and indirect objects.

A. For each activity, list at least four items (with articles and plural forms) associated with it.

> MODEL: Einkaufen → die Tasche, -n; das Portmonee, -s; der Scheck, -s;
> die Liste, -n

1. Schreiben
2. Wandern
3. Ski fahren
4. Geburtstag feiern
5. Kochen

B. Make two lists, one of people (friends, family members) and another of items that one might give as a gift. Then state what present you will give to each person. Use verbs such as **schenken**, **kaufen**, **mitbringen**, and **besorgen**.

MODEL: Opa   Hausschuhe   <u>Ich werde dem Opa Hausschuhe</u>
                                       <u>besorgen.</u>
         Frauke   CD   <u>Ich werde der Frauke die CD kaufen.</u>

§8   For Reference: The Declension of Nouns

1. Most masculine nouns and all neuter nouns add **-s** or **-es** to the genitive singular.

2. A small group of masculine nouns (weak nouns) adds **-n** or **-en** in all forms, except in the nominative singular. This is the weak declension.

3. All nouns add **-n** to the dative plural, unless the nominative plural ends in **-n** or **-s**.

4. Feminine nouns never take an ending in the singular.

5. The last word of a compound noun is declined, i.e., the compound takes its article, number, and case endings.

6. Similar to the principal parts of verbs, from which all tenses can be derived, there are principal parts of nouns, from which all cases can be derived. They are:
   a. the nominative singular (the case in which nouns are listed in all vocabularies and dictionaries)
   b. the genitive singular
   c. the nominative plural

Good dictionaries list information on declension in some form or other. Here is one example of how information on nouns will be listed:

Film *m.* (-[e]s/-e)

nominative	gender	genitive singular	nominative plural
singular noun	(masculine)	ending added to	ending added to
		noun (if any)	singular form (if any)

Studentin *f.* (-/-nen)   **Drama** *n.* (-s/Dramen)

   if no ending is added,   if the plural nominative
   this is indicated with   is unusual, it will be
   a hyphen   indicated here

If a compound noun is not listed in a dictionary, find information on declension by looking up the last noun element of the compound.

In this book, the nominative singular and plural of each noun are given, as the genitive singular for most nouns is predictable.

   a. Feminine nouns never add an ending in the genitive singular
   b. Masculine and neuter nouns add **-(e)s** in the genitive singular, with the exception of weak nouns, which add **-(e)n**. The latter are marked *weak* in this book.

The genitive is only marked as such in those rare instances when it has the weak ending plus **-s**, as in

> **der Name** (*weak; genitive* **-ns**), **-n**.

For the use of nouns with **der**-words and **ein**-words, see Kapitel 6; with prepositions, see Kapitel 7; in time expressions, see Kapitel 11.

Themen und Vokabular

Geben und Schenken

besorgen	*to get, buy*
bringen, brachte, hat gebracht	*to bring*
mit•bringen	*to bring along (also: to bring as a token or gift)*
geben, gab, hat gegeben	*to give, to hand*
jemandem (dat) etwas (acc) leihen, lieh, hat geliehen	*to loan something to somebody*
kaufen	*to buy*
schenken	*to give as a gift*
schicken	*to send, to mail*

Schicken

der Brief, -e	*letter*
die E-mail	*e-mail*
die Postkarte, -n	*postcard*
das Paket, -e	*package*
das Päckchen, -	*small package*
die Post	*mail*
der Scheck, -s	*check*

Familienmitglieder

der Bruder, ⸚	*brother*
der Cousin, -s	*cousin (m.)*
die Eltern (pl.)	*parents*
die Geschwister (pl.)	*siblings*
die Großeltern (pl.)	*grandparents*
die Großmutter, ⸚	*grandmother*
der Großvater, ⸚	*grandfather*
das Kind, -er	*child*
die Kusine, -n	*cousin (f.)*

die Mutter, ⸚	*mother*
der Nachbar, -n (weak)	*neighbor (m.)*
die Nachbarin, -nen	*neighbor (f.)*
der Neffe, -n (weak)	*nephew*
die Nichte, -n	*niece*
der Onkel, -	*uncle*
die Schwester, -n	*sister*
die Tante, -n	*aunt*
der Teenager, -	*teenager*
der Vater, ⸚	*father*
die Verwandten (pl.)	*relatives*

Besitztum

das Auto, -s	*car, automobile*
das Bild, -er	*picture*
der Bildband, ⸚e	*photo book*
das Buch, ⸚er	*book*
der CD-Spieler, -	*CD-player*
der Computer, -	*computer*
das Fahrrad, ⸚er (Rad)	*bicycle (bike)*
der Fernseher, -	*TV set*
das Fotoalbum, Fotoalben	*photo album*
der Fotoapparat, -e	*camera*
das Gemälde, -	*painting*
das Haus, ⸚er	*house*
die Kleidung (sing. only)	*clothing, clothes*
das Kleidungsstück, -e	*article of clothing*
das Motorrad, ⸚er	*motorcycle*
die Stereoanlage, -n	*stereo*
die Videokamera, -s	*video camera*
der Wagen, -	*car*

KAPITEL

6

der-Words and ein-Words; Personal Pronouns

der-Words

§1 Forms

Compare the boldface words in the following sentence pairs:

> **Der** Wagen gefällt mir nicht.
> **Dieser** Wagen gefällt mir nicht.
>
> Ich kaufe **den** Wagen.
> Ich kaufe **diesen** Wagen.

Dieser is one of several words that are called *der-words* because their declensional endings resemble those of the definite article. The most common **der**-words are listed below.

dieser	*this*
jener	*that*
jeder	*every*
mancher	*some, many a;* plural: *some, a few* (not: *many*)
solcher	*such a;* plural: *such*
welcher	*which*
alle	*all*
beide	*both*

Declension of der-words

Compare the declension of the definite article with the declension of the **der**-word **dieser**.

	MASCULINE	NEUTER	FEMININE	PLURAL
NOMINATIVE	der dieser	das dies**es**	die diese	die diese
ACCUSATIVE	den diesen	das dies**es**	die diese	die diese
DATIVE	dem diesem	dem diesem	der dieser	den diesen
GENITIVE	des dieses	des dieses	der dieser	der dieser

The endings of the **der**-words in boldface are slightly different from the endings of the definite article.

100

Übung 6-1

ANWENDEN A. Respond to each question by using the appropriate **der**-word equivalent for the English article given in parentheses. You may begin your sentences with various introductory clauses (**Ja, ich finde,... Ich glaube,... Ich denke,...** etc.).

MODEL: Annette: Welchen Blazer soll ich mitnehmen? (*this*)
         Mutter: <u>Also, ich denke, du sollst diesen Blazer mitnehmen.</u>

Annette bespricht Reisevorbereitungen mit ihrer Mutter.

1. Welche Tasche soll ich mitnehmen? (*this*)
2. Und welchen Freunden soll ich eine Postkarte schreiben? (*all*)
3. Aus welcher Stadt soll ich anrufen? (*every*)
4. Welcher Mantel passt am besten? (*this*)
5. Soll ich (Leder)schuhe mitnehmen? (*such*)
6. Kann ich mir ein Buch ausleihen? (*this*)
7. Soll ich den Verwandten schreiben? (*some*)
8. Brauche ich die Ausweise? (*both*)

B. Now, form questions that combine the German word for *which* with the items given. Use verbs such as **mitnehmen**, **einpacken**, and **brauchen**.

MODEL: der Rock   →   <u>Welchen Rock soll ich einpacken?</u>

Annette braucht weiterhin die Hilfe ihrer Mutter.

der Seidenschal, das Kostüm, die Strümpfe, das Medikament, die Brille, der Anorak, der Regenmantel

C. Use **all-** or **jed-** to form five statements that generalize about people or things. You may use the suggested nouns or provide your own.

MODEL: <u>Alle Deutschen sind fleißig.</u>

Politikerin, Student, Professor, Grammatikbuch, Film von Spielberg, Anwalt, Ärztin

§2   The Use of *dieser* and *jener*

Zuerst müssen wir **dieses** und nicht **jenes** Problem besprechen.
First we have to discuss this problem, not that one.

The **der**-words **dieser** and **jener** are sometimes used together to express a contrast, as in the example above. **Jener** is rarely used otherwise. When no contrast is expressed, **dieser** is used as the equivalent of both *this* and *that*.

Niemand kann **diese** Frage beantworten.   *Nobody can answer this/that question.*
Niemand kennt **diese** Leute.   *Nobody knows these/those people.*

§3   The Definite Article Meaning *this/these* or *that/those*

In conversational German, the definite article, when spoken with heavy stress, is often the equivalent of English *this/these* or *that/those*. Compare

Dieser Wagen ist mein Traum. ⟶
Der Wagen ist mein Traum. ⟶ *This/That car is my dream.*

Diesen Wagen möchte ich haben. ⟶
Den Wagen möchte ich haben. ⟶ *I'd like to have this/that car.*

Dieses Mädchen möchte ich kennenlernen. ⟶
Das Mädchen möchte ich kennenlernen. ⟶ *I'd like to meet this/that girl.*

Diese Mädchen sind sehr nett. ⟶
Die Mädchen sind sehr nett. ⟶ *These/Those girls are very nice.*

§4   The German Equivalents of *this/that is* and *these/those are*

Compare the following sentences.

a. **Dieser** Wein ist großartig.	*This wine is great.*
b. **Das** (dies) **ist** der beste Wein.	*That is the best wine.*
c. **Das sind** die besten Weine.	*Those are the best wines.*

In sentence a., **diese** is a demonstrative adjective preceding the noun **Wein**. It is declined and its ending agrees with **Wein**.

In sentence b., **das** does not take an ending because it does not precede the noun. It is a demonstrative pronoun pointing out **Wein**.

In sentence c., the noun being pointed out, **Weine**, is plural and the verb agrees with it (**sind**). There is no plural form of **das**.

Übung 6-2

ANWENDEN Provide the correct form of **dies-** or **das**. Insert the appropriate third person singular or plural form of **sein** after **das**.

MODEL: _____ Sessel möchte Franz. <u>Diesen Sessel möchte Franz.</u>
_____ die Vitrine für Onkel Karl. <u>Das ist die Vitrine für Onkel Karl.</u>

Familie Kolleg verteilt den Besitz ihrer Großmutter.

1. _____ Antikschrank bekommt Gerda.
2. _____ Porzellanservice gehört jetzt Tante Erika.
3. _____ Teppich hat bestimmt ein Vermögen gekostet.
4. _____ die Kristallgläser von unserer Urgroßmutter.
5. _____ Couchgarnitur passt gut in Gerhards Zimmer.
6. Und _____ der Eichentisch für Sabine.
7. _____ die Holzstühle für den Tisch.
8. _____ das Himmelbett für Annes Tochter.

ein-Words

The *ein-words* take the endings of the indefinite article **ein** (*a, an*). Including the indefinite article, **ein**-words are **ein**, the negative article **kein** (*no*), and the possessives **mein** (*my*), **dein** (*your*, fam.), **sein** (*his, its*), **ihr** (*her*), **unser** (*our*), **euer** (*your*, fam.), **ihr** (*their*), and **Ihr** (*your*, formal).

§5   *Ein - kein*

Compare the declension of **der** and **(k)ein**.

	MASCULINE		FEMININE	
NOMINATIVE	der Mann	(k)ein Mann	die Frau	(k)eine Frau
ACCUSATIVE	den Mann	(k)ein**en** Mann	die Frau	(k)ein**e** Frau
DATIVE	dem Mann	(k)ein**em** Mann	der Frau	(k)ein**er** Frau
GENITIVE	des Mannes	(k)ein**es** Mannes	der Frau	(k)ein**er** Frau

	NEUTER		PLURAL	
NOMINATIVE	das Kind	(k)ein Kind	die/kein**e**	Männer, Frauen, Kinder
ACCUSATIVE	das Kind	(k)ein Kind	die/kein**e**	Männer, Frauen, Kinder
DATIVE	dem Kind	(k)ein**em** Kind	den/kein**en**	Männern, Frauen, Kindern
GENITIVE	des Kindes	(k)ein**es** Kindes	der/kein**er**	Männer, Frauen, Kinder

Note: **Ein**, naturally, does not have a plural, but its negation **kein** does. The **ein**-words have the same endings as the definite article, with the exception of the three singular forms (boxed above) that take no ending:

nominative masculine **(k)ein Mann**   nominative neuter **(k)ein Kind**

accusative neuter   **(k)ein Kind**

Übung 6-3

ANWENDEN Respond to each question with an appropriate sentence that contains a noun preceded by the correct form of **ein-**.

MODEL: Susanne muss einen Brief schreiben. Was braucht sie?
<u>Sie braucht einen Stift.</u> Or: <u>Sie braucht einen Kuli.</u>

1. Doris möchte einen Kaffee trinken. Was holt sie?
2. Ankes Mann möchte die Resultate von den Fußballspielen wissen. Was gibt Anke ihm?
3. Anke muss ein Paar Schuhe bezahlen. Wem gibt sie das Geld?
4. Anke und ihr Mann haben Gäste. Was besorgen sie vielleicht für die Einladung?
5. Die Kinder gehen schlafen. Was haben oder hören Kinder gern im Bett?

The use of kein

When preceding a noun, **kein** may mean *no, not a,* or *not any.*

Ich habe **kein** Auto. ⎯⎯⎯ *I have no car.*
I don't have a car.

Sie hat **keine** Geduld. ⎯⎯⎯ *She has no patience.*
She doesn't have any patience.

Das ist **kein** Wein—   *That isn't wine—it's grape juice.*
das ist Traubensaft.

Übung 6-4

ANWENDEN   Complete the sentences logically with a phrase that contains the correct form of **kein**. Form a separate phrase for each item given in parentheses.

> MODEL: Christa soll eine Bekannte vom Flughafen abholen, aber... (Zeit)
> aber sie hat keine Zeit.

Gewisse Leute haben die Dinge, die sie brauchen, nicht.

1. Kurt möchte gern Tennis spielen, aber... (Partner, Partnerin)
2. Nadja muss eine Arbeit fertig schreiben, aber... (Computer, Ideen, Lust)
3. Lisa kann ihre Wäsche nicht waschen, weil... (Waschmaschine)
4. Die Freunde von Martin können nicht bei ihm übernachten, weil... (Platz, Gästezimmer)

Nicht ein is used instead of **kein** when **ein** is emphasized (often having the meaning of *one*).

Ordinary stress

Ich habe **kein** Wort verstanden.   *I did not understand a word.*

Ein emphasized

Ich habe **nicht ein** Wort verstanden.   *I didn't understand one (a single) word.*

The uses of manch ein, so/solch ein, *and* was für ein/welch ein

1. manch ein (*many a*)

The singular inflected forms of **manch-** mean *many a* or *some*. They are much less common than the plural form **manche**. When the singular form occurs, it is usually combined with **ein-**. Note that **manch** remains uninflected and **ein-** is inflected to agree with the noun that follows it.

Manch eine Frau ist in diesem   *Many a woman is successful in this*
Geschäft erfolgreich.   *business.*

2. so/solch ein (*such a*)

Solche, like **manche**, also occurs mostly in the plural. In conversational German, the singular form **so ein** is most commonly used as the equivalent of *such a*.

So ein/solch ein Haus möchte ich haben.	*I'd like to have such a house. I'd like to have a house like that.*

3. was für ein/welch ein (*what a*)

Was für ein, more commonly than **welch ein**, is used mainly in exclamations and questions. When it introduces a question, it has the meaning of *what kind of (a)*.

Was für ein/welch ein Dummkopf!	*What a blockhead! What a dummy!*
Was für eine/welch eine Zeitverschwendung!	*What a waste of time!*

Was für ein, reflects the gender, number, and case of the singular noun following it.

Was für ein Hund ist das?	*What kind of (a) dog is that?*
Was für einen Hund haben Sie?	*What kind of (a) dog do you have?*

Note that the expression is reduced to **was für** when used with plural nouns.

Was für Filme gefallen Ihnen?	*What kind of films do you like?*
Was für Leute sind das?	*What kind of people are these?*

Übung 6-5

ANWENDEN A. Form questions with **was für (ein-)**.

MODEL: Pflanzen   <u>Was für Pflanzen sind das?</u>

Richard hat viele interessante Dinge (und Menschen) in seinem Haus. Erik will genaueres über sie erfahren.

Videokamera, Computer, Gemälde, Skulptur, Leute, Kinder, Kostüme

B. Provide an exclamation with **was für ein** that fits the situation.

MODEL: Sie haben Ihr Portmonee verloren.
          <u>Was für ein Ärger!</u>

1. Ein Freund von Ihnen hat seinen Schlüssel in der Wohnung vergessen.
2. Ihre beste Freundin steht plötzlich vor Ihrer Tür!
3. Sie haben drei Stunden beim Arzt gewartet.
4. Seit drei Tagen regnet es ohne Pause.

§6   The Possessives

The possessives are

mein	*my*
dein	*your* (familiar singular)
sein	*his, its*
ihr	*her, its*
unser	*our*
euer	*your* (familiar plural)
ihr	*their*
Ihr	*your* (formal)

When preceding a noun, the possessive takes the ending of **ein/kein**. This ending is determined by the gender, number (singular or plural), and case of the noun that follows it.

Das ist **mein** Vater.
Das ist **meine** Mutter.
Das sind **meine** Eltern.

The nominative case

	MASCULINE	FEMININE	NEUTER	PLURAL
(my)	mein Freund	meine Freundin	mein Auto	meine Hobbys
(your)	dein Freund	deine Freundin	dein Auto	deine Hobbys
(his, its)	sein Freund	seine Freundin	sein Auto	seine Hobbys
(her, its)	ihr Freund	ihre Freundin	ihr Auto	ihre Hobbys
(our)	unser Freund	uns(e)re Freundin	unser Auto	uns(e)re Hobbys
(your)	euer Freund	eu(e)re Freundin	euer Auto	eu(e)re Hobbys
(their)	ihr Freund	ihre Freundin	ihr Auto	ihre Hobbys
(your)	Ihr Freund	Ihre Freundin	Ihr Auto	Ihre Hobbys

Note: a. **unser, euer**: **-er** is part of the stem, not a declensional ending.

   b. **uns(e)re, eu(e)re**: The **e** before the **r** may be omitted when a declensional ending is added.

   c. *your* ──
   dein (singular familiar) — referring to someone addressed as **du**
   euer (plural familiar) — referring to two or more persons addressed as **ihr**
   Ihr (formal) — referring to one or more persons addressed as **Sie**

   d. **ihr**: may have the meaning of *her* or *their* depending on the context.

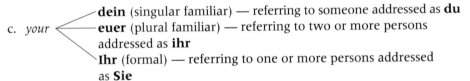

ihr Hobby ──
   her hobby
   their hobby

Declension of the possessives

As mentioned before, the possessives preceding nouns have the same case ending as **ein** and **kein**.

The three forms in boxes (nominative masculine, nominative neuter, and accusative neuter) have no endings.

	MASCULINE	NEUTER	FEMININE	PLURAL
NOMINATIVE	mein	mein	mein**e**	mein**e**
ACCUSATIVE	mein**en**	mein	mein**e**	mein**e**
DATIVE	mein**em**	mein**em**	mein**er**	mein**en**
GENITIVE	mein**es**	mein**es**	mein**er**	mein**er**

Übung 6-6

VERSTEHEN A. Identify all the possessors to which the possessive pronoun in boldface could refer.
1. Das ist **ihr** Wagen.   Hans / Christine / Herr und Frau Sommer
2. Willst du **seinen** Wagen kaufen?   Thomas / Thomas und Gerd / Anne
3. Das sind **ihre** Fotos.   Anne / Anne und Petra / Kurt / Herr Sommer
4. Warum wollen sie **ihr** Haus verkaufen?   Brigitte / Herr und Frau Sommer/ Frau Hahn / Anton

B. Complete each sentence by inserting the correct possessive pronoun.

Chaos! Alle Leute suchen etwas!

1. Sind das _____ Schuhe? (*your* [three forms])
2. Wo ist _____ Mantel? (*my, her, his*)
3. Ich finde den Hut von _____ Mutter nicht. (*my, our*)
4. Gehört diese Jacke _____ Freund? (*your* [familiar, singular; formal]; *their*)
5. Ist das die Brille _____ Kollegin? (*your* [formal], *our, his*)
6. Siehst du irgendwo _____ Anorak? (*my, his, her*)

The German equivalent of the English *its*

The German equivalent of *its* can be **sein-** or **ihr-**.

1. **der** Staat und **seine** Einwohner
   the nation and its inhabitants

2. **das** Dorf und **seine** Einwohner
   the village and its inhabitants

3. **die** Stadt und **ihre** Einwohner
   the city and its inhabitants

In 1. and 2., the possessors (**Staat/Dorf**) are masculine and neuter; the possessive **sein-** is used. In 3., the possessor (**Stadt**) is feminine; the possessive **ihr-** is used.

Übung 6-7

ANWENDEN Insert the German equivalent of *its*.

1. die Universität und _____ Professorinnen
2. das Krankenhaus und _____ Ärzte
3. der Klub und _____ Mitglieder
4. die Maschine und _____ Erfinder
5. das Buch und _____ Autorin

Uses of the Articles

§7 Uses of the Definite Article

1. Most names of countries are neuter. They are used without an article except when preceded by an adjective.

Deutschland	**in Deutschland**	but: **das** neue Deutschland
Schweden	**in Schweden**	**das** liberale Schweden
Italien	**in Italien**	**das** schöne Italien

The names of feminine, masculine, and plural countries require the definite article.

a. Feminine

   die Schweiz
   die Türkei
   die Bundesrepublik Deutschland (die BRD)

b. Masculine

   der Irak
   der Iran
   der Libanon

c. Plural

   die Niederlande (*The Netherlands*)
   die Vereinigten Staaten von Amerika (die USA)

Note the use of the definite article with the following countries:

Wir fahren **in die** Schweiz.
            in die Türkei.
            in die BRD.
            in die USA.
            in den Libanon.

2. German normally uses the definite article rather than the possessive with parts of the body and articles of clothing where reference to the subject of the sentence may be assumed.

Sie können das Huhn mit **den** Fingern essen.
You can eat the chicken with your fingers.

Er hat immer **die** Hände in **den** Taschen.
He always has his hands in his pockets.

Ich verliere **den** Verstand.
I'm losing my mind.

3. In prepositional phrases with verbs of motion, the article is used in German but not in English.

in die Stadt gehen	*to go to town*
in die Schule gehen	*to go to school*

mit dem Auto fahren	*to go by car*
mit dem Wagen fahren	

mit dem Bus fahren — *to go by bus*

mit der Bahn fahren	*to go by train*
mit dem Zug fahren	

mit der U-Bahn fahren — *to go by subway*

4. The article is used in English but not in German to express playing an instrument.

Klavier spielen	*to play the piano*
Violine/Geige spielen	*to play the violin*
Trompete spielen	*to play the trumpet*

but: ein Musikinstrument spielen   *to play a musical instrument*

The German equivalents of *the Wagners, at the Winklers'*, etc., may be expressed with or without the article.

Die Wagners haben Gäste.	*The Wagners have guests.*
Wir waren bei **Winklers**.	*We were at the Winklers'.*

§8 Uses of the Indefinite Article

Unlike English, German does not use the indefinite article with the verbs **sein**, **bleiben**, and **werden** when the following noun denotes a profession, nationality, or social status.

Andreas ist Student.	*Andreas is a student.*
Karin ist Studentin.	*Karin is a student.*
Barbara wird Ärztin.	*Barbara is going to be a doctor.*
Herr Schmidt will nicht Rechtsanwalt bleiben.	*Mr. Schmidt does not want to remain a lawyer.*
Er ist Witwer.	*He is a widower.*
Sie ist Witwe.	*She is a widow.*

However, the article is used when the noun is modified by an adjective.

Sie ist **eine geduldige Lehrerin**.
Du wirst bestimmt **ein guter Arzt** werden.

Vokabulartip: **Freunde** *und* **Bekannte**

To express that someone is a friend or an acquaintance, German speakers use the indefinite article and a possessive pronoun.

Gerd ist **ein Freund (von mir)**.	*Gerd is a friend (of mine).*
Frau Engel ist **eine Bekannte (von uns)**.	*Ms. Engel is an acquaintance (of ours).*

When a possessive pronoun precedes the noun, the meaning of *friend* is usually *girlfriend* or *boyfriend*.

Gerd ist **ihr Freund**.	*Gerd is her boyfriend.*
Inge ist **seine Freundin**.	*Inge is his girlfriend.*

Übung 6-8

ANWENDEN   A. State the country in which the different people live. Use a prepositional phrase with **in**.

> MODEL: Margret, Amsterdam
> <u>Margret wohnt in den Niederlanden.</u>

1. Familie Rütli, Zürich
2. Sefgül, Ankara
3. Bill, Washington
4. Herr und Frau Strauß, München
5. Hussein, Bagdad

B. State the country to which these people would travel.

> MODEL: Ruth ist fasziniert von Teheran.
> <u>Sie fährt in den Iran.</u>

1. Jutta möchte das Weiße Haus sehen.
2. Uwe möchte das UN-Gebäude in Genf besuchen.
3. Andreas findet Ankara hochinteressant.
4. Oliver ist Reporter und berichtet über die Konflikte in Beirut.
5. Pierre möchte eine Woche in Berlin verbringen.
6. Dagmar liebt Tulpen und Windmühlen.

C. Name five friends (or acquaintances, or boyfriends/girlfriends) and state their occupations.

> MODEL: <u>Ein Freund von mir ist Lehrer. Sein Name ist Richard.</u>
> <u>Eine Bekannte von mir ist Kinderärztin. Ihr Name ist Brigitte.</u>

Übung 6-9

ZUSAMMENFASSUNG **Der-**words, **ein-**words, and uses of the articles.

A. Restate the questions with the correct form of **welch-**.

> MODEL: Wollt ihr etwas lesen?
> <u>Und welches Buch wollt ihr lesen?</u>

Karin hat Leute zu Besuch und macht ihnen verschiedene Vorschläge.

1. Wollt ihr einen Wein trinken?
2. Soll ich eine Pizza bestellen?
3. Wollt ihr einen Film sehen?
4. Wollen wir ein Museum besuchen?
5. Findet ihr Kunstgallerien interessant?
6. Kommt später ein Freund von euch?

B. Answer the personalized questions.

1. Was sind Sie? Was sind Ihre Geschwister? Was sind Ihre Eltern von Beruf?
2. Wie kommen Sie zur Uni? Zur Arbeit?
3. Wie fahren Sie in den Urlaub?
4. Spielen Sie ein Instrument? Spielt jemand in Ihrer Familie ein Instrument? Welches? Spielt ein Freund/eine Freundin von Ihnen ein Instrument?
5. Was ist Ihr Hauptfach an der Uni? Was ist Ihr Nebenfach?

Stellen Sie diese Fragen jetzt einer Studienkollegin und einem Studienkollegen.

6. Wie heißt ein Professor/eine Professorin von dir?
7. Wie heißt deine Freundin/dein Freund? dein Mann/deine Frau?

Personal Pronouns

§9   The Cases of Personal Pronouns and Their Uses

The personal pronouns are declined as follows:

	1ST PERSON	2ND PERSON FAMILIAR	3RD PERSON MASCULINE	3RD PERSON FEMININE	3RD PERSON NEUTER	
SINGULAR NOMINATIVE	ich	du	er	sie	es	
ACCUSATIVE	mich	dich	ihn	sie	es	
DATIVE	mir	dir	ihm	ihr	ihm	
						FORMAL SINGULAR + PLURAL
PLURAL NOMINATIVE	wir	ihr		sie		Sie
ACCUSATIVE	uns	euch		sie		Sie
DATIVE	uns	euch		ihnen		Ihnen

Note: All cases of the formal address **Sie** are capitalized. The forms are the same as those of the third-person plural **sie** except for the capitalization.

The genitive forms, which are rare and occur only in literary German, are as follows:

SINGULAR	meiner	deiner	seiner	ihrer	seiner	
PLURAL	unser	euer		ihrer		Ihrer

Examples: Gedenke meiner!   *Think of me.*
             (commonly: Denk an mich!)

             Erbarme dich unser!   *Have mercy on us.*
             (used in prayers)

Übung 6-10

ANWENDEN   A. Insert the correct German equivalents in the accusative or dative.

Gabi (8 Jahre alt) hat schlechte Laune. Sie macht negative Kommentare über verschiedene Leute. Sie spricht mit ihren Eltern.

1. Meine Schwester hasst _____ *mich*_____. (*you* [familiar plural], *me*)
2. Meine Freunde helfen _____*mir*_____ nie! (*me, us*)
3. Ihr versteht _*mich, ihn, sie*_ (*me, her, him*) nicht.
4. Thomas hat immer gute Laune. Ich beneide _____! (*him*)

B. Formulate a logical follow-up question to each statement. Replace the boldface noun subject or object with a pronoun.

MODEL: Ich habe gestern **den Film** „Die Titanik" gesehen.
          <u>Und wie fandest du ihn?</u>

1. Ulrich, **meine Mutter** hat am Wochenende angerufen.
2. Ich habe **meiner Freundin** ein Geburtstagsgeschenk gekauft.
3. Und **meinem Bruder** habe ich eine CD geschenkt.
4. Ich habe **einen Freund** von mir im Kino getroffen.
5. **Eine Kollegin** von mir heiratet nächste Woche.

Personal pronouns referring to inanimate objects

Because inanimate objects in German are masculine, feminine, or neuter (according to their grammatical gender, cf. Kap. 5 §1), they are referred to by masculine, feminine, or neuter personal pronouns.

Dieser Wagen ist nicht zu teuer.   Vielleicht kaufe ich **diesen Wagen**.
Er ist nicht zu teuer.   Vielleicht kaufe ich **ihn**.
It is not too expensive.   *Maybe I'll buy it.*

Übung 6-11

ANWENDEN A. Substitute pronouns for the boldface subjects and objects and answer the questions.

> MODEL: Hast du **die Post** abgeholt?   <u>Ja, ich habe sie abgeholt.</u>

Karin fragt Erich, welche Dinge er erledigt hat.

1. Hast du **den Scheck** von Anton eingelöst?
2. Hast du **deine Eltern** angerufen?
3. Haben wir **die Rechnung** für die Autoreparatur bezahlt?
4. Ist **das Paket** von deiner Tante angekommen?
5. Hast du **Hannelore** zum Geburtstag gratuliert?
6. Hast du **unserem Nachbarn** für seine Hilfe gedankt?
7. Hast du **den Brief** an deine Oma geschrieben?

B. Answer the following questions in the negative, substituting pronouns for the nouns.

Einiges haben Karin und Erich nicht erledigt.

1. Hast du **das Wohnzimmer** aufgeräumt?
2. Hast du **deine Autoschlüssel** gefunden?
3. Haben wir **das Video** zurückgebracht?
4. Steht **der Grill** jetzt im Garten?
5. Und ist **unser Auto** sauber?
6. Hast du **die Katze** gefüttert?

A note on the use of personal pronouns referring to **das Mädchen**

The noun **Mädchen** is neuter. Normally personal pronouns must be in the same gender as the nouns to which they refer; however, for this neuter noun, the feminine **sie** is often used instead.

> **Das Mädchen** da drüben wohnt im Studentenheim. **Es/Sie** ist sehr nett.

When the name is mentioned, the feminine form must be used.

> **Das Mädchen** heißt Maria Schreiber. **Sie** hat zwei Brüder.

The use of personal pronouns with **gefallen**

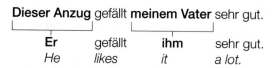

As mentioned in Kapitel 5 §4, the person or thing liked or disliked is the subject of the German sentence. The person who does the liking or disliking is the dative object of the verb.

Übung 6-12

ANWENDEN A. Respond positively or negatively, as indicated in parentheses, by replacing the boldface noun with a personal pronoun.

> MODEL: Gefällt Ihnen **Ihre Wohnung**? (Ja)
> <u>Ja, sie gefällt mir.</u>

Maximilians Nachbarin möchte wissen, ob Maximilian die Uni und sein Studium gefallen.

1. Gefallen Ihnen **die Kurse** an der Uni? (Ja)
2. Gefällt Ihnen **der Deutschkurs** dieses Semester? (Ja)
3. Hat Ihnen **der Kurs** letztes Semester gefallen?(Nein)
4. Gefällt Ihnen **die Universität**? Gefällt **die Uni** Ihren Freunden/Freundinnen? (Ja)
5. Gefallen Ihnen **die Aktivitäten an der Uni**? (Ja)
6. Gefällt Ihnen **die Mensa** hier? (Nein)

B. Now respond to the same questions by stating whether *you* like or dislike the things that are mentioned.

§10   Position of Personal Pronoun Objects

1. One personal pronoun object and one noun object

Compare the following three sentences:

Sie hat **meinem Bruder diesen Koffer** gebracht.   *She brought my brother*
    ⌐INDIRECT OBJECT⌐DIRECT OBJECT⌐   *this suitcase.*
    (DATIVE/PERSON) (ACCUSATIVE/THING)

Sie hat   **ihm**   **diesen Koffer** gebracht.   *She brought him this suitcase.*

Sie hat   **ihn**   **meinem Bruder** gebracht.   *She brought it to my brother.*

When there are two noun objects, the indirect object usually precedes the direct object, as in the first sentence. Personal pronoun objects precede noun objects regardless of which one is the direct or indirect object, as in the second and third sentences. In English, the indirect object is preceded by *to* when it follows the direct object, as in the third sentence.

2. Two personal pronoun objects

When there are two personal pronoun objects, the accusative always precedes the dative.

Barbara hat   **Martin diesen Koffer**   geschenkt.

Barbara hat   **ihn**   **ihm**   geschenkt.
Barbara gave   *it*   *to him.*

To summarize 1. and 2.: When the objects in a sentence include one pronoun and one noun, the pronoun always precedes the noun, regardless of case. When both objects are pronouns, the accusative pronoun must precede the dative pronoun.

Übung 6-13

ANWENDEN Replace the boldface noun(s) with a personal pronoun.

> MODEL: Hast du **deiner Mutter** etwas geschickt?   (ein Brief)
> <u>Ja, ich habe ihr einen Brief geschickt.</u>

Marianne hat viele Geschenke besorgt. Jakob möchte genau wissen, wer welche Dinge bekommt oder bekommen hat.

1. Hast du **deinem Vater** etwas zum Geburtstag geschenkt? (ein Hemd)
2. Und wem hast du **diese CD** gekauft? (ein Freund)
3. Hast du **deinen Eltern** etwas besorgt? (Bücher)
4. Hast du **deiner Oma** etwas gebracht? (Kekse)
5. Wem hast du **die Fotos** gezeigt? (meine Eltern)
6. Hast du **den Kindern** etwas mitgebracht? (Malbücher)
7. Was hast du **den Nachbarn** mitgebracht? (Wein)
8. Und wem bringst du **die Pralinen**? (eine Bekannte)

3. A personal pronoun object and a noun subject

Personal pronoun objects commonly precede noun subjects in sentences with inverted word order or dependent word order.

Inverted word order

STATEMENT	Hoffentlich hat der Film meinem Freund gefallen.
	Hoffentlich hat der Film ihm gefallen.
MORE COMMON	Hoffentlich hat **ihm der Film** gefallen.
QUESTION	Hat der Film deiner Freundin gefallen?
	Hat der Film ihr gefallen?
MORE COMMON	Hat **ihr der Film** gefallen?

Dependent word order

	Ich glaube nicht, dass der Film meinen Freunden gefallen hat.
	Ich glaube nicht, dass der Film ihnen gefallen hat.
MORE COMMON	Ich glaube nicht, dass **ihnen der Film** gefallen hat.

Übung 6-14

ZUSAMMENFASSUNG Personal pronouns. Cases and position of pronouns.

A. Form sentences with two noun objects from the two lists. Use various verbs
(**schenken**, **bringen**, **schreiben**, etc.).

> MODEL: Ich habe dem Polizisten meinen Führerschein gezeigt.

ProfessorIn	Schokolade
PolizistIn	Führerschein
Beamte/Beamtin	Wahrheit
VerkäuferIn	Ausweis
Chef	Geld
NachbarIn	Postkarte
Familie	Geschenk
FreundIn	Bildband
Bekannte	Zettel
Kinder	Geschichte
Eltern	Ring

B. Now restate each sentence you formed in **A.** by replacing the accusative object
with a pronoun.

> MODEL: Ich habe ihn dem Polizisten gezeigt.

C. Respond to each personalized question with two sentences. Replace the repeated
object with a pronoun in the second sentence.

1. Wem haben Sie diesen Monat etwas geschenkt? Was war es?
2. Wem haben Sie etwas geschickt? Was?
3. Wem haben Sie etwas gebracht? Was?
4. Wem haben Sie etwas geliehen? Was war es?

Themen und Vokabular

Kleidung

der Anorak, -s	parka, windbreaker
der Anzug, ¨e	suit (men's)
der Blazer, -	blazer
die Bluse, -n	blouse
das (Ober)hemd, -en	dress shirt
die Hose. -n	pants
die Jacke, -	jacket
das Jacket, -s	coat
das Kleid, -er	dress
das Kostüm, -e	women's suit; costume
die Krawatte, -n	tie
der Mantel, ¨	overcoat
der Parka, -s	parka
der Rock, ¨e	skirt
die Sandale, -n	sandal
der (Seiden)schal, -s	(silk) scarf
der Schlips, -e	tie
der Schuh, -e	shoe
die Socke, -n	sock
der Strumpf, ¨e	sock, stocking

Personen und Berufe

der Arzt, ¨e	doctor, physician (m.)
die Ärztin, -nen	doctor, physician (f.)
der Bekannte, -n (adj. noun)	acquaintance (m.)
die Bekannte, -n	acquaintance (f.)
der Einwohner, -	inhabitant (m.)
die Einwohnerin, -nen	inhabitant (f.)
der Erfinder, -	inventor (m.)
die Erfinderin, -nen	inventor (f.)
der Freund, -e (ein Freund)	friend (m.); boyfriend
die Freundin, -nen (eine Freundin)	friend (f.); girlfriend
der Professor, -en	professor (m.)
die Professorin, -nen	professor (f.)

Im Haus

der Antikschrank, ¨e	antique cabinet, closet
die Couchgarnitur, -en	matching couch set
der Eichentisch, -e	oak table
das Himmelbett	canopy bed
der Holzstuhl, ¨e	wooden chair
das Kristallglas, ¨er	crystal glass
das Porzellanservice	china
der Teppich, -e	carpet, rug

7 Prepositions; *da-/wo-* Compounds; Interrogatives

Prepositions

A preposition usually precedes a noun or pronoun, which is called its *object*. The preposition and its object constitute a phrase, called a *prepositional phrase*, e.g., *with a friend, for my friends, without them*. The use of prepositions is highly idiomatic. It is therefore imperative to pay close attention to these tricky words.

German prepositions are commonly divided into four groups.

1. Prepositions that govern the dative case
2. Prepositions that govern the accusative case
3. Prepositions that govern either the dative or accusative case
4. Prepositions that govern the genitive case

In our treatment of these groups we will consider only the most commonly used prepositions and their meanings. (For a more detailed treatment of the use of prepositions in time expressions, see Kap. 10 §3 ff.)

§1 Prepositions That Govern the Dative Case

1. aus

    a. *out of* (expressing motion)

        Sie kommt gerade **aus dem Haus**.
        She's just coming out of the house.

        Ich komme gerade **aus einer Vorlesung**.
        I'm just coming from a lecture.

    b. *from* (being or coming from a place)

        Schreibers kommen **aus Deutschland**.
        The Schreibers come (are) from Germany.

c. *made of* (a certain material)

Aus welchem Stoff ist dieser Anzug?
What material is this suit made of?

Das Denkmal ist **aus Marmor**.
The monument is made of marble.

d. idiomatic expression: **aus diesem Grund** *for this/that reason*

Aus diesem Grund haben wir die Einladung nicht angenommen.
For this/that reason we did not accept the invitation.

2. außer *except for, besides*

Außer meiner Schwester waren alle gekommen.
Except for my sister, everybody had come.

Außer diesem Paket habe ich noch einen Scheck bekommen.
Besides this package, I also received a check.

3. bei

a. *at, near*

Wir haben das Auto **beim Postamt** geparkt.
We parked the car at/near the post office.
Das ist eine Stadt **bei Nürnberg**.
That's a city near Nuremberg.

b. *at, with* (someone's home, business, or office)

Er wohnt **bei seinen Eltern**. *He lives with his parents.*
Ich war gestern **bei Monika**. *I was at Monika's yesterday.*

Sie arbeitet **bei der Firma Köhler**. *She works at the Köhler company.*
Andreas ist **beim Arzt**. *Andreas is at the doctor's.*
        (**bei dem**)

Inge hat die Handschuhe **bei Hertie** gekauft. *Inge bought gloves at Hertie's.*

c. *in* (when used in connection with the weather)

bei diesem Wetter	*in this weather*
bei Regen	*when it rains*
bei Schnee	*when it snows*
bei dieser Kälte	*in this cold*
bei dieser Hitze	*in this heat*

4. gegenüber von *opposite, across from*

Das Postamt ist **gegenüber vom Bahnhof**.
                    (**von dem**)
The post office is across from the railway station.

Sabine wohnt **gegenüber von uns**.
Sabine lives across from us.

Gegenüber von precedes a noun or pronoun. **Gegenüber** used by itself follows a noun or pronoun.

Herr Schmidt saß **mir gegenüber**.
Mr. Schmidt was sitting across from me.

5. mit

a. *with*

Wir fliegen **mit Freunden** nach Europa.   *We are flying to Europe with friends.*
Er arbeitet gern **mit den Händen**.   *He likes to work with his hands.*

Mit corresponds very closely to the English *with*.

b. *by* (with means of transportation)

Wir fahren **mit dem Wagen**.   *We are going by car.*
        mit dem Bus.   *by bus.*
        mit dem Zug/mit der Bahn. *by train.*

Note the use of the definite article in German (cf. Kap. 6 §7, 3).

6. nach

a. *after* (in connection with time)

nach einer Stunde   *after an hour*
nach der Vorlesung   *after the lecture*
nach der Deutschstunde   *after German class*

b. *to* (with names of villages, towns, countries, islands, continents)

Wir fahren **nach Wien**. (*to Vienna*)
but: Wir fahren **in die Schweiz**. (*to Switzerland*)

Place names that are used with the definite article use the preposition **in**. (cf. Kap. 6 §7, 1)

expression: **nach Hause gehen** *to go home*

c. *according to*

Man kann nicht nur **nach dem Aussehen** urteilen.
One cannot judge by appearances only.

Idiomatic expression: **meiner (seiner, ihrer) Meinung nach**
                    in my (his/her) opinion
The preposition **nach** in this expression normally follows the noun.

7. seit *since, for a period of time*

> Käte schwänzt **seit Montag**. *Käte has been skipping class since Monday.*
> Klaus schwänzt **seit einer Woche**. *Klaus has skipped class for a week.*

Note the use of the present tense in German and the present perfect in English to express a stretch of time that began in the past and continues into the present (cf. Kap. 2 §6, 3).

8. von

    a. *from* (indicating the starting point of some action or state of things)

> Wir sind mit dem Wagen **von Hamburg nach Berlin** gefahren.
> *We drove from Hamburg to Berlin.*

> Ich komme **von zu Hause**.
> *I am coming from home.*

> Dieser Brief ist **von meinen Eltern**.
> *This letter is from my parents.*

    b. *of* (used figuratively)

> Das ist sehr nett **von Ihnen**.
> *That is very nice of you.*

> Das war sehr dumm **von mir**.
> *That was very stupid of me.*

von can be used in phrases that function as the genitive case (cf. Kap. 5 §4, 4). Compare the following:

> Das ist die Adresse **eines Freundes**.
> Das ist die Adresse **von einem Freund**.
> *That is the address of a friend.*

    c. *by* (author)

> Das ist ein Roman **von Thomas Mann**.   *This is a novel by Thomas Mann.*
> Das ist eine Komposition **von Beethoven**. *That is a composition by Beethoven.*

9. zu *to*

    a. direction, goal (cf. §6)

> Ich gehe **zum Arzt**.   *I am going to the doctor.*
>   (zú dem)
> Sie geht **zum Briefkasten**.   *She is going to the mailbox.*
> Wir gehen **zur Bushaltestelle**.   *We are going to the bus stop.*
>   (zú der)

    b. attitude

> Er ist sehr nett **zu mir**.   *He is very nice to me.*

c. idiomatic expressions

(keine) Lust haben zu   *(not) to be in the mood to...*
                                   (not) to feel like...

zu Fuß gehen   *to go on foot, to walk*

zu Hause   *at home*

Remember:

The following prepositions may be contracted with the definite article:

bei dem	=> **beim**	Ich war **beim Arzt.**
von dem	=> **vom**	Ich komme **vom Arzt.**
zu dem	=> **zum**	Ich gehe **zum Arzt.**
zu der	=> **zur**	Ich gehe **zur Bushaltestelle.**

Übung 7-1

ANWENDEN A. Provide the appropriate preposition with the items given in parentheses. Contract the preposition and the article when appropriate.

MODEL: Ich besuche meine beste Freundin. Ich fahre _____ . (Dresden)
          <u>Ich fahre nach Dresden.</u>

1. Kai hat schreckliche Kopfschmerzen. Er ist _____ . (Arzt)
2. Anke hat Zahnschmerzen. Sie geht _____ . (Zahnarzt)
3. Korinna möchte ein Paket nach Hause schicken. Sie ist _beim_ . (Postamt) *Postamt*
4. Herr und Frau Sandner haben zu Mittag gegessen. Sie kommen gerade *aus dem Restaurant* . (Restaurant)
5. Dieses Musikstück gefällt mir gut. Es ist _Von_ _____ . (Mozart)
6. Ich wohne allein. *mit mir* ist nur meine Katze hier. (ich)
7. Evas Mutter kommt *aus Schweiz* . (Schweiz) *außer / der*
8. Ich hatte gestern Geburtstag. Ich habe _Von meiner_ ein neues Fahrrad bekommen. (Mutter) *der*
9. Vielen Dank für die 100 Mark. Das ist wirklich nett _von dir_ . (du)
10. Ich gehe gern _____ spazieren. Ich nehme einen Regenschirm mit. (Regen)

B. Formulate sentences that contain appropriate prepositional phrases.

1. Nennen Sie drei Freunde/Freundinnen oder Bekannte und woher sie kommen.

   MODEL: <u>Peter kommt aus Philadelphia.</u>

2. Nennen Sie die Transportmittel für verschiedene Aktivitäten.

   MODEL: Urlaub in Kalifornien.
   <u>Ich fahre mit dem Auto nach Kalifornien.</u>
   zur Uni, einkaufen, von Boston nach Washington, Freunde besuchen

3. Sie verbringen den Sommer in Europa. Nennen Sie drei Reiseziele.

   Ich fahre _____. Ich fliege _____.

4. Nennen Sie drei Gegenstände und sagen Sie, aus welchem Material sie sind.

5. Geburtstagsgeschenke (oder Weihnachtsgeschenke). Sagen Sie, wer ihnen was geschenkt hat. (drei Geschenke)

   MODEL: <u>Ich habe von meiner Schwester ein T-Shirt bekommen.</u>

6. Nennen Sie drei Familienmitglieder oder Verwandte, wo sie wohnen und wie lange sie schon dort wohnen.

   MODEL: <u>Meine Tante wohnt seit zehn Jahren in Arizona.</u>

§2 Prepositions That Govern the Accusative Case

1. bis

a. *till, until, by* (time)

   Ich bin **bis Ende August** in Stuttgart.
   I'll be in Stuttgart until the end of August.

   Die Arbeit soll **bis nächste Woche** fertig sein.
   The work is supposed to be finished by next week.

b. *as far as, to, up to* (location)

   Ich fahre nur **bis Köln**.
   I'm only going to /as far as Cologne.

   Ich habe den Roman **bis Seite 200** gelesen.
   I read the novel up to page 200.

Bis is frequently used with a numeral or a place name, and then the accusative case of the object is not evident. When **bis** occurs with another preposition, the latter one determines the case of the noun.

   Wir haben **bis zur Kaffeepause** auf Sie gewartet.
   We waited for you until the coffee break.

Wir sind **bis zu einem Dorf** bei Stuttgart gefahren.
We went as far as a village near Stuttgart.

2. durch

a. *through*

Wir sind **durch die Stadt** gelaufen.
We walked through the town.

b. *by means of*

Ich habe den Job **durch einen Freund** bekommen.
I got the job through a friend.

3. entlang *along, down*

Wir fuhren **die Straße entlang**.
We were driving down the street.

Entlang generally follows its noun object. Occasionally, it precedes its noun object, in which case **entlang** then governs the dative case.

Entlang der Straße standen viele Zuschauer.
Many onlookers were standing along the street.

4. für *for*

a. denoting possession

Hier ist ein Brief **für dich**.
Here is a letter for you.

b. denoting agreement

Ich bin **für die Todesstrafe**.
I am for/I agree with capital punishment.

5. gegen *against; around*

a. denoting opposition, adversity

Die ganze Welt ist **gegen mich**.
The whole world is against me.

Haben Sie etwas **gegen mich**?
Do you have something against me?

b. denoting impact

Ich bin **gegen einen Baum** gefahren.
I ran/crashed into a tree.

c. (with time phrases) *around, approximately*

Wir holen dich **gegen 7 Uhr** ab.
We'll pick you up around 7.

6. ohne *without*

> Ich kann nicht **ohne dich** leben.
> *I can't live without you.*

7. um

> a. *around*

The adverb **herum** is frequently added.

> Wir sind **um den See (herum)** gefahren.
> *We drove around the lake.*

> b. (with time phrases) *at*

> Das Konzert fängt **um 20 Uhr** an.
> *The concert starts at 8 P.M.*

The following prepositions may be contracted with **das**:

durch das = **durchs**	Der Dieb ist **durchs** Feld gelaufen.
für das = **fürs**	Diese Milch ist **fürs** Baby.
um das = **ums**	Der Hund ist **ums** Haus gerannt.

Übung 7-2

ANWENDEN A. Insert an appropriate accusative preposition and combine it with the item given in parentheses. Contract the preposition and the article when possible.

Eine Reise in und um Norddeutschland.

1. Auf unserer Reise durch Deutschland sind wir zuerst _____ gekommen. (Kiel) [handwritten: *durch die Stadt*]
2. Wir sind stundenlang _____ gelaufen. (Stadt) [handwritten: *durch die stadt / ohne die*]
3. Wir sind nach dem Aufenthalt in Kiel _____ gefahren. (Straßenkarte) [handwritten: *mit der*]
4. Dann sind wir _____ gesegelt. (Küste) [handwritten: *entlang die*]
5. Ich habe ein paar Souvenire _____ gekauft. (meine Eltern) [handwritten: *für*]
6. Auf der Rückfahrt ist mein Freund _____ gefahren. (ein Baum) [handwritten: *gegen einen Baum*]

B. Write a coherent paragraph in the present perfect tense. Select items from the first list given below (e.g., **der Fluss, der See**) and combine them with accusative prepositions from the second list.

Ein Spaziergang

1. der Fluss, der See, die Wiese, der Pfad, der Weg, 9 Uhr/4 Uhr, die Wanderkarte
2. durch, entlang, um, von...bis, bis zu, ohne

C. Provide five statements that include prepositional phrases with **ohne**.

Was oder wen brauche ich?

MODEL: Ohne meinen Walkman gehe ich nicht joggen.

D. State your own or someone else's opinion by using prepositional phrases with **für** and **gegen**. Come up with five sentences. You may refer to the vocabulary at the end of the chapter for some useful words.

> MODEL: Ich bin gegen Studiengebühren.
> Meine Eltern sind für höhere Steuern.

§3   Prepositions That Govern both the Dative and the Accusative

Two-way prepositions can govern either the dative or accusative, depending on the context. The following rules will help you determine the appropriate case.

1. Motion to a place: The preposition governs the **accusative**.

Peter und Linda gehen **in den** Park.
(INTO/TO THE)

The sentence answers the question:
> **Wohin gehen Peter und Linda?** (*where to/ to what place*)
or: **Wo gehen Peter und Linda hin?**

Wohin or **wo...hin** are used in the sense of "where to ...," asking for the direction of a motion.

2. Being in a place: The preposition governs the **dative**.

Peter und Linda sind **im** Park.
(IN DEM)

The sentence answers the question:
Wo sind Peter und Linda? (*where/in what place?*)

3. Motion at or **within a place**: The preposition governs the **dative**.

Peter und Linda laufen **im** Park herum.
Peter and Linda are walking around in the park.

Sie gehen **im** Park spazieren.
They are taking a walk in the park.

The sentences answer the questions: **Wo** laufen Peter und Linda **herum**?
Wo gehen sie spazieren?

Remember:

> **ACCUSATIVE:**
> <u>motion to a place</u>
> answering **wohin** (*where to*) questions
> **DATIVE:**
> <u>being somewhere or motion within a place</u>
> answering **wo** (*where/in or at what place*) questions

Vokabulartip: Standort (wo) *und* placieren (wohin)

In English, location is generally expressed with the verb *to be*, while the general placement of people and things is expressed with *to put*. German requires more specific information and supplies it with certain verb pairs that are used frequently.

1. sitzen; (sich) setzen   *to sit; to sit down*

Sitzen and **setzen** are used with animate subjects and objects only, never with things.

Das Kind **sitzt auf dem** Boden.	*The child is sitting on the floor.*
Der Vater **setzt das Kind auf den** Stuhl.	*The father sits (puts) the child on the chair.*

2. liegen; (sich) legen   *to lay; to lie down*

Liegen and **legen** are used when the end result is that someone or something is lying down completely flat or horizontally.

Anne **liegt im Gras**.	*Anne is lying in the grass.*
Leg das Buch bitte **hierher**.	*Lay (put) the book down here.*

3. stehen; (sich) stellen   *to stand; to put or place upright*

Das Glas **steht in der Küche**.	*The glass is [standing] in the kitchen.*
Stell bitte den Wagen **in die** Garage.	*Please put the car in the garage.*

Note how the English verb *put* is rendered with three different verbs in German. Each denotes how the item or person is positioned(upright, horizontal, or seated) once it has been placed somewhere.

Stell das Buch ins Regal.	*Put the book into the shelf* (upright).
Leg die Servietten dahin.	*Put the napkins there* (flat).
Setz das Kind in den Stuhl.	*Put the child in the chair* (seated).

The three verbs that denote motion (**setzen, legen, stellen**) combine with a reflexive pronoun (**sich, mich, dich,** etc.) when the subject and the object are the same. (In English, these pronouns are understood.) The reflexive pronoun does not occur with the *non-motion* verbs (**sitzen, liegen, stehen**).

Setzt euch!	*Sit [yourself] down.*
Stell dich in die Ecke!	*Go stand [yourself] in the corner.*
Ich bin müde. Ich **lege** mich hin.	*I am tired. I am going to lie down.*

Übung 7-3

VERSTEHEN Determine if the sentence indicates motion to a place or location/motion within a place.

1. Werner ist heute den ganzen Tag in der Schule.
2. Frau Kraicek unterrichtet in einem Gymnasium.
3. Um wie viel Uhr gehen die Kinder in den Kindergarten?
4. Mein Vater macht jeden Abend Sport im Fitnesscenter.
5. Stehen die Gläser im Schrank?
6. Ich treffe Freunde in der Bibliothek.
7. Wir gehen jeden Tag in die Stadt.
8. Leg das Kind ins Bett. Es ist todmüde.
9. Sitzen die Gäste schon im Wohnzimmer?
10. Gehen wir ein bisschen im Wald wandern?

The following prepositions use the dative or the accusative case, depending on meaning. They are often called *two-way prepositions*.

ACCUSATIVE	DATIVE
wohin? *(where to?)*	**wo**? *(where? in or at what place?)*

1. an

    a. **an** *on* (vertical surface)

Ich hänge das Bild **an die Wand**. *I am hanging the picture on the wall.*	Jetzt hängt das Bild **an der Wand**. *Now the picture is hanging on the wall.*

    b. **an** *to go to* or *to be at something*

Ich gehe **ans Fenster**. **(an das)** *I am going to the window.*	Jetzt stehe ich **am Fenster**. **(an dem)** *Now I am standing at the window.*
Der Kellner kommt **an den Tisch**. *The waiter is coming to the table.*	Jetzt steht er **am Tisch**. **(an dem)** *Now he is standing at the table.*

    c. location on a body of water.

Wir fahren **an die Ostsee**. *We are going to the Baltic Sea.*	Jetzt sind wir **an der Ostsee**. *Now we are at the Baltic Sea.*

2. auf

    a. **auf** *on* (horizontal surface)

Ich stelle die Lampe **auf den Tisch**. *I am putting the lamp on the table.*	Die Lampe steht **auf dem Tisch**. *The lamp is standing on the table.*

b. **auf** *to; in;* and *at*

Ich gehe **auf den Fußballplatz**.
I am going to the soccer field.

Jetzt bin ich **auf dem Fußballplatz**.
Now I am on the soccer field.

aufs Postamt.
(**auf das**)
to the post office.

auf dem Postamt.
at/in the post office.

3. hinter *behind*

Ich habe mein Fahrrad **hinter die**
Garage gestellt.
*I put my bicycle behind the
garage.*

Das Fahrrad steht **hinter der** Garage.
*The bicycle is [standing] behind
the garage.*

4. in *in; into; to*

Wir gehen **ins Museum**.
(**in das**)
We are going to the museum.

Jetzt sind wir **im Museum**.
Now we are in the museum.

5. neben *next to; beside*

Ich habe die Schlüssel **neben die**
Brille gelegt.
I laid (put) the keys next to my glasses.

Die Schlüssel liegen **neben der** Brille.
*The keys are lying next to my
eyeglasses.*

6. über *above; over; across*

Heute sind viele Flugzeuge
über die Stadt geflogen.
Today many planes flew over the city.

Jetzt kreist ein Flugzeug **über der** Stadt.
Now a plane is circling over the city.

7. unter *under*

Bitte stellen Sie den Papierkorb
unter den Schreibtisch.
*Please put the wastebasket
under the desk.*

Der Papierkorb steht **unter dem**
Schreibtisch.
*The wastebasket is standing
under the desk.*

8. vor *in front of; before*

Ich habe das Fahrrad **vor die** Tür
gestellt.
I put the bicycle in front of the door.

Das Fahrrad steht **vor der** Tür.
*The bicycle is [standing] in front of the
door.*

9. zwischen *between*

Ich habe das Lesezeichen **zwischen
die** Seiten 10 und 11 gelegt.
*I placed the bookmark between
pages 10 and 11.*

Das Lesezeichen liegt aber nicht mehr
zwischen den Seiten 10 und 11.
*But the bookmark isn't between pages
10 and 11 anymore.*

Parking, landing, and *arriving* are done within an area. Thus, two-way prepositions used with the verbs **parken, landen,** and **an•kommen** require the dative.

Ich habe den Wagen **auf dem** Marktplatz geparkt.
I parked the car on the town square.

Das Privatflugzeug kann nicht **auf diesem** Flugplatz landen.
The private plane cannot land on this airfield.

Wir sind um 10 Uhr **in der** Schweiz angekommen.
We arrived in Switzerland at 10 o'clock.

The following are contractions of two-way prepositions with the definite article:

DATIVE	ACCUSATIVE	DATIVE	ACCUSATIVE
an dem = **am**	an das = **ans**	über das = **übers**	über dem = **überm**
in dem = **im**	auf das = **aufs**	unter das = **unters**	unter dem = **unterm**
	in das= **ins**	vor das = **vors**	vor dem = **vorm**

Übung 7-4

VERSTEHEN Determine if the surface is horizontal or vertical and then insert the correct preposition (**an** or **auf**).

Kai und seine Mutter räumen Kais Zimmer um.

1. Stell doch das Bett hier _____ die Wand.
2. Soll dein Schreibtisch _____ diesem Fenster stehen?
3. Leg die Decke _____ dein Bett!
4. Und stell den Stuhl nicht _____ den Teppich!
5. Den Computer kannst du _____ den Schreibtisch stellen.
6. Und ich finde, das Bild soll _____ dieser Wand hängen.

Übung 7-5

ANWENDEN A. Insert a logical preposition and the correct article before the noun.

Frauke kommt nach Hause und findet ein Chaos vor. Nichts ist an seinem Platz!

1. Eine Menge Gläser stehen _____ Tisch.
2. Und viele Dosen liegen _____ Küche.
3. Jemand hat alle Stühle _____ Balkon gestellt.
4. Und einige Bücher liegen _____ Couch.
5. Wer hat alle Zeitschriften _____ Badewanne gelegt?
6. Ich sehe eine Menge CDs _____ Boden.
7. Mein Fahrrad steht _____ Garage.
8. Und _____ Fenster habe ich einen fremden Herrn gefunden!

B. Provide an appropriate counterpart to each sentence. If the sentence states location, provide a logical sentence with motion, or vice versa.

> MODEL: Die Zeitung liegt auf dem Tisch.
> <u>Mein Vater legt sie auf den Tisch.</u>

1. Die Gläser stehen schon auf dem Tisch.
2. Maria legt die Servietten auf die Teller.
3. Die Kollegen sitzen schon am Tisch.
4. Die Mutter hat Niko ins Bett gelegt.
5. Liegt die Decke auf dem Sessel?
6. Stell die Tassen bitte neben die Teller.
7. Die sechs Teller stehen im Schrank.
8. Du kannst das Baby in seinen Wagen setzen.

§4   Prepositions That Govern the Genitive Case

1. anstatt; statt *instead of*

> **Anstatt des Wagens** hat er das Motorrad repariert.
> or: **Statt des Wagens**...
> *Instead of the car, he repaired the motorcycle.*

Nouns immediately following the preposition have no genitive ending.

> **Statt Fisch** haben wir Sauerkraut mit Bratwurst gegessen.
> *Instead of fish, we ate sauerkraut with bratwurst (fried sausage).*

> **Statt Dieter** habe ich Frank eingeladen.
> *Instead of Dieter, I invited Frank.*

2. trotz *in spite of*

> **Trotz des Gewitters** sind wir in die Stadt gefahren.
> *In spite of the thunderstorm, we went downtown.*

Idiomatic expression: **trotzdem** *in spite of it; anyway*

> Er hatte zu viel getrunken und ist **trotzdem** mit dem Auto gefahren.
> *He had too much to drink and drove the car in spite of it (anyway).*

3. während *during*

> **Während des Vortrags** habe ich die Zeitung gelesen.
> *During the lecture I read the newspaper.*

4. wegen *because of*

> **Wegen meiner Eltern** haben wir die Reise verschoben.
> *Because of my parents, we postponed the trip.*

In formal speech, **wegen** sometimes follows the noun.

Meiner Eltern wegen haben wir die Reise verschoben.

When used with pronouns, two forms are possible.

genitive + **wegen**   or   **wegen** + dative

meinetwegen	wegen mir	*because of me, for my sake*
deinetwegen	wegen dir	*because of you, for your sake*
seinetwegen	wegen ihm	*because of him, for his sake*
ihretwegen	wegen ihr	*because of her, for her sake*
seinetwegen	wegen ihm	*because of it, for its sake*
unsertwegen	wegen uns	*because of us, for our sake*
euretwegen	wegen euch	*because of you, for your sake*
ihretwegen	wegen ihnen	*because of them, for their sake*
Ihretwegen	wegen Ihnen	*because of you, for your sake*

Idiomatic expression: **meinetwegen** *for all I care, as far as I am concerned*

Meinetwegen kannst du machen, was du willst.
For all I care, you can do what you want.

Colloquially, the preceding prepositions are often used with the dative.

statt **dem** Wagen, während **dem** Vortrag, wegen **meinen** Eltern

5. The following prepositions are less frequently used:

diesseits (*on this side of*)   diesseits
jenseits (*on the other side of*)   jenseits   ⟩ **der** Grenze, **des** Rheins

oberhalb (*above, upstream*)   oberhalb
unterhalb (*below, downstream*)   unterhalb   ⟩ **der** Stadt, **des** Mississippis

innerhalb (*inside of, within*)   innerhalb
außerhalb (*outside of*)   außerhalb   ⟩ **der** Stadt, **der** Bürostunden

The preceding prepositions are often used with **von** + dative.
diesseits vom Rhein, **innerhalb von einem** Jahr,
außerhalb von Köln

Übung 7-6

ANWENDEN Use the cues to supply a genitive (or dative) prepositional phrase.

Peter und Karen Johnson sehen sich eine Landkarte an. Sie planen eine Reise nach Süddeutschland.

1. Siehst du dieses Dorf? Es liegt _____ . (außerhalb / Konstanz)   [des]
2. Und der Bodensee liegt _____ . (innerhalb / Bundesland Baden-Württemberg)   [des]

3. Konstanz ist _____ , aber Schaffhausen liegt _____ .
   (diesseits / Grenze / unterhalb von / Bodensee)
4. Wir besuchen diese verschiedenen Orte _____ . (während / die
   Sommerferien)
5. Wir planen mit dem Zug _____ zu fahren. (statt / das Auto)
6. _____ werden wir viel laufen und wandern. (trotz / Wetter)
7. Das Wetter ist _____ ! (jenseits / unsere Kontrolle)
8. Leider können wir _____ nur zehn Tage bleiben. (wegen / die Arbeit von
   Peter)

§5 Summary of Common Prepositions and Their Basic Meanings

DATIVE	ACCUSATIVE	DATIVE OR ACCUSATIVE	GENITIVE
aus *out of, from* **außer** *except, besides* **bei** *at, near, at someone's place* **gegenüber (von)** *across from* **mit** *with, by* **nach** *after, to, according to* **seit** *since* **von** *from, of, by* **zu** *to, toward*	**bis** *until, to, as far as* **durch** *through* **entlang** *along* **für** *for* **gegen** *against* **ohne** *without* **um** *around*	**an** *on (vertically) by, at the edge of* **auf** *on (horizontally)* **hinter** *behind* **in** *in, into, to* **neben** *next to, beside* **über** *above, over, across* **unter** *under* **vor** *in front of, before* **zwischen** *between* Use the accusative when the verb denotes motion toward a place (answering the question "where to?"). Use the dative when the verb denotes either position in a place or motion within a place (answering the questions "where?" "in or at what place?")	**anstatt, statt** *instead of* **trotz** *in spite of* **während** *during* **wegen** *because of* **diesseits** *on this side of* **jenseits** *on the other side of* **oberhalb** *above* **unterhalb** *below* **innerhalb** *inside of, within* **außerhalb** *outside of*

The following are common contractions of the preposition with the definite article:

preposition + **das = ans, aufs, durchs, fürs, ins, übers, ums, unters, vors**
preposition + **dem = am, beim, im, vom, überm, unterm, vorm, zum**
preposition + **der = zur**

Contractions are not used

1. When the article is stressed

> Wir gehen **ins** Kino.
> *We are going to the movies.*

> but: **In das** Kino gehen wir nie wieder.
> *We'll never go to that movie theater again.*

2. When the noun is modified

> Wir gehen **in das Kino da drüben**.
> *We are going to the movie theater over there.*

§6   The German Counterparts of *to* with Verbs of Motion

Various German prepositions correspond to the English *to* with verbs of motion.

1. *to* = **nach**

This is the normal preposition used with names of towns, cities, regions, countries, or continents. It is not used when the name is accompanied by the article.

> Wir fahren   **nach** Frankfurt.
>   **nach** England.
> but: Wir fahren   **in die** Schweiz.
>   **in die** Vereinigten Staaten.

2. *to* = **zu**

This is the most generally acceptable word, and the only one possible if the object is a person.

a. Going to a person's home or business

> Ich gehe **zum Arzt**.
> Er fährt **zu seiner Schwester**.
> Wir gehen **zu (den) Neumanns**.

b. Used with names of stores

> Wir gehen **zu Hertie**.

c. Going to places other than cities, regions, countries

> Sie geht **zum Briefkasten**.
> Ich gehe **zur Bushaltestelle**.
> Wir fahren **zum Flughafen**.

3. In many instances **in**, **auf**, or **an** with the accusative may, or must be, used. This is especially true for public buildings and events in them.

a. *to* = **in** meaning *into a place, into a building*

Wir gehen **in die Stadt.**	*We are going to town, downtown, uptown.*
in die Deutschstunde.	*to the German class.*
ins Kino/Konzert.	*to the movies/the concert.*

b. *to* = **in** meaning *to a geographic region* (not a city or state)

Wir fahren **in den Schwarzwald.**	*We're driving to the Black Forest.*
in die Alpen.	*to the Alps.*
in die Lüneburger Heide.	*to the Lüneburg Heath.*

c. *to* = **auf** meaning *onto a surface, base of operation*

Wir gehen **auf den Tennisplatz.**	*We are going to the tennis court.*
auf den Marktplatz.	*to the town square.*

Idiomatic:

Wir gehen **auf die Bank/Post.**	*We are going to the bank/post office.*
or: **zur Bank/Post.**	
Wir gehen **auf den Bahnhof.**	*to the railway station.*
or: **zum Bahnhof.**	
Wir gehen **auf eine Party.**	*to a party.*
or: **zu einer Party.**	
Wir fahren **aufs Land.**	*We're driving out to the country.*

d. *to* = **an** meaning *up to, to the edge of*:

Ich gehe **ans Fenster.**	*I am going to the window.*
an den Tisch.	*to the table.*
ans Telefon.	*to (answer) the phone.*

Übung 7-7

ZUSAMMENFASSUNG Dative, accusative, genitive, and two-way prepositions.

A. Use two-way prepositions to describe where ten kitchen items (tools, utensils, foods) are located or where Sara or Erika might place them. For five items, mention location; for the five others, placement.

Sara und Erika sind in ihrer Küche und bereiten eine Einladung vor. Einige Dinge sind schon dort, wohin sie gehören, andere noch nicht.

MODEL: Der Sprudel steht im Eisschrank. *(location)*
Wir müssen die Teller auf den Tisch stellen. *(placement)*

B. Answer the personalized questions.

1. Woher kommen Sie? Wie ist Ihre Heimatstadt gelegen? (Was ist oberhalb/unterhalb?)
2. Wie liegt Ihre Wohnung/Ihr Haus/das Haus Ihrer Eltern? (Was ist gegenüber?)

3. Wer wohnt außer Ihnen da?
4. Seit wann wohnen Sie schon dort? Seit wann wohnen Ihre Eltern da?
5. Wohin fahren Sie in den Ferien? Wo waren Sie in den letzten Ferien?
6. Sind Sie für oder gegen Abtreibung/die Todesstrafe/Grenzen zwischen Ländern/Streiks?
7. Was machen sie nur wegen Ihren Eltern?
8. Beschreiben Sie einen Raum in Ihrer Wohnung. Wo genau stehen und liegen verschiedene Dinge?

Verbs and Adjectives Used with Prepositions

In combinations of verbs or adjectives with prepositions, the rules governing the use of the dative and the accusative with two-way prepositions do not apply. The case for each must be learned individually. Most such constructions use the accusative.

§7 Verbs Used with Prepositions

Many verbs and adjectives complete their meanings with prepositional phrases. Some common ones are listed below.

1. Verbs with dative prepositions

gratulieren (dat.) **zu**	*to congratulate on*
halten **von** (hält), hielt, hat gehalten	*to think of*
handeln **von**	*to deal with, be about*
sprechen **mit** (spricht), sprach, gesprochen	*to talk with or to*
sprechen **von**	*to talk of or about*

2. Verbs with accusative prepositions

bitten **um**, bat, hat gebeten	*to ask for, to request*
danken (dat.) **für**	*to thank for*

3. Verbs with two-way prepositions

antworten **auf** + acc.	*to answer something*
arbeiten **an** + dat.	*to work on*
denken **an** + acc.	*to think of or about*
lachen **über** + acc.	*to laugh at or about*
reagieren **auf** + acc.	*to react to*
warten **auf** + acc.	*to wait for*

Übung 7-8

VERSTEHEN Match each question with the most logical response.

1. Wie reagieren viele Leute auf Hitze?
2. Was machen Großeltern oft?
3. Was machen Studenten oft?
4. Wie verbringen Professorinnen die Semesterferien?
5. Was machen Redner nach einer Rede?

a. Sie arbeiten an Forschungsprojekten.
b. Sie danken den Zuhörern für Ihre Aufmerksamkeit.
c. Sie bitten ihre Eltern um Geld.
d. Sie sprechen oft von ihren Enkelkindern.
e. Sie haben schlechte Laune und sind müde.

Übung 7-9

ANWENDEN Respond to each scenario with a sentence that contains one of the verbs with prepositions from the list given. Use each verb with preposition only once.

MODEL: Sie erzählen einer Freundin einen Witz. Was macht sie? (lachen über)
<u>Sie lacht über den Witz.</u>

gratulieren zu, handeln von, sprechen mit, denken an, danken für

1. Ein Freund von Ihnen hat Geburtstag. Was machen Sie?
2. Ihre Oma hat Ihnen 100 Mark geschenkt. Was machen Sie?
3. Lesen Sie gerade ein interessantes Buch? Beschreiben Sie es kurz.
4. Sie haben finanzielle Probleme. Was machen Sie?
5. Ihr Freund/Ihre Freundin wohnt weit weg. Was macht er/sie hoffentlich?

§8 Adjectives Used with Prepositions

The following frequently used adjectives complete their meanings with prepositional phrases:

befreundet sein **mit** + dat.	*to be friends with*
begeistert sein **von** + dat.	*to be enthusiastic about*
böse sein **auf** + acc.	*to be angry with*
or: **mit** + dat.	
froh sein **über** + acc.	*to be glad about*
geschieden sein **von** + dat.	*to be divorced from*
getrennt sein **von** + dat.	*to be separated from*
glücklich sein **über** + acc.	*to be happy about*
stolz sein **auf** + acc.	*to be proud of*
verheiratet sein **mit** + dat.	*to be married to*
verliebt sein **in** + acc.	*to be in love with*
verlobt sein **mit** + dat.	*to be engaged to*
verrückt sein **auf** + acc.	*to be crazy about*
verwandt sein **mit** + dat.	*to be related to*
zufrieden sein **mit** + dat.	*to be satisfied, content with*

Example:

> Ich war **von diesem Film** begeistert. —— *I was enthusiastic about this film.*
> or: Ich war begeistert **von diesem Film**. ——

Begeistert functions as a predicate adjective (following the verb **sein**; cf. Kap. 8 Introduction). Predicate adjectives may precede or follow prepositional phrases.

Vokabulartip: ein Wörterbuch benutzen

We have treated only a few common verbs and adjectives that complete their meanings with prepositional phrases. There are, of course, many more. A good dictionary will tell you what prepositions and cases are used with those verbs and adjectives.

Übung 7-10

ANWENDEN A. Use the cues to construct sentences. Supply the prepositions that are used with the adjectives and the correct form of **sein**.

Bei einem Klassentreffen erfahren die Anwesenden alles über verschiedene Beziehungen.

> MODEL: Alle/froh/das Treffen
> <u>Alle sind froh über das Treffen.</u>

1. Susanne/verlobt/ein Musiker
2. Kurt/nicht mehr/verheiratet/die Rechtsanwältin
3. Er/verrückt/eine Schauspielerin
4. Seine Frau/natürlich/böse/er
5. Kurt/jetzt/geschieden/seine Frau
6. Aber/Birgit und Kai/zufrieden/ihr Leben
7. Birgit/immer noch/total verliebt/ihr Mann
8. Sie (plural)/sein/besonders glücklich/ihr Baby
9. Christiane/stolz/ihre Kinder

B. Use expressions from exercise A to answer the following personalized questions.

1. Beschreiben Sie, welche Geschwister (mit wem) verheiratet oder verlobt (oder getrennt/geschieden) sind.
2. Ist eine gute Freundin/ein guter Freund von Ihnen im Moment in jemanden verliebt? Wen?
3. Und Sie? Sind Sie verlobt oder verheiratet? Oder verliebt?
4. Mit wem sind Sie gut befreundet?
5. Sind Sie auf jemanden böse? Warum?

Da-Compounds

§9 *da*- as Pronoun Substitute

Compare these sentence pairs.

Haben Sie etwas **gegen Herrn Klein**? Haben Sie etwas **gegen ihn**?	*Do you have something against Mr. Klein?* *Do you have something against him?*
Haben Sie etwas **gegen den Vorschlag**? Haben Sie etwas **dagegen**?	*Do you have something against the suggestion?* *Do you have something against it?*

When referring to people, the appropriate dative or accusative pronoun is used as the object of the preposition, as in the first sentence pair. When referring to things or concepts, as in the second pair, a **da**-compound replaces the preposition plus pronoun; **da**- (**dar**- before vowels) is attached as a prefix to the preposition.

Commonly used **da**-compounds:

dabei	damit	daran
dadurch	danach	darauf
dafür	davon	daraus
dagegen	davor	darin
	dazu	darüber
		darum

Since the **da**- does not change, this construction does not reflect the gender, number (singular or plural), or case of the noun it replaces.

Ich weiß nichts **von dieser Sache.**
   von diesen Dingen.
   von seinen Plänen.
> Ich weiß nichts **davon.**
> *I know nothing about it/them.*

Ich habe keine Lust **zur Arbeit.**
   zum Lernen.
   zum Kochen.
> Ich habe keine Lust **dazu.**
> *I'm not in the mood for it.*

Normally the accent is on the preposition: **da<u>zu</u>, da<u>mit</u>, da<u>von</u>**, etc. When the **da**-compound is emphasized, the accent shifts to da: **<u>da</u>zu, <u>da</u>mit, <u>da</u>von**, etc.

   <u>Da</u>zu habe ich keine Lust.
   <u>Da</u>von weiß ich nichts.

The emphatic **da**-compound is generally in first position.

A commonly used expression:

> **Es kommt (ganz) darauf an.**   *It (all) depends.*

Übung 7-11

VERSTEHEN Substitute the prepositional phrase in each sentence with a **da**-compound or keep the preposition and replace the object with a personal pronoun.

MODEL: Kai ist gegen den Vorschlag.   Anne hat wenig zeit für ihre Mutter.
<u>dagegen</u>   <u>für sie</u>

1. Klaus hat viele Fotos von seinem Sohn gemacht.
2. Ich habe viel für diese Bücher bezahlt.
3. Für meine Kinder nehme ich mir viel Zeit.
4. Bist du stolz auf deinen Bruder?
5. Warum bittest du deine Eltern nicht um Hilfe?
6. Er erzählt viel von seiner Reise in den Nahen Osten.
7. Bist du böse auf deinen Freund?

§10   Prepositions That Do Not Form *da*-Compounds

Da-compounds cannot be formed with the following prepositions:

ohne, seit, außer,

nor with any preposition governing the genitive case (cf. Kap. 7 §4).

Pronouns or set expressions which convey the idea to be expressed are used instead.

ohne seine Hilfe	*without his help*
ohne sie	*without it*
seit seiner Krankheit	*since his illness*
seitdem	*since then*
außer seinem Geld	*except for, or aside from, his money*
außerdem	*aside from that, besides*
wegen seines Fleißes	*because of his diligence*
deswegen, deshalb	*because of that, that's why*
trotz meiner Faulheit	*in spite of my laziness*
trotzdem	*in spite of that*
statt eines Erfolgs	*instead of a success*
stattdessen	*instead of that*

§11   Anticipatory *da*-Compounds

Compare the following three sentences:

Renate ist stolz **auf ihre Aussprache**.
Renate ist stolz **darauf**.
Renate ist stolz **darauf**, dass sie so eine gute Aussprache hat.
Renate is proud (of the fact) that she has such good pronunciation.
or: *Renate is proud of having such good pronunciation.*

In the third sentence, the **da**-compound anticipates what is expressed in the following clause. It is an anticipatory **da**-compound. Depending on the context, the English translation of such a construction either disregards the **da**-compound or uses a prepositional phrase or gerund, as shown above.

This construction must be used when the prepositional object is a phrase rather than a noun.

> Andrea ist froh **darüber**, dass ihr Auto wieder funktioniert.
> *Andrea is glad (about the fact) that her car is working again.*
> or: *Andrea is glad about her car working again.*

Übung 7-12

ANWENDEN Introduce each sentence with a clause that contains an anticipatory **da**-compound.

> MODEL: Daniel vergisst nie die Geburtstage seiner Familie. (stolz sein auf).
> <u>Daniel ist stolz darauf, dass er nie die Geburtstage seiner Familie vergisst</u>

1. Annette fährt morgen in den Urlaub. (denken an)
2. Helga wird nächstes Jahr in Afrika arbeiten. (viel sprechen von)
3. Andreas hat immer recht. (überzeugt sein von)
4. Karin hat noch eine Chance bekommen. (froh sein über)
5. Svens Eltern rufen an. (warten auf)

§12   The Position of Prepositional Phrases and *da*-Compounds

Prepositional phrases and **da**-compounds are generally placed near the end of the sentence.

	PREPOSITION + NOUN OR PRONOUN, *DA*-COMPOUND	
Margot hat Renate	bei den Hausaufgaben	geholfen.
Sie hat ihr	dabei	geholfen.
Ich habe die Uhr	von meinen Eltern	bekommen.
Ich habe sie	von ihnen	bekommen.

§13   The Interrogative Pronouns *wer* and *was*

The interrogative pronoun **wer**

The interrogative **wer** is used to refer to people of either gender in the singular and plural. Its forms are as follows:

NOMINATIVE	**wer**	*who*
ACCUSATIVE	**wen**	*who(m)*
DATIVE	**wem**	*to whom, who(m)*
GENITIVE	**wessen**	*whose*

Herr Schmidt hat Peter angerufen.   **Wer** hat Peter angerufen?

NOMINATIVE   NOMINATIVE   *Who called Peter?*
(SUBJECT)   (SUBJECT)

Herr Schmidt hat **Peter** angerufen.   **Wen** hat Herr Schmidt angerufen?

ACCUSATIVE   ACCUSATIVE   *Who(m) did Mr. Schmidt call?*
(DIRECT OBJECT)   (DIRECT OBJECT)

Das Gemälde gehört **meinen Eltern**.   **Wem** gehört das Gemälde?

DATIVE   DATIVE   *To whom does this painting
belong?*

Das sind **Barbaras** Kinder.   **Wessen** Kinder sind das?

GENITIVE   GENITIVE   *Whose children are these?*

The genitive **wessen** is often replaced with some other construction, such as:

Wem gehört dieser Regenschirm?   *To whom does this umbrella belong?*

Übung 7-13

VERSTEHEN Name the element in the first sentence to which the boldface question word in the second sentence refers.

Ein Telefongespräch: Klaus muss bei jeder Information nachfragen.

1. Meine Oma hat mir gestern einen Tennisschläger geschenkt.
   Wer hat dir den geschenkt?
2. Und Tante Gerda hat meiner Schwester eine wertvolle Kette gekauft.
   Wem hat sie sie geschenkt?
3. Sag Martin, er soll Utes Wörterbuch zurückgeben.
   Was soll er ihr zurückgeben?
4. Ute will es ihrem Bruder leihen.
   Wem will sie es leihen?
5. Heute Nachmittag treffe ich Sandra zum Kaffee.
   Wen triffst du zum Kaffee?
6. Und heute Abend werde ich Karins Eltern kennenlernen.
   Wessen Eltern wirst du kennenlernen?

Using **wer** *with prepositions*

Das Geschenk ist **für** einen Freund.

eine Freundin.   **Für wen** ist das Geschenk?

Herrn und Frau Becker.   *Who is the present for?*
or: *For whom is the present?*

Das Geschenk ist **von** einem Freund.

einer Freundin. ⟶ **Von wem** ist das Geschenk?

Herrn und Frau Becker.

Who is the present from?
or: From whom is the present?

In German, the preposition always precedes the interrogative and determines its case.

Übung 7-14

ANWENDEN Formulate questions following the model by referring to the boldface element with the correct interrogative pronoun or preposition and interrogative pronoun.

MODEL: Klaus hat **Ute** angerufen.
        <u>Wie bitte? Wen hat Klaus angerufen?</u>

Roland ruft Jutta an und berichtet den neuesten Klatsch. Jutta muss nachfragen.

1. Werner hat endlich **Ingrids** Telefonnummer bekommen.
2. Weißt du, dass Sabine **Ulrich** hasst?
3. Und sie ist böse **auf dich**!
4. Veronika ist verliebt **in Bernd**.
5. Ich habe **Tom** eine E-Mail geschickt.
6. Und ich habe **Lars** gestern angerufen.
7. Morgen gehe ich **mit Oliver und Patrick** zum Essen aus.

The interrogative pronoun **was**

The interrogative **was** refers to things and concepts of any gender in the singular and plural. It has only one form, which is both nominative and accusative.

Was ist nicht richtig?   *What is not correct?*

NOMINATIVE
(SUBJECT)

Was verstehen Sie nicht?   *What don't you understand?*

ACCUSATIVE
(DIRECT OBJECT)

Using **was** *with prepositions*

Compare:

STATEMENT	Ich habe Angst **vorm Fliegen**.	*I am afraid of flying.*
	Ich habe Angst **davor**.	*I am afraid of it.*
QUESTION	**Wovor** hast du Angst?	*What are you afraid of?*

Wo- is added as a prefix to the preposition **vor: wovor**. In colloquial German, the preposition is followed by **was: Vor was** hast du Angst?

Compare the following **da**-compounds and **wo**-compounds.

DA-COMPOUNDS (USED IN STATEMENTS)		WO-COMPOUNDS (USED IN QUESTIONS)	
damit	*with it/them*	**womit?**	*with what?*
dafür	*for it/them*	**wofür?**	*for what?*
davon	*of it/them*	**wovon?**	*of what?*

An **r** is inserted when the preposition begins with a vowel.

da<u>r</u>in	*in it/them*	**wo<u>r</u>in?**	*in what?*
da<u>r</u>an	*on or of it/them*	**wo<u>r</u>an?**	*on or of what?*
da<u>r</u>aus	*from it/them*	**wo<u>r</u>aus?**	*from what?*
da<u>r</u>auf	*on it/them*	**wo<u>r</u>auf?**	*on what?*

Ich denke **daran**.   **Woran** denkst du?   > *What are you thinking of?*
colloquial: **An was** denkst du?

Ich warte **darauf**.   **Worauf** warten Sie?   > *What are you waiting for?*
colloquial: **Auf was** warten Sie?

The genitive prepositions and **außer, ohne,** and **seit** do not form **wo**-compounds, just as they do not form **da**-compounds.

Ich kann nicht **ohne den Fernseher** leben.   > **Ohne was** kannst du nicht leben?
Ich kann nicht **ohne ihn** leben.

Übung 7-15

ZUSAMMENFASSUNG Verbs and adjectives with prepositions; **da-** and **wo**-compounds; interrogatives **wer** and **was**.

Answer the personalized questions.

1. An wen denken Sie oft? Warum?
2. Woran denken Sie oft? Ihre Zukunft? Wo Sie arbeiten und wohnen werden?
3. Wem schreiben Sie oft? Wen rufen Sie oft an? Mit wem sprechen Sie viel?
4. Auf wen sind Ihre Eltern stolz? Warum?
5. Auf wen sind Sie böse? Warum?
6. Worüber sind Sie glücklich? Worüber sind Freunde von Ihnen glücklich?
7. Wofür sind Sie? Wogegen sind Sie? Ihre Eltern? Ein Freund/eine Freundin von Ihnen? Ihr Chef?
8. Über welche Person im Fernsehen lachen Sie oft?
9. Was haben Sie kürzlich gelesen? Wovon handelt das Buch? Welchen Film haben sie gesehen? Wovon handelt er?
10. Woran arbeiten Sie im Moment?

Themen und Vokabular

Im Freien

der Bach, ¨e	creek
der Berg, -e	mountain
das Feld, -e	field
der Fluss, ¨e	river
der Hügel, -	hill
der See, -n	lake
der Spaziergang, ¨e	walk
der Spazierweg, ¨e	walking trail
der Teich, -e	pond
der Wald, ¨er	forest
der Waldweg, -e	forest trail
die Wanderkarte, -n	hiking map, guide
die Wanderung, -en	hike
der Weg, -e	trail
die Wiese, -n	lawn, meadow

In der Stadt

das Dorf, ¨er	village
die Grenze, -n	border
das Land, ¨er	country, nation
	(also: federal state)
auf dem Land	in the country
das (Bundes) land	federal state
der Marktplatz	market square
der Ort, -e	town (also: place)
der Park, -s	park
der Platz, ¨e	square
der Sportplatz, ¨e	sports field
die Stadt, ¨e	city

Standort und Placieren

setzen	to sit down, put
sitzen, saß,	
hat gesessen	to sit (no motion)
stehen, stand	
hat gestanden	to stand (upright)
stellen	to place (upright), put
legen	to lay down, place (horizontal), put
liegen, lag, hat gelegen	to lie (no motion)

Politische Themen

die Abtreibung	abortion
die Demokratie, -n	democracy
die Gewerkschaft, -en	union
die Lobby, -s	(political) lobby
die Monarchie, -n	monarchy
die Partei, -en	(political) party
die Steuer, -n	tax
der Streik, -s	strike
die Studiengebühr, -en	college tuition
die Todesstrafe	capital punishment
die Wahl, -en	election
das Wahlrecht	right to vote

Beziehungen

die Freundschaft, -en	friendship
die Beziehung, -en	relationship

8 Adjectives

Introduction

Note the use of **vorsichtig** in the following sentences:

a. Herr Kästner ist **vorsichtig**.	*Mr. Kästner is careful.*
b. Herr Kästner fährt **vorsichtig**.	*Mr. Kästner drives carefully.*
c. Herr Kästner ist ein **vorsichtiger** Fahrer.	*Mr. Kästner is a careful driver.*

In sentence a, **vorsichtig** is a predicate adjective with the verb **sein**; in sentence b, it is an adverb modifying **fahren**. In both situations, the base form **vorsichtig** is used with no ending. German does not distinguish between the base forms of adverbs and adjectives.

In sentence c, **vorsichtig** is an *attribute adjective* directly preceding the noun **Fahrer**, which it modifies. Attributive adjectives have endings which are determined by the gender, number (singular or plural), and case of the nouns they modify.

In this chapter, we will consider only attributive adjectives. We will simply call them *adjectives*.

The Declension of Adjectives

There are three basic groups of adjectives.

1. Adjectives that are not preceded by **der**-words or **ein**-words, referred to as *unpreceded adjectives*

2. Adjectives preceded by **der**-words

3. Adjectives preceded by **ein**-words

§1 Unpreceded Adjectives

SINGULAR	PLURAL
Das ist ⟨ kalt**er** Kaffee. kalt**es** Wasser. kalt**e** Milch.	Das sind kalt**e** Getränke.

Unpreceded adjectives are declined almost exactly like **der**-words.

The chart below reviews the declension of the **der**-word **dieser**.

	MASCULINE	NEUTER	FEMININE	PLURAL
NOMINATIVE	dies**er** Kaffee	dies**es** Wasser	dies**e** Milch	dies**e** Getränke
ACCUSATIVE	dies**en** Kaffee	dies**es** Wasser	dies**e** Milch	dies**e** Getränke
DATIVE	dies**em** Kaffee	dies**em** Wasser	dies**er** Milch	dies**en** Getränken
GENITIVE	dies**es** Kaffees	dies**es** Wassers	dies**er** Milch	dies**er** Getränke

The endings attached to the **der**-words are known as strong endings. Compare them with the endings of the unpreceded adjectives below.

	MASCULINE	NEUTER	FEMININE	PLURAL
NOMINATIVE	kalt**er** Kaffee	kalt**es** Wasser	kalt**e** Milch	kalt**e** Getränke
ACCUSATIVE	kalt**en** Kaffee	kalt**es** Wasser	kalt**e** Milch	kalt**e** Getränke
DATIVE	kalt**em** Kaffee	kalt**em** Wasser	kalt**er** Milch	kalt**en** Getränken
GENITIVE	kalt**en** Kaffees	kalt**en** Wassers	kalt**er** Milch	kalt**er** Getränke

The difference between the strong endings and the endings of unpreceded adjectives occurs in the genitive singular masculine and neuter—the attributive adjective has the ending -**en** instead of -**es**.

Übung 8-1

ANWENDEN A. Place the appropriate forms of the adjectives in parentheses before the noun, replacing any article given.

MODEL: Trinken Sie gern Tee? (englisch, heiß, kalt)
<u>Trinken Sie gern englischen Tee? heißen Tee? kalten Tee?</u>

1. Wo kann man Käse kaufen? (holländisch, französisch, deutsch)
2. Der Kaviar schmeckt wirklich gut. (russisch, schwarz, rot)
3. In dieser Bibliothek finden Sie Zeitungen. (ausländisch, europäisch, interessant)
4. Kann ich hier Eier bekommen? (frisch, braun, groß, klein)
5. Wo ist der Zucker? (braun, weiß)
6. Dieses Brot schmeckt köstlich. (schwarz, dunkel)
7. Ich liebe das Aroma dieses Kaffees. (frisch, geröstet, schwarzen)
8. Ich backe viel mit Mehl. (braun, fein)

B. Respond to each question with a few items that contain an unpreceded adjective and a noun. You may use the adjectives that are suggested.

1. Welche Getränke trinken Sie gern?
2. Welcher Käse schmeckt Ihnen?
3. Welche Zeitungen lesen Sie oft?
4. Welche Filme sehen Sie? (lustig, spannend, historisch, dokumentarisch)
5. Bei welchem Wetter gehen Sie spazieren? Bei welchem bleiben Sie zu Hause? (schön, schlecht, sonnig, regnerisch)

§2   Adjectives Preceded by *der*-Words

Including the definite article, the **der**-words are **der, dieser, jeder, jener, mancher, solcher, welcher, alle,** and **beide** (cf. Kap. 6, §1). Adjectives preceded by **der-** words have *weak endings,* meaning that the endings do not clearly indicate gender, number or case. The following table shows the combinations of **der** and **dieser** + weak adjective + noun.

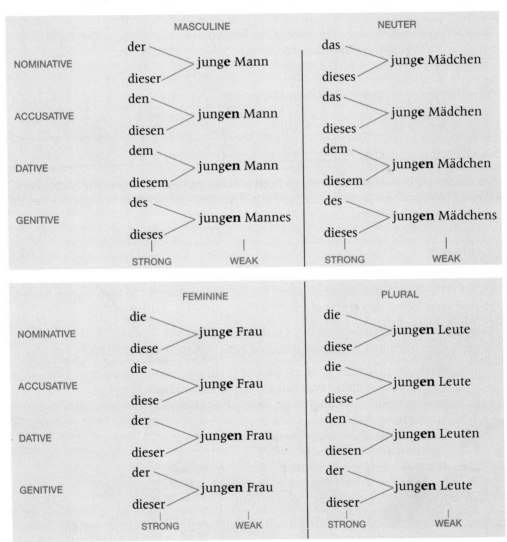

The weak adjective endings are either **-e** or **-en**.

> **-e** in the nominative masculine singular
> the nominative and accusative neuter singular
> the nominative and accusative feminine singular
> **-en** in all other cases

The following key shows the distribution of the endings **-e** and **-en** of adjectives preceded by **der**-words.

	MASCULINE	NEUTER	FEMININE	PLURAL
NOMINATIVE	-e	-e	-e	-en
ACCUSATIVE	-en	-e	-e	-en
DATIVE	-en	-en	-en	-en
GENITIVE	-en	-en	-en	-en

The *strong declension* of **der**-words includes a greater variety of endings, which helps to identify the gender, number, and case of the nouns that follow. The weak declension with the two endings **-e** and **-en** is less distinctive. Remember that weak adjective endings do not occur unless preceded by a strong ending.

Übung 8-2

ANWENDEN Write the phrases with the correct adjective endings.

1. dieser jung_ Mann; die nett_ Frau; der alt_ Herr; die freundlich_ Dame
2. diese braun_ Handschuhe; dieser weiß_ Blazer; diese bequem_ Jacke; das gestreift_ Hemd
3. während des heftig_ Gewitters; wegen des heiß_ Sommers; trotz der lang_ Nächte
4. mit den nett_ Leuten; mit den alten Freunden; beide französischen Studentinnen; alle ausländische Studenten
5. durch das nasse Gras; über den reißenden Fluss; die markierten Wanderwege entlang; in die alte Stadt

Omission of the noun

Observe the omission of the noun in the second response to the question.

Welche Handschuhe willst du kaufen?	Vielleicht kaufe ich **die braunen Handschuhe.**
	or: Vielleicht kaufe ich **die braunen.**
	Perhaps I'll buy the brown ones.

The fact that the noun **Handschuhe** is not repeated in the second sentence does not affect the adjective ending: **die braunen** is used in both sentences. In English, *one(s)* is added when the noun is omitted.

Übung 8-3

ANWENDEN Follow each question with another that contains the two adjectives given in parentheses, omitting the noun they modify.

> MODEL: Hast du meinen Blazer gesehen? (schwarz; blau)
>   <u>Meinst du den schwarzen oder den blauen?</u>

Anja sucht alle möglichen Dinge und fragt ihren Mann.

1. Wo ist meine Bluse? (seidene; ander-)
2. Ist meine Aktentasche im Wohnzimmer? (neu; alt)
3. Hast du meinen Mantel gesehen? (hell; warm)
4. Und weißt du, wo mein Portmonee ist? (ledern; ander-)

§3   Adjectives Preceded by *ein*-Words

The **ein**-words are **ein**, **kein**, and the possessives (cf. Kap. 6, §5 and §6). The **ein**-words have the same strong endings as the **der**-words except in three cases where they have no ending at all (see the boxed forms).

The declension of **(k)ein** + adjective + noun is as follows:

	MASCULINE	NEUTER	FEMININE
NOMINATIVE	(k)ein junger Mann	(k)ein junges Mädchen	(k)eine junge Frau
ACCUSATIVE	(k)einen jungen Mann	(k)ein junges Mädchen	(k)eine junge Frau
DATIVE	(k)einem jungen Mann	(k)einem jungen Mädchen	(k)einer jungen Frau
GENITIVE	(k)eines jungen Mannes	(k)eines jungen Mädchens	(k)einer jungen Frau

	PLURAL
NOMINATIVE	keine jungen Leute
ACCUSATIVE	keine jungen Leute
DATIVE	keinen jungen Leuten
GENITIVE	keiner jungen Leute

If an **ein**-word has an ending, the adjective has the same weak ending as after a **der**-word. But if the **ein**-word has no ending, the adjective has a strong ending: **-er** (masculine) or **-es** (neuter).

The following key shows the endings of adjectives preceded by **ein**-words:

	MASCULINE	NEUTER	FEMININE	PLURAL
NOMINATIVE	-er	-es	-e	-en
ACCUSATIVE	-en	-es	-e	-en
DATIVE	-en	-en	-en	-en
GENITIVE	-en	-en	-en	-en

The following are examples of possessive + adjective + noun combinations:

> Ist das dein neu**es** Auto?
> Ist das Ihr neu**er** Wagen?
> Das ist seine neu**e** Freundin?
> Das ist unser neu**es** Haus.

Keep in mind that **-er** of **unser** and **euer** is not a declensional ending (cf. Kap. 6, §6). The **e** before **r** is usually omitted when strong endings are added.

> Das ist uns**(e)re** neue Nachbarin.
> Wir haben uns**(e)rer** neuen Nachbarin geholfen.
> Ist das eu**(e)re** neue Nachbarin?
> Helft ihr eu**(e)rer** neuen Nachbarin?

Übung 8-4

ANWENDEN A. Respond to each question, using the adjective that appears in parentheses.

> MODEL: Hast du einen Film gesehen? (toll)
> <u>Ja, ich habe einen tollen Film gesehen.</u>

1. Hat Dieter einen Brief bekommen? (lang)
2. Stellt das ein Problem für deine Frau dar? (riesig)
3. Hast du ein Kleid gekauft? (schick)
4. Hilfst du deinem Bruder? (klein)
5. Gehst du mit der Chefin zum Mittagessen? (neu)
6. Wohnen viele Leute in Wohnungen und Apartments? (modern)

B. Respond to each question with a phrase consisting of an indefinite article, an adjective, and a noun. For plural nouns, use adjectives only.

> MODEL: Haben Sie heute morgen etwas getrunken?
> <u>Ja, einen heißen Kaffee.</u>

1. Und haben Sie heute morgen etwas gegessen?
2. Lesen Sie im Moment etwas?
3. Haben Sie in letzter Zeit etwas im Kino gesehen?
4. Haben Sie Freunde oder Verwandte hier?
5. Und was für Kurse machen Sie dieses Semester?

§4   Slightly Irregular Forms of Adjectives

The **c** is omitted from adjectives ending in **-ch** when an ending is added.

    hoch (*high*)   Das Gebäude ist **hoch**.
                                  das **hohe** Gebäude/ein **hohes** Gebäude

Adjectives ending in **-el** omit **e** before **l** when an ending is added.

    dunkel (*dark*)   Das Zimmer ist **dunkel**.
                                  das **dunkle** Zimmer/ein **dunkles** Zimmer

Adjectives ending in **-er** after **eu** and **au** omit **e** before **r** when an ending is added.

    teuer (*expensive*)   Die Bücher sind **teuer**.
                                  die **teuren** Bücher

    sauer (*sour*)   Die Milch ist **sauer**.
                                  die **saure** Milch

§5   Adjectives Derived from City Names

City names used as adjectives add **-er** regardless of the gender, number, or case of the following noun. These adjectives are capitalized.

    Das Flugzeug ist auf dem **Berliner** Flughafen gelandet.
    The plane landed at the Berlin airport.

    Das ist ein Bild vom **Kölner** Dom.
    That's a picture of the cathedral of Cologne.

    Wo haben Sie diese **Frankfurter** Würstchen gekauft?
    Where did you buy these frankfurters?

§6   Several Adjectives Modifying the Same Noun

When several adjectives modify the same noun, they have the same adjective ending.

    Das ist ein **schöner** Sommertag.
    Das ist ein **schöner**, **warmer** Sommertag.
    Das ist ein **schöner**, **warmer** und **klarer** Sommertag.

§7   *alle* Followed by a *der*-Word or *ein*-Word

Alle (or in some instances, **all**) may be followed by a **der**-word or **ein**-word; both have the same strong ending. Added adjectives have weak endings.

    all**e** dies**e** Sachen
    all**e** mein**e** Freunde

    alle meine gut**en** Freunde
    alle meine gut**en**, alt**en** Freunde

Übung 8-5

ANWENDEN A. Place the city names as adjectives before the nouns.

> MODEL: Die **Würstchen in Frankfurt** isst man mit viel Senf.
> <u>Frankfurter Würstchen isst man mit viel Senf.</u>

1. Der Dom in Köln ist berühmt für seine Geschichte.
2. Eine Menge Leute besuchen jedes Jahr das Münster in Freiburg.
3. Und viele Menschen betrachten täglich Gemälde in den Museen in London.
4. Alle Leute mögen Lebkuchen aus Nürnberg.
5. Auf dem Oktoberfest in München (change **-en** to **-n**) befinden sich immer Touristen.
6. Seit 1989 gibt es die Mauer in Berlin nicht mehr.

B. Describe each item with two or three adjectives. Try to use as many different adjectives as possible.

> MODEL: Haus   →   <u>ein gemütliches, kleines und billiges Haus</u>

1. Tisch	5. Kind
2. Park	6. Sommertag
3. Lehrerin	7. Hut
4. Pullover	8. Auto

§8   Summary of the Main Features of Adjective Endings

1. Two sets of endings have to be kept in mind.

a. The strong endings of the **der**-words

	MASCULINE	NEUTER	FEMININE	PLURAL
NOMINATIVE	-er	-es	-e	-e
ACCUSATIVE	-en	-es	-e	-e
DATIVE	-em	-em	-er	-en
GENITIVE	-es	-es	-er	-er

b. The weak endings of the adjectives

	MASCULINE	NEUTER	FEMININE	PLURAL
NOMINATIVE	-e	-e	-e	-en
ACCUSATIVE	-en	-e	-e	-en
DATIVE	-en	-en	-en	-en
GENITIVE	-en	-en	-en	-en

2. In the sequence (article)-adjective-noun, at least one strong ending must be present to signal gender, number, and case. Thus, we find the following patterns:

a. Unpreceded adjectives have the strong **der**-word endings.

junger Mann	junges Mädchen	junge Frau	junge Leute
NOMINATIVE	NOMINATIVE/ACCUSATIVE	NOMINATIVE/ACCUSATIVE	NOMINATIVE/ACCUSATIVE

Exception: In the singular, the genitive masculine and neuter have the weak ending -**en** instead of the strong -**es**.

b. Adjectives preceded by **der**-words have weak endings, i.e., -**e** in the nominative (masculine, feminine, neuter) and the accusative (feminine, neuter).

der junge Mann	das junge Mädchen	die junge Frau
NOMINATIVE	NOMINATIVE/ACCUSATIVE	NOMINATIVE/ACCUSATIVE

In all other cases the ending is -**en**.

c. Adjectives preceded by **ein**-words

When the **ein**-word has a strong ending, the adjective has a weak ending. When the **ein**-word has no ending, the adjective has the strong ending -**er** or -**es**.

ein junger Mann	ein junges Mädchen	eine junge Frau
NOMINATIVE	NOMINATIVE/ACCUSATIVE	NOMINATIVE/ACCUSATIVE

In all other cases the ending is -**en**.

3. Adjectives in a series

Series of adjectives modifying the same noun take the same endings.

ein netter, langer Brief   ein hübsches, aber altmodisches Kleid

---

Übung 8-6

ZUSAMMENFASSUNG Unpreceded adjectives; adjectives after **der**- and **ein**-words; irregular adjectives.

A. Respond to each question with a noun preceded by an adjective. Use an article only if it appears in parentheses.

1. Was für Möbelstücke haben Sie in Ihrer Wohnung? (ein)
2. Nennen Sie drei Getränke, die Sie oft trinken.
3. Welche Art von Leuten (was für Leute) mögen Sie?
4. Was für Kleidung tragen Sie gern?
5. Was tragen Sie jetzt? (ein)

B. Write a paragraph about a particularly beautiful place, for example, a garden, a beach, a forest, or a cathedral.

C. Make five statements about some particularly awful things, for example, a piece of clothing, a movie, or a person you dislike.

> MODEL: Das ist ein scheußlicher Hut!
> *Aliens* ist ein grausiger Film.

Additional Uses of Adjectives

§9   Adjectives Preceded by Uninflected Elements

Adjectives preceded by uninflected elements have strong endings to signal the gender, number, and case of the noun that follows.

1. etwas *some, a little*

> Wo kann ich **etwas** heiß**es** Wasser bekommen?

2. ein wenig *a little*

> Hier ist noch **ein wenig** schwarz**er** Kaffee.

Etwas and **ein wenig** are interchangeable.

3. ein paar *a few, some* (generally more than two)

> Wir haben **ein paar** alte Freunde besucht.

4. genug *enough*

> Haben wir **genug** kalte Getränke für unser Picknick?

5. cardinal numbers **zwei**, **drei**, **vier**, etc.

With the exception of **ein-**, cardinal numbers remain uninflected

> drei neu**e** Experimente

When the cardinal number is preceded by a strong **der**-word or **ein**-word, the adjective has a weak ending.

die	drei	neu**en** Experimente
seine	drei	neu**en** Experimente
STRONG	UNINFLECTED	WEAK

6. so ein, was für ein

So ein gut**er** Freund ist unbezahlbar.	*Such a good friend is priceless.*
So gut**e** Freunde habe ich leider nicht.	*Unfortunately, I don't have such good friends.*
Was für ein gut**er** Freund!	*What a good friend!*
Was für gut**e** Freunde!	*What good friends!*

In literary German, **mancher**, **solcher**, and (in exclamations) **welcher** occur without endings.

manch gut**er** Freund	solch gut**er** Freund	Welch gut**er** Freund!
or: manch ein gut**er** Freund	solch ein gut**er** Freund	Welch ein gut**er** Freund!
many a good friend	*such a good friend*	*What a good friend!*

Übung 8-7

ANWENDEN Make up sentences using the cues given. Except for items 7. and 8., include **ein wenig**, **etwas**, **ein paar**, or **genug** before the food and drink items. Use the present tense unless otherwise indicated.

Was haben wir zum Essen und Trinken zu Hause?

> MODEL: im Brotkasten / liegen / frisch / Scheiben Brot
> <u>Im Brotkasten liegen ein paar frische Scheiben Brot.</u>

1. im Kühlschrank / liegen / grün / Salat
2. hier / stehen / Flaschen Mineralwasser
3. wir / haben / kalt / Bier?
4. du / kaufen / deutsch / Käse? (present perfect)
5. sein / im Keller / französisch / Wein
6. wir / haben / dunkle Schokolade
7. was für ein / köstlich / Braten!
8. so ein / lecker / Gemüse!

§10   Adjectives Preceded by *andere, einige, mehrere, viele, wenige*

Like attributive adjectives, the indefinite numerals **andere** (*other*), **einige** (*some, a few*), **mehrere** (*several*), **viele** (*many*), and **wenige** (*few, not many*) may occur with either strong or weak endings, depending on whether or not they are preceded.

UNPRECEDED	PRECEDED
viel**e** Studenten	die viel**en** Studenten
ander**e** Projekte → strong endings	keine ander**en** Projekte → weak endings
wenig**e** Freunde	meine wenig**en** Freunde

When another adjective is added, it has the same strong or weak ending.

UNPRECEDED	PRECEDED
viel**e** neu**e** Studenten	die viel**en** neu**en** Studenten
ander**e** groß**e** Projekte	keine ander**en** groß**en** Projekte
wenig**e** gut**e** Freunde	meine wenig**en** gut**en** Freunde

When used in the singular, unpreceded **viel** and **wenig** are usually not inflected; adjectives that follow them have strong endings.

> viel/wenig Geld   viel/wenig ausländisch**es** Geld

For the use of **ander-** in the singular, see Kap. 18 §1.

Übung 8-8

ANWENDEN A. Make up a sentence using **es gibt...**, **wir haben...**, **hier sind...**, and **in meinem Deutschkurs sind...** for each item. Place an appropriate number, followed by an adjective, before the noun.

> MODEL: Fenster
> <u>Es gibt drei hohe Fenster.</u>

1. Schreibtisch
2. Tafel
3. Wand
4. Tür

5. Fernseher
6. Studenten und Studentinnen
7. ProfessorIn
8. Computer

B. Now, do the same for another locale, for example, your workplace, the house you share with people, or a gathering you attended at someone's home.

§11 Forms and Use of *derselbe* (the same)

The English expression *the same* corresponds to German **der + selbe**, which is written as one word. **Der** has a strong ending, **selbe** a weak one.

SINGULAR
Das ist ⟨
— **derselbe** Mann.
— **dasselbe** Mädchen.
— **dieselbe** Frau.

PLURAL
Das sind **dieselben** Leute.

⌊der⌋ ⌊selbe⌋
STRONG   WEAK

The full declension is as follows:

	MASCULINE	NEUTER	FEMININE	PLURAL
NOMINATIVE	derselbe	dasselbe	dieselbe	dieselben
ACCUSATIVE	denselben	dasselbe	dieselbe	dieselben
DATIVE	demselben	demselben	derselben	denselben
GENITIVE	desselben	desselben	derselben	derselben

Any additional adjective takes the same ending as **selbe**.

Das ist derselbe junge Mann.
⌊STRONG⌋ ⌊WEAK⌋ ⌊WEAK⌋

Übung 8-9

ANWENDEN Insert the appropriate form of **derselbe** before each noun phrase.
Include the adjective when it is given in parentheses.

Georg und Frank haben viele Dinge gemeinsam. Georg erklärt es:

1. Wir machen immer _____ .
2. Und oft machen wir _____ Fehler. (dumm)
3. Frank trägt manchmal _____ Pullover.
4. Und manchmal trägt er sogar _____ Strümpfe. (bunt)
5. An der Uni treffen wir uns mit _____ Freunden.
6. Und oft haben wir _____ Meinung.

§12   Adjectival Nouns

Adjectives referring to persons, things, or abstractions may assume the function of
nouns.

1. Adjectives referring to persons

Das ist ein Programm für Blind**e**.
That's a program for the blind.

Ein Fremd**er** und eine Fremd**e** kamen gestern zu unserem Haus.
A man and a woman we didn't know came to our house yesterday.

Diese Deutsch**en** besuchen New York.
These Germans are visiting New York.

Adjectival nouns are capitalized. They follow the rules for the declension of
adjectives and hence may have either strong or weak endings. They are
frequently rendered into English by adding *man, woman,* or *people.*

SINGULAR		PLURAL	
male	female	male and female	
der Arm**e**	die Arm**e**	die Arm**en**	viele Arm**e**
ein Arm**er**	eine Arm**e**	keine Arm**en**	
		alle Arm**en**	
der Fremd**e**	die Fremd**e**	die Fremd**en**	einige Fremd**e**
ein Fremd**er**	eine Fremd**e**	keine Fremd**en**	
		alle Fremd**en**	
der Deutsch**e**	die Deutsch**e**	die Deutsch**en**	mehrere Deutsch**e**
ein Deutsch**er**	eine Deutsch**e**	keine Deutsch**en**	
		alle Deutsch**en**	

UNPRECEDED

Sind Sie Deutsch**er**? (*male*)	Sind diese Touristen Deutsch**e**?
Sind Sie Deutsch**e**? (*female*)	

An attributive adjective has the same ending as the adjectival noun

ein mysteriös**er** Fremder   viele jung**e** Deutsche
eine freundlich**e** Blinde

2. Adjectives referring to things or abstractions

The neuter forms of adjectives used as nouns are generally collectives or abstractions.

das Neue	*the new, new things, that which is new*
das Alte	*the old, etc.*
das Gute und das Böse	*good and evil*

Das Gute an der Sache ist, dass ich jetzt mehr Zeit für meine Familie habe.
The good thing (or part) about the matter is that I now have more time for my family.

These neuter forms are frequently preceded by **etwas, nichts, viel, wenig,** or **alles.**

der – word

etwas Schön**es**	*something beautiful*	all**es** Schöne	*all that is beautiful*
UNINFLECTED STRONG		STRONG WEAK	
wenig Neu**es**	*little that is new* *little news*	all**es** Neu**e**	*all that is new*
nichts Interessant**es**	*nothing interesting*	all**es** Interessante	*all that is interesting*
viel Gut**es**	*much that is good* *many good things*	all**es** Gute	*all that is good*
		idiom: **Alles Gute!**	*All the best!* or: *Good luck!*

Übung 8-10

ANWENDEN A. Use the adjectives given in parentheses as nouns.

Oskar ist zu Besuch bei Freunden in der Schweiz. Sie antworten auf seine Kommentare.

1. Oskar: Ein _____ hat mich am Bahnhof um Geld gebeten. (arm)
   Jörg: Leider gibt es in unserer Stadt einige _____. (arm)
2. Oskar: Sind im Sommer viele _____ in der Stadt? (fremd)
   Agnes: Ja, gerade gestern hat uns eine _____ nach dem Weg gefragt. Und
            diese _____ war sehr höflich. (fremd)
3. Oskar: Sind eure Nachbarn _____? (deutsch)
   Jörg: Ja, hier wohnen viele _____? Eine Kollegin von uns ist mit einem
            _____ verheiratet. (deutsch)

B. Insert in the blank the correct form of an adjective that logically fits into the sentence.

neu, böse, gut, alt, interessant

1. Habt ihr etwas _____ von Anneliese gehört? Ich habe sie schon ewig nicht mehr gesehen.
2. Wir wünschen dir alles _____ zum Geburtstag!
3. Gibt es etwas _____ im Fernsehen?
4. Wir werfen alles _____ weg. Wir haben nicht genug Platz für die Sachen.
5. Der Junge hat etwas _____ gesagt. Jetzt ist das Mädchen traurig.

§13 Participles Used as Adjectives and Nouns

There are two types of participles: present participles and past participles.

1. Present participles

In English, the present participle has the ending **-ing**; in German a **-d** is added to the infinitive.

lachen**d**	*laughing*	schlafen**d**	*sleeping*	gutaussehen**d**	*handsome*
weinen**d**	*crying*	folgen**d**	*following*	passen**d**	*suitable*

When the participle is used as an adjective preceding a noun, it follows the rules for the adjective declension.

der folgend**e** Satz	die folgend**en** Sätze	folgend**e** Sätze
das passend**e** Kleid	die passend**en** Kleider	passend**e** Kleider
ein weinend**es** Kind	die weinend**en** Kinder	weinend**e** Kinder

Some present participles are commonly used as nouns. They follow the pattern of adjectival nouns, explained in the preceding section.

der/die Reisend**e**	die Reisend**en**	Reisend**e**
the traveler (male/female)	*the travelers*	*travelers*
ein Reisend**er** (male)		
eine Reisend**e** (female)		
der/die Überlebend**e**	die Überlebend**en**	Überlebend**e**
the survivor (male/female)	*the survivors*	*survivors*
ein Überlebend**er** (male)		
eine Überlebend**e** (female)		

2. Past participles

When a past participle precedes a noun, it has normal adjective endings.

INFINITIVE	PAST PARTICIPLE
verdienen	**verdient**
(*to earn, deserve*)	das verdient**e** Geld (*the earned money*)
	eine verdient**e** Strafe (*a deserved punishment*)
gebrauchen	**gebraucht**
(*to use*)	die gebraucht**en** Bücher (*the used or second-hand books*)
stehlen	**gestohlen**
(*to steal*)	der gestohlen**e** Wagen (*the stolen car*)

Several past participles have come to be used as nouns. Like other adjectival nouns, they may have strong or weak adjective endings, depending on their usage. Here are some common examples:

der/die Angestellt**e** (*the employee*)   der/die Gelehrt**e** (*the scholar*)
ein Angestellt**er**   ein Gelehrt**er**
eine Angestellt**e**   eine Gelehrt**e**
der/die Erwachsen**e** (*the adult*)   der/die Verlobt**e** (*the fiancé*)
ein Erwachsen**er**   ein Verlobt**er**
eine Erwachsen**e**   eine Verlobt**e**

When another adjective is added, it has the same ending as the participle.

der/die neu**e** Angestellt**e**   plural: die neu**en** Angestellt**en**
ein neu**er** Angestellt**er**   neu**e** Angestellt**e**
eine neu**e** Angestellt**e**   viel**e** neu**e** Angestellt**e**

Übung 8-11

ANWENDEN Use the adjectives given in parentheses as nouns.

Frau Helm organisiert einen Empfang. Sie bespricht mit einer Kollegin, wer die Gäste sind.

1. Zu diesem Empfang kommen nur _____. (erwachsen)*e*
2. Alle Gäste sind _____ der Firma Siemens. (angestellt)*e (employees)*
3. Herr Richter ist ein neuer _____. (angestellt)*er*
4. Seine _____ heißt Frau Berger. Sie ist sehr nett. (verlobt)*e*
5. Frau Herzog ist eine neue _____ in der Verkaufsabteilung. (angestellt)*e*
6. Und Klaus Neumann ist ihr _____. (verlobt)*er*
7. Dr. Fuchs ist ein berühmter _____. (gelehrt)*er*
8. Wir laden oft _____ ein. Sie halten einen Vortrag für die Gäste. (gelehrt)*e*

§14 Summary of Additional Uses of Adjectives

1. Adjectives have strong endings when preceded by uninflected elements, such as **etwas, ein wenig, ein paar,** and **genug;** cardinal numbers (except **ein-**); and **so ein,** and **was für ein** (also **manch, solch, welch**).

2. Adjectives following **andere, einige, mehrere, viele,** and **wenige** have the same strong or weak endings as these forms.

3. **Derselbe** combines the strong declension of **der** and the weak declension of **selbe** in one word. Additional adjectives take weak endings.

4. Participles preceding nouns follow the rules for the declension of adjectives.

5. Adjectives and participles used as nouns have the usual adjective endings. They are listed as follows:

> **der/die Fremde** (adjective noun) *stranger*
> **der/die Verwandte** (adjective noun) *relative*

Übung 8-12

ZUSAMMENFASSUNG Additional uses of adjectives.

A. Restate each sentence by using the boldface verb as an adjective.

> MODEL: Sind diese Bücher neu oder **gebraucht?**
> <u>Das sind gebrauchte Bücher.</u>

1. Ist das eine Strafe, die er **verdient hat?**
2. Hast du das Kind gehört? Es hat **geweint.**
3. Kinder sind zufrieden, wenn sie **schlafen.**
4. Die Gewerkschaft spricht mit den Arbeitern die **streiken.**
5. Ich suche ein Kleid, das für den Empfang **passt.**
6. Ist der Herr da drüben nicht **gut aussehend?**

B. Write a paragraph using uninflected elements (**etwas, ein wenig, ein paar, genug, einige, mehrere, viele,** and **wenige**).

Sie und ein paar Freunde planen eine Party. Beschreiben Sie, welche Dinge (Essen, Getränke, Musik, Möbel, usw.) sie dafür haben.

C. Combine the words into a headline or the first sentence of a news item. Add your own words to those that are given as cues.

> MODEL: 500 Angestellte Firma Krupp entlassen
> <u>500 Angestellte der Firma Krupp entlassen!</u>

1. Flugzeugabsturz Überlebende (plural)
2. Diebe Reisende (singular masculine) in Italien
3. Streikende (plural) ablehnen Verhandlungen
4. Blinde (singular feminine) nach Operation sehen

Themen und Vokabular

Positive Gefühle		Negative Gefühle	
einmalig	unique	abartig	abnormal, deviant
faszinierend	fascinating		
hervorragend	outstanding, superb	abscheulich	disgusting, repulsive
hochinteressant	highly interesting	abstoßend	revolting
		entsetzlich	dreadful, horrible
glänzend	brilliant		
köstlich	delicious	furchtbar	frightful, awful
lecker	tasty		
toll	great, super	grausig	ghastly
wunderbar	wonderful, miraculous	hässlich	ugly
		krankhaft	sick, sickening
wunderschön	beautiful		
		scheußlich	ugly, hideous
		schockierend	shocking
		schrecklich	terrible
		widerlich	disgusting, nauseating

9 Comparison of Adjectives and Adverbs

Forms of Comparison

§1 Basic Pattern

There are three degrees of comparison.

1. *the positive degree (base form)*	*fast*	*My car is fast.*
2. *the comparative degree*	*faster*	*Your car is faster.*
3. *the superlative degree*	*fastest*	*Her car is the fastest.*

In English, short adjectives form the comparative and superlative by adding the endings **-er** and **-est** to the base form, whereas longer adjectives use *more* and *most: more elegant, most elegant.*

Regardless of length, German adjectives add **-er** to form the comparative and **-st** or **-est** to form the superlative.

The German forms for the three degrees of comparison are

POSITIVE	schnell	elegant	_____
COMPARATIVE	schnell**er**	elegant**er**	_____**er**
SUPERLATIVE	schnell**st**-	elegant**est**-	_____**(e)st**-

For the sake of pronunciation, **-est** is added to adjectives ending in **-d, -t, -s, -sch, -ß, -ss,** or **-z.**

mild	laut	hübsch (*pretty*)	heiß
milder	lauter	hübscher	heißer
mild**est**-	laut**est**-	hübsch**est**-	heiß**est**-

Polysyllabic adjectives (adjectives with more than one syllable) ending in **-d, -t,** or **-sch** add **-st** in the superlative when the last syllable is unstressed.

interessant	but: dringend (*urgent*)	praktisch
interessanter	dringender	praktischer
interessant**est**-	dringend**st**-	praktisch**st**-

§2   Variations and Irregularities

1. Most monosyllabic adjectives (adjectives with one syllable) with the stem vowels **a**, **o**, or **u** require an umlaut in the comparative and superlative.

alt	kalt	lang	warm	groß	jung	kurz (*short*)	dumm
älter	k**ä**lter	l**ä**nger	w**ä**rmer	gr**ö**ßer	j**ü**nger	k**ü**rzer	d**ü**mmer
ältest-	k**ä**ltest-	l**ä**ngst-	w**ä**rmst-	gr**ö**ßt-	j**ü**ngst-	k**ü**rzest-	d**ü**mmst-

Note the irregular form **größt-**: only **-t** is added to the stem in the superlative. §3 of the Appendix offers a list of adjectives that add an umlaut in the comparative and superlative.

2. Adjectives ending in **-e**, **-el**, and **-er** show a variation in the comparative.

leise (*soft*)	dunkel (*dark*)	teuer (*expensive*)
leiser (only **r** added)	**dunkler** (**e** omitted)	**teurer** (**e** omitted)
leisest-	dunkelst-	teuerst-

3. Hoch drops **c** in the comparative; **nahe** adds **c** in the superlative.

hoch	nahe (*close, near*)
höher	näher
höchst-	**nächst-**

4. The comparative and superlative of **gut** and **viel** are irregular, as are the forms of their English counterparts.

gut	(*good)*	**viel**	(*much)*
besser	(*better*)	**mehr**	(*more*)
best-	(*best*)	**meist-**	(*most*)

Note that in contrast to their English equivalents, the comparative and superlative of **schlecht** and **wenig** are regular.

schlecht	(*bad*)	wenig	(*little*)
schlecht**er**	(*worse*)	wenig**er**	(*less*)
schlecht**est-**	(*worst*)	wenig**st-**	(*least*)

Using the Forms of Comparison

In German, all three forms of adjectives—positive, comparative, and superlative—may function as predicate adjectives, adverbs, or attributive adjectives (cf. Kap. 8, Introduction).

§3   Comparison of Predicate Adjectives and Adverbs

The comparative of a predicate adjective or adverb has the ending **-er**, the superlative **-(e)sten**. The superlative is preceded by **am**. These forms do not change.

Heute ist es **kalt**.	Inge fährt **schnell**.	_____
kälter.	**schneller**.	_____er
am kältesten.	**am schnellsten**.	am _____(e)sten

Übung 9-1

ANWENDEN A. Respond to each statement with a new person or thing. Use the comparative forms of the adjective in the original sentence and the ones given in parentheses.

MODEL: Ich finde Politik interessant. (Kunst; wichtig, sinnvoll)
<u>Ich finde Kunst interessanter, wichtiger und sinnvoller.</u>

1. Ich finde Frau Kern nett. (Frau Roth; freundlich, intelligent)
2. Meine Chemieprofessorin spricht langsam. (meine Chinesischprofessorin; deutlich, laut)
3. Ich finde die Schauspielerin Kate Winslow hübsch. (Emma Thompson; attraktiv, elegant)
4. Meine Freundin Sabine ist groß. (meine Freundin Klara; dünn, neugierig, tolerant)
5. Schokoladeneis ist gut. (Erdbeereis; lecker, gesund)
6. Ich finde Russisch kompliziert. (Chinesisch; schwierig)
7. Mein Vater fährt langsam. (meine Mutter; vorsichtig, sicher)
8. Dein braunes Kleid ist elegant. (dein rotes Kleid; modern, passend, schick, lang)
9. Mein Zimmer ist dunkel. (meine Wohnung; klein, gemütlich, teuer)

B. Use the superlative form to describe a specific item (person or thing). If two adjectives are given, provide two examples for the category.

MODEL: Ein Gebäude (hoch)   <u>Das Empire State Building ist am höchsten.</u>

1. Ein Schauspieler/eine Schauspielerin (gutaussehend)
2. Wagen (schnell)
3. Eissorte (gut)
4. Ein Kurs (langweilig, interessant)
5. Das Wetter in _____ (heiß, kalt)
6. _____ (wichtig)

Phrases of comparison expressing equality and inequality

In phrases of comparison, the positive degree is expressed with **so ... wie** (*as...as*) and the comparative degree with **als** (*than*).

Marlene ist **so groß wie** ich. *Marlene is as tall as I (am).*	**so _____ wie**	as _____ as
Klaus ist **größer als** ich. *Klaus is taller than I (am).*	**_____ er als**	_____er than more _____ than
Helga ist **intelligenter als** ich. *Helga is more intelligent than I (am).*		more _____ than

Strengthening the comparison

Certain words or prefixes may be added to strengthen a comparison.

1. So may be expanded to **ebenso** or **genauso**.

Walter ist **ebenso/genauso** groß wie ich.

2. The comparative form may be preceded by **noch, etwas,** or **viel**.

Dieter ist **noch** fauler als ich.	*Dieter is even lazier than I (am).*
Helga ist **etwas** dicker als du.	*Helga is somewhat (a little) heavier than you.*
Ich bin **viel** kleiner als er.	*I am much shorter than he (is).*

3. In the superlative, **aller-** (*the very...*)may be added as a prefix.

Das ist am **allerbesten**.   *That is the very best of all.*

Übung 9-2

ANWENDEN A. Complete each sentence with a clause that contains a strengthened comparative (**noch, etwas, viel**) or superlative (**aller-**).

MODEL: Mein Deutsch ist gut, aber... (viel)
          Mein Deutsch ist gut, aber Evas Deutsch ist viel besser.

1. Ich bin groß, aber... (etwas)
2. Schokolade schmeckt gut, aber... (aller-)
3. Ich bin faul, aber... (noch)
4. Die Englischprüfung war schwer und... (genauso)
5. Ich arbeite viel, aber... (viel)
6. Ich fahre schnell, aber... (aller-)

B. Compare various people with one another using the elements given with the phrases **so ... wie** and **-er als**.

MODEL: Kollegen/Innen (groß)
          Martin ist so groß wie Gerd. Franziska ist größer als Monika.

1. Freunde/Innen (schlank [no umlaut])
2. Verwandte (hübsch)
3. Teenager (höflich)
4. Geschwister oder Zimmerkollegen/Innen (ordentlich)
5. Professoren/Innen (geduldig)
6. bekannte Schauspieler/Innen
7. Politiker/Innen

§4   Comparison of Attributive Adjectives

Used attributively, comparative and superlative adjectives have the same strong or weak endings as any other adjective (cf. Kap. 8). The endings are added to the base forms as given in §1 and §2 of this Kapitel.

Der groß**e** Koffer gehört mir.
Der größer**e** Koffer gehört mir.
Der größt**e** Koffer gehört mir.

STRONG   WEAK

Das ist ein groß**er** Koffer.
Das ist kein größer**er** Koffer.
Das ist mein größt**er** Koffer.

UN-   STRONG
INFLECTED

Übung 9-3

ANWENDEN   A. For each sentence with a comparison, respond with a sentence that states the opposite. Adjust personal pronouns as appropriate to the response.

MODEL: Das ist der kürzere Weg.
<u>Nein, das stimmt nicht. Das ist der längere Weg.</u>

1. Ich habe jüngere Kollegen.
2. Hannelore trägt billigere Schuhe.
3. Du hast einen ältereren Wagen.
4. Jürgen Klinsmann ist der schlechtere Fußballspieler.
5. Das ist der längere Film.
6. Er hat ein leichteres Leben als wir.
7. Das war eine einfachere Prüfung.
8. Gabi wiegt weniger als du.

B. Use the cues to make statements that contain an attribute in the superlative form.

MODEL: Tante Elisabeth / Haus / groß / haben
<u>Tante Elisabeth hat das größte Haus!</u>

Reiche Verwandte in Monaco.

1. mein Onkel / Wagen / teuer / besitzen
2. Und / meine Kusine / reich / Mann / heiraten (present perfect)
3. Onkel Richard / Anzüge / elegant / tragen
4. Tante Greta / Kostüme / schick / kaufen
5. Thomas / in / schön / Haus / wohnen

Comparative and superlative forms of **viel** *and* **wenig**

viel	SINGULAR	Sie hat **viel** Zeit.	(*much*)
		mehr Zeit>	(*more*)
		die meiste Zeit.	(*the most*)
	PLURAL	**Viele** Leute sind dagegen.	(*many*)
		Mehr Leute	(*more*)
		Die meisten Leute	(*most*)

wenig	SINGULAR	Sie hat **wenig** Zeit.	(*little*)
		weniger **Zeit.**	(*less*)
		die wenigste Zeit.	(*the least*)
	PLURAL	**Wenige** Leute sind dagegen.	(*few*)
		Weniger Leute	(*fewer*)
		Die wenigsten Leute	(*the fewest*)

Note: a. **Viel** and **wenig** usually have endings in the plural but not in the singular.

b. The comparatives **mehr** and **weniger** never add an ending.

c. **Meist-** requires the definite article: **die meisten Leute** (*most people*).

d. Whereas English often uses *more* to form the comparatives of longer adjectives, German relies exclusively on the **-er** ending.

Das ist wirklich ein **interessanterer** Film als sein letzter.
This is really a more interesting movie than his last one.

Übung 9-4

ZUSAMMENFASSUNG Comparative and superlative forms of adjectives.

A. Select any two items from each set of words and provide a sentence comparing them with each other. Use the adjectives given. Provide six such comparisons for each of the three sets.

MODEL: Jogurt, Milch, Eis, Käse
gesund, flüssig, kalt, weich
Jogurt ist gesünder als Eis. Milch ist flüssiger als Jogurt.
Eis ist kälter als Jogurt. Käse ist weicher als Eis.

1. Auto, Fahrrad, Motorrad, Rollerblades, Bahn, Flugzeug
schnell, teuer, laut, bequem, langsam, umweltfreundlich, gut
2. Kind, Teenager, Baby, Erwachsene, Großeltern, Mann, Frau, Eltern
alt, klein, schwierig, hilflos, erfahren, geduldig
3. Wald, Wiese, Bach, Fluss, See, Berge, Hügel, Stadt, Dorf
klein, groß, tief, hoch, dunkel, schnell, ruhig

B. Make up a list of, for example, celebrities, TV shows, cities, or countries and then a list of appropriate adjectives. Then provide six comparisons between any two items from each list.

C. Now, use a superlative to distinguish one item from all the others in the sets of words in A.

MODEL: Milch ist am gesündesten.

Vokabulartip: sensibel *und* vernünftig

To describe a person as sensitive, one would use the word **sensibel** in German. (**Sensibel** does not mean *sensible*.) To describe someone as being sensible or reasonable, use **vernünftig**.

D. Compare yourself with relatives and friends by forming sentences that express equality or inequality.

MODEL: schlank sein

Meine Kusine Charlotte ist so schlank wie ich.
Meine Kusine Charlotte ist genauso schlank wie ich.
Meine Kusine Charlotte ist schlanker als ich.

1. dick sein
2. sensibel sein
3. neugierig sein
4. egoistisch sein
5. vernünftig sein
6. vorsichtig fahren
7. etwas schnell lernen
8. langsam arbeiten
9. viel essen
10. viel helfen

E. Answer the following personalized questions.

1. Wer in Ihrer Familie spricht am wenigsten? Wer spricht am lautesten?
2. Wer in Ihrer Familie hat die meiste Geduld? Wer hat die wenigste Geduld?
3. Und wer isst am meisten?
4. Wer von Ihren Freunden und Freundinnen hat die meiste Willensstärke?
5. Wen von Ihren Freunden und Freundinnen finden Sie am nettesten?
6. Welcher Freund oder welche Freundin (oder welcher Lehrer/welche Lehrerin) hat die besten Einfälle?
7. Welchen Schauspieler und welche Schauspielerin bewundern Sie am meisten?
8. Welche Fernsehsendung gefällt Ihnen am besten oder hat Ihnen am besten gefallen?
9. Welche bekannte Person hat Ihrer Meinung nach die meiste Toleranz?
10. Welche bekannte Person hat die meiste Arroganz?

Additional Features of Comparatives and Superlatives

§5   Two Ways of Expressing the Superlative of Predicate Adjectives

Meine Freunde sind sehr nett.
My friends are very nice.

or: Rainer ist **am nettesten**.
Rainer ist **der netteste** (Freund).
Rainer is the nicest (one).

When persons or things of a distinctive group are compared, the superlative predicate adjective may appear in the attributive form without the noun (but in agreement with the noun to which it refers) rather than in the form that requires **am...(e)sten**.

Additional examples:

Die Töchter von Körners sind sehr intelligent.	*The Körners' daughters are very intelligent.*
Astrid ist **am intelligentesten**. or: Astrid ist **die intelligenteste**.	*Astrid is the most intelligent (one).*
Sie sehen hier sehr wertvolle Gemälde.	*You are seeing very valuable paintings here.*
Dieses Gemälde ist **am wertvollsten**. or: Dieses Gemälde ist **das wertvollste**.	*This painting is the most valuable (one).*

Übung 9-5

ANWENDEN Answer the personalized questions with the *am...* superlative and then the attributive form.

MODEL: Haben Sie freundliche Nachbarn?
Ja, Herr Mohr ist am freundlichsten. Von meinen Nachbarn ist Herr Mohr der freundlichste.

1. Sind Ihre Freunde und Freundinnen tolerant?
2. Sind Ihre Freunde/Freundinnen intelligent?
3. Haben Sie geduldige Professoren und Professorinnen?
4. Sind Ihre Prüfungen dieses Semester schwierig?
5. Lesen Sie spannende und interessante Bücher?
6. Sind Ihre Eltern streng? Ihr Vater oder ihre Mutter?

§6 The Comparatives and Superlatives of the Adverbs *bald, oft,* and *gern*

bald	*soon*	Besuchst du uns **bald**?
eher	*sooner*	Kannst du nicht **eher** kommen?
am ehesten	*(the) soonest*	Er hat **am ehesten** reagiert.
oft	*often*	Er hat **oft** angerufen.
öfter	*more often*	Sie hat **öfter** angerufen.
am öftesten	*most often*	Wir haben **am öftesten** angerufen.
am häufigsten	*most frequently*	Du hast **am häufigsten** angerufen.

The superlative **am häufigsten** is more commonly used than **am öftesten**.

Gern(e), **lieber**, **am liebsten** are used together with a verb to express various degrees of liking.

An **e** may be added to **gern**.

gern(e)	etwas **gern** tun	*to like to do something*
lieber	etwas **lieber** tun	*to prefer to do something*
am liebsten	etwas **am liebsten** tun	*to like to do something most, best*

Note the use of **essen** and **trinken** when referring to food and drink.

Er **trinkt gern** Kaffee.	*He likes coffee.*
Ich **trinke lieber** Tee.	*I prefer tea.*
Sie **isst am liebsten** Hummer.	*She likes lobster the best.*

Übung 9-6

ANWENDEN A. Express a preference for one of the two activities in each item by using **lieber**.

MODEL: Fahrrad fahren   Auto fahren.
<u>Ich fahre gern Rad, aber ich fahre lieber Auto.</u>

1. Kaffee trinken   Kola trinken
2. sich mit Leuten unterhalten   in Ruhe lesen
3. Videos anschauen   ins Kino gehen
4. zu Hause kochen   zum Essen ausgehen
5. zwei Sportarten

B. Respond to the following personalized questions.

1. Was essen und trinken Sie am liebsten? Was isst Ihr Bruder/Ihre Schwester am liebsten? Was isst ein Freund von Ihnen am liebsten?
2. Was machen Sie am Wochenende am häufigsten?
3. Was macht Ihre Familie am häufigsten, wenn Sie Ferien haben?
4. Welchen Sport/welche Aktivitäten machen Sie am liebsten im Sommer? Und im Winter?
5. Wen treffen Sie am häufigsten? Mit wem telefonieren Sie am häufigsten? Wer schickt Ihnen am häufigsten Post oder E-mail?

§7   The Use of *immer* + Comparative

The construction **immer** + comparative indicates a progressive change.

Es wird **immer kälter**.
It is getting colder and colder. It keeps getting colder. (literally, *It is always/ever colder.*)

Du wirst **immer egoistischer**.
You are becoming more and more egotistical.

Immer mehr Arbeiter verlieren ihren Arbeitsplatz.
More and more workers are losing their jobs.

Übung 9-7

ANWENDEN A. Make five statements using the **immer...** construction. Use the cued adjectives.

> MODEL: Menschen / aktiv
> <u>Die Menschen werden immer aktiver.</u>

Die Zeiten haben sich geändert!

1. Arbeitstage / lang
2. Junge Leute / träge (*sluggish*)
3. Ozonloch / groß
4. Politiker / korrupt
5. Häuser / teuer

B. Now, make two such statements with elements of your own.

§8   The Use of *je ... desto* or *je ... um so*

> **Je** schneller **desto** besser.
> or: **Je** schneller **um so** besser.   *The faster the better.*
>
> **Je** bequemer **desto** besser.
> or: **Je** bequemer **um so** besser.   *The more comfortable the better.*

Observe the word order in the following example:

Je mehr ich für dich **tue**, desto mehr **verlangst du** von mir.
— DEPENDENT CLAUSE— — MAIN CLAUSE —
verb at the end   inverted word order

The more I do for you, the more you demand from me.

Übung 9-8

ANWENDEN Follow each phrase (**je ...**) with a logical (or maybe absurd!) one that begins with **desto...**.

> MODEL: Je mehr ich schlafe, ...
> <u>Je mehr ich schlafe, desto müder werde ich.</u>

1. Je eher du gehst, ...
2. Je mehr du schimpfst, ...
3. Je weniger ich esse, ...
4. Je mehr Geld ich verdiene, ...
5. Je mehr sie über ihn nachdenkt, ...
6. Je öfter ich diese Schuhe trage, ...

§9   Absolute Comparatives and Superlatives

Absolute comparatives

In certain expressions, a comparative form is used where no comparison is actually implied.

ein **älterer** Herr	*an elderly gentleman*
ein **größerer** Geldbetrag	*a rather large amount of money*
eine **längere** Reise	*a rather long trip*
neuere Sprachen	*modern languages*

Absolute superlatives

Superlative forms may be used to indicate a very high degree of some quality. As adjectives, some superlatives are often unpreceded.

Liebste Barbara!	*Dearest Barbara!*
Liebster Peter!	*Dearest Peter!*
Beste Grüße!	*Best regards!*

As adverbs, these superlatives modify an adjective or another adverb; they lack **am** and the ending **-en**:

Das war **höchst** interessant.	*That was incredibly interesting.*
Das ist **äußerst** unangenehm.	*That is extremely unpleasant.*

Special adverbial superlatives with the ending -ens

höchstens	*at the most*	Sie ist **höchstens** 20 Jahre alt.
mindestens	*at least*	Er arbeitet **mindestens** 8 Stunden am Tag.
frühestens	*at the earliest*	Ich komme **frühestens** am Freitag zurück.
spätestens	*at the latest*	Wir rufen Sie **spätestens** am Sonnabend an.
meistens	*mostly, most of*	
meist	*the time, usually*	Ich komme **meistens/meist** zu spät.

Übung 9-9

ANWENDEN Give a response that contains the superlative given in parentheses.

> MODEL: Was kosten Ihre Bücher für die Uni jedes Semester? (mindestens)
> <u>Sie kosten mindestens 350 Mark.</u>

1. Wann kommen Sie abends nach Hause? (spätestens)
2. Wann stehen Sie morgens auf? (frühestens)
3. Wie viel Geld geben Sie pro Semester für Bücher aus? (höchstens)
4. In welches Restaurant gehen Sie zum Mittagessen? (meistens)
5. Was wiegen Sie? (höchstens)
6. Wie lange werden Sie noch studieren? (mindestens)

§10   Comparatives and Superlatives Used as Nouns

Like other adjectives, comparatives and superlatives may be used as nouns. They
retain their usual adjective endings (cf. Kap. 8, §12) and are capitalized.

Comparatives

der/die/das Stärker**e**	*the stronger one*
die Stärker**en**	*the stronger ones*
nichts Schöner**es**	*nothing more beautiful*
nichts Besser**es**	*nothing better*
etwas Billiger**es**	*something cheaper, something less expensive*
etwas Interessanter**es**	*something more interesting*

Superlatives

Thomas ist **der Beste** in Chemie.	*Thomas is the best (one) in chemistry.*
Du bist **die Allerschönste**.	*You are the most beautiful one of all.*
Der Nächste, bitte!	*Next (person), please.*
Das ist **das Wichtigste**.	*That is the most important thing.*
Haben Sie **das Neu(e)ste** gehört?	*Have you heard the latest?*
Ich habe **mein Bestes** getan.	*I did my best.*

Übung 9-10

ZUSAMMENFASSUNG Additional features of comparatives and superlatives (cf. §5
to §10 in this Kapitel).

A. Describe each item with an absolute superlative.

    MODEL: Pelé   →   der beste Fußballspieler

1. Mount Everest (hoch)
2. Tokio (teuer)
3. Viper (giftig)
4. Der Film „Vom Winde verweht" (lang)
5. Jupiter (groß)
6. Cheetah (schnell)
7. Provide one such statement of your own.

B. Answer the personalized questions. Include the superlative that is used as a noun in your response.

1. Was ist für Sie das Wichtigste im Leben?
2. Was ist das Schwerste im Leben für Sie?
3. Was ist für Sie das Leichteste?
4. Was ist das Neuste für Sie und Ihre Freunde? (Musik, Kleidung, Worte)
   Musik: Das Neuste ist/sind...
   Kleidung: Das Neuste ist...
5. Beschreiben Sie Familienmitglieder:
   Wer ist der/die Stärkste? Schwächste? Bei einem Sport der/die Beste?
   Wer der/die Schönste? Toleranteste? Bescheidenste? Begabteste? Der/die Ordentlichste?

Themen und Vokabular

Charaktereigenschaften: Hauptwörter

die Arroganz	*arrogance*
die Ausdauer	*endurance, stamina*
die Bescheidenheit	*modesty*
der Einfall, ⸚e	*idea*
die Idee, -en	*idea*
die Geduld	*patience*
die Selbstbeherrschung	*self-control*
die Toleranz	*tolerance*
die Willensstärke	*willpower*

Charaktereigenschaften: Adjektive

aktiv	*active*
begabt	*talented*
bescheiden	*modest, humble*
egoistisch	*egotistical, selfish*

freundlich	*friendly*
geduldig	*patient*
großzügig	*generous*
intelligent	*intelligent*
intolerant	*intolerant*
ordentlich	*neat, orderly*
sensibel	*sensitive*
streng	*strict*
tolerant	*tolerant, accepting*
träge	*sluggish*
unfreundlich	*unfriendly*
ungeduldig	*impatient*
unordentlich	*disorderly*
vernünftig	*sensible, reasonable*

10 Numerals; Time Expressions

Cardinal and Ordinal Numbers

§1 Cardinal Numbers and Their Uses

0 null	80 achtzig
1 eins	90 neunzig
2 zwei, zwo	100 (ein)hundert
3 drei	101 hunderteins
4 vier	102 hundertzwei
5 fünf	150 hundertfünfzig
6 sechs	151 hunderteinundfünfzig
7 sieben	199 hundertneunundneunzig
8 acht	200 zweihundert
9 neun	201 zweihunderteins
10 zehn	300 dreihundert
11 elf	400 vierhundert
12 zwölf	500 fünfhundert
13 dreizehn	600 sechshundert
14 vierzehn	700 siebenhundert
15 fünfzehn	800 achthundert
16 sechzehn	900 neunhundert
17 siebzehn	999 neunhundertneunundneunzig
18 achtzehn	1 000 (ein)tausend
19 neunzehn	2 000 zweitausend
20 zwanzig	10 000 zehntausend
21 einundzwanzig	100 000 (ein)hunderttausend
22 zweiundzwanzig	250 320 zweihundertfünfzigtausend-
23 dreiundzwanzig	dreihundertzwanzig
30 dreißig	1 000 000 eine Million
31 einunddreißig	10 000 000 zehn Millionen
40 vierzig	100 000 000 hundert Millionen
41 einundvierzig	200 500 000 zweihundert Millionen
50 fünfzig	fünfhunderttausend
60 sechzig	1 000 000 000 eine Milliarde (one billion)
70 siebzig	1 000 000 000 000 eine Billion (one trillion)

1. Eins is used in counting. It is the only cardinal number that changes when modifying a noun. It then uses the endings of the **ein**-words (cf. Kap. 6 §5).

> Ich habe nur **einen Freund.**
> Ich habe **zwei Freunde.**

2. Eins is written **1**, with the initial stroke below the line.

> **Sieben** is usually written **7** to distinguish it from **eins**.
> In spoken German, **zwo** is often used instead of **zwei**, to avoid confusion with **drei**.

3. The boldface numbers are irregular.

> **eins** but **einundzwanzig** (**s** omitted)
> **sechs** but **sechzehn, sechzig** (**s** omitted)
> **sieben** but **siebzehn, siebzig** (**en** omitted)
> **dreißig** (ending **-ßig** instead of **-zig**)

4. To separate thousands, German leaves a space or inserts a period. It does not insert a comma, as English does.

> 10 570 or 10.570 or zehntausendfünfhundertsiebzig

5. All numbers of less than one million are written in lowercase letters. Numbers of one million or more are capitalized; they are feminine nouns, and their plural forms end in **-en**.

> **zwei Millionen, Milliarden, Billionen**

Remember:	**eine Milliarde**	= *one billion*
	eine Billion	= *one trillion (one thousand billion)*

Übung 10-1

VERSTEHEN A. Read the following figures aloud.

1.	26	5.	126	9.	1 317	13.	431 690
2.	67	6.	247	10.	4 255	14.	919 900
3.	88	7.	739	11.	19 387	15.	1 500 000
4.	94	8.	966	12.	51 674	16.	10 800 750

B. Write the numerals for the numbers written out below.

1.	sieben	6.	dreizehn
2.	fünfzehn	7.	null
3.	eine Milliarde	8.	zwölf
4.	zwanzig	9.	einundzwanzig
5.	siebzehn	10.	hundert

Approximate figures

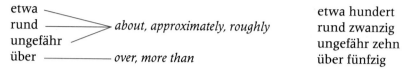

etwa hundert
rund zwanzig
ungefähr zehn
über fünfzig

Decimals

The German equivalent of a decimal point is a comma.

0,5   (read: **null Komma fünf**)
2,75   (read: **zwei Komma sieben fünf**)

Monetary amounts in **Deutsche Mark (DM)** *and* **Pfennig**

Mark and **Pfennig** are used in the singular.

Diese CD kostet DM 30,50. (read: **dreißig Mark** und **fünfzig Pfennig**)
(or: **dreißig Mark fünfzig**)
Ich habe nur noch **50 Pfennig**.

Simple arithmetic

$12 + 4 = 16$ zwölf **und** vier ist sechzehn
                    or: zwölf **plus** vier...

$12 - 4 = 8$ zwölf **weniger** vier ist acht
                    or: zwölf **minus** vier...

$\left.\begin{array}{l}12 \times 4 \\ \text{or: } 12 \cdot 4\end{array}\right\} = 48$ zwölf **mal** vier ist achtundvierzig

$12 : 4 = 3$ zwölf **geteilt durch** vier ist drei
                    (short: zwölf **durch** vier ist drei)

German uses a colon to express division.

Übung 10-2

VERSTEHEN   Read the following sentences with figures aloud.

Wie viel kostet das?

1. Diese Uhr kostet DM 124,95.
2. Diese Wohnung kostet über 100 000 Mark.
3. Wir haben für dieses Auto ungefähr 30 000 Mark bezahlt.

Wie viele Leute wohnen hier?

4. Unsere Stadt hat rund 600 000 Einwohner.
5. In Deutschland leben rund 79,1 Millionen Menschen.
6. München hat eine Einwohnerzahl von ungefähr 1,2 Millionen.

Rechnen.

7. $56 + 21 = 77$
8. $75 - 45 = 30$
9. $7 \times 9 = 63$
10. $150 : 10 = 15$

Übung 10-3

ANWENDEN Write out and then say aloud the numbers in response to the personalized questions.

1. Was ist Ihre Telefonnummer?
2. Was ist Ihre Hausnummer?
3. Was ist die Vorwahl für Ihre Heimatstadt?
4. Wie viele Einwohner hat Ihre Heimatstadt?
5. Wie viele Menschen leben in den USA?

§2   Ordinal Numbers and Their Uses

der, das, die		der, das, die	
1.		**erste**	*the first*
2.		zweite	*the second*
		or: **der zwote**	
3.		**dritte**	*the third*
4.		vierte	
5.		fünfte	
6.		sechste	
7.		siebente	
		or: **siebte** (more common)	
8.		**achte**	
9.		neunte	
10.		zehnte	
11.		elfte	
12.		zwölfte	
13.		dreizehnte	
19.		neunzehnte	
20.		zwanzigste	
21.		einundzwanzigste	
22.		zweiundzwanzigste	
23.		dreiundzwanzigste	
30.		dreißigste	
31.		einunddreißigste	
40.		vierzigste	
50.		fünfzigste	
60.		sechzigste	
70.		siebzigste	
80.		achtzigste	
90.		neunzigste	

100.	der, die, das hundertste
200.	zweihundertste
1000.	tausendste
1.000.000.	millionste

1. The ordinal numbers **erst-**, **dritt-**, **siebt-**, and **acht-** are irregular. The others from *second* to *nineteenth* are formed by adding **-t** to the cardinal number. Higher numbers add **-st**.

2. Ordinal numbers take normal adjective endings (cf. Kap. 8 §8).

der erst**e** Sonntag	die erst**e** Frage
am erst**en** Sonntag	nach der erst**en** Frage

3. When numerals are used, ordinal numbers are indicated by placing a period after the number.

Mein Büro ist im 19. Stock. *My office is on the nineteenth floor.*

The use of the adverbs erstens, zweitens, drittens, etc.

erstens	*first(ly), in the first place*
zweitens	*second(ly), in the second place*
drittens	*third(ly), in the third place*

Warum willst du nicht mit uns ins Kino gehen?
Erstens bin ich müde, **zweitens** habe ich keine Zeit, und **drittens** bin ich pleite.

The use of -mal and Mal with cardinal and ordinal numbers

Cardinal number + **-mal**		Ordinal number used as adjective	
einmal	*once*	das erste Mal	*the first time*
noch einmal	*once more*	zum ersten Mal	*for the first time*
zweimal	*twice, two times*	das zweite Mal	
dreimal	*three times*	das dritte Mal	
zehnmal	*ten times*	das vierte Mal	
hundertmal	*a hundred times*		
tausendmal	*a thousand times*		

Fractions

With the exception of **ein halb-** and **die Hälfte**, fractions are neuter nouns. They are formed by adding **-l** to the ordinal number. **Ein halb-** takes the normal adjective endings. In compounds like **eineinhalb** and **anderthalb** ($1\frac{1}{2}$), no adjective ending is used.

$\frac{1}{2}$	ein halb-	Das ist **ein halber** Kuchen.	*This is half a cake.*
	die Hälfte	**Die Hälfte** gehört mir.	*Half of it is mine.*
$\frac{1}{3}$	ein Drittel		
$\frac{1}{4}$	ein Viertel		
$\frac{2}{5}$	zwei Fünftel		
$\frac{3}{10}$	drei Zehntel		

1/100	ein Hundertstel	
1½	eineinhalb	Wir haben **eineinhalb (anderthalb) Jahre** in
	or: anderthalb	Zürich gewohnt.
2½	zweieinhalb	Martin hat **zweieinhalb** Jahre Deutsch gelernt.
3½	dreieinhalb	Helgas Eltern sind **dreieinhalb** Wochen in Florida geblieben.

Übung 10-4

ANWENDEN A. Insert an appropriate numeral in each blank.

1. Ein Semester an der Uni dauert genau _____ Monate.
2. Ich lerne seit _____ Jahren Deutsch.
3. Ich sitze in meinem Deutschkurs in der _____ Reihe.
4. Wir sind im Moment im _____ Kapitel in diesem Deutschbuch.
5. Ich lese gerade _____ (Name eines Buches). Ich bin im _____ Kapitel.
6. Wir sind jetzt im _____ Jahrhundert.
7. Letztes Jahr war ich nur einmal im Urlaub. Und Sie?

B. Provide an appropriate adverb for each blank.

1. Ich kann dir nur ein halbes Brot geben. Die andere _____ brauche ich selbst.
2. Die Kinder hören nicht zu! Ihre Mutter muss alles _____ sagen.
3. Möchten Sie noch einen Kaffee? Eine ganze oder eine _____ Tasse?
4. Ich habe in dem Film, „Himmel über Berlin," beim ersten Mal nichts verstanden, aber beim _____ bin ich viel besser mitgekommen.
5. Ihre Freundin war nicht zu Hause. Sie ruft sie später _____ an.
6. Wer war der _____ Mensch auf dem Mond?

The use of ordinal numbers with dynastic names

Papst Paul **der Erste**	written: Papst Paul I.
Kaiser Wilhelm **der Zweite**	Kaiser Wilhelm II.
König Ludwig **der Vierzehnte**	König Ludwig XIV.

Here the ordinal numbers are capitalized, since they are regarded as part of a proper name. They have the usual adjective endings.

NOMINATIVE	Kaiser Friedrich **der Dritte**	Kaiser Friedrich III war sein Freund.
ACCUSATIVE	Kaiser Friedrich **den Dritten**	Er hasste Kaiser Friedrich III.
DATIVE	Kaiser Friedrich **dem Dritten**	Sie halfen Kaiser Friedrich III.
GENITIVE	Kaiser Friedrichs **des Dritten**	Sie war die Tochter Kaiser Friedrichs III.

Note that the genitive **-s** is attached to the name only, not to the title.

Übung 10-5

VERSTEHEN Read the sentences aloud. Pay special attention to the numerals.

1. Viele Künstler und Philosophen kamen ins Schloss Sanssouci zu Kaiser Friedrich II.
2. Kaiser Karl V. regierte zur Zeit der Reformation.
3. Viele Menschen besuchen das Schloss Neuschwanstein Ludwigs II.
4. Papst Gregor VII. bannte König Heinrich IV.
5. Elisabeth I. regierte viele Jahre in England.

Time Expressions

When using time expressions, one must pay particular attention to the gender of the noun. Here is a list of frequently occurring nouns grouped according to gender.

MASCULINE	MASCULINE	FEMININE
der Monat, -e	**Monate**	die Sekunde, -n
der Tag, -e	der Januar	die Minute, -n
	der Februar	die Stunde, -n
Wochentage/	der März	die Nacht, ¨e
Wochenende	der April	die Mitternacht, ¨e
der Sonntag, -e	der Mai	die Zeit, -en
der Montag, -e	der Juni	die Jahreszeit, -en (*season*)
der Dienstag, -e	der Juli	die Woche, -n
der Mittwoch, -e	der August	die Uhr, -en (*clock, watch*)
der Donnerstag, -e	der September	
der Freitag, -e	der Oktober	NEUTER
der Sonnabend, -e	der November	
or: der Samstag, -e	der Dezember	das Jahr, -e
		das Wochenende, -n
Tageszeiten	**Jahreszeiten**	
der Morgen, -	der Frühling, -e	
der Vormittag, -e	der Sommer, -	
der Mittag, -e	der Herbst, -e	
der Nachmittag, -e	der Winter, -	
der Abend, -e		
(*but:* die Nacht)		

§3   Time Expressions Referring to Seasons, Months, Days of the Week, and Parts of the Day

Most time expressions that include a preposition are in the dative case.

1. Seasons and months

im Frühling	*in the spring*	**im** Januar	*in January*
im Sommer	*in the summer*	**im** Februar	*in February*
im Herbst	*in the fall*	**im** März	*in March*
im Winter	*in the winter*		

In contrast to English usage, German names of the months require the definite article.

Wir heiraten **im** Januar.
(IN + DEM)

Der Juli war dieses Jahr sehr heiß.

2. Days of the week

am (**an** + **dem**) may be omitted.

(am) Sonntag	*on Sunday*	(Am) Sonntag bin ich in Berlin.
(am) Montag		
(am) Dienstag		

3. Parts of the day

am Morgen	*in the (early) morning (before 10 A.M.)*	Am Morgen war ich zu Hause.
am Vormittag	*in the (late) morning or forenoon*	
am Mittag **zu** Mittag	*at noon*	
am Nachmittag	*in the afternoon*	
am Abend	*in the evening* *at night (before bedtime)*	
in der Nacht	*at night (after bedtime)*	

Note that *at night* (before bedtime) is expressed by **am Abend**.

4. The days of the week combined with parts of the day

(am) Sonntagmorgen   (Am) Sonntagmorgen ist unser Hund davongelaufen.
(am) Montagvormittag
(am) Dienstagmittag
(am) Mittwochabend (*Wednesday evening/night*)

in der Nacht ⟨ vom Donnerstag zum/auf den Freitag
                 vom ersten bis/zum zweiten Mai
(*during the night from … to …*)

5. Adverbial forms ending in **-s**

Forms ending in **-s** normally denote repeated occurrences. Because they are adverbs, they are not capitalized.

sonntags, montags, dienstags, mittwochs, donnerstags, freitags, samstags/sonnabends
on Sundays, Mondays ...

Parts of the day functioning as adverbs

morgens, vormittags, mittags, nachmittags, abends, nachts
in the morning(s) ...

Meistens lerne ich **abends.**   *I usually study at night.*

These forms may also refer to one event.

Ich war gestern zu Hause.   Nur **am Nachmittag**
                               or: Nur **nachmittags** ⟩ war ich bei Kleins.

I was at home yesterday. I was at the Kleins' only in the afternoon.

Note the difference between using **am** + day and the adverbial form ending in **-s**.

Herr Zimmermann arbeitet **am Montag** nicht.
Herr Zimmermann arbeitet **montags** nicht.

The first sentence may mean that Mr. Zimmermann will not work this coming Monday or that he usually does not work on Mondays. The use of **montags** in the second sentence has only one meaning: that he does not work on Mondays.

The days of the week combined with parts of the day have two forms.

Frau Berger ist **donnerstags nachmittags** immer in ihrem Büro.
(two adverbs)
or: **donnerstagnachmittags**
(one adverb)

Übung 10-6

ANWENDEN A. Insert a logical time expression in the blank.

1. Die meisten Familien machen Urlaub _____, wenn die Kinder Schulferien haben.
2. Die meisten Hochzeiten gibt es _____.
3. Die Arbeitswoche beginnt _____ und ist normalerweise _____ zu Ende.
4. Viele Leute gehen _____ in die Kirche oder _____ in die Synagoge.
5. Ins Kino gehen Leute oft am _____ oder _____ .

B. State in six sentences what you did yesterday from morning to night: in the early morning, in the late morning, at noon, in the afternoon, in the evening and at night. Begin your sentences with the time expression.

C. Describe a routine for each of the days of the week. Use adverbial **s**-forms.

   MODEL: Sonntags machen wir oft einen Spaziergang.

D. Now, modify them to include the time of the day.

   MODEL: Sonntag nachmittags machen wir oft einen Spaziergang.

§4 Additional Time Expressions

1. Adverbs

vorgestern	gestern	heute	morgen	übermorgen
the day before yesterday	*yesterday*	*today*	*tomorrow*	*the day after tomorrow*

Parts of the day may be used with **heute, gestern**, and **morgen**: Note that the parts of the day are nouns and are capitalized. Only the adverb **früh** is not.

heute Morgen		gestern Morgen	
	this morning		*yesterday morning*
heute früh		gestern früh	
heute Vormittag	*this morning*	gestern Vormittag, *etc.*	
	this afternoon		
heute Mittag	*this noon*		
heute Nachmittag	*this afternoon*		
	this evening	morgen früh	*tomorrow morning*
heute Abend	*tonight*	(only this form)	
heute Nacht	*tonight*	morgen Vormittag, *etc.*	

The adverb **morgen** may have two meanings: *morning* or *tomorrow*. When it follows another time expression, it has the meaning of *morning*.

   Heute Morgen habe ich den Wecker nicht gehört.
   This morning I didn't hear the alarm clock.

When it precedes another time expression or stands alone, it has the meaning of *tomorrow*.

Ich fahre **morgen Nachmittag** nach Münster.
I'm going to Münster tomorrow afternoon.

Dieter fährt **morgen** auch nach Münster.
Dieter is also going to Münster tomorrow.

Keep in mind that until bedtime (about 11 P.M.), **Abend** corresponds to the English *night*.

tonight	heute Abend
tomorrow night	morgen Abend
last night	gestern Abend

Last night (*after bedtime*) is expressed by **letzte Nacht**. Compare:

Ich habe **gestern Abend** in der Bibliothek gearbeitet.
I worked in the library last night.

Ich habe **letzte Nacht** nicht gut geschlafen.
I didn't sleep well last night.

Übung 10-7

ANWENDEN Respond by stating during which part of the day you did things today and yesterday.

1. Was haben Sie gestern Abend gemacht?
2. Was haben Sie gestern oder heute Mittag gemacht?
3. Wie haben Sie letzte Nacht geschlafen?
4. Wer oder was hat Sie gestern Morgen aufgeweckt?
5. Wann haben Sie gestern gelernt oder Hausaufgaben gemacht?
6. Welche Kurse hatten Sie gestern Vormittag? Welche gestern Nachmittag?
7. Welcher Tag war vorgestern? Welcher Tag ist übermorgen?

2. Time expressions in the accusative case

Most time expressions that do not include a preposition are in the accusative case.

dies**e** Woche	nächst**e** Woche	jed**e** Woche
this week	*next week*	*every week*
dies**es** Wochenende	nächst**es** Wochenende	jed**es** Wochenende
dies**en** Monat	nächst**en** Monat	jed**en** Monat
dies**es** Jahr	nächst**es** Jahr	jed**es** Jahr
dies**en** Freitag	nächst**en** Freitag	jed**en** Freitag
	but: <u>am</u> nächsten Tag	jed**en** Tag
	the next day	

| vorige
letzte | Woche
last week | **den** ganz**en** Tag
all day long /the whole day |

voriges/letztes Wochenende

den ganzen Abend

vorigen/letzten Monat

die ganze Nacht
den ganzen Monat

voriges/letztes Jahr

das ganze Jahr
die ganze Zeit

3. Time expressions with prepositions + dative case

   a. Answering the question **wann**? (*when?*)

in ein paar Minuten *in a few minutes*	vor ein paar Minuten *a few minutes ago*	nach einer Weile *after a while*
in einer Stunde	vor einer Stunde	nach der Deutschstunde
in einer Woche	vor drei Wochen	nach ein paar Tagen
in einem Monat	vor fünf Monaten	nach einer Woche
in einem Jahr	vor zwei Jahren	nach einem Jahr

heute in einer Woche	heute vor einer Woche
heute in acht Tagen	*a week ago today*
(idiomatic expression)	
a week from today	
heute in einem Monat	heute vor einem Monat
a month from today	*a month ago today*
heute in einem Jahr	heute vor einem Jahr
a year from today	*a year ago today*

   b. Answering the question **wie oft**? (*how often?*)

einmal, zweimal, dreimal am Tag	*once, twice, three times a day*
in der Woche	*a week*
or: die Woche	
(accusative)	
im Monat	*a month*
im Jahr	*a year*

   c. Exception: preposition + accusative

   This is one explanation answering the question, **für/auf wie lange**? (*for how long?*)

   Heike und Detlef fahren **für (auf) einen Tag** nach Köln.
   für eine Woche
   für ein paar Monate

   Heike and Detlef are going to Cologne for one day.
   for a week.
   for a few months.

Der Präsident wird **für** vier Jahre gewählt.
The president is elected for four years.

Für… is used more often than **auf**…
Note that **ein paar** is not inflected (cf. Kap. 9 §9).
(For the use of **seit** + dative, cf. Kap. 2 §6, 3 and Kap. 7 §1, 7.)

4. Set expressions in the genitive case denoting indefinite time

Eines Tages ist Frank davongelaufen.	*One day Frank ran away.*
Eines Morgens	*One morning*
Eines Abends ⟶ ist er zurückgekommen.	*One evening* ⟶ *he came back.*
Eines Nachts	*One night*

Although **Nacht** is feminine, the masculine form **eines Nachts** is used by analogy with **eines Morgens** and **eines Abends**.

Übung 10-8

ANWENDEN A. State when the events that are marked on the calendar took place, or will take place in the future. Try to use as many different accusative and preposition + dative time expressions as you can. Use **etwa**, **rund**, **ungefähr**, and **über** when appropriate. Assume that the current date is Thursday, August 20th.

MODEL:

20. Juni	Dagmar und Gerd heiraten

Vor zwei Monaten haben Dagmar und Gerd geheiratet.

Wann haben Mitglieder der Familie Martens, Freunde und Bekannte verschiedene Dinge gemacht?

25. Juni	Muttis Geburtstag	15./16. August	Badezimmer renoviert
29./30. Juni	Besuch von Rosi und Karl	22./23. August	Besuch bei Oma und Opa
25. Juli–3. August	im Urlaub	30. August	Papa aus Holland zurück
13. August	Zum Abendessen bei Schusters eingeladen	13. September	Schulbeginn
16.–19. August	Mutti und Papi Amsterdam	6., 13., 20., 27. September	Tennismatch

B. Respond to the personalized questions.

1. Wo werden Sie vielleicht in ein paar Jahren wohnen?
2. In wie vielen Jahren (oder Monaten) sind Sie mit dem Studium fertig?
3. Routine: Was machen Sie jedes Wochenende? Jeden Freitag? Jede Woche? Einmal in der Woche? Einmal im Monat? Einmal im Jahr?
4. Wann sind Sie mit den Hausaufgaben fertig? In ein paar Minuten?
5. Was haben Sie genau heute vor einer Woche gemacht?

5. Expressing dates

	written:
a. Heute ist **der elfte Mai.**	Heute ist **der 11. Mai.**
b. Heute haben wir **den elften Mai.**	Heute haben wir **den 11. Mai.**
den elften fünften	**den 11.5.**
c. Ich habe **am elften Mai** Geburtstag.	Ich habe **am 11. Mai** Geburtstag.
am elften fünften	**am 11.5.**

In sentence **a.**, **der elfte Mai** is a predicate nominative (after **sein**). In sentence **b.**, **den elften Mai** is in the accusative (direct object). In sentence **c.**, **am elften Mai** is in the dative (prepositional phrase).

Asking about today's date

Welches Datum haben wir heute?
or: **Den wie vielten haben wir heute?** *What is today's date? What's the date today?*

Dates in letterheads and documents

Berlin, **den 11. Mai 1972**
(spoken: den elften Mai neunzehnhundertzweiundsiebzig)
Bonn, **den 31. Oktober 2003**
(spoken: den einunddreißigsten Oktober zweitausenddrei)

The day always precedes the month, even when the month is indicated by an ordinal number.

31.10.1985 = 31. Oktober 1985

The English phrase *in 1950* is in German **im Jahr(e) 1950** or simply **1950.**

Der Komponist starb **im Jahr(e) 1929.**
or: Der Komponist starb **1929.** *The composer died in 1929.*

Übung 10-9

VERSTEHEN Write out the following dates in German, then read them aloud.

MODEL: Berlin, November 9, 1989   Berlin, den neunten November
neunzehnhundertneunundachtzig.
or: den neunten elften

1. Hamburg, August 3, 1982
2. Berlin, December 31, 1946
3. Vienna, January 1, 1985

Übung 10-10

ANWENDEN Insert the correct date in each sentence.

> MODEL: Den Tag der Wiedervereinigung feiern die Deutschen _____.
> <u>Den Tag der Wiedervereinigung feiern die Deutschen am 3. Oktober.</u>

1. Weihnachten ist _____.
2. Neujahr ist immer _____.
3. _____ machen viele Leute Scherze.
4. Heute ist _____. (today's date)
5. Ich bin _____ geboren. (insert year; two different ways)
6. Mein Geburtstag ist _____. (date, month)

Übung 10-11

ZUSAMMENFASSUNG Time expressions.

A. Form sentences by combining the time expressions in the left column with the events in the right column. Use the tense in parentheses when it is given; otherwise, use the tense most appropriate to the sentence.

> MODEL: heute Nachmittag   Freundin zum Flughafen bringen
> <u>Heute Nachmittag bringe ich meine Freundin zum Flughafen.</u>

1. vorgestern   eine Prüfung ablegen
2. gestern Abend   nur Unsinn reden
3. heute Morgen   mit Professor Zimmermann sprechen müssen (past)
4. morgen früh   mein Zimmer saubermachen müssen
5. nächsten Sonnabend   mit meiner Freundin ausgehen
6. am ersten August   Peter Geburtstag haben (present tense)
7. vorigen Sonntag   spät aufstehen
8. voriges Wochenende   für eine Prüfung lernen müssen
9. jeden Donnerstag   schwimmen gehen
10. einmal in der Woche   meine Eltern anrufen
11. mittwochs nachmittags normalerweise einkaufen gehen
12. heute Abend   nichts vorhaben
13. die ganze Zeit   zu Hause bleiben (future)
14. übermorgen   die Semesterferien beginnen
15. im Sommer   einen Job suchen (future)

B. Respond to the following personalized questions with complete sentences.

1. Welches Datum haben wir heute?
2. In welchem Jahr sind Sie geboren? Ihre Mutter? Ihr Vater? Ihr Freund/Ihre Freundin oder Ihr Ehemann/Ihre Ehefrau?
3. In welchem Monat ist Ihr Geburtstag? Der Geburtstag Ihrer Mutter? Ihres Vaters?

4. Zu welcher Jahreszeit sind Sie am aktivsten? Zu welcher gehen Sie zur Uni?
5. Nennen Sie drei regelmäßige Aktivitäten an drei verschiedenen Wochentagen.
6. Nennen Sie drei regelmäßige Aktivitäten zu drei verschiedenen Tageszeiten.
7. Finden Sie das Geburtsdatum für drei berühmte Personen aus verschiedenen Jahrhunderten heraus. Schreiben Sie jedes genau auf und lesen Sie es dann laut.

Clock Time

In official statements of time (such as timetables, office hours, performance time), the twenty-four-hour system is used (explained in §6 of this Kapitel). Otherwise, time is expressed according to the twelve-hour system.

§5   Using the Twelve-Hour System

There are three common ways to ask for the time in German.

Wie spät ist es?
Wie viel Uhr ist es? → *What time is it?*
Welche Uhrzeit haben wir?

Time is most commonly expressed as follows:

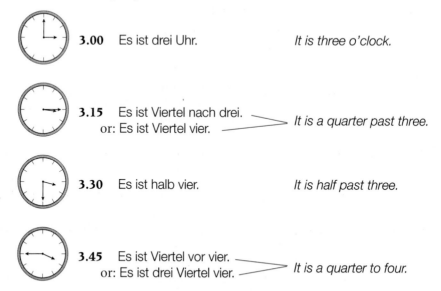

3.00   Es ist drei Uhr.   *It is three o'clock.*

3.15   Es ist Viertel nach drei.
        or: Es ist Viertel vier.   *It is a quarter past three.*

3.30   Es ist halb vier.   *It is half past three.*

3.45   Es ist Viertel vor vier.
        or: Es ist drei Viertel vier.   *It is a quarter to four.*

In German, hours are separated from minutes by a period rather than a colon. Alternatively, the minutes may be raised: 3.15 or 3^{15}.

Note the use of **ein** when it precedes **Uhr**, and **eins** when it stands alone.

1.00   Es ist **ein Uhr**.
1.15   Es ist **Viertel nach eins**.
12.30   Es ist **halb eins**.
12.45   Es ist **Viertel vor eins**.

Übung 10-12

VERSTEHEN   Match the time given in each sentence with the correct clock.

a.   b.   c.   d.   e.   f.   g.

1. Die Vorlesung beginnt um Viertel zehn.
2. Ich esse um halb zwei zu Mittag.
3. Sabine, treffen wir uns heute um Viertel acht?
4. Mein Bus fährt Viertel vor sieben.
5. Um Viertel nach acht beginnt der Film.
6. Er ist um halb elf zu Ende.
7. Ich gehe um zwölf ins Bett.

Übung 10-13

ANWENDEN   Give the time in German. Provide options when appropriate.

MODEL: 8.15   Es ist Viertel nach acht.
Es ist Viertel neun.

1. 10.15	5. 6.15	9. 11.45	13. 1.00
2. 10.30	6. 7.15	10. 12.45	14. 2.15
3. 10.45	7. 8.30	11. 1.45	15. 3.45
4. 11.00	8. 9.30	12. 7.00	16. 12.30

Five-minute intervals

The most common forms of five-minute intervals are shown below.

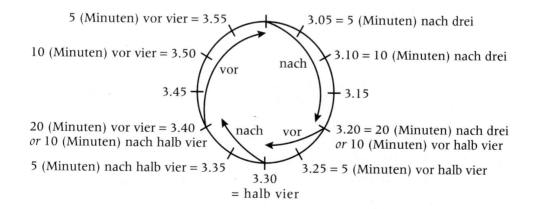

5 (Minuten) vor vier = 3.55   3.05 = 5 (Minuten) nach drei

10 (Minuten) vor vier = 3.50   3.10 = 10 (Minuten) nach drei

vor   nach

3.45   3.15

20 (Minuten) vor vier = 3.40   3.20 = 20 (Minuten) nach drei
or 10 (Minuten) nach halb vier   or 10 (Minuten) vor halb vier

nach   vor

5 (Minuten) nach halb vier = 3.35   3.25 = 5 (Minuten) vor halb vier

3.30
= halb vier

Other intervals may be expressed the same way.

3.02	Es ist zwei (Minuten) nach drei.
3.32	Es ist zwei (Minuten) nach halb vier.
3.38	Es ist acht (Minuten) nach halb vier.
3.48	Es ist zwölf (Minuten) vor vier.
3.58	Es ist zwei (Minuten) vor vier.

Minute cannot be omitted after **eine**.

3.01	Es ist **eine Minute** nach drei.
3.59	Es ist **eine Minute** vor vier.

Übung 10-14

ANWENDEN Give the time in German following the pattern in the model.

MODEL: 6.20   Es ist 20 (Minuten) nach sechs.
or: Es ist 10 (Minuten) vor halb sieben.

1.	5.20	5.	9.05	9.	12.25	13.	7.50
2.	5.40	6.	9.25	10.	12.35	14.	2.20
3.	11.20	7.	9.35	11.	12.55	15.	9.40
4.	11.40	8.	12.05	12.	1.55	16.	10.35

Übung 10-15

ANWENDEN Give the time in German following the pattern in the model.

MODEL: 10.04   Es ist vier (Minuten) nach zehn.

1.	10.13	5.	6.09	9.	12.07	13.	2.01
2.	10.29	6.	6.17	10.	12.39	14.	3.29
3.	10.36	7.	6.27	11.	1.06	15.	11.59
4.	10.57	8.	6.54	12.	1.33		

Note: If you don't remember the above ways of expressing time, you may resort to a simpler way.

5.10	Es ist fünf Uhr zehn.
7.20	Es ist sieben Uhr zwanzig.
1.55	Es ist ein Uhr fünfundfünfzig.
12.33	Es ist zwölf Uhr dreiunddreißig.

People will understand you if you say this. However, when German-speaking people express the time as explained in this section, you should be able to understand them.

To make clear whether A.M. or P.M. is meant, **morgens**, **vormittags**, **mittags**, **nachmittags**, **abends**, or **nachts** is frequently added.

7:00 A.M. = 7 Uhr morgens	10:00 A.M. = zehn Uhr vormittags
7:00 P.M. = 7 Uhr abends	10:00 P.M. = zehn Uhr abends
	1:00 A.M. = ein Uhr nachts
	1:00 P.M. = ein Uhr mittags/nachmittags

§6   Using the Twenty-Four-Hour System

Official statements of time are based on the twenty-four-hour system.

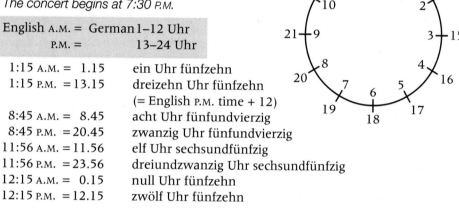

Der Zug fährt 13.40 (dreizehn Uhr vierzig) ab.
The train leaves at 1:40 P.M.

Das Konzert beginnt 19.30 (neunzehn Uhr dreißig).
The concert begins at 7:30 P.M.

English A.M. =	German 1–12 Uhr
P.M. =	13–24 Uhr

1:15 A.M. =	1.15	ein Uhr fünfzehn
1:15 P.M. =	13.15	dreizehn Uhr fünfzehn
		(= English P.M. time + 12)
8:45 A.M. =	8.45	acht Uhr fünfundvierzig
8:45 P.M. =	20.45	zwanzig Uhr fünfundvierzig
11:56 A.M. =	11.56	elf Uhr sechsundfünfzig
11:56 P.M. =	23.56	dreiundzwanzig Uhr sechsundfünfzig
12:15 A.M. =	0.15	null Uhr fünfzehn
12:15 P.M. =	12.15	zwölf Uhr fünfzehn

Note: **Viertel**, **halb**, **drei Viertel**, **vor**, and **nach** are not used in the twenty-four-hour system.

Übung 10-16

ANWENDEN   Give the time according to the twenty-four-hour system.

MODEL:	4:13 A.M.	<u>vier Uhr dreizehn</u>
	4:13 P.M.	<u>sechzehn Uhr dreizehn</u>

1.	7:20 A.M.	3.	10:45 A.M.	5.	3:15 A.M.
	7:20 P.M.		10:45 P.M.		3:15 P.M.
2.	9:30 A.M.	4.	6:10 A.M.	6.	12:30 A.M.
	9:30 P.M.		6:10 P.M.		12:30 P.M.

B. Convert to English P.M. time.

MODEL: 14.30 = <u>2:30 P.M.</u>

1.	19.00	3.	20.45	5.	15.10
2.	17.15	4.	13.30	6.	23.50

§7   Common Expressions Used When Telling Time

um 1 Uhr   *at 1 o'clock*

> **Um** 1 Uhr esse ich zu Mittag und **um** 7 Uhr zu Abend.
> *At 1 o'clock I have lunch/dinner* (noon meal) *and at 7 o'clock supper/dinner (evening meal).*

When telling time, **um** is the German equivalent of English *at.*

Punkt 3 Uhr	*3 o'clock sharp*	
gegen 3 Uhr so gegen 3 Uhr	*around 3 o'clock, approximately at 3*	
von...bis...	*from ... to ...*	Das Postamt ist **von 9 bis 5** (Uhr) geöffnet.
vor•gehen (Uhr)	*to be fast*	Meine Uhr **geht etwas vor.** *My watch is a little fast.* Diese Uhr **geht 5 Minuten vor.**
nach•gehen (Uhr)	*to be slow*	Meine Uhr **geht etwas nach.** *My watch is a little slow.* Diese Uhr **geht 10 Minuten nach.**
richtig gehen (Uhr)	*to be correct*	**Geht** diese Uhr **richtig?** *Is that clock correct?* *Is that the right time?*
nicht gehen	*not work, not run*	Meine Uhr **geht nicht.** *My watch doesn't work.*
stehen bleiben	*to stop*	Meine Uhr **ist** schon wieder **stehen geblieben.** *My watch has stopped again.*
die Uhr stellen	*to set the clock*	Ich habe vergessen **den Wecker** zu **stellen.** *I forgot to set the alarm clock.*
nach meiner Uhr	*according to my watch*	**Nach meiner Uhr** ist es 3 Uhr. *According to my watch it is 3 o'clock.*

Übung 10-17

ANWENDEN A. Provide statements or questions appropriate to the scenarios given.

1. Marianne ist schon wieder zu spät zur Arbeit gekommen. Was für ein Problem hat sie vielleicht mit ihrer Uhr? (give two possibilities.)
2. Auf Toms Uhr ist es Viertel nach acht, aber auf Hannos erst acht. Was kann mit den Uhren sein?
3. Lars muss morgen ganz früh aufstehen. Was soll er machen?
4. Jutta will, dass Walter sie um acht Uhr abholt und keine Minute später. Was sagt sie zu Walter?
5. Frau Witte hat ihre Uhr zur Reparatur gebracht. Warum? Was ist mit der Uhr?
6. Günter will seine Freunde zum Abendessen treffen, aber er will die Zeit nicht so genau festlegen. Was sagt er?

B. Respond to the following personalized questions.

    1. Wie viel Uhr ist es jetzt?

    2. Geht Ihre Uhr vor?

    3. Wann sind Sie heute Morgen aufgestanden? Für wie viel Uhr hatten Sie den Wecker gestellt?

    4. Wann müssen Sie bei der Arbeit/auf der Uni sein? Um Punkt acht?

    5. Von wann bis wann sind Sie bei der Arbeit? Wie lange sind Sie jeden Tag an der Uni?

Übung 10-18

ZUSAMMENFASSUNG Clock time.

A. Include the time in the sentences you form from the cues. *Wie verläuft Margots Tag?*

MODEL: _____ Margot / auf•stehen
<u>Um Viertel vor sieben steht Margot auf.</u>

1. _____ / zur Universität / fahren

2. _____ / im Hörsaal / sitzen

3. _____ / zu Mittag / essen

4. _____ / in die Bibliothek / gehen

5. _____ / mit dem Bus / nach Hause / fahren

6. _____ / gemütlich / zu Abend / essen

7. _____ / Dieter / anrufen

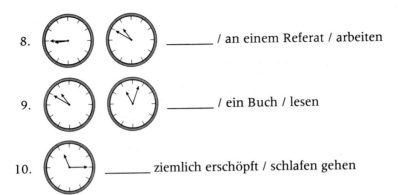

8. _____ / an einem Referat / arbeiten

9. _____ / ein Buch / lesen

10. _____ ziemlich erschöpft / schlafen gehen

B. Write a paragraph in which you describe a day in detail. You can choose a typical day (present tense) or a day that was in some way exceptional (present perfect tense).

Themen und Vokabular			
Am Telefon		**das Jahrzehnt, -e**	*decade*
die Auskunft	*directory information*	**das Neujahr**	*New Year's Day*
		das Silvester	*New Year's Eve*
die Telefonnummer, -n	*telephone number*	**die Tageszeit, -en**	*time of the day*
die Vorwahl	*area code*	**die Uhrzeit**	*clock time, time*
	country code	**das Wochenende, -n**	*weekend*
		der Wochentag, -e	*weekday, workday*
Zeit			
die Jahreszeit, -en	*season*		
das Jahrhundert, -e	*century*		
die Jahrhundertwende	*turn of the century*		

KAPITEL

11 Conjunctions; Infinitive Phrases

Conjunctions

There are two basic types of conjunctions: coordinating and subordinating.

§1 Coordinating Conjunctions

Coordinating conjunctions connect words, phrases, and clauses of equal importance. The following coordinating conjunctions are used frequently:

aber	*but (however, nevertheless)*
denn	*because, for*
oder	*or*
sondern	*but (rather)*
und	*and*

Coordinating conjunctions have no effect on word order. The sentences they join retain their normal or inverted word order, as the following sentences illustrate. Two clauses joined by **und** or **oder** need not be separated by a comma.

1. Monika spielt gern Tennis. Ihr Freund spielt lieber Fußball.
   Monika spielt gern Tennis, **aber** ihr Freund spielt lieber Fußball.
   Monika likes to play tennis, but her friend prefers to play soccer.

2. Ich rufe Martin um 7 Uhr an. Dann ist er bestimmt zu Hause.
   Ich rufe Martin um 7 Uhr an, **denn** dann ist er bestimmt zu Hause.
   I'll call Martin at 7 o'clock, because he definitely will be home then.

3. Wir treffen uns heute Abend in einem Restaurant. Eva bringt ihren neuen Freund mit.
   Wir treffen uns heute Abend in einem Restaurant **und** Eva bringt ihren neuen Freund mit.
   We'll meet in a restaurant tonight, and Eva is bringing her new boyfriend.

In **2.**, the inversion is caused by the adverb **dann**.

Vokabulartip: **denn** *und* **dann**

Do not confuse:

> **denn** = *because, for* (coordinating conjunction)
> **dann** = *then* (adverb)

§2   The German Equivalents of *but*

Sondern means *but* when used in the sense of "but on the contrary" or "but rather" after a negative.

> Klaus ist **nicht** dumm, **sondern** sehr intelligent.
> *Klaus is not stupid but (on the contrary) very intelligent.*

> Wir sprechen **nicht** von dir, **sondern** von Klaus.
> *We are not talking about you but (rather) about Klaus.*

Note the use of **sondern** in the phrase **nicht nur…sondern auch**.

> Diese Transaktion ist **nicht nur** kompliziert, **sondern auch** riskant.
> *This transaction is not only complicated but also risky.*

But is equivalent to **aber** in all other instances. **Aber** is also used in the sense of "however" or "nevertheless." In these cases the preceding clause may or may not be negated.

> Ulrich ist nicht dumm, **aber** er hat immer schlechte Noten.
> *Ulrich is not stupid, but (however, nevertheless) he always has bad grades.*

> Sabine ist intelligent, **aber** ihre Noten sind nicht gut.
> *Sabine is intelligent, but (however, nevertheless) her grades are not good.*

Übung 11-1

VERSTEHEN A. Insert **sondern** or **aber** and state the reason for your choice.

1. Wir wohnen in einem kleinen, alten Haus, _____ es gefällt uns sehr.
2. Müllers fahren nicht nach Spanien, _____ nach Italien.
3. Dieses Dokument ist nicht das Original, _____ eine Kopie.
4. Ich habe nicht viel Geld, _____ einmal im Monat kaufe ich mir etwas Besonderes.
5. Nicht Lore, _____ Klaus hat das Geschirr gespült.
6. Ich verstehe nicht immer alles, was mein amerikanischer Freund sagt, _____ meistens weiß ich, was er sagen will.

Übung 11-2

ANWENDEN A. Respond to each question by supplying another item that is logically related. Use the expression **nicht nur...sondern auch**.

> MODEL: Haben Sie einen Rucksack dabei?
> <u>Ich habe nicht nur einen Rucksack dabei, sondern auch mein Portmonee.</u>

1. Ist es heute heiß?
2. Haben Sie zu Hause einen Fernseher?
3. Ist Ihre Freundin/Ihr Freund gut aussehend?
4. Tragen Sie heute einen Schal?
5. Haben Sie einen Kuli dabei?

B. Complete each sentence logically and with the conjunction provided.

1. Ich bin sehr böse auf Klaus, denn...
2. Ich fand den Film todlangweilig, aber...
3. Heute Morgen sind wir schwimmen gegangen und...
4. Sie hat nicht nur vergessen mich anzurufen, sondern...
5. Er hat das vergessen oder...

§3   Subordinating Conjunctions

Subordinating conjunctions introduce dependent clauses. Compare the following sentences:

a. **Ich bin** jetzt oft in der Bibliothek,   denn **ich schreibe** eine Semesterarbeit.
   MAIN CLAUSE   DEPENDENT CLAUSE

b. **Ich bin** jetzt oft in der Bibliothek,   weil **ich** eine Semesterarbeit **schreibe.**
   MAIN CLAUSE   DEPENDENT CLAUSE

c. Weil **ich** eine Semesterarbeit **schreibe,**   **bin ich** jetzt oft in der Bibliothek.
   DEPENDENT CLAUSE   MAIN CLAUSE

Sentence **a.** consists of two equal clauses that are joined by **denn**.

In sentence **b.**, the clause introduced by the subordinating conjunction **weil** has dependent word order: the inflected verb is in last position. When the dependent clause precedes the main clause, as in sentence **c.**, the latter has inverted word order (cf. Kap. 1 §3).

Here is a list of subordinating conjunctions that are used frequently.

als	*when*
bevor	
ehe	*before*
bis	*until*
da	*since* (stating reason), *because*
damit	*so that, in order that*
dass	*that*

indem	*by* (doing something)
nachdem	*after*
ob	*whether, if*
obwohl ⟍	⟍ *although*
obgleich ⟋	
seit ⟍	⟍ *since* (referring to time)
seitdem ⟋	
sobald	*as soon as*
solange	*as long as*
während	*while*
weil	*because*
wenn	*when, whenever, if*

§4   The German Equivalents of *when, if,* and *since*

1. Three German equivalents of *when:* **wann**, **als**, and **wenn**

a. *when* = **wann** used in the sense of "at what time" in direct and indirect questions.

Direct questions

> **Wann** kommt Sonja nach Hause?
> *When (at what time) is Sonja coming home?*

Indirect questions (cf. Kap. 1 §5)

> Weißt du, **wann** Sonja nach Hause **kommt**?
> Ich weiß nicht, **wann** Sonja nach Hause **kommt**.

b. *when* = **als** in clauses that refer to a single past occurrence or state.

> Leider hat es gestern geregnet, **als** wir ein Picknick machen wollten.
> *Unfortunately it rained yesterday when we were planning to have a picnic.*

> Sie war sehr vorsichtig, **als** sie am Montag mit dem Chef sprach.
> *She was very careful when she talked to the boss on Monday.*

> Ich habe mich erkältet, **als** ich gestern in der Stadt war.
> *I caught a cold when I was in town yesterday.*

The occurrence or state may cover a period of time.

> Sabine hat Peter kennengelernt, **als** sie in München studiert hat.
> *Sabine met Peter when she was studying in Munich.*

> Er hatte viele Freunde, **als** er jung und unternehmungslustig war.
> *He had many friends when he was young and enterprising.*

Als is also used in present tense summaries of such past events in stories, plays, films, etc. (cf. Kap. 2 §6, 4).

> **Als** der Held seinen Gegner kommen **sieht**, stellt er sich tot.
> *When the hero sees his opponent coming, he pretends to be dead.*

c. *when* = **wenn** in all other instances.

When is equivalent to **wenn** in all other instances when referring to repeated occurences in the past. In such cases, English often uses *whenever*.

> Leider hat es immer geregnet, **wenn** wir ein Picknick machen wollten.
> *Unfortunately, it always rained when (whenever) we wanted to have a picnic.*

> Sie war immer sehr vorsichtig, **wenn** sie mit dem Chef gesprochen hat.
> *She was always very careful when (whenever) she talked to the boss.*

When = **wenn** in all clauses referring to the present and future (single or repeated occurrences).

> Hoffentlich regnet es nicht, **wenn** ihr morgen ein Picknick macht.
> Sie ist immer sehr vorsichtig, **wenn** sie mit dem Chef spricht.

Remember: *when*
- = **wann** (at what time) in direct and indirect questions
- = **als** referring to a single past occurrence or state (including present tense summaries of such past events)
- = **wenn** in all other instances

Übung 11-3

VERSTEHEN Supply the German equivalent of *when*.

1. Ich habe mich sehr gefreut, __*als*__ ich am Montag die gute Nachricht bekam.
2. Ich habe mich immer gefreut, __*wenn*__ du mich angerufen hast.
3. __*Wann*__ rufst du Renate an? Ich weiß noch nicht, __*wenn*__ ich sie anrufen kann.
4. Natürlich werde ich dir alles erzählen, ~~*wenn*~~ *wenn* du morgen zu mir kommst.
5. __*als*__ ich ihn gestern gesehen habe, ging es ihm noch ganz gut.
6. __*Wenn*__ ich ihn sehe, geht es ihm immer gut.
7. Weißt du noch, _____ du den Brief abgeschickt hast?
8. _____ Sonja in Frankfurt studierte, hatte sie einen französischen Freund.
9. Wir haben Goethes Faust gesehen, _____ wir vorige Woche im Theater waren. Faust sieht Margarete zum ersten Mal, _____ sie gerade aus der Kirche kommt.

2. The German equivalents of *if*: **wenn** and **ob**

if = **wenn** in conditional statements.

> **Wenn** das wahr ist, (dann) gibt es bestimmt einen Skandal.
> *If that is true, (then) there will certainly be a scandal.*

if = **ob** in indirect questions. (English also uses *whether* in this context; (cf. Kap. 1 §5).

> Ist das wahr? Ich weiß nicht, **ob** das wahr ist.
> *Is that true? I don't know if (whether) that is true.*

Remember:
> *if* = **wenn** unless it is replaceable by *whether*, in which case it is **ob**

Übung 11-4

VERSTEHEN Supply the German equivalent of *if*.

1. Ich weiß nicht, _____ er die Wahrheit gesagt hat.
2. Sie wird bestimmt sehr böse, _____ er ihr nicht die Wahrheit sagt.
3. Ich möchte wissen, _____ Kästners jetzt zu Hause sind.
4. _____ ich mein Stipendium verliere, muß ich mit dem Studium aufhören.
5. Wissen Sie, _____ der Zug aus München Verspätung hat?
6. _____ der Zug pünktlich abfährt, kommen wir um 12 Uhr in Bonn an.

3. The German equivalents of *since*

a. *since* = seitdem or seit when it refers to time.

Seitdem and **seit** (**erst seit, schon seit**) are used with the present tense if the action is not yet completed, while in English *since* is used with the present perfect (often in the progressive form). (See Kap. 2 §6, 3.)

> **Seitdem** (seit) Maria in Bonn studiert, schreibt sie mir nicht mehr.
> *Since Maria has been studying at Bonn, she does not write to me anymore.*

Seitdem and **seit** are used with the present perfect tense if the action was completed in the past. English uses the simple past in this situation.

> Wir haben noch nicht von Alexander gehört, **seitdem** (seit) er nach Bonn gezogen ist.
> *We have not yet heard from Alexander since he moved to Bonn.*

b. *since* = da when it indicates causal connection (replaceable by *because*).

> Wir können ihn nicht anrufen, **da** wir nicht wissen, wo er jetzt ist.
> *We cannot call him since (because) we don't know where he is now.*

Both **da** and **weil** indicate causal connection. The following examples show the difference between their uses.

> Ich muß heute zur Bibliothek, **weil** diese zwei Bücher bereits überfällig sind.
> *I have to go to the library today because these two books are overdue.*

Da Katrin in der Nähe von der Bibliothek wohnt, werde ich sie auf dem
Heimweg besuchen.
Since Katrin lives near the library, I'll visit her on my way home.

In the first sentence, the decisive reason for the trip to the library is expressed
in the clause introduced by **weil**: the overdue books must be returned.

In the second sentence, there is no compelling reason to visit Katrin. The clause
introduced with **da** implies that the speaker wants to take advantage of the
opportunity, since Katrin lives near the library.

In general, the choice of **weil** or **da** depends on how important the causal
connection is. **Weil** is more commonly used than **da**. In particular, **da** cannot
be used to answer the question *why*.

Warum hast du die Bücher nicht zurückgebracht?
Weil ich sie vergessen habe.

Remember: **Weil** indicates a strong, definite causal connection.
Da indicates a less definite causal connection.

Übung 11-5

VERSTEHEN Supply the German equivalent of *since*.

1. _____ es nicht aufhörte zu regnen, sind wir den ganzen Sonntag zu
Hause geblieben.
2. Wir haben nichts von Winklers gehört, _____ sie nach Basel gezogen sind.
3. Leider kann ich Martin nicht schreiben, _____ ich seine Adresse nicht
weiß.
4. _____ Maria für eine Prüfung lernen mußte, bin ich mit Sonja ins Kino
gegangen.
5. _____ die Wagners im Urlaub sind, versorgen wir ihre Katze.

§5   Additional Uses of Subordinating Conjunctions

1. The use of **indem**

The German dependent clause introduced by **indem** states a means by which
something is, was, or will be done. The English equivalent is usually expressed
with *by* plus an *-ing* form (a gerund) with only an implied subject.

Wir haben das Problem gelöst, **indem** wir einen Kompromiss
geschlossen haben.
We solved the problem by making a compromise.

2. The use of tenses in clauses introduced by **nachdem**

The clause introduced by **nachdem** expresses an action which preceded that of the main clause. If the verb in the main clause is in the present or future tense, the **nachdem** clause is in the present perfect tense.

Er **duscht** meistens, nachdem er den Rasen **gemäht hat**.

PRESENT

He usually takes a shower

PRESENT PERFECT

after he has mowed the lawn.
or: *after he mows the lawn.*
or: *after mowing the lawn.*

If the main clause is in the past, present perfect, or past perfect tense, the **nachdem** clause is in the past perfect tense.

Er **duschte** gestern, **nachdem** er den Rasen **gemäht hatte**.

PAST

He took a shower yesterday

PAST PERFECT

after he had mowed the lawn.
or: *after he mowed the lawn.*
or: *after mowing the lawn.*

In colloquial German, the past perfect is often replaced with a present perfect or past tense.

Er hat **geduscht**, nachdem er nach Hause **gekommen ist**.

PRESENT PERFECT

PRESENT PERFECT

3. Subordinating conjunctions frequently confused with other words

Da may be used as a subordinating conjunction or as an adverb.

da ⟨ *since* (subordinating conjunction)
there (adverb of place)
then (adverb of time)

The best way to recognize a subordinating conjunction is to check whether the inflected verb appears at the end of the clause.

Da Martin nicht weit von mir **wohnt**, sehe ich ihn oft.
(verb last: dependent clause)
Since Martin doesn't live far from me, I often see him.

Da wohnt Martin.
Martin lives there.

Da war es schon zu spät.
(verb second: main clause with inverted word order; cf. Kap. 1 §2)
Then it was already too late.

Während may be used as a subordinating conjunction or as a preposition.

während — *while* (subordinating conjunction)
während — *during* (preposition + genitive or dative)

Während wir uns **unterhielten**, hat Dietmar geraucht.
While we were talking, Dietmar was smoking.

Während unserer Unterhaltung rauchte Dietmar.
During our conversation Dietmar was smoking.

Übung 11-6

VERSTEHEN This exercise provides practice with the rules in §5 of this Kapitel. Explain the function of each word in boldface type.

Norbert erzählt, was er und seine Freundin gestern gemacht haben.

Gestern war ich auf der Bank. **Da** stand plötzlich meine Freundin neben mir. **Während** wir gewartet haben, hat sie mir von ihrer langweiligen Vorlesung erzählt. **Nachdem** ich auf der Bank alles erledigt hatte, sind wir noch einkaufen gegangen. **Da** ich sowieso einen Spaziergang machen wollte, gingen wir zu Fuß. Meine Freundin hat geschimpft, **weil** sie zu müde war. **Da** habe ich ein Taxi geholt. **Während** der Fahrt ist sie prompt eingeschlafen.

Übung 11-7

ANWENDEN Complete each sentence with a subordinate clause and the appropriate tense from the cues given in parentheses.

Ein hektischer Abend im Hause Wagner. Die Eltern von Gerd und Iris sind bis acht Uhr bei einem Empfang.

1. Am Nachmittag musste Gerd nach Hause eilen, da... (Eltern einen Termin haben)
   sie ihren ___
2. Iris kam erst nach Hause, nachdem... (ihren Nachmittagsunterricht beenden)
3. Nach dem Abendessen räumt Iris die Küche auf, während ihr Bruder Gerd... (sich um das Baby kümmern) *es den Becher*
4. Das Baby zeigt seine Ungeduld, indem... (Becher auf den Boden werfen)
5. Iris badet das Baby, während... (Gerd Hausaufgaben machen)
6. Die Eltern kommen nach Hause, nachdem... (sich alles zu Hause beruhigen)
7. Sie schicken Iris und Gerd ins Kino, da... (so schön helfen)

Übung 11-8

ZUSAMMENFASSUNG   Additional uses of subordinating conjunctions.

A. Complete the sentences using personalized information. Note that not all sentences require a subordinate clause.

1. Ich studiere _____, (Ihr Hauptfach an der Uni), da...
2. Ich habe einen Job als _____ (z.B., Kellner/in, Verkäufer), damit...
3. Während der Semesterferien...
4. Ich wohne hier in _____ seit...
5. Gestern war es furchtbar heiß, als...
6. Ich mag _____ (Name eines Freundes/einer Freundin), obwohl...
7. Ich finde _____ (Name einer Politikerin) gut, weil...
8. Ich werde _____ (zukünftiger Beruf), wenn...

B. Respond to each question by beginning with the subordinate clause. Remember that the conjugated verb of the main clause immediately follows the subordinate clause.

1. Wo werden Sie wohnen, solange Sie studieren? *(stay as long as you study)*
2. Was machen Sie, sobald Sie mit den Hausaufgaben fertig sind? *(as soon as)*
3. Was haben Sie gestern gemacht, nachdem Sie mit aller Arbeit fertig waren?
4. Was machen Sie während der Semesterferien?
5. Was machen Sie, wenn Sie einen Freund lange nicht gesehen haben?
6. Was machen Sie, nachdem Sie Streit mit Ihrem Freund/Ihrer Freundin hatten? *(disagreement)*
7. Was trinken Sie, während Sie fernsehen?

Infinitive Phrases

§6   Basic Structure

The German infinitive phrase is normally at the end of a sentence and is composed of **zu** and an infinitive. All modifiers and objects precede the infinitive phrase, although in English they would follow it. The infinitive phrases are not set off by commas (see Appendix §1).

Ich hatte nicht den Mut **zu fragen**.
I didn't have the courage to ask.

Ich hatte nicht den Mut ihn **zu fragen**.
I didn't have the courage to ask him.

Ich hatte nicht den Mut ihn gestern **zu fragen**.
I didn't have the courage to ask him yesterday.

Zu, when accompanying a verb with a separable prefix, stands between the prefix and verb.

Ich habe vor dieses Mal nach**zu**geben.
I am planning to give in this time.

Übung 11-9

ANWENDEN A. Provide the appropriate response by using an infinitival phrase.

> MODEL: Hast du die Dias mitgebracht? (Leider habe ich vergessen...)
> <u>Leider habe ich vergessen sie mitzubringen.</u>

Roland hat Probleme mit seinem Chef. Gabi stellt ein paar Fragen.

1. Habt ihr heute das Projekt abgeschlossen? (Nein, wir hatten nicht die Absicht...)
2. Bist du mit deinen Kollegen zum Mittagessen gegangen? (Sie hatten keine Zeit...)
3. Hast du mit deinem Chef über die lange Arbeitszeit gesprochen? (Ich hatte keine Gelegenheit...)
4. Sage ich nichts dazu? (Vielleicht ist es besser...)
5. Sprichst du morgen mit ihm? (Ich habe nicht vor...)
6. Stellen deine Kollegen den Chef zur Rede? (Niemand traut sich...) *den Chef zur Rede zu stellen*

B. Rephrase each sentence by beginning with the introductory clause given. Adjust the infinitival clauses as needed.

Frauke und ihr Mann streiten sich. Frauke sagt zu ihrem Mann:

1. Ich will nicht mit dir streiten. (Ich habe keine Lust)
   Ich habe keine Lust... *mit dir zu streite*
2. Du kannst nie nachgeben. *nachzugeben*
   Es ist schwer für dich...
3. Aber ich höre immer gut zu. (leicht sein)
   Für mich ist es leicht... *zuzuhören*
4. Du brauchst nicht laut zu werden.
   Es hat keinen Zweck... *zu werden*
5. Denkst du über alles nach? (vor•haben)
   Hast du vor... *über alles nach zudenken*

§7 Infinitive Phrases Introduced with *um, ohne, anstatt,* or *statt*

Um introduces infinitive phrases that express a purpose or intention. **Um** is obligatory in such phrases where *in order* is optional in English:

Ich habe das getan **um** Geld **zu** sparen.	*I did this (in order) to save money.*
um nicht in Schulden **zu** geraten.	*in order not to run up debts.*

When the infinitive phrase is introduced with **ohne**, **anstatt**, or **statt**, the English equivalents include gerunds.

> Monika legte den Hörer auf **ohne** ein Wort **zu** sagen.
> *Monika put down the receiver without saying a word.*
> or: *Monika hung up without saying a word.*

Ich bin auf eine Party gegangen **anstatt/statt** für die Prüfung **zu** lernen.
I went to a party instead of studying for the exam.

Übung 11-10

ANWENDEN A. Provide an appropriate infinitival phrase that completes each sentence.

Bärbel hat Probleme mit den Leuten in ihrer Wohngemeinschaft.

1. Kurt hat Bärbels Kamera verliehen ohne...
2. Manfred sieht immer abends fern statt...
3. Gerd hat einfach Bärbels Auto genommen ohne...
4. Und Bärbel musste sich beeilen um...
5. Angelika isst das ganze Eis alleine statt...

B. Respond to the following personalized questions.

1. Was machen Sie um fit zu bleiben? Um gesund zu bleiben?
2. Was machen Sie um mit Freunden in Kontakt zu bleiben? *schick sie Post*
3. Was machen Ihre Eltern um mit Ihnen in Kontakt zu bleiben?
4. Was kann man tun um einen Streit zu vermeiden?
5. Was machen Sie um erfolgreich an der Uni zu sein?
6. Haben Sie wichtige Entscheidungen getroffen ohne mit Ihren Eltern zu sprechen?
7. Was machen Sie manchmal statt zu lernen?

§8   The Infinitive Phrase Preceding the Main Clause

The main clause has inverted word order when it is preceded by an infinitive phrase. Compare

Ich habe geschwiegen um Anita nicht zu ärgern.
Um Anita nicht zu ärgern **habe ich** geschwiegen.

Übung 11-11

ANWENDEN Combine the sentences with a logical infinitival phrase.

MODEL: Erich hat die Hausaufgaben nicht gemacht. Er hat Fußball gespielt.
<u>Statt die Hausaufgaben zu machen hat Erich Fußball gespielt.</u>

1. Dagmar hat nicht im Garten geholfen. Sie ist schwimmen gegangen.
2. Anton hat sein Zimmer nicht aufgeräumt. Er hat die ganze Zeit vorm Fernseher gesessen.
3. Petra hat kein Wort gesagt. Sie hat das Zimmer verlassen.
4. Martin will Freunde treffen. Er ist in die Stadt gegangen.
5. Man kann Teenager [schwer] verstehen! Man muss Geduld haben.

§9   English Infinitive Constructions Expressed in German by Dependent Clauses

1. English infinitives with subjects in the objective case

As the following example illustrates, an English infinitive may have a subject in the objective case.

My parents want *me* to continue with my studies.

In this sentence, *me* is not a direct object, since it does not mean "My parents want me," but rather "My parents want that I continue with my studies." *Me* is the implied subject of the infinitive *to continue*.

In German, the above sentence can only be expressed by means of a **dass** clause. There is no equivalent infinitival rendering.

Meine Eltern wollen, **dass ich** weiterstudiere.

Additional examples

Sie erwartet, **dass ich sie heute abend anrufe**.	*She expects me to call her tonight.*
Ich glaube, **dass er ein ehrlicher Mensch ist**.	*I believe him to be an honest person.*
Meine Eltern wollen, **dass wir heiraten**.	*My parents want us to get married.*

Übung 11-12

VERSTEHEN Identify the implied subject of the infinitival clause and then restate it as a subject in English.

MODEL: We believe him to be an honest man.
          him ⟶ he

1. He asked her to marry him.
2. She told you to call the police.
3. Did you ask me to come along?
4. I advised her to contact a lawyer.
5. I want you to fix the VCR.

Übung 11-13

ANWENDEN A. Write the following sentences in German.

1. a. I want you to tell me the truth.
   b. He wants me to tell him the truth.
   c. Do you want me to tell you the truth? (formal)
   d. We all want you to tell us the truth. (formal)

2. a. I don't expect him to pay the bill.
   b. They expect me to pay the bill.
   c. Do you expect me to pay the bill? (familiar singular)
   d. Nobody expects you to pay the bill. (familiar singular)

B. Form sentences by providing subordinate clauses introduced by **dass**. Use the cues and supply additional elements (e.g., pronouns, articles) where necessary.

MODEL: Ruth möchte, ... / Mutter / Frühstück / machen
          <u>Sie möchte, dass ihre Mutter das Frühstück macht.</u>

Ruth hat (zu) viele Erwartungen.

1. Ruth will, ... / Bruder / Auto / waschen
2. Sie erwartet, ... / Freund / sie / zum Essen / einladen
3. Sie will, ... / Freundin Veronika / Buch / besorgen
4. Und sie glaubt, ... / Eltern / Wohnung / bezahlen
5. Sie erwartet, ... / ihre Schwester / Wäsche / waschen
6. Ihre Familie will, ... / Ruth / endlich / selbständig / werden!

2. English infinitives introduced with a question word

In English, but not in German, infinitives may be introduced with a question word. Compare

I don't know
what I am supposed to do.
what to do.

Ich weiß nicht,
was ich machen soll.

She told me
where I should buy the book.
where to buy the book.

Sie hat mir gesagt,
wo ich das Buch kaufen soll.

He will tell you
how you can solve this problem.
how to solve this problem.

Er wird dir sagen,
wie du dieses Problem lösen kannst.

Because German does not permit an infinitive phrase after a question word, the English infinitival clause in each case has no German counterpart.

Übung 11-14

ANWENDEN A. Express the following sentences in German. Use the modals in parentheses in the subordinate clause.

MODEL: I don't know who(m) to invite. (sollen)
          <u>Ich weiß nicht, wen ich einladen soll.</u>

1. I don't know who(m) to ask. (sollen)
2. I don't know what to say. (sollen)
3. I can't tell you what to do. (müssen [formal])
4. Peter can tell you how to do that. (müssen [familiar singular])

5. I don't know how to solve this problem. (sollen)
6. We can tell you who(m) to call. (können)
7. Do you know how to explain that? (sollen)

B. Formulate the questions that Herr and Frau Fuchs ask in different situations, following the model.

MODEL: *They want to know...*
          where to get souvenirs
          Wissen Sie, wo wir Souvenire kaufen können?
    or: Wissen Sie, wo man Souvenire kaufen kann?

Herr and Frau Fuchs are visiting Vienna and are asking for some information at their hotel. They want to know...

1. how to get to the city center
2. where to exchange money
3. where to eat Italian food
4. how to find the restaurant *Dolce Vita*
5. where to buy a city map

Übung 11-15

ZUSAMMENFASSUNG Infinitive constructions.

A. Express in German.

Ihre Zimmerkollegin/Ihr Zimmerkollege geht Ihnen auf die Nerven. Sie sagen ihm/ihr, was er tun und nicht tun soll.

1. Don't tell me what to eat and drink.
2. Don't tell me when to get up.
3. Don't tell my friends to leave earlier.
4. They will tell you to leave them alone.
5. I don't want us to argue all the time.
6. But I want us to make compromises.
7. I want you to be more tolerant.
8. Or I will tell you to move out.

B. Complete the following sentences with an appropriate clause.

Sie geben einem guten Freund Ratschläge.

1. Um erfolgreich zu sein...
2. Um gesund zu bleiben...
3. Man kann seine Freunde nicht behalten ohne...
4. Du musst mehr schlafen statt...
5. Du musst früher aufstehen um...
6. Man kann keinen guten Job finden ohne...
7. Statt im Internet zu surfen...

Themen und Vokabular

Probleme

das Argument, -e	argument, fight
argumentieren	to argue
die Auseinandersetzung,	
-en	controversy, fight
diskutieren	to discuss
der Grund, ⁻e	reason
das Problem, -e	problem
die Rede, -n	talk
jemanden (acc.) zur	to confront
Rede stellen	somebody
der Streit, -s	quarrel, fight

(sich) streiten, stritt,	to argue,
hat gestritten	quarrel, fight
der Zweck, -e	purpose
es hat keinen Zweck	it's no use

Lösungen

besprechen, besprach,	
hat besprochen	to talk over
der Kompromiss, -e	compromise
einen Kompromiss	
schließen, schloss,	to make a
hat geschlossen	compromise
die Lösung, -en	solution

12 The Subjunctive Part 1

Introduction

Both English and German use two sets of verb forms that indicate how real or how likely a speaker believes a statement to be. The more usual forms, called *indicative*, indicate that an utterance is either factual or relatively likely.

She is Miss America.	Sie ist „Miss Amerika".
I am not Mr. Körner.	Ich bin nicht Herr Körner.
Perhaps he'll come tomorrow.	Vielleicht kommt er morgen.

The other set of forms, called *subjunctive*, indicates that a statement is relatively unlikely, implausible, conjectural, or simply contrary to fact.

*If he **were** to come tomorrow,…*	Wenn er morgen **käme**,…
*If I **were** Miss America,…*	Wenn ich „Miss Amerika" **wäre**,…
*If I **were** Mr Körner,…*	Wenn ich Herr Körner **wäre**,…

Were, **wäre**, and **käme** in the sentences above are subjunctive forms. English has few distinct subjunctive forms, whereas German has many recognizable subjunctives.

German distinguishes between a conditional, or general, subjunctive (also called *subjunctive II*), and a special subjunctive (also called *subjunctive I*). This chapter (The Subjunctive Part 1) deals only with the conditional subjunctive and how it is used to express contrary to fact conditions and wishes in the past, present, and future. For convenience, we shall refer to it simply as the *subjunctive*. It is used mainly to signal unreal conditions. These unreal conditions are divided into two time categories: those that deal with the present or future and those that deal with the past.

Kapitel 13 (The Subjunctive Part 2) will treat additional uses of the conditional subjunctive and the special subjunctive for indirect discourse.

Contrary to Fact Conditions Referring to the Present or Future

§1 Contrary to Fact Conditions in English

Compare these two sentences.

When I lived in Vienna, I often went to the opera.
If I lived in Vienna, I would go to the opera often.

In the first sentence, *lived* is the past tense indicative: the speaker once lived in Vienna. In the second sentence, *lived* refers to the present and is called *present tense subjunctive.* "If I lived in Vienna" is a hypothesis, or unreal condition.

Note the difference between a factual indicative conditional sentence and a subjunctive (contrary to fact) conditional sentence.

> If **I have** the money, **I'll go** to Europe.
> If **I had** the money, **I would go** to Europe.

In the first sentence, the speaker considers it possible that he/she will have the money. Because the condition may be fulfilled, it is real and hence in the indicative. In the second sentence, the condition is purely hypothetical. The speaker does not have the money (but if he/she had it ...); hence the verb *had* is subjunctive (identical in form, but not in meaning, to the past indicative).

Hypothetical conditions are generally accompanied by equally hypothetical conclusions. Note the verb forms used in the following sentences:

CONDITION	CONCLUSION	FACT
If I **had** the money,	I **would go** to Europe.	(But I don't have the money...)
If she **had** the time,	she **would join** us.	(But she doesn't have the time...)
If I **could** pay my debts,	I **would be** very relieved.	(But I can't pay my debts...)
If he **got** angry,	I **would get** angry, too.	(But he isn't getting angry...)
SUBJUNCTIVE		CONDITIONAL

(usually identical in form to the past indicative)   *would* + verb

The subjunctive and the conditional may refer to the present, future, or the past.

PRESENT   PRESENT
If I had more money, I would not be living in such a small apartment.
    (But I don't have more money...)

PRESENT   FUTURE
If I had the money, I would buy this boat tomorrow.
    (But I don't have the money...)

FUTURE   FUTURE
If I lost my scholarship, I would have to quit school.
    (But I'm not losing my scholarship...)

Übung 12-1

VERSTEHEN A. Indicate which of the sentences contain real conditions and which contain contrary to fact conditions.

1. If she invites me, I will not accept.
2. If I could, I'd help you.
3. If we had a choice, we wouldn't be here.
4. If that is true, I'll never speak to her again.

5. If I didn't call them, they'd be very angry with me.
6. If she loves me, she'll forgive me.

B. The following sentences contain real conditions. Change them to contrary to fact conditions.

1. If she invites me, I will not accept.
2. If I can, I'll help you.
3. If you have a fever, you'll have to see a doctor.
4. If that is true, I'll never speak to her again.
5. If we have a choice, we won't sign the contract.
6. If I don't call them, they'll be very angry with me.
7. If she loves me, she'll forgive me.

§2   Contrary to Fact Conditions in German

	CONDITION	CONCLUSION
Real condition	Wenn wir müde **sind**, *When we are tired,*	**schlafen** wir ein bisschen. *we sleep a little.*
Unreal condition	Wenn wir müde **wären**, *If we were tired,*	**würden** wir ein bisschen **schlafen**. *we would sleep a little.*

The real condition and conclusion are expressed in the indicative; their contrary to fact counterparts are expressed in the subjunctive. **Würden** is equivalent to the English *would*.

The conclusion may be introduced by **dann** or **so** (the latter has a literary flavor).

Wenn er wirklich in Gefahr wäre, **dann (so)** müssten wir ihn warnen.
If he were really in danger, then we would have to warn him.

Note: In the example above, the conditional clause, or **wenn**-clause, is a dependent clause; hence, the verb stands at the end. The conclusion is the main clause. It has inverted word order because it is preceded by a dependent clause (cf. Kap. 11 §3).

§3   Contrary to Fact Conditions with Questions

Contrary to fact conditions may follow questions.

Was würdest du sagen, wenn ich nicht zurückkäme?
What would you say if I didn't come back?

Was würden Sie tun, wenn Sie an ihrer Stelle wären?
What would you do if you were in her place?

§4   Forms of the Present Subjunctive

1. The verbs **haben, sein, werden** (cf. Kap. 3 §9)

Haben, sein, and **werden** form the subjunctive by adding an umlaut to the past indicative forms.

haben	sein	werden
ich hätte	ich wäre	ich würde
du hättest	du wär(e)st	du würdest
er ⎫	er ⎫	er ⎫
sie ⎬ hätte	sie ⎬ wäre	sie ⎬ würde
es ⎭	es ⎭	es ⎭
wir hätten	wir wären	wir würden
ihr hättet	ihr wär(e)t	ihr würdet
sie hätten	sie wären	sie würden
Sie hätten	Sie wären	Sie würden

(The **e** of the familiar singular and plural is usually omitted.)

Übung 12-2

ANWENDEN   A. Restate the **wenn**-clauses, substituting the subjects in parentheses.

1. Wenn ich nicht so egoistisch wäre, ... (du, ihr, wir)
2. Wenn ich krank würde, ... (Rita, die Kinder, ihr, du, Sie)
3. Wenn ich Ferien hätte, ... (er, Sie, ihr, du)

B. Insert a phrase that logically completes the sentences. Use only **haben**, **sein**, or **werden**, as indicated.

1. Wenn ich _____, würde ich zum Arzt gehen. (werden)
2. Wenn wir _____, würden wir länger im Urlaub bleiben. (haben)
3. Wenn du _____, würdest du nicht mehr weitergehen. (werden)
4. Wenn ihr _____, würden wir zusammen ausgehen. (sein)
5. Wenn ihr _____, würdet ihr nicht so oft mit dem Bus fahren. (haben)
6. Wenn er _____, würde er eine Weltreise machen. (sein)

2. Modal auxiliaries (cf. Kap. 4 §2)

The present subjunctive and past indicative of modals are alike, with one exception. Those modals that have an umlaut in the infinitive add an umlaut in the subjunctive. Remember also that **möchten** is often used as an indicative in the place of **mögen** (cf. Kap. 4 §1).

INFINITIVE	PAST INDICATIVE	PRESENT SUBJUNCTIVE	
können	ich konnte	ich könnte	
dürfen	ich durfte	ich dürfte	
müssen	ich musste	ich müsste	(with umlaut)
mögen	ich mochte	ich möchte	
wollen	ich wollte	ich wollte	(without umlaut)
sollen	ich sollte	ich sollte	

Remember: **wollen** and **sollen** never have an umlaut.

Übung 12-3

ANWENDEN A. Supply the appropriate subjunctive forms of the modals in parentheses.

1. Wenn wir laufen _____,... (müssen, wollen, können, dürfen, sollen)
2. Wenn Monika zu Hause bleiben _____,... (müssen, mögen, wollen, sollen)
3. Wenn du mitkommen _____,... (dürfen, mögen, können, wollen)
4. Wenn Sie weggehen _____,... (sollen, können, müssen)
5. Wenn ihr das nicht _____,... (wollen, mögen, dürfen, können)

B. Provide three suggestions for each scenario. Use the suggested modal verbs in the present subjunctive.

1. Erklären Sie einem Freund, was er in Ihrer Heimatstadt tun könnte.
2. Sie sind Babysitter für zwei kleine Kinder. Sagen Sie den Kindern, was sie nicht machen dürften oder könnten und was sie machen müssten, wenn die Eltern zu Hause wären.
3. Sie haben eine Bekannte zu Besuch [formal address]. Sie wollen herausfinden, was sie machen möchte. Machen Sie Vorschläge.
4. Was könnten/dürften/sollten Sie nicht tun, wenn Sie Teenager wären? Was müssten Sie tun?

3. Weak verbs

The forms of the present subjunctive and the past indicative are identical (cf. Kap. 3 §1). Precisely because they are identical, they are rarely used. Instead, a form of **würde** + infinitive is used (cf. §5).

ich sagte	ich arbeit**e**te
du sagtest	du arbeit**e**test
er	er
sie⟩ sagte	sie⟩ arbeit**e**te
es	es
wir sagten	wir arbeit**e**ten
ihr sagtet	ihr arbeit**e**tet
sie sagten	sie arbeit**e**ten
Sie sagten	Sie arbeit**e**ten

(An **e** is added when the stem ends in **-d**, **-t**, or consonant clusters.)

Übung 12-4

VERSTEHEN Indicate whether the statement is in the past tense or the present tense subjunctive.

1. Wenn es Sommer wäre, arbeitete ich im Restaurant.
2. Sie sagten den Eltern Bescheid, wenn sie spät nach Hause kamen.
3. Wir tanzten bis spät in die Nacht, wenn wir gute Musik hätten.

4. Wenn er lustig wäre, lachte ich über seinen Witz.
5. Wenn es schön war, machten wir ein Picknick.
6. Sie weinte immer, wenn ein Film traurig war.
7. Wir suchten das Geschäft nicht so lange, wenn der Stadtplan klar wäre.

4. Strong verbs (cf. Kap. 3 §4, §6; Appendix §2)

The personal endings of the subjunctive are identical to the past tense endings of weak verbs minus **t**.

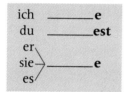

ich _____**e**	wir _____**en**
du _____**est**	ihr _____**et**
er	sie _____**en**
sie→_____**e**	Sie _____**en**
es	

These endings are attached to the past tense stem of strong verbs, i.e., the second principal part.

gehen   **ging**   ist gegangen

PAST INDICATIVE		PRESENT SUBJUNCTIVE
ich ging		ich ging**e**
du ging**st**		du ging**est**
er		er
sie→ging		sie→ging**e**
es		es
wir ging**en**	(identical)	wir ging**en**
ihr ging**t**		ihr ging**et**
sie ging**en**	(identical)	sie ging**en**
Sie ging**en**	(identical)	Sie ging**en**

Strong verbs with the vowels **a**, **o**, and **u** in the past indicative require an umlaut in the present subjunctive.

	PAST INDICATIVE	PRESENT SUBJUNCTIVE
kommen	kam	k**ä**me
fliegen	flog	fl**ö**ge
fahren (fährt)	fuhr	f**ü**hre

A few strong verbs have irregular present subjunctives.

beginnen	begann	beg**ö**nne (also: begänne)
helfen (hilft)	half	h**ü**lfe (also: hälfe)
stehen	stand	st**ü**nde (also: stände)

Many present subjunctives are felt to be stilted or obsolete. Students may, however, encounter them in literature and will need to recognize them. These subjunctives are shown in parentheses in §2 of the Appendix.

The present subjunctives of the following verbs are still current, including the compound forms, some of which are listed here.

		PAST INDICATIVE	PRESENT SUBJUNCTIVE
finden		fand	**fände**
geben (gibt)		gab	**gäbe**
auf•geben	*to give up*		
zu•geben	*to admit*		
zurück•geben	*to give back, to return*		
gehen		ging	**ginge**
aus•gehen	*to go out*		
zurück•gehen	*to go back, to return*		
halten (hält)	*to hold, stop*	hielt	**hielte**
behalten	*to keep*	behielt	**behielte**
heißen	*to be named*	hieß	**hieße**
kommen		kam	**käme**
an•kommen	*to arrive*		
bekommen	*to receive, get*		
mit•kommen	*to come along*		
lassen (läßt)	*to let; to leave*	ließ	**ließe**
tun	*to do*	tat	**täte**

5. Mixed verbs (cf. Kap. 3 §8)

Mixed verbs form the present subjunctive by adding an umlaut to their past indicative forms.

	PAST INDICATIVE	PRESENT SUBJUNCTIVE
denken	d**a**chte	d**ä**chte
bringen	br**a**chte	br**ä**chte
wissen	w**u**sste	w**ü**sste

These three verbs are commonly used in conversational German.
The following mixed verbs change the stem vowel to **e** in the subjunctive:

	PAST INDICATIVE	PRESENT SUBJUNCTIVE
brennen	es br**a**nnte	es br**e**nnte
kennen	ich k**a**nnte	ich k**e**nnte
nennen	ich n**a**nnte	ich n**e**nnte
rennen	ich r**a**nnte	ich r**e**nnte

These four subjunctives are now obsolete. The use of substitute forms is explained in §5.

§5   The Subjunctive with *würde* + Infinitive

Verbs other than **haben, sein, werden**, and also **wissen** use a form of **würde** (subjunctive of **werden**) + infinitive of the main verb to express unreal conditions. This corresponds to the English use of *would* + verb.

> Wenn wir hier parken **könnten**, **würden** wir Zeit und Geld **sparen**.
>   (instead of **sparten**)
> *If we could park here, we would save time and money.*

Würde plus the infinitive of the main verb is structurally the future subjunctive (cf. Kap. 12 §6); however, it frequently serves as a substitute for the present subjunctive.

Do not confuse the following two uses of **würde**:

> Wenn ich diese Rechnung nicht bezahlen könnte, **würde** ich nervös.
>   (**werden** as main verb)

> Wenn ich hier parken könnte, **würde** ich Zeit und Geld **sparen**.
>   (auxiliary)   (main verb in the infinitive)

In the first sentence, **würde** is the main verb, accompanied by the predicate adjective **nervös**. Its meaning is "to become, get." In the second sentence, the infinitive **sparen** is the main verb and **würde** functions as its auxiliary. This construction will be referred to as "**würde** + infinitive form."

Übung 12-5

VERSTEHEN Restate the main clause by substituting the present subjunctive with the **würde**-form.

MODEL: Er behielte das Geld, wenn es seins wäre. <u>Er würde das Geld behalten.</u>

1. Er spräche länger, wenn er etwas zu sagen hätte.
2. Wenn sie Ferien hätten, kämen sie zu Besuch.
3. Wir gingen ins Kino, wenn ein guter Film laufen würde.
4. Du tätest mir den Gefallen, wenn ich dich darum bitten würde.
5. Wenn er nicht so langweilig wäre, ließet ihr ihn weiterreden.
6. Ich fände es gut, wenn sie uns in Ruhe lassen würden.
7. Wenn er netter wäre, gäbe er mir sein Auto.

Übung 12-6

ANWENDEN Respond to the following personalized questions. You need not repeat the **wenn**-clause.

1. Was würden Sie machen, wenn Sie heute keine Uni hätten?
2. Was würden Sie und Ihre Freunde machen, wenn es Samstagabend wäre?

3. Was würde ihre Familie machen, wenn heute Sonntag wäre?
4. Wohin würden Sie gern fahren, wenn Sie eine Woche Ferien hätten?
5. Wen würden Sie einladen, wenn Sie eine Party hätten? Wen würden Sie nicht einladen?
6. Wer würde Sie vielleicht einladen, aber wer würde Sie nicht einladen?
7. Wem würden Sie schreiben, wenn Sie in Deutschland wären?

§6   Use of *würde* + Infinitive in the *wenn*-Clause

In formal German, **würde** + infinitive was traditionally not used in **wenn**-clauses. This rule has now been relaxed, and the **würde**-construction occurs both in the main clause and the **wenn**-clause.

> Wenn ihr mitkommen **würdet**, könnten wir das besprechen.
> *If you would come along, we could talk about it.*

> Wenn sie das Haus kaufen **würden**, hätten sie mehr Platz für Gäste.
> *If they would buy the house, they would have more room for guests.*

It is, however, considered poor practice in formal style to have **würde** + infinitive forms in both the **wenn**-clause and the conclusion.

> poor formal style: Wenn die Regierung helfen **würde**, **würde** diese Firma nicht bankrott machen.
> *If the government would help, this company would not go bankrupt.*
> rephrased: Wenn die Regierung helfen **könnte**, **würde** diese Firma nicht bankrott machen.
> or: Wenn die Regierung helfen **würde**, **machte** diese Firma nicht bankrott.

In informal German, few present subjunctive forms are used. However, studies have shown that the forms listed in §4, 4 and 5 are current and occur in written German as frequently as the equivalents with **würde** + infinitive.

The use of the conditional subjunctive in spoken German parallels that of the simple past (cf. Kap. 3 §9). The verbs that occur in the simple past also occur in the conditional subjunctive: **ginge**, **käme**, and **gäbe**. These forms, as well as **wäre**, **hätte**, **würde**, **wüsste**, and the subjunctives of modal verbs, are common in everyday speech.

With all other verbs, **würde** + infinitive is used. This means that **würde** often occurs both in the **wenn**-clause and in the conclusion.

> Wenn Peter nicht soviel **angeben würde**, **würde** ich ihn auch zu meiner Party **einladen**.

Note: Always use the present subjunctives of **haben, sein, werden, wissen,** and the modals. In everyday spoken German, you can use the **würde** + infinitive forms of virtually all other verbs both in the **wenn**-clause and in the conclusion.

Übung 12-7

ANWENDEN Supply the cued **wenn**-clause with **würde** + infinitive of the cued verb.

Doris ist mit einer Freundin beim Kaffeetrinken. Sie sprechen über verschiedene Menschen in ihrem Leben.

1. Ich würde verrückt, / mein Freund / mich / nicht anrufen
2. Würdest du böse, / dein Mann / ohne dich / ausgehen?
3. Würden wir glücklich, / wir / alleine / leben?
4. Ich würde vielleicht mehr arbeiten, / meine Kinder / nicht / zu Hause / wohnen
5. Und mein Mann würde mehr helfen, / ich / nicht alles / machen

§7   Omission of *wenn*

Compare the following sentences:

> **Wenn** ich eine Schreibmaschine **hätte**, würde ich dir öfter schreiben.
> **Hätte** ich eine Schreibmaschine, **dann/so** würde ich dir öfter schreiben.

Note: The inflected verb is at the beginning of the condition. The particles **dann** (common) or **so** (literary flavor) may be added.

Literal translations of such sentences are stilted.

> *Had I a typewriter, then I would write to you more often.*
> idiomatic: *If I had a typewriter, I would write to you more often.*

§8   Reversal of the *wenn*-Clause and Conclusion

Compare the following two sentences in German:

> **Ich würde** die Rechnung nicht bezahlen, wenn ich an seiner Stelle wäre.
> *I would not pay the bill if I were in his place. (...if I were him)*

> Wenn ich an seiner Stelle wäre, **würde** ich die Rechnung nicht bezahlen.
> *If I were in his place (If I were him), I would not pay the bill.*

Note the change to normal word order when the conclusion (main clause) precedes the **wenn**-clause.

§9   Conclusions Standing Alone

Although an unreal condition is not always expressed, one is often implied. In such instances, the main clause (conclusion) stands alone.

> **Ich würde den Vertrag nicht unterschreiben.** (wenn ich an deiner Stelle wäre)
> *I would not sign the contract. (if I were you)*

Ich würde ihm gern helfen. (wenn ich es könnte)
I would gladly help him. (if I could)

Das wäre schade. (wenn das passierte)
That would be a pity. (if that happened)

Übung 12-8

ANWENDEN Express the conclusions in German. The condition is implied.

Ilse reagiert auf die Vorschläge von ihren Kindern für Ferienaktivitäten.

1. Gehen wir heute Nachmittag schwimmen?
   That would be a good idea.
2. Vielleicht regnet es aber heute Nachmittag.
   That would be a pity.
3. Sollen wir zuerst unser Zimmer aufräumen?
   That would be great!
4. Nimmt Klaus es uns übel, wenn wir ihn nicht anrufen?
   Yes, he would resent it.
5. Sollen wir Anne einladen?
   Yes, you should invite her.

§10   *wenn*-Clauses Standing Alone

Wishes expressed with a **wenn-**clause standing alone are those not expected to be fulfilled. In German, they end with an exclamation point. Just as English uses the particle *only*, German uses **nur**. In most instances, **nur** follows the subject and pronoun objects but precedes all other elements.

	Wenn ich nur mehr Zeit **hätte!**	*If only I had more time.*
less common:	**Hätte** ich nur mehr **Zeit!**	
	Wenn Sie mich nur verstehen **könnten!**	*If only you could understand me.*
less common:	**Könnten** Sie mich nur verstehen!	
	Wenn ich nur ihren Namen **wüsste!**	*If only I knew her name.*
less common:	**Wüsste** ich nur ihren Namen!	

§11   Wishes Introduced by *ich wollte* or *ich wünschte*

The introductory statement **Ich wollte,...** or **Ich wünschte,...** is a form of the present subjunctive. The English counterpart *I wish* is, of course, present indicative. Wishes with the introductory statement end in a period rather than an exclamation point.

Ich wollte,	ich **hätte** mehr Freizeit.	*I wish I had more leisure time.*
Ich wünschte,	ich **wäre** nicht so schüchtern.	*I wish I weren't so shy.*
	ich **wüsste** es.	*I knew it.*
	ich **könnte** Sie überzeugen.	*I could convince you.*

The wish itself is expressed in the present subjunctive with **haben**, **sein**, **werden**, **wissen**, and the modals; with other verbs, **würde** + infinitive forms are commonly used.

Übung 12-9

ANWENDEN   A. Provide a wish without an introductory clause appropriate to the complaints stated. You may use a negative or an opposite statement.

> MODEL: Klaus ist immer schlecht gelaunt.
> <u>Wenn er nur nicht so schlecht gelaunt wäre!</u>
> or: <u>Wenn er nur besser gelaunt wäre!</u>

Ute wünscht, dass verschiedene Dinge anders wären. (Sie haben etwas mit Arbeit zu tun.)

1. Mein Mann hat immer zu viel Arbeit.
2. Und meine Kollegen arbeiten zu wenig.
3. Mein Chef ist sehr arrogant.
4. Und meine Sekretärin kennt nicht genug Computerprogramme.
5. Leider bin ich ziemlich ungeduldig.

B. Supply five similar wishes of your own.

C. Now, rephrase your wishes by beginning them with **Ich wünschte,**...or **Ich wollte,**....

Contrary to Fact Conditions Referring to the Past

§12   In English

	CONDITION	CONCLUSION
PRESENT	If I knew,	I would tell you.
	PRESENT SUBJUNCTIVE	PRESENT CONDITIONAL
PAST	If I had known,	I would have told you.
	PAST SUBJUNCTIVE	PAST CONDITIONAL

Note: The past subjunctive form (*I had known*) in the conditional clause is identical to the past perfect indicative. The conclusion is expressed in the past conditional (*would have told*).

Übung 12-10

VERSTEHEN Indicate whether the statement refers to a contrary to fact condition in the past or in the present, then state the implied facts in the indicative in English.

1. If I had told you, you would not have believed it.
2. If they had had the courage, they would have refused.
3. If they printed that, they would ruin our reputation.
4. If I did not call her, she would become very angry.
5. If they had been in trouble, we would have helped them.
6. If I had the money, I would study abroad for a year.

§13   In German

	WENN-CLAUSE	CONCLUSION
PRESENT	Wenn ich es wüsste,	(dann) würde ich es dir sagen.
PAST	Wenn ich es **gewusst hätte**, PAST SUBJUNCTIVE	(dann) **hätte** ich es dir **gesagt**. PAST SUBJUNCTIVE

Both the **wenn**-clause and the conclusion are expressed in the past subjunctive.

The **würde**-substitute is not used when referring to the past. Note that while there are three past tenses in the indicative (simple past, present perfect, and past perfect), there is only one past subjunctive tense.

The forms of the past subjunctive will be practiced first in main clauses (conclusions), then in **wenn**-clauses, and finally in sentences consisting of a **wenn**-clause plus a conclusion.

§14   Main Clauses in the Past Subjunctive

1. Using weak, strong, and irregular verbs

The forms of the past subjunctive are derived from the past perfect indicative (cf. Kap. 3 §10).

The auxiliaries **haben** and **sein** are in the subjunctive; the past participle remains unchanged.

PAST PERFECT INDICATIVE	PAST SUBJUNCTIVE	ENGLISH EQUIVALENT
Verbs with auxiliary **haben**		
ich hatte gefragt	ich hätte gefragt	*I would have asked*
ich hatte eingeladen	ich hätte eingeladen	*I would have invited*
ich hatte gehabt	ich hätte gehabt	*I would have had*
Verbs with auxiliary **sein**		
ich war geblieben	ich wäre geblieben	*I would have stayed*
ich war gewesen	ich wäre gewesen	*I would have been*
ich war geworden	ich wäre geworden	*I would have become*

Übung 12-11

ANWENDEN A. Provide an opposite statement (main clause only) in the past subjunctive. Try to provide new items rather than merely negate the given sentences.

MODEL: Oskar hat Sport gemacht.
          <u>Kai hätte auf der Couch gelegen.</u>

Wenn Oskar etwas macht, macht Kai immer genau das Gegenteil! Was hätte er wohl gemacht?

1. Oskar hat seiner Mutter zum Geburtstag gratuliert.
2. Er hat für die Prüfung gelernt.
3. Er hat sich etwas zum Abendessen gekocht.
4. Oskar ist zu der Party von Rudi gegangen.
5. Er hat sich auf der Party mit vielen Leuten unterhalten. → *to have conversation*
6. Er hat die Freunde angerufen und sich bedankt.
7. Er ist joggen gegangen.

B. Provide an appropriate sentence (main clause only) in the past subjunctive.

Was hätten Sie oder andere Leute in den verschiedenen Situationen gemacht?

MODEL: Sie haben ein defektes Video gekauft.
          <u>Ich hätte es zurückgebracht.</u>

1. Ihr Chef hat Ihnen mitgeteilt, dass Ihre Firma dieses Jahr viel Profit gemacht hat.
2. Eine Freundin von Ihnen (denken Sie an eine bestimmte Person) hat einen wichtigen Termin verpasst.
3. Ein guter Freund hat Sie nicht auf seine Party eingeladen.
4. Ihre Eltern haben schon lange nicht mehr angerufen.
5. Ihre Kollegen im Deutschkurs hatten eine Diskussion über Politik.
6. Sie haben den Geburtstag von Ihrer Mutter vergessen.
7. Sie haben die ganzen Ferien zu Hause verbracht.

2. Using modals

Modals always use the auxiliary **haben** for the present and past perfect tenses (cf. Kap. 4 §3, §4).

a. Modals with a dependent infinitive

Ich **hätte** ihm **helfen können.**	*I could have helped him.*
or:	*I would have been able to help him.*
Ich **hätte** ihm **helfen sollen.**	*I should have helped him.*
Er **hätte** dort nicht **parken dürfen.**	*He would not have been allowed to park there.*
Sie **hätte** lange **warten müssen.**	*She would have had to wait for a long time.*
Niemand **hätte** das **essen wollen.**	*Nobody would have wanted to eat that.*
Niemand **hätte** das **essen mögen.**	*Nobody would have liked to eat that.*

hätte + _____
DOUBLE INFINITIVE

b. Modals without a dependent infinitive

Ich hätte es **gekonnt, gesollt, gedurft, gemußt, gewollt,** and **gemocht.**

hätte + _____
PAST PARTICIPLE

Note the difference between the German and English constructions.

Ich hätte ihm helfen können.	Ich hätte es gekonnt.
I could have helped him.	*I could have (done it).*
Ich hätte ihm helfen sollen.	Ich hätte es gesollt.
I should have helped him.	*I should have (done it).*

Übung 12-12

ANWENDEN A. Rephrase each sentence using a past subjunctive and the modal in parentheses.

MODEL: Du hast deine Großeltern nicht angerufen.
          Du hättest sie anrufen sollen!

Frau Baumann spricht mit ihren Kindern über Dinge im Haus.

1. Richard, du hast den Fernseher nicht ausgemacht. (können)
2. Und Tim und Sven, ihr habt die Spielsachen nicht weggeräumt. (sollen)
3. Ich habe die Wäsche nicht gewaschen. (müssen)
4. Und Anke, du hast das Video nicht ausgeliehen. (dürfen)
5. Papa, wir haben keinen Wein gekauft. (können)
6. Und die Möllers haben unsere Zeitung nicht zurückgebracht. (sollen)

B. Now, restate your answers from **A.** with the modal only.

MODEL: Du hättest sie anrufen sollen.
          Du hättest das gesollt.

§15 *wenn*-Clauses in the Past Subjunctive

The following wishes refer to the past:

Wenn er mich nur **angerufen hätte**!	*If only he had called me.*
Wenn ich nur mehr Zeit **gehabt hätte**!	*If only I had had more time.*
Wenn ich nur zu Hause **gewesen wäre**!	*If only I had been at home.*

The **wenn**-clause has dependent word order: the inflected form is in final position.

Exception: The inflected form must precede a double infinitive (cf. Kap. 4 §7).

Wenn ich dir nur **hätte** helfen können!	*If only I could have helped you.*
but: Wenn ich es nur gekonnt **hätte**!	*If only I could have (done it).*

§16   Wishes in the Past Introduced by *ich wollte* or *ich wünschte*

The expression of wishes in past subjunctive involves two different tenses: A present wish (expressed in the present subjunctive) that something occurred in the past, i.e., yesterday (expressed in the past subjunctive).

Ich **wollte,**
Ich **wünschte,** du **hättest** mich gestern **angerufen.**   *I wish you had called me yesterday.*
PRESENT SUBJUNCTIVE   PAST SUBJUNCTIVE

Additional examples

Ich **wollte,**	ich **wäre** vorsichtiger **gewesen.**	*I wish I had been more careful.*
Ich **wünschte,**	ich **hätte** das im voraus **gewusst.**	*I had known that beforehand.*
	ich **hätte** das voraussehen **können.**	*I could have foreseen that.*

Übung 12-13

ANWENDEN A. Provide a wish in the past tense appropriate to each given situation. First, state the wish without an introductory clause. Then, restate the wish with an introductory clause.

MODEL: Ein Kellner hat heute Morgen Kaffee verschüttet.
          <u>Wenn der Kellner nur nicht den Kaffee verschüttet hätte!</u>
          <u>Ich wünschte, der Kellner hätte den Kaffee nicht verschüttet.</u>

Probleme im Hotel Sonnenhof. Der Manager klagt.

1. Vier Hotelgäste sind früher abgereist.
2. Und eine Familie hat ihren Aufenthalt abgesagt.
3. Meine Buchhalterin (*accountant*) hat gekündigt.
4. Und eine Bedienung (*service person*) ist heute Morgen nicht zur Arbeit gekommen.
5. Gestern Abend war das Restaurant leer.
6. Und heute Morgen gab es keine Brötchen zum Frühstück.
7. Warum habe ich diesen Job angenommen?

B. Express five wishes of your own about something in the past. First, state these wishes without introductory clauses. Then, restate the wishes with introductory clauses.

§17   *wenn*-Clause + Conclusion in the Past Subjunctive

When the **wenn**-clause precedes the conclusion, the conjugated verb remains the second element of the main clause, followed immediately by its subject.

Wenn ich es gewusst hätte, (dann/so) hätte ich es dir gesagt.
If I had known it, I would have told you.

When the conclusion precedes the **wenn**-clause, normal word order is observed in the main clause and dependent word order is used in the dependent clause.

Ich hätte es dir gesagt, **wenn** ich es gewusst hätte.

Übung 12-14

ANWENDEN A. Restate each sentence by supplying an appropriate **wenn**-clause and changing the conclusion to the past subjunctive. The **wenn**-clause should precede the conclusion.

> MODEL: Ich habe mein Studium abgebrochen.
> <u>Wenn meine Noten besser gewesen wären, hätte ich es nicht</u>
> <u>abgebrochen.</u>

Andrea hat ihr Leben in den letzten Wochen drastisch verändert.

1. Ich habe mein Auto verkauft.
2. Ich bin in eine kleine Wohnung gezogen.
3. Ich habe meinen Freund verlassen.
4. Ich habe einen Job gefunden.
5. Ich habe in den letzten Wochen viel gearbeitet.

B. Now, restate the sentences you wrote in **A.** by beginning each with the conclusion, followed by the **wenn**-clause.

Omission of wenn

One may begin a sentence with the inflected verb and omit **wenn**; the particle **dann** is then commonly added in the main clause.

> Wenn ich es gewusst hätte, hätte ich es dir gesagt.
> **Hätte** ich es gewusst, **dann** hätte ich es dir gesagt.

Übung 12-15

ANWENDEN Restate each sentence. Omit **wenn**, change the word order, and add **dann**.

1. Wenn ich an seiner Stelle gewesen wäre, hätte ich den Chef um eine Gehaltserhöhung gebeten.
2. Wenn es nach mir gegangen wäre, wären wir etwas länger in Wien geblieben.
3. Wenn wir nicht so schnell gefahren wären, wäre der Unfall vielleicht nicht passiert.
4. Wenn ich es gekonnt hätte, hätte ich Ihnen den Gefallen getan.

§18   *wenn*-Clause and Conclusion in Different Tenses

Observe the use of the tenses in the **wenn**-clause and conclusion.

1. Wenn Ute nicht krank **wäre**, **könnten** wir jetzt ins Konzert gehen.
         PRESENT PRESENT
   If Ute weren't sick, we could go to the concert now.

Jte nicht krank **gewesen wäre**, **wären** wir gestern ins Konzert **gegangen**.
        PAST   PAST   PAST

e hadn't been sick, we would have gone to the concert yesterday.

3. Wenn Ute nicht krank **wäre**, **wären** wir gestern ins Konzert **gegangen**.
        PRESENT   PAST   PAST

If Ute weren't sick, we would have gone to the concert yesterday.

In sentence **3.**, the **wenn**-clause is in the present, since Ute is still sick. The conclusion is in the past tense, since the concert was yesterday.

Übung 12-16

ANWENDEN Provide a logical counterstatement in the **wenn**-clause for each situation. Try not to merely negate the one that is given.

MODEL: Der Roman ist sehr lang. Deshalb habe ich ihn nicht gelesen.
                <u>Wenn der Roman kürzer wäre, hätte ich ihn gelesen.</u>

1. Das Benzin ist sehr teuer. Wir haben einen kleinen Wagen gekauft.
2. Kurt ist sehr geizig. Er hat die Rechnung nicht bezahlt.
3. Ich habe nicht viel Ausdauer. Ich habe mit dem Studium aufgehört.
4. Mein Vater hat keine bessere Stelle gefunden. Wir können diese moderne Wohnung nicht mieten.
5. Wir haben nicht in der Lotterie gewonnen. Wir machen keine Reise um die Welt.

§19 Summary of the Main Features

Contrary to fact conditions

1. General pattern

	WENN-CLAUSE		CONCLUSION
PRESENT AND FUTURE	Wenn ich es **wüsste**, PRESENT SUBJUNCTIVE		(dann) **würde** ich es dir sagen. WÜRDE + INFINITIVE
		OR:	PRESENT SUBJUNCTIVE (especially with **haben, sein, wissen**, and the modals)
PAST	Wenn ich es **gewusst hätte**, PAST SUBJUNCTIVE		(dann) **hätte** ich es dir **gesagt**. PAST SUBJUNCTIVE

2. Omission of **wenn**

Wüsste ich es, dann **würde** ich es dir sagen.
Hätte ich es gewusst, dann **hätte** ich es dir **gesagt**.

3. The conclusion precedes the **wenn**-clause

Ich würde es dir sagen, wenn ich es wüsste.
Ich hätte es dir gesagt, wenn ich es gewusst hätte.

4. The **wenn**-clause and the conclusion in different tenses

Wenn ich es **wüsste**, dann **hätte** ich es dir **gesagt**.

5. The **wenn**-clause standing alone

Wenn ich es nur wüsste!
Wenn ich es nur gewusst hätte!

6. The main clause (conclusion) standing alone

Ich würde es dir sagen.
Ich hätte es dir gesagt.

§20   Reference Table

Selected verbs

fragen	weak verb (using **haben**)
gehen	strong verb (using **sein**)
haben	
sein	functioning as main verbs
werden	
können	modal without dependent infinitive
gehen können	modal with dependent infinitive

WENN-CLAUSES

PRESENT	PAST
Wenn ich...**fragte**	Wenn ich...**gefragt hätte**
If I asked	*If I had asked*
Wenn ich...**ginge**	Wenn ich...**gegangen wäre**
If I went	*If I had gone*
Wenn ich...**hätte**	Wenn ich...**gehabt hätte**
If I had	*If I had had*
Wenn ich...**wäre**	Wenn ich...**gewesen wäre**
If I were	*If I had been*
Wenn ich...**würde**	Wenn ich...**geworden wäre**
If I became	*If I had become*
Wenn ich...**könnte**	Wenn ich...**gekonnt hätte**
If I could	*If I could have*
Wenn ich...**gehen könnte**	Wenn ich...**hätte gehen können**
If I could go	*If I could have gone*

MAIN CLAUSES

PRESENT	PAST
Ich **würde...fragen**	Ich **hätte...gefragt**
I would ask	*I would have asked*
Ich **würde...gehen**	Ich **wäre...gegangen**
I would go	*I would have gone*
Ich **hätte**	Ich **hätte...gehabt**
I would have	*I would have had*
Ich **wäre**	Ich **wäre...gewesen**
I would be	*I would have been*
Ich **würde...werden**	Ich **wäre...geworden**
I would become	*I would have become*
Ich **könnte (es)**	Ich **hätte (es) gekonnt**
I could (do it)	*I could have (done it)*
Ich **könnte...gehen**	Ich **hätte...gehen können**
I could go	*I could have gone*

Übung 12-17

ZUSAMMENFASSUNG Unreal conditions and wishes in the present and past.

A. Begin each sentence with the **wenn**-clause.

> Model: Mein Fernseher ist kaputt und ich möchte unbedingt die Serie „*Gesetz und Ordnung*" sehen. (familiar)
> <u>Wenn ich an deiner Stelle wäre, würde ich zu einem Nachbarn gehen.</u>

Was würden Sie tun, wenn Sie an meiner (seiner, Ihrer) Stelle wären?

1. Mein Auto funktioniert nicht, aber ich muss schnell zur Arbeit. (familiar)
2. Jemand ist in Sabines Haus eingebrochen.
3. Peter ist furchtbar hungrig und hat nichts im Eisschrank.
4. Ich brauche unbedingt einen neuen Job. (formal)
5. Unsere Haus ist zu klein geworden, nachdem wir die Zwillinge bekommen haben.
6. Es ist 7 Uhr morgens und wir haben keinen Kaffee im Haus.
7. Ulrikes Kurs beginnt in einer halben Stunde und sie hat vergessen, ihre Hausaufgaben zu machen.

B. Personalized questions. Respond with two or three sentences to each question.

Was wäre, wenn? Was würden Sie machen, wenn?

1. wenn Sie nicht studieren würden?
2. wenn Sie Ihre Traumreise machen könnten?
3. wenn Ihre Freunde böse auf Sie wären?

4. wenn ein Freund Sie plötzlich ignorieren würde?
5. wenn es tagelang regnen würde?
6. wenn es keine Fernseher gäbe?
7. wenn Sie Präsident/in wären?
8. wenn Sie keine Verpflichtungen hätten?

C. Sagen oder schreiben Sie in fünf Sätzen, was Sie tun würden, wenn Sie eine Million Dollar in der Lotterie gewonnen hätten.

Themen und Vokabular		
Idiomatische Ausdrücke	**wenn ich du (sie, er, usw.) wäre**	*if I were you (her, he, etc.)*
an jemands Stelle sein — *to be in someone's place*	**wenn es nach mir (dir, uns, usw.) ginge**	*if it were up to me (you, us, etc.)*
wenn ich (du, er, usw.) an seiner (ihrer, deiner, usw.) Stelle wäre — *if I (you, he, etc.) were in his (her, your, etc.) place*	**sich vorstellen, dass**	*to imagine that*

13 The Subjunctive Part II

Various Uses of the Subjunctive

§1 *As if*-Clauses Introduced by *als ob, als wenn,* or *als*

As if-clauses in English. Compare the use of the tenses in the following examples:

1. The *as if*-clause is expressed in the present subjunctive.

MAIN CLAUSE	*AS IF* CLAUSE
Today he **looks**	as if he **were** ill.
PRESENT INDICATIVE	PRESENT SUBJUNCTIVE

Yesterday he **looked** as if he **were** ill. (like he **was** ill)
PAST INDICATIVE — PRESENT SUBJUNCTIVE

In the first sentence, the main clause is in the present tense and in the second it is in the past tense. However, in both sentences the *as if*-clause is in the present subjunctive. Why? The reason is what is called in German **Gleichzeitigkeit**, meaning *simultaneity*. Hans looks ill at the time of the statement of the main clause, i.e. today or yesterday. In other words, the action or state of the *as if*-clause is simultaneous with the main clause.

Additional examples

> She **acts** as if she **were** Miss America.
> She **acted** as if she **were** Miss America.

2. The *as if*-clause is expressed in the past subjunctive.

> Today Hans **looks** as if he **had been** ill.
> Yesterday Hans **looked** as if he **had been** ill.

The *as if*-clause refers to a time prior to the main clause. It is expressed in the past subjunctive (identical in form to the past perfect indicative, cf. Kap. 12 §12). The German term is **Vorzeitigkeit**, meaning *prior occurrence*.

Additional examples

> She **feels** so much better, as if she **had been** at a health spa.
> She **felt** so much better, as if she **had been** at a health spa.

Note: English often uses the indicative after *as if*.

> *He looks as if he (is / was / has been) ill.*

As if-clauses in German. The German equivalents of the above sentences in **1.** and **2.** are stated below.

1. The *as if*-clause is in the present subjunctive because of **Gleichzeitigkeit**.

> Er **sieht** heute so **aus**, als ob er krank **wäre**.
> Er **sah** gestern so **aus**, als ob er krank **wäre**.

2. The *as if*-clause is in the past subjunctive because of **Vorzeitigkeit**.

> Er **sieht** heute so **aus**, als ob er krank gewesen wäre.
> Er **sah** gestern so **aus**, als ob er krank gewesen wäre.

The subjunctive is used here just as in English. However, as noted previously, English often uses the indicative in as if-clauses, whereas German sentences like those above are very common.

> Rule 1   The *as if*-clause is expressed in the present subjunctive, if its action or state is simultaneous with the main clause.
>
> Rule 2   The *as if*-clause is expressed in the past subjunctive, if its action or state was prior to the main clause.

In German, the **als ob**-clause may also be introduced by **als wenn** (used less frequently) or the shortened form, **als**. When the shortened form is used, the inflected verb follows immediately after **als**.

> Er sieht/sah so aus, **als wenn** er krank wäre.
>   or: **als** wäre er krank.

Additional examples

> Cornelia hat ihr Geld verschwendet, **als ob (wenn) sie Millionärin wäre.**
>   **als wäre sie Millionärin.**
> *Cornelia wasted her money, as if she were a millionaire.*

> Krauses tun (taten) so, **als ob (wenn) sie viele Freunde hätten.**
>   **als hätten sie viele Freunde.**
> *The Krauses act (acted) as if they had many friends.*

> Katrin tut (tat) so, **als ob (wenn) sie noch nie Angst gehabt hätte.**
>   **als hätte sie noch nie Angst gehabt.**
> *Katrin acts (acted) as if she had never been afraid.*

Unusual or obsolete present subjunctives are replaced by **würde** + infinitive forms (cf. Kap. 12 §6).

> Diese Kinder sehen so aus, **als ob (wenn) sie frieren würden.** (instead of **frören**)
>   **als würden sie frieren.**
> *These children look as if they were freezing.*

Vokabulartip: Idiomatische Ausdrücke mit **als ob**

Several idiomatic uses of verbs often occur in conjunction with an *as if*-phrase in German. They are **scheinen, aussehen, jemand (dative) vorkommen, klingen,** and **tun.**

> Du **klingst so, als ob** du schlechte Laune hättest.
> *You sound as if you were in a bad mood.*

> Es **sieht so aus, als ob** es zu spät dafür wäre.
> *It looks as if it is too late for that.*

> Mir **kommt es so vor, als** würde ich etwas hören.
> *It seems to me like I am hearing something.*

> Es **scheint so, als ob** wir nicht genug Zeit hätten.
> *It seems as if we didn't have enough time.*

When **nur** is added, the implication is that the opposite of what is stated is true.

> Er klingt **nur** so, als wäre er arrogant.
> *He only sounds as if he were arrogant.*

Observe the following idiomatic uses of **tun**:

> Idioms: Tun Sie so, als ob (wenn) Sie zu Hause wären.
>   als wären Sie zu Hause.
> *Make yourself at home.*

> Sie tut nur so.
> *She is only pretending.*

Übung 13-1

ANWENDEN State your response with an *as if*-clause (**als ob** and **als**). Paraphrase the original question in your respose instead of merely repeating it.

> MODEL: Ist Herr Körner wirklich so intelligent oder klingt er nur so?
>   Er klingt nur so, als ob er alles wüsste.
>   or: Er klingt nur so, als wüsste er alles.

Der Schein trügt!

1. Sind Lehmanns wirklich Millionäre oder sehen sie nur so aus?
2. Hat Jutta wirklich so viel Arbeit oder tut sie nur so?
3. Hast du wirklich keine Ahnung davon oder scheint das nur so?
4. Bin ich zu dick oder kommt mir das nur so vor?
5. Helfen deine Freunde dir oder sieht das nur so aus?
6. Hast du schlechte Laune oder scheint das nur so?
7. Macht Frau Ohnesorge sich wirklich keine Sorgen oder tut sie nur so?

B. Make five statements about people who act *as if/like*. Use **tun so, als ob**.

MODEL: Meine Freundin Brigitte tut immer so, als hätte sie kein Geld.

In literary German, **als ob**-clauses are also expressed in the special subjunctive (cf. §7). There is no difference in meaning.

Er sah so aus,
  — als ob er krank **sei**.
  — als **sei** er krank.

Es schien,
  — als ob er krank **gewesen sei**.
  — als **sei** er krank **gewesen**.

§2   *beinah(e)* or *fast*, Indicating That Something Almost Occurred

To indicate that something almost happened, German often uses the past subjunctive while English uses the past indicative.

The **-e** of **beinahe** may be omitted. **Beinah(e)** and **fast** mean *almost* and are used interchangeably. **Beinah(e)** and **fast** normally follow subjects and personal pronoun objects, but precede all other elements.

Ich hätte es beinah(e) (fast) vergessen.	*I almost forgot it.*
Ich wäre vor Lachen beinah(e) (fast) gestorben.	*I almost died laughing.*

Übung 13-2

ANWENDEN   A. Use **beinah(e)** or **fast** and the past subjunctive in your responses.

Beinahe! Sabine und ihr Freund hatten eine aufregende Reise. Sabines Mutter stellt Fragen.

MODEL: Habt ihr den Flug verpasst?
         <u>Nein, aber wir hätten ihn beinahe verpasst.</u>

1. Hattet ihr einen Autounfall?
2. Habt ihr das Hotel nicht gefunden?
3. Sabine, hast du deinen Pass vergessen?
4. Seid ihr zur Insel Mainau gefahren?
5. Habt ihr vor dem Rückflug verschlafen?
6. Haben die Roths euch getroffen?

B. Now make five statements about things that almost happened to you or others. Follow the format of **A**.

§3   Tentative and Polite Statements and Questions

In German, the subjunctive is frequently used to make statements and pose questions in a more tentative, modest, or polite way. Compare

INDICATIVE   Ich **rate** Ihnen diese dumme Bemerkung zu ignorieren.
               I advise you to ignore this stupid remark.

SUBJUNCTIVE   Ich **würde** Ihnen **raten** diese dumme Bemerkung zu ignorieren.
               I would advise you to ignore this stupid remark.

The use of the subjunctive **würde** + **raten** in the second sentence makes the statement more tentative. It expresses the advice with modesty and caution in contrast to the somewhat blunt tone of the first sentence. This distinction is clear in the two English sentences above. However, subjunctive constructions occur more frequently in German than in English. They often have to be rendered into English with indicative forms, as the following examples illustrate:

Wir **hätten** also wieder einmal Glück **gehabt**.
So we have been lucky again.

Damit **hätte** ich endlich mein Ziel **erreicht**.
With that, I have finally achieved my goal.

Questions are frequently made more polite by using the subjunctive. Compare

INDICATIVE	SUBJUNCTIVE
Haben Sie einen Zettel für mich?	**Hätten** Sie einen Zettel für mich?
Do you have a piece of paper for me?	*Would you have a piece of paper for me?*
Ist Ihnen das recht?	**Wäre** Ihnen das recht?
Is that OK with you?	*Would that be OK with you?*
Können Sie einen Augenblick warten?	**Könnten** Sie einen Augenblick warten?
Can you wait a moment?	*Could you wait a moment?*
Tun Sie mir diesen Gefallen?	**Würden** Sie mir diesen Gefallen tun?
Are you going to do me this favor?	*Would you do me this favor?*

Note that the **würde** + infinitive forms are used with most verbs other than **haben**, **sein**, **wissen** and the modals.

Übung 13-3

ANWENDEN Express the requests more politely.

MODEL: Passen Sie ein paar Minuten auf meine Sachen auf?
         Würden Sie ein paar Minuten auf meine Sachen aufpassen?

Im Büro einer Tageszeitung bittet Bruno seine Mitarbeiter um verschiedene Dinge.

1. Anke, hilfst du mir mit dem Computer?
2. Herr Krause, zeigen Sie mir Ihren Artikel?
3. Kurt, bring mir doch einen Kaffee!

4. Frau Rosbacher, können wir das Interview besprechen?
5. Kurt und Sabine, sollen wir uns erst morgen treffen?
6. Herr Zahn, haben Sie eine Diskette für mich?

Übung 13-4

ZUSAMMENFASSUNG Various uses of the subjunctive.

A. Formulate polite requests and questions appropriate to the different situations. Use the verbs in parentheses.

1. Sie haben einen schweren Koffer und brauchen Hilfe. (können)
2. Sie sind in einem Kaufhaus und suchen die Sportabteilung. (würden)
3. Sie sind in einem Café und möchten einen Kaffee. (könnten)
4. Ihre Freundin soll Sie morgen anrufen. (möchten)
5. Sie wissen nicht, ob Ihre Eltern nächstes Wochenende zu Hause sind. (sein)
6. Zwei Nachbarn sollen Ihre Blumen gießen, während Sie unterwegs sind. (könnten)

B. Complete these personalized questions.

1. Was gefällt Ihnen an bestimmten Freunden und Freundinnen von Ihnen nicht? (drei Sätze)
    Ich wollte, _____(Name)…
    Ich wünschte, _____ (Name)...
2. Welche Wünsche haben Sie im Moment? Nennen Sie drei Dinge.

MODEL: Ich wollte, ich hätte mehr Zeit für meine Freunde!

3. Haben Sie in letzter Zeit etwas getan oder gesagt, was Sie jetzt bereuen? Nennen Sie drei Dinge.

MODEL: Ich wollte, ich wäre nicht so schnell gefahren!

4. Hätten Sie diesen Monat beinahe etwas gekauft? Was?
5. Hätten Sie beinahe etwas vergessen oder etwas verpasst? Was?
6. Hätte ein Freund beinahe etwas vergessen? Was?
7. Wären Sie letztes Jahr beinahe irgenwohin gefahren? Wohin?

Using the Indicative and Subjunctive in Indirect Discourse

Compare the following direct and indirect quotes:

Mrs. Stern said, "My husband is depressed." (direct quote)
Mrs. Stern said her husband was depressed. (indirect quote)

In indirect discourse, one person reports what another has said without quoting him/her directly. In the example, the possessive *my* changed to *her*. The verb tense was also shifted in the indirect quote. If the introductory statement (Mrs. Stern said) has a past time form, *is* may change to *was* in the indirect quote.

In German, indirect discourse may be expressed in the indicative or in the subjunctive. Native speakers of German choose indicative or subjunctive forms according to what they want to imply and what they feel would sound right in a given context. Even native speakers, however, may use indicative and subjunctive somewhat haphazardly. This can be quite puzzling to those who study German as a foreign language. Not yet being able to resort to a German **"Sprachgefühl"** (*feeling for the language*), they need some rules and guidelines as a basis to work with. The following detailed explanations are designed to provide it.

Indirect discourse is treated somewhat differently in informal German (everyday speech, informal writing) than in formal German (literary works, lectures, papers, official statements).

§4   Informal German Using the Indicative

When speakers use the indicative to report what someone has said, they indicate that they do not doubt the correctness of what they are reporting.

Compare the following German direct and indirect quotes with the previous English example:

> Frau Stern sagte: „**Mein** Mann ist deprimiert." (direct quote)
> Frau Stern sagte, **ihr** Mann **ist** deprimiert. (indirect quote)
> > or: **dass ihr** Mann deprimiert ist.

Note: a. As in English, the possessive changes from **mein** to **ihr**. But, unlike English, the time of the verb is not shifted. In German, an indirect quote normally uses the same time as the direct quote, regardless of the tense in the introductory statement.

b. A direct quote is preceded by a colon. The opening quotation mark is not raised. Indirect quotes are separated from opening statements by a comma, and never use quotation marks.

c. Indirect quotes in the indicative are often introduced by **dass**, which helps to make clear that the quote is indirect.

These additional examples illustrate that the tense of the direct quote is usually retained in the indirect quote.

> Köhlers sagen: „**Unsere** Kinder arbeiten nicht gern im Garten."
> Köhlers sagen, dass **ihre** Kinder nicht gern im Garten arbeiten.

> Frau Köhler sagte: „**Mein** Mann arbeitet im Garten."
> Frau Köhler sagte, dass **ihr** Mann im Garten arbeitet.

> Herr Köhler hat gesagt: „**Meine** Frau und **ich** haben im Garten gearbeitet."
> Herr Köhler hat gesagt, dass **seine** Frau und **er** im Garten gearbeitet haben.

Übung 13-5

ANWENDEN A. Restate the messages as indirect quotes in the indicative. Follow the model.

> MODEL: Sigrid: „Ich rufe euch Freitagabend an."
> <u>Sigrid hat gesagt, dass sie uns Freitagabend anruft.</u>

Janosch hat den Anrufbeantworter abgehört und gibt seiner Mitbewohnerin Anke verschiedene Nachrichten weiter.

1. Klaus: „Ich hole Sandra um 7 Uhr ab."
2. Elke: „Ich habe Franks Telefonnummer vergessen. Ich brauche sie heute."
3. Frau Berger (Ankes Chefin): „Ich bin nur drei Tage in Hamburg geblieben. Ich bin morgen wieder im Büro."
4. Zimmermanns: „Wir wollen euch dieses Wochenende besuchen. Wir rufen nochmal an."
5. Ankes Mutter: „Alles hat geklappt. Ich bin gut in München angekommen."
6. Uwe: „Ich habe eine neue Stelle gefunden. Ich feiere das am Freitagabend."
7. Waltraud: „Du hast unsere Verabredung vergessen! Ich bin sauer!"

B. Say or write five things someone else told you. Begin each statement with an introductory clause that contains **sagen** or **erzählen**.

Questions are quoted indirectly as follows:

DIRECT QUOTE	INDIRECT QUOTE
Herr Schreiber hat Herrn Köhler gefragt:	Herr Schreiber hat Herrn Köhler gefragt,
a. „Wann arbeiten Sie in Ihrem Garten?"	a. **wann** er in seinem Garten arbeitet.
b. „Arbeiten Sie oft in Ihrem Garten?"	b. **ob** er oft in seinem Garten arbeitet.

> *Note:*   Indirect questions always have dependent word order. They are introduced either by a question word, as in sentence **a.**, or by **ob**, as in sentence **b.**, and they never include quotation marks (cf. Kap. 1 §5.).

Additional example

Ich habe Andreas gefragt:	Ich habe Andreas gefragt,
a. „Warum hast du Renate eingeladen?"	a. **warum** er Renate eingeladen hat.
b. „Hast du Renate eingeladen?"	b. **ob** er Renate eingeladen hat.

Übung 13-6

ANWENDEN Formulate indirect quotations from the direct ones, using the introductory clause provided.

> MODEL: „Kommt Renate heute Abend vorbei?"
> <u>Ich habe Martin gefragt, ob Renate heute Abend vorbeikommt.</u>
> „Warum fährt Renate weg?"
> <u>Ich habe Martin gefragt, warum Renate wegfährt.</u>

Wolfgang wiederholt ein Gespräch mit seinem Freund Martin.

1. „Hat Renate angerufen?"
   Martin hat mich gefragt,...
2. „Wer ist Renate?"
   Dann habe ich Martin gefragt,...
3. „Wo hast du Renate kennengelernt?"
   Und ich habe ihn gefragt,...
4. „Warum willst du das wissen?"
   Martin hat mich gefragt,...
5. „Stellst du Renate deinen Freunden bald vor?"
   Ich habe Martin gefragt,...

§5   Informal German Using the Subjunctive

The subjunctive tends to be used when the reporter has reservations about the validity of what was said or, at least, wants to distance himself or herself from what was said.

In indirect discourse, the subjunctive occurs in three tenses: present, past, and future.

1. The direct quote is in the present tense.

Indirect quotations expressed in the subjunctive are usually not introduced by **dass**. The subjunctive alone suffices to mark the indirect quote.

Sandra hat gesagt:	Sandra hat gesagt,
„Professor Bauer **ist** nicht fair."	Professor Bauer **wäre** nicht fair.
	PRESENT SUBJUNCTIVE

The use of the present subjunctive **wäre** instead of **ist** indicates that the reporter has reservations about the validity of Sandra's statement.

Additional examples

Sie sagte:	Sie sagte,
Ich **habe** Angst.	sie **hätte** Angst.
Ich **kann** das nicht essen.	sie **könnte** das nicht essen.
Ich **werde** verrückt.	sie **würde** verrückt.
Ich **weiß** seinen Namen nicht mehr.	sie **wüsste** seinen Namen nicht mehr.

Übung 13-7

VERSTEHEN Indicate whether the quote restates a fact (indicative) or expresses reservations (subjunctive).

1. Herr Kästner hat gesagt, dass er bei seinen Kinder oft nachgeben muss.
2. Professor Wagner hat gesagt, die Prüfung wäre gar nicht schwer.
3. Margot hat mir gesagt, sie hätte keine Willenskraft.
4. Ihr Freund hat mich angerufen und gesagt, er war krank.

5. Frau Schmidt hat gesagt, sie wüsste nichts davon.
6. Herr Stern hat gesagt, die Kinder würden nie müde.

In informal German, few present subjunctives are used other than those of **haben**, **sein**, **werden**, **wissen**, and the modals. As stated in Kapitel 12 §6, studies have shown that in written informal German (personal letters, diaries, etc.), the following present subjunctives of some strong verbs occur as frequently as their **würde +** infinitive substitutes.

fände	würde finden	hieße	würde heißen
gäbe	würde geben	käme	würde kommen
ginge	würde gehen	ließe	würde lassen
hielte	würde halten	täte	würde tun

The same is true of their compound forms, such as:

gäbe an	würde angeben	käme an	würde ankommen
ginge aus	würde ausgehen	bekäme	würde bekommen

Übung 13-8

ANWENDEN Change the direct quotations to indirect quotations, introducing them with „Alexandra hat geschrieben." First, use the present subjunctive. Then, restate the sentence using **würde +** the infinitive.

Alexandra besucht einen Sommerkurs und hat einen Brief an ihre Mutter geschrieben. Ihre Mutter berichtet Alexandras Oma, was darin stand. (Alexandras Mutter ist nicht sicher, ob alles wirklich stimmt, was Alexandra geschrieben hat.)

MODEL: „Ich gehe selten aus."
          a. Alexandra hat geschrieben, sie ginge selten aus.
          b. Alexandra hat geschrieben, sie würde selten ausgehen.

1. „Und ich komme immer früh nach Hause."
2. „Wir alle finden die Stadt ziemlich langweilig."
3. „Ich lasse mein Auto immer stehen und gehe zu Fuß."
4. „Ich halte nicht viel von Professor Kern."
5. „Er lässt den Studenten wenig Freiheit."
6. „Susanne bekommt nie Geld von ihren Eltern."
7. „Susanne tut mir leid."

2. Because the present subjunctive of weak verbs is identical in form to the past indicative, the **würde +** infinitive substitute is preferred. (cf. Kapitel 12, §4, 3; §5.)

Frau Schneider schrieb: „Mein Mann **bezahlt** alle Rechnungen."
Frau Schneider schrieb, ihr Mann **bezahlte** alle Rechnungen.
                    PAST SUBJUNCTIVE = PAST INDICATIVE
          preferred: ihr Mann **würde** alle Rechnungen **bezahlen**.

3. The direct quote is in the past, present perfect, or past perfect.

The past subjunctive is used in indirect discourse to replace any past tense in the original statement.

Maria hat gesagt:
„Ich **wusste** nichts davon."
„Ich **habe** nichts davon **gewusst**."
„Ich **hatte** nichts davon **gewusst**."

Maria hat gesagt:
sie **hätte** nichts davon **gewusst**.
(PAST SUBJUNCTIVE)
Maria said she had known nothing about it.

Additional examples

Er hat gesagt:
„Ich hatte keine Angst."
„Das war eine Lüge."
„Der Film hat niemand gefallen."
„Viele Leute sind im Kino eingeschlafen."

„Ich musste immer nachgeben."

„Ich wollte es nicht."

Er hat gesagt,
er **hätte** keine Angst **gehabt**.
das **wäre** eine Lüge **gewesen**.
der Film **hätte** niemand **gefallen**.
viele Leute **wären** im Kino **eingeschlafen**.
er **hätte** immer **nachgeben müssen**.
er **hätte** es nicht **gewollt**.

Übung 13-9

ANWENDEN A. Change the following direct quotations to indirect discourse using the subjunctive.

MODEL: Peter: „Ich konnte meinen Chef nicht überzeugen."
          <u>Peter hat gesagt, er hätte seinen Chef nicht überzeugen können.</u>

Viele Gerüchte in der Nachbarschaft.

1. Eine Nachbarin: „Herr Schubert ist gestorben."
2. Eine andere Nachbarin. „Die Familie hat nur sein Geld gewollt."
3. Bauers: „Wir hatten keine Schwierigkeiten mit der Polizei."
4. Sabine: „Thomas hat mir einen Heiratsantrag gemacht."
5. Thomas: „Sabine hat mich missverstanden."
6. Renate: „Mein Freund hat gelogen."
7. Und ihr Freund: „Ich habe das nur zum Spass gesagt."
8. Frau Müller: „Wir wollten in Berlin ein Haus kaufen."

B. State five things others have told you that you consider to be rumors.

4. The direct quote is in the future tense.

So far, the **würde** + infinitive form of the main verb has been used as a substitute for the present subjunctive; however, as mentioned in Kap. 12 §5, these forms are actually the future subjunctive. They are used as such in indirect discourse.

Frau Morgenstern hat gesagt:	Frau Morgenstern hat gesagt,
„Ich **werde** das bei der Polizei **melden**."	sie **würde** das bei der Polizei **melden**.
	Mrs. Morgenstern said she would
	report that to the police.

The use of the future subjunctive does not necessarily imply having reservations about what was said. It is virtually required if the event has already happened when reported.

Rainer und Monika haben im Juni geheiratet.
Sie haben mir schon im Februar gesagt, sie **würden** im Juni heiraten.

Übung 13-10

ANWENDEN A. Change the following direct quotations to indirect discourse using the future subjunctive.

Versprechen von Politikern.

1. Der Kanzler sagte: „Ich werde die Steuern senken."
2. Die Abgeordneten haben gesagt: „Wir werden protestieren."
3. Der Finanzminister sagte: „Ich werde den Kanzler unterstützen."
4. Der Außenminister hat gesagt: „Die Delegation wird den Besuch verschieben."
5. Der Kandidat hat gesagt: „Wir werden gewinnen."

B. Look in a newspaper and choose five statements made by politicians about the future. Rewrite these statements in German indirect discourse.

Keep the following two uses of **würde** + infinitive in mind:

würde + infinitive = subjunctive in the future tense

Bettina sagte: „Ich **werde** Holger bei den Hausaufgaben **helfen**."
FUTURE INDICATIVE

Bettina sagte, sie **würde** Holger bei den Hausaufgaben **helfen**.
FUTURE SUBJUNCTIVE

würde + infinitive = substitute for present subjunctive

Bettina sagte: „Ich **helfe** Holger bei den Hausaufgaben."
PRESENT INDICATIVE

Bettina sagte, sie **würde** Holger bei den Hausaufgaben **helfen**.
FUTURE SUBJUNCTIVE

Bettina sagte, sie **würde** Holger bei den Hausaufgaben **helfen**.
SUBSTITUTE FOR THE OBSOLETE PRESENT SUBJUNCTIVE **HÜLFE**

Remember: The **würde** + infinitive forms may refer to the present or future. Their meaning has to be derived from context.

Indirect reporting of commands

Commands are reported in indirect discourse with the modal **sollen**. Either the indicative or the subjunctive may be used; the latter option does not imply having reservations.

> Bitte rufen Sie mich an!
> Er hat mir gesagt, ich **soll** ihn anrufen. (indicative)
>   or: ich **sollte** ihn anrufen. (subjunctive)
>   *He told me I should call him.*
> or: *He told me to call him.*

In English, indirect commands are frequently expressed with the infinitive, as in the example above. German does not have this option.

Übung 13-11

ANWENDEN Complete the sentences with an indirect command that is equivalent to the direct command given.

> MODEL: „Habt keine Angst!"
>   <u>Herr Rauscher hat den Kindern gesagt,</u>
>   <u>dass sie keine Angst haben sollen/sollten.</u>

Herr Rauscher verteilt Ratschläge und bekommt selbst einige.

1. „Seid fleißig!"
   Herr Rauscher hat den Schülern gesagt,...
2. „Versuchen Sie es noch einmal!"
   Er hat seinem Chef gesagt,...
3. „Rauchen Sie nicht soviel!"
   Die Ärztin hat Herrn Rauscher geraten,...
4. „Gib die Hoffnung nicht auf!"
   Er hat seiner Tochter gesagt,...
5. „Glaubt diese Gerüchte nicht!"
   Er hat den Nachbarn gesagt,...
6. „Rede nicht so viel!"
   Seine Frau hat ihm geraten,...

§6 Indirect Discourse in Formal German

Indirect discourse in formal German is normally a matter of noncommittal reporting requiring the subjunctive. Here the subjunctive forms merely denote indirectness of speech, and not reservations as to what is reported.

So far, only the forms of the general subjunctive have been used. Formal German uses the forms of the special subjunctive in indirect discourse, but only where they are not identical to indicative forms. If they are identical, the general subjunctive is used, as the following paradigms illustrate.

1. Present Subjunctive

The forms of the special subjunctive are based on the stem of the infinitive.

Example: sprechen (spricht), sprach, hat gesprochen

SPECIAL SUBJUNCTIVE	GENERAL SUBJUNCTIVE
subjunctive endings added to infinitive stem **sprech-**	subjunctive endings added to past tense stem **sprach** + umlaut
ich spreche	ich spräche
du sprechest	du sprächest
er sie→spreche es	er sie→spräche es
wir sprechen	wir sprächen
ihr sprechet	ihr sprächet
sie sprechen	sie sprächen
Sie sprechen	Sie sprächen

Some forms of the special subjunctive are identical to present indicative forms and hence cannot be readily recognized as subjunctive. These forms are replaced by forms of the general subjunctive, as indicated by the arrows in the following table.

INDICATIVE		SPECIAL SUBJUNCTIVE	GENERAL SUBJUNCTIVE
ich spreche	identical to	(ich spreche) ——→	ich spräche
du sprichst		du sprechest	du sprächest
er sie→spricht es		er sie→spreche es	er sie→spräche es
wir sprechen	identical to	(wir sprechen) ——→	wir sprächen
ihr sprecht		ihr sprechet	ihr sprächet
sie sprechen	identical to	(sie sprechen) ——→	sie sprächen
Sie sprechen	identical to	(Sie sprechen) ——→	Sie sprächen

Der Konsul sagte: „Meine Frau **spricht** zwei Fremdsprachen und meine Kinder **sprechen** sogar drei Fremdsprachen."

Der Konsul sagte, seine Frau **spreche** zwei Fremdsprachen und seine Kinder **sprächen** sogar drei Fremdsprachen.

Roughly ninety percent of the subjunctives used in formal indirect discourse are either third-person singular or third-person plural. The special subjunctive is used in the third-person singular, while the general subjunctive replaces it in the third-person plural.

	SPECIAL SUBJUNCTIVE	GENERAL SUBJUNCTIVE
machen	er sie ⟩mache es	sie machten
geben	gebe	gäben
gehen	gehe	gingen
haben	habe	hätten
werden	werde	würden
wissen	wisse	wüssten
können	könne	könnten

stem of infinitive + **e**

Exception: All forms of the special subjunctive of **sein** differ from the indicative forms and are not replaced by the general subjunctive **wäre**.

PRESENT INDICATIVE	PRESENT SPECIAL SUBJUNCTIVE
ich bin	ich **sei**
du bist	du **sei(e)st**
er	er
sie ist	sie **sei**
es	es
wir ⟩sind	wir ⟩**seien**
ihr seid	ihr **seiet**
sie sind	sie **seien**
Sie sind	Sie **seien**

Note: ich **sei**⟶
er, sie, es **sei** ⟶ no -**e** added to the stem of the infinitive
The **e** in **seiest** is generally omitted.

Using the special subjunctive of **sein**

> Der Direktor sagte: „Das ist ein großes Problem, aber meine Mitarbeiter sind sehr optimistisch, dass sie es lösen können."
> Der Direktor sagte, das **sei** ein großes Problem, aber seine Mitarbeiter **seien** sehr optimistisch, dass sie es lösen könnten.

Übung 13-12

ANWENDEN Change the following direct quotations to indirect discourse. Begin each sentence with **Sie sagte,...**

MODEL: „Man kann die Unzufriedenheit der Arbeiter verstehen."
<u>Sie sagte, man könne die Unzufriedenheit der Arbeiter verstehen.</u>

Frau Petri, eine Kommentatorin im Fernsehen, hat über die Probleme der Firma Motiva berichtet.

1. „Die Firma Motiva hat finanzielle Schwierigkeiten, aber andere Firmen haben noch größere Schwierigkeiten."

2. „Die Spannung zwischen dem Chef und seinen Mitarbeitern wird immer
   größer, und die Debatten werden immer länger."
3. „Der Chef ist nicht diplomatisch, und seine Mitarbeiter sind es auch nicht."
4. „Der Chef und die Arbeiter müssen zusammenarbeiten."
5. „Der Chef weiß das und die Arbeiter wissen das auch."
6. „Man muss solche Probleme in Ruhe besprechen."

2. Past Subjunctive

The auxiliary **haben** uses the special subjunctive in the third-person singular
and the general subjunctive in the third person plural. The auxiliary **sein** uses
the special subjunctive in both forms.

	THIRD-PERSON SINGULAR **special subjunctive**	THIRD-PERSON PLURAL **general subjunctive**
verbs requiring **haben**	er sie →habe vergessen es	sie hätten vergessen
	habe gehabt habe fahren können habe gekonnt	hätten gehabt hätten fahren können hätten gekonnt
	special subjunctive	**special subjunctive**
verbs requiring **sein**	er sie →sei gefahren es	sie seien gefahren
	sei gewesen sei geworden	seien gewesen seien geworden

DIRECT QUOTE IN ANY PAST TENSE	INDIRECT QUOTE IN THE PAST SUBJUNCTIVE
Sie sagten:	Sie sagten,
„Wir waren in großer Gefahr."	sie **seien** in großer Gefahr **gewesen**.
„Niemand konnte uns helfen."	niemand **habe** ihnen **helfen können**.
„Zwei Polizisten haben es versucht."	zwei Polizisten **hätten** es **versucht**.

Übung 13-13

ANWENDEN Change the following direct quotations to indirect discourse, using the
special subjunctive wherever possible.

MODEL: „Man konnte nicht alles verstehen, was der Zeuge sagte."
         <u>Sie hat behauptet, man habe nicht alles verstehen können, was der
         Zeuge gesagt habe.</u>

In der Zeitung erscheint ein Bericht über einen Prozess.

1. „Die zwei Zeugen haben sich widersprochen."
   Der Richter erklärte,...
2. „Ich bin die ganze Zeit in meinem Wagen geblieben."
   Ein Zeuge sagte,...

3. „Ich bin schnell über die Straße gelaufen."
   Dann sagte er,...
4. „Der Mann hat eine Sonnenbrille getragen."
   Der andere Zeuge sagte,...
5. „Ich habe den Mann nur von hinten gesehen."
   Später sagte er,...
6. „Ich habe den Prozess verloren, weil die Zeugen ihre Aussagen geändert
   haben."
   Die Rechtsanwältin betonte,...

3. Future Subjunctive

The auxiliary **werden** uses the special subjunctive in the third-person singular
and the general subjunctive in the third-person plural.

SPECIAL SUBJUNCTIVE	GENERAL SUBJUNCTIVE
er sie →**werde** fahren es	sie **würden** fahren
Die Direktorin sagte: „Ich werde den Fall klären. Meine Mitarbeiter werden den Fall klären."	Die Direktorin sagte, sie **werde** den Fall klären. ihre Mitarbeiter **würden** den Fall klären.

Übung 13-14

ANWENDEN Change the following direct quotations to indirect discourse.

Zwischen der Bürgermeisterin und dem Stadtrat besteht ein Konflikt.

1. „Die Bürgermeisterin wird zurücktreten."
   Ein Stadtrat kommentierte,...
2. „Viele Stadträte werden das begrüßen."
   Ein anderer prophezeite,...
3. „Ich werde im Amt bleiben."
   Die Bürgermeisterin erklärte,...
4. „Wir werden die Bürgermeisterin unterstützen."
   Viele Bürger der Stadt sagten,...

Indirect reporting of questions

The rules for use of the subjunctive in formal indirect discourse apply to questions as
well as to statements. Note that dependent word order is required.

Die Reporterin fragte:	Die Reporterin fragte,
„Wann ist der Unfall passiert?"	wann der Unfall passiert **sei**.
„Hat man die Polizei informiert?"	ob man die Polizei informiert **habe**.
„Ist der Fahrer an dem Unfall schuld?"	ob der Fahrer an dem Unfall schuld **sei**.

Indirect reporting of commands

The special subjunctive of **sollen** is used in the singular and the general subjunctive is used in the plural.

> „Bitte stören Sie mich nicht!"
> Sie sagte ihm, er **solle** sie nicht stören.

> She told him ⎯⎯⎯ he should not disturb her.
>   ⎯⎯⎯ not to disturb her.

> Sie sagte ihnen, sie **sollten** sie nicht stören.

> She told him ⎯⎯⎯ they should not disturb her.
>   ⎯⎯⎯ not to disturb her.

Longer indirect quotations

In German, lengthy statements may be quoted indirectly by using the subjunctive. In English, remarks such as *he continued*, *he also mentioned*, or *he stated further* have to be added as reminders to the listener or reader to indicate that the indirect quotation continues. This is not necessary in German, because the subjunctive itself signals the continuation of the indirect quote. Compare

> A direct quotation by councilman Schmidt:

> „Die Sitzung war sehr stürmisch. Der Bürgermeister und die Stadträte führten lange Debatten. Man konnte sich nicht einigen, und der Bürgermeister drohte mit seinem Rücktritt."

> The newspaper account of his statement:

> Stadtrat Schmidt sagte, die Sitzung **sei** sehr stürmisch **gewesen**. Der Bürgermeister und die Stadträte **hätten** lange Debatten **geführt**. Man **habe** sich nicht **einigen können**, und der Bürgermeister **habe** mit seinem Rücktritt **gedroht**.

Übung 13-15

ANWENDEN Change the direct quotations to indirect discourse using the introductory clauses provided.

1. „Stadtrat Schubert hatte eine geniale Idee. Sein Vorschlag war ein Kompromiss. Der Bürgermeister und die Stradträte fanden diesen Kompromiss akzeptabel."
   Die Reporterin sagte,...
2. „Die Debatte mit meinen Mitarbeitern hat mich sehr enttäuscht. Zwei Mitarbeiter sind nicht objektiv geblieben. Ich musste die Diskussion abbrechen."
   Die Chefin sagte,...

3. „Der Vortrag war hochinteressant. Die Rednerin sprach über die politischen und wirtschaftlichen Probleme Chinas. Am Schluss stellten einige Zuhörer Fragen. Leider konnte die Rednerin nur kurz darauf antworten."
Der Journalist schrieb,...

§7 Final Remarks on the Use of the Indicative and Subjunctive in Indirect Discourse

1. As discussed, informal indirect discourse is expressed in the indicative when the person providing the account has no doubt about the validity of what is reported. The general subjunctive is used in cautious reporting, usually when the speaker has reservations about what was said.

2. In formal German, the subjunctive is normally required for indirect discourse. The special subjunctive is used unless it is identical to the indicative, in which case the general subjunctive is substituted.

However, the indicative is used in the following cases:

a. When quoting oneself, because one is usually willing to vouch for one's own claims

Ich sagte vor Gericht: „Der Polizist hat mich missverstanden."
Ich sagte vor Gericht, **dass** der Polizist mich missverstanden **hat**.

b. When reporting something that is undeniably true

Galilei hat als Erster gesagt, **dass** sich die Erde um die Sonne **bewegt**.

In order to distinguish the indirect quote from the direct quote, a **dass**-clause is normally used.

3. Subjunctives in original statements are retained in both formal and informal indirect discourse.

Frau Morgenstern sagte: „Ich **möchte** Architektin werden."
Frau Morgenstern sagte, sie **möchte** Architektin werden.

Herr Morgenstern sagte: „Wenn meine Frau Architektin **wäre**, **würden** wir in einem Palast wohnen."
Herr Morgenstern sagte, wenn seine Frau Architektin **wäre**, **würden** sie in einem Palast wohnen.

§8 Other Uses of the Special Subjunctive

The special subjunctive is found chiefly in formal indirect discourse. Otherwise, it is rarely used. All of the following examples are in the third-person singular, and except for **sei**, they all end in -**e**.

1. Set phrases

wie dem auch sei   *be that as it may*

Dieses Problem ist sehr kompliziert und schwer zu lösen. **Wie dem auch sei**, eine
  Lösung muss gefunden werden.
This problem is very complicated and hard to solve. Be that as it may, a solution
  must be found.

es sei denn   *unless*

Sie sollte das nicht tun, **es sei denn**, sie kann einfach nicht anders.
She shouldn't do that unless she simply can't help it.

Komme, was wolle.   *Come what may.*

Komme, was wolle, ich lasse mich nicht umwerfen.
Come what may, I won't let it throw me.

2. Set wishes

Es lebe die Freiheit!   *Long live freedom!*
Er lebe hoch!   *Hooray for him!*

3. General imperatives, usually with the indefinite pronoun **man** as subject

Man täusche sich nicht.   *One shouldn't deceive oneself.*
                        Don't deceive yourself.

Beim Einnehmen dieser Tabletten **folge man** den Anweisungen des Arztes.
When taking these tablets, follow your doctor's instructions.

Man nehme ein Pfund Mehl und ein halbes Pfund Zucker.
Use a pound of flour and half a pound of sugar.

Remember: Apart from formal indirect discourse, the special subjunctive occurs
only in a few expressions and in general imperatives with **man**.

Themen und Vokabular

Vorwände

aus•sehen als ob, sah...aus, hat ausgesehen	*to look as if*
sich etwas ein•bilden	*to exist in one's imagination*
das Gerücht, -e	*rumor*
klingen als ob, klang, hat geklungen	*to sound as if*
scheinen als ob, schien, hat geschienen	*to seem as if*
tun als ob, tat, hat getan	*act as if*
jemand (dat.) vor•kommen als ob, kam...vor, ist vorgekommen	*to appear to someone as if*

Das Gesetz

die Aussage, -n	*testimony*
ändern	*to change*
das Gericht	*court of law*
vor Gericht	*in court*
formulieren	*to phrase*
der Prozess, -e	*trial*
den Prozess verlieren, verlor, hat verloren	*to lose the case*
der Rechtsanwalt, ¨e	*lawyer (m.)*
die Rechtsanwältin, -nen	*lawyer (f.)*
der Richter, -	*judge (m.)*
die Richterin, -nen	*judge (f.)*
(sich) widersprechen, widersprach, hat widersprochen	*to contradict (oneself)*
der Zeuge, -n (weak noun)	*witness (m.)*

die Zeugin, -nen	*witness (f.)*

Die Politik

der/die Abgeordnete, -n	*representative*
der Bürgermeister, -	*mayor (m.)*
die Bürgermeisterin, -nen	*mayor (f.)*
drohen	*to threaten*
der Rücktritt, -e	*resignation*
mit dem Rücktritt drohen	*to threaten to resign*
der Stradtrat, ¨e	*town councilor, councilman (m.)*
die Stadträtin, -nen	*town councilor, councilman (f.) (also: city council)*
zurück-treten (tritt zurück) trat zurück, ist zurückgetreten	*to resign*

Zitieren

aus•sagen	*to state, make a statement*
behaupten	*to claim*
betonen	*to emphasize, stress*
erklären	*to explain*
erzählen	*to tell, narrate*
informieren über	*to inform about*
(jemand [dat.] etwas) mit•teilen	*to share, tell*
prophezeien	*to prophesy, predict*
sagen	*to say*
das Zitat, -e	*citation, quote*
zitieren	*to cite, quote*

14 der-Words and ein-Words as Pronouns; Indefinite Pronouns; Relative Clauses

der-Words and ein-Words Used as Pronouns

§1 der-Words Used as Pronouns

The definite article denotes the gender, number, and case of nouns; it is a *determiner*.

The **der**-words, **dieser**, **jeder**, **jener**, **mancher**, **solcher**, **welcher**, **alle**, and **beide**, function much like the definite article and are also referred to as determiners when they precede nouns. When they stand alone, they function as pronouns. In either case, they have the same endings.

DETERMINER	PRONOUN
Welchen Wagen wollen Sie kaufen?	**Welchen** wollen Sie kaufen?
Which car do you want to buy?	*Which one do you want to buy?*
Jeder Student ist dagegen.	**Jeder** ist dagegen.
Every student is against it.	*Everyone is against it.*

§2 der, das, die Used as Demonstrative Pronouns

When used as *demonstrative pronouns*, that is, as pronouns that distinguish one person or thing from another, **der**, **das**, **die** are declined as follows:

	MASCULINE	NEUTER	FEMININE	PLURAL
NOMINATIVE	der	das	die	die
ACCUSATIVE	den	das	die	die
DATIVE	dem	dem	der	**denen**
GENITIVE	**dessen**	**dessen**	**deren**	**deren**

The forms in boldface differ from the forms of the definite article. The genitive singular and plural and the dative plural have the long forms **dessen**, **deren**, and **denen**.

The demonstrative pronouns occur frequently in informal German.

1. Pointing out persons and things

In informal German, *this one* and *that one* (plural: *these* and *those*) are generally expressed by **der**, **das**, **die + hier** (close to the speaker) or **+ da** (more distant from the speaker). The pronoun is always stressed and always reflects the gender, number, function, and case of the noun it refers to, called the *antecedent*.

(direct object)
Welches <u>Bild</u> gefällt dir besser? **Das hier** oder **das da**?
ANTECEDENT   *This one or that one?*

(object of dative preposition)
Mit welchem <u>Mechaniker</u> hast du gesprochen? Mit **dem hier** oder mit **dem da**?
ANTECEDENT   *With this one or with that one?*

Übung 14-1

ANWENDEN Respond to each question with an appropriate answer that contains the correct forms of **der**, **das**, **die + hier** or **+ da**. Use various introductory clauses, such as **Ich weiß nicht genau, ob…**; **Ich bin nicht sicher, ob…**.

MODEL: (Im Zentrum) In welchem Geschäft gibt es Levis Jeans?
<u>Ich weiß nicht, ob es sie in dem hier oder in dem da gibt.</u>

Karla und Vera erledigen einiges zusammen in der Stadt. In verschiedenen Situationen gibt es Fragen.

1. (*Im Zentrum*) Karla, in welchen Laden willst du gehen?
2. (*Im Kaufhaus*) Welches Kleid willst du denn kaufen?
3. (*Sie fragen eine Verkäuferin*) Entschuldigung, welche Strümpfe sind im Sonderangebot?
4. (*Sie stehen vor zwei Restaurants*) In welchem Restaurant hast du letzte Woche gegessen, Vera?
5. (*Im Restaurant*) Und welcher Kellner hat dich letztes Mal bedient?
6. (*An der Straßenbahnhaltestelle*) Welche Straßenbahn müssen wir Richtung Stadtmitte nehmen?
7. (*In der Straßenbahn*) Welchen Fahrschein soll ich stempeln?

2. Third-person pronouns

Conversational German frequently uses **der**, **das**, and **die** as third-person pronouns. They may be stressed or unstressed and are translated into English with the usual third-person pronouns. The stressed pronouns are frequently placed at the beginning of main clauses.

In the following examples, stress is indicated by underlining:

Herr Müller	kann uns nicht helfen.
Er	kann uns nicht helfen.
Der	kann uns nicht helfen.
or: **Der**	
He	*cannot help us.*

Ich spreche nicht mehr mit	diesen Leuten.
Ich spreche nicht mehr mit	ihnen.
Ich spreche nicht mehr mit	**denen**.

or: Mit **denen** spreche ich nicht mehr.
I don't talk to them any more.

Übung 14-2

ANWENDEN   A. Respond to each question with two sentences. First, replace the object with a personal pronoun. Then replace the personal pronoun with an article used as a pronoun.

MODEL: Triffst du dich oft mit deinen Nachbarn? (ja)
<u>Ja, ich treffe mich oft mit ihnen.</u>
<u>Mit denen treffe ich mich oft.</u>

Nachbarschaftliche Beziehungen.

1. Könnt ihr das Problem in der Nachbarschaft lösen? (ja)
2. Hat Frau Winter ihren Hund gefunden? (nein)
3. Wirst du alle Nachbarn zu deiner Party einladen? (ja)
4. Hast du die Einladungen? (nein)
5. Schreibst du den Einkaufszettel morgen? (ja)

B. Use the cues in parentheses to give an appropriate answer. Provide the correct forms of the demonstrative pronouns for the nouns.

MODEL: Rufst du morgen Andreas an? (nie wieder)
<u>Nein, d e n rufe ich nie wieder an.</u>

Kurt und Walter unterhalten sich über verschiedene Leute. Walter äußert seine Meinungen.

1. Wie verstehst du dich mit Ruth? (gut)
2. Lädst du Franziska zu deiner Party ein? (bestimmt)
3. Hast du Post von Monika bekommen? (schon lange nicht mehr)
4. Geht Monika noch mit Udo aus? (nie wieder)
5. Vermisst du deine Eltern? (selten)
6. Sprichst du oft mit deinen Nachbarn? (selten)

3. Alternatives to **da**-Compounds

Normally pronoun objects of prepositions that refer to inanimate objects are replaced by **da**-compounds (cf. Kap. 7 §9).

Er ist stolz **auf seinen Sportwagen.**
Er ist stolz **darauf.**

However, when speakers wish to emphasize the pronoun, they have two choices. They may stress the **da**-element

<u>Darauf</u> ist er stolz.

or use a demonstrative pronoun as the object of the preposition

Auf <u>den</u> ist er stolz.

The second option is even more emphatic than the stressed **da**-compound.

Übung 14-3

ANWENDEN Respond to the following sentences using the preposition + an appropriate demonstrative pronoun.

MODEL: Interessierst du dich für diesen neuen Film?
<u>Ja, für d e n interessiere ich mich sehr.</u>
or: <u>Nein, für d e n interessiere ich mich überhaupt nicht.</u>

1. Ist Anneliese von diesem Buch begeistert?
2. Hast du über die letzte Seinfeld-Episode laut gelacht?
3. Bist du auf diese neue Musikgruppe ganz verrückt?
4. Hat Jürgen viel für diese CD bezahlt?
5. Haben deine Freunde mit diesem Videospiel gern gespielt?

4. Special use of the genitive forms **dessen** and **deren**

Hans, sein Freund Peter und **dessen** Schwester Barbara haben uns besucht.
Hans, his friend Peter, and the latter's sister Barbara visited us.

Seine Schwester would leave the question open as to whether Barbara is the sister of Hans or of Peter. **Dessen** (*the latter's*) makes it clear that she is Peter's sister. The gender and number of **dessen** is determined by the possessor, i.e., Peter; thus the masculine singular is used.

Additional examples

Helga, Margot und **deren** Schwester / **deren** Bruder
Helga, Margot, and the latter's sister / the latter's brother

Margot is the possessor, thus the feminine singular is used.

Schmidts, Müllers und **deren** Sohn / **deren** Tochter
The Smiths, the Müllers, and the latter's son / the latter's daughter

The Müllers are the possessors, thus the plural form is used.

The genitive pronouns, **dessen** and **deren**, are not influenced in any way by the cases of the nouns that follow them.

Wir sind mit <u>dem Opa</u>, <u>Elke</u> und **deren** <u>Brüdern</u> nach Wien gefahren.
DATIVE   DATIVE   GENITIVE DATIVE

Übung 14-4

ANWENDEN A. Restate the relationships between the people (and their pets) using **dessen** or **deren**.

MODEL: Hans, Martin und die Freundin von Martin waren gestern zusammen im Kino.
<u>Hans, Martin und dessen Freundin</u>

1. Barbara und Hannelore gehen mit dem Hund spazieren. Der Hund gehört Hannelore.
2. Frau Zimmermann und die Körners machen ein Picknick im Park. Die zwei Kinder von Körners sind auch dabei.
3. Das Geschenk ist von Monika und Renate. Die Eltern von Renate haben auch etwas Geld beigesteuert.
4. Wolfgang, sein Bruder und seine Schwägerin, also die Frau von Wolfgang, haben uns besucht.

B. Think of three groups of people you know and describe what they recently did together. State their relationships to one another using **dessen** and **deren**.

§3 *ein*-Words Used as Pronouns

The **ein**-words (**ein**, **kein**, and the possessives) are determiners when preceding nouns, but pronouns when standing alone.

1. ein and kein

DETERMINER	PRONOUN
Ist das **ein** Fehler?	Ja, das ist **einer**. *Yes, that is one.*
	Nein, das ist **keiner**. *No, that isn't one.*
Ist das **ein** Problem?	Ja, das ist **ein(e)s**.
	Nein, das ist **kein(e)s**.
Ist das **eine** Warnung?	Ja, das ist **eine**.
	Nein, das ist **keine**.

Used as determiners, the **ein**-words have three forms without endings: the nominative masculine singular, the nominative neuter singular, and the accusative neuter singular. All other forms have the same endings as the **der**-words (cf. Kap. 6 §5).

Used as pronouns, the **ein**-words have the same endings as the **der**-words in all forms, including the nominative masculine singular (-**er**) and the nominative and accusative neuter singular (-**es**, usually shortened to -**s**).

The following table combines the declension of the determiner and the pronoun:

	MASCULINE		FEMININE	NEUTER		PLURAL
NOMINATIVE	ein	einer	eine	ein	ein(e)s	keine
ACCUSATIVE	einen		eine	ein	ein(e)s	keine
DATIVE	einem		einer	einem		keinen
GENITIVE	eines		einer	eines		keiner

Remember: The forms of the determiner and pronoun differ only in three cases in the singular.

Übung 14-5

ANWENDEN Answer the questions using **ein**-words as pronouns and the phrases cued in parentheses.

> MODEL: Wo ist eine Post? (an / Bahnhof)
> <u>Am Bahnhof ist eine.</u>

Ein Fremder fragt Veronika nach verschiedenen Orten in der Stadt.

1. Wo ist bitte ein Supermarkt? (an / der Kirchplatz)
2. Und wo ist ein großer Parkplatz? (außerhalb / die Stadt)
3. Wissen Sie, wo es ein gutes Restaurant gibt? (gegenüber von / der Dom)
4. Und eine Sparkasse? Wo ist eine Sparkasse? (neben / der Supermarkt)
5. Und kennen Sie ein gutes Theater? (mitten in / das Zentrum)

B. Answer the questions both positively and negatively. If you own the item asked about, say who doesn't have one. If you don't own it, say who does.

> MODEL: Haben Sie einen Computer?
> <u>Ja, ich habe einen, aber meine Mutter hat keinen.</u>

1. ein Auto?
2. Ihre eigene Wohnung?
3. ein Mountainbike? (neuter)
4. ein Mobiltelefon? (masculine)
5. eine Videokamera?
6. einen Fernseher?

2. The possessives

The possessives take the same endings as **ein** and **kein**, as the following nominative masculine and neuter forms illustrate:

DETERMINERS		PRONOUNS	
Das ist mein Wagen.	(*my car*)	Das ist mein**er**.	(*mine*)
mein Auto.		mein**(e)s**.	
Das ist dein Wagen.	(*your car*)	Das ist dein**er**.	(*yours*)
dein Auto.		dein**(e)s**.	
Das ist sein Wagen.	(*his car*)	Das ist sein**er**.	(*his*)
sein Auto.		sein**(e)s**.	
Das ist ihr Wagen.	(*her car*)	Das ist ihr**er**.	(*hers*)
ihr Auto.		ihr**(e)s**.	
Das ist unser Wagen.	(*our car*)	Das ist uns(e)r**er**.	(*ours*)
unser Auto.		uns(e)r**es**.	
Das ist euer Wagen.	(*your car*)	Das ist eu(e)r**er**	(*yours*)
euer Auto.		eu(e)r**es**.	
Das ist ihr Wagen.	(*their car*)	Das ist ihr**er**.	(*theirs*)
ihr Auto.		ihr**(e)s**	
Das ist Ihr Wagen.	(*your car*)	Das ist Ihr**er**	(*yours*)
Ihr Auto.		Ihr**(e)s**	

Note: German equivalents of *your* and *yours*:

your car ⟨ **dein** Wagen / **euer** Wagen / **Ihr** Wagen   yours ⟨ **deiner** (familiar singular) / **eu(e)rer** (familiar plural) / **Ihrer** (formal, singular + plural)

The **e** of **unser** and **euer** may be omitted when the ending **-e** or an ending beginning with **-e** is added (cf. Kap. 6 §6).

Übung 14-6

ANWENDEN A. Insert the German equivalents of the pronouns given in parentheses.

Wem gehört was?

1. Hier ist Peters CD-Spieler, (masculine)
   und da drüben ist auch _____. (mine, yours [three forms])
2. Das ist Karins Radio, (neuter)
   und da drüben ist auch _____. (mine, yours [three forms])
3. Die Kamera gehört Herrn Berger,
   und da drüben ist auch _____. (mine, yours [three forms])
4. Das hier sind alle Sachen von Helga,
   und da drüben sind _____. (mine, ours, theirs)
5. Wir fahren nicht mit meinem Wagen;
   fahren wir mit _____! (his, hers)

B. Respond with the appropriate forms of **ein**, **kein**, and the possessives. Include what is in the parentheses.

> MODEL: Hat Frau Rütli ein Glas Wein? (ihr Mann)
> <u>Ja, sie hat eins, aber ihr Mann hat keins.</u>

Bei einer Party kümmern sich Konstanze und Valentin um ihre Gäste.

1. Hat Helmut einen Teller? (seine Eltern)
2. Hat Erika ein Getränk? (ihre Freundin)
3. Hat Herr Lehnert einen Stuhl? (seine Kollegin)
4. Und Frau Horn, hat sie ein Sandwich? (ihr Freund)
5. Und du, hast du ein Bier? (du)

3. The German equivalents of the possessive phrases *of mine, of yours*, etc.

German uses the preposition **von** with the dative case of the personal pronoun to express the English possessive phrases *of mine, of yours*, etc.

He is a friend of mine.	Er ist ein Freund **von mir**.
	(lit.: *He is a friend of me.*)
He is a friend of his.	Er ist ein Freund **von ihm**.
of hers.	**von ihr**.
of ours.	**von uns**.
of theirs.	**von ihnen**.
	— **von dir**.
of yours. ←	— **von euch**.
(three forms)	— **von Ihnen**.

Übung 14-7

ANWENDEN A. Respond by replacing the **von**-phrase in the question with **von** + pronoun. Use pronouns for the other nouns as well. Begin your sentence with the elements given in parentheses.

> MODEL: Ist Gerda eine Bekannte von euch? (ja)
> <u>Ja, sie ist eine Bekannte von uns.</u>

Wer sind all diese Leute?

1. Ist Thomas ein Freund von Barbara? (ich glaube, dass)
2. Sind Schmidts Verwandte von Brauns? (ja)
3. Sind Tim und Lorena gute Freunde von Brauns? (ich bin nicht sicher)
4. Und ist Frederike eine Kollegin von dir? (nein)
5. Frau Paschke, ist Herr Schubert ein Kollege von _____? (ja)

B. Name five people and describe your relationship with each.

> MODEL: Matthew ist ein Kollege von mir in meinem Deutschkurs.
> Zoe ist eine gute Freundin von uns.

Indefinite Pronouns

§4   Uses of *man, jemand,* and *niemand*

1. man

The English equivalents of **man** may be *one, you, they,* or *people,* depending on the context.

Man weiß das nicht im voraus.	**One** *doesn't know that beforehand.*
	You *don't know that beforehand.*
Man hat mich gewarnt.	**They** *warned me.*
	People *warned me.*

The form **man** exists only in the nominative case as a third person subject pronoun. For the accusative and dative, **einen** and **einem** are used instead.

Diese Unsicherheit macht **einen** nervös.
This insecurity makes one (you, people) nervous.

Frau Braun dankt **einem** nie.
Ms. Braun never thanks you (anyone).

Sein is used as the possessive of **man**.

Man sollte immer **seine** Meinung sagen.
One should always speak one's mind.

In English, a second occurrence of **one** is sometimes replaced by *he*. This cannot be done in German.

If one wants to help, one/he/she will find a way.
Wenn **man** helfen will, findet **man** einen Weg.

Expressions: **Man** kann nie wissen.   *One never knows.*
You never know.

Er kann **einem** leid tun. *One feels sorry for him.*
I feel sorry for him.
Das tut **man** nicht!   *People don't do that!*

Übung 14-8

ANWENDEN Respond to the following sentences substituting **man**, **einen**, or **einem** for the pronouns and making all other necessary changes.

Remember that **man** only occurs in the nominative case, i.e., as the subject of a sentence.

MODEL: Können wir unsere Kinder ins Museum mitbringen?
          <u>Ja, man kann Kinder mitbringen.</u>

Christa und Franz bekommen Besuch. Am Telefon stellen ihnen die Besucher viele Fragen.

1. Kommen wir von der Autobahn gut in die Stadt?
2. Können wir dort schön spazieren gehen?
3. Brauchen wir einen Stadtplan?
4. Macht uns das Wetter vielleicht müde?
5. Christa, hilft es dir, wenn Gäste etwas kochen?
6. Freut es euch (accusative), wenn Gäste kommen?
7. Tut es euch (dative) leid, wenn die Gäste abreisen?

2. jemand and niemand

Jemand (*somebody, someone, anybody, anyone*) and **niemand** (*nobody, no one*) may remain uninflected or take the ending **-en** in the accusative and **-em** in the dative.

Expression: Das geht **niemand(en)** etwas an.
         That is nobody's business.

Note the following use of **jemand** and **niemand** with **anders**:

jemand anders (als)   *somebody/someone else (but)*
niemand anders (als)   *nobody/no one else (but)*

Nicht Frank, sondern **jemand anders** hat mir das erzählt.
Not Frank, but someone else told me that.

Ich habe mit **niemand anders** als Helga darüber gesprochen.
I talked with no one else but Helga about it.

Übung 14-9

ANWENDEN Complete the sentences using the German equivalents of *somebody, nobody* (uninflected forms), and *one*.

Karin ist furchtbar neugierig und fragt ihre Freundin Brigitte über ihr Privatleben.

1. Du fährst nach Berlin. Kennst du dort _____. (somebody)
2. Hast du den Ring von Werner bekommen oder _____? (somebody else)
3. _____, aber warum heiratest du Werner nicht? (it's naturally nobody's business)
4. Hast du _____ darüber gesprochen oder redest du _____? (with somebody else, with nobody)
5. Du kannst _____ wirklich auf die Nerven gehen! (one)
6. _____ kann dir helfen! (nobody)

§5   Uses of *irgend*

1. **Irgend** expresses indefiniteness. It is often used to intensify an indefinite pronoun. Compare the sentence pairs.

> **Jemand** hat das bei der Polizei gemeldet.
> *Someone reported that to the police.*

> **Irgend jemand** hat das bei der Polizei gemeldet.
> *Someone or other reported that to the police.*

> Ich möchte Monika **etwas** geben.
> *I'd like to give Monika something.*

> Ich möchte Monika **irgendetwas** geben.
> *I'd like to give Monika something or other.*

2. **Irgend** may be prefixed to other words.

irgendein *a, some, any* (singular)
irgendwelche *some, any* (plural)

> Haben Sie **irgendeinen** Vorschlag?
> *Do you have any suggestion (at all)?*

> Haben Sie **irgendwelche** Vorschläge?
> *Do you have any suggestions (at all)?*

irgendwann *some time or other, sometime, anytime*

> **Irgendwann** ist sie zur Vernunft gekommen.
> *At some time or other she came to her senses.*

> Hoffentlich sehe ich Sie **irgendwann** mal wieder.
> *I hope to see you again sometime.*

irgendwie *somehow (or other)*

Wir müssen das Problem **irgendwie** lösen.
We have to solve this problem somehow (or other).

irgendwo *somewhere (or other), anywhere* (denoting the place where something occurs)
irgendwohin *somewhere (or other), anywhere* (denoting motion to a place)

Ich habe Hannelore **irgendwo** in der Stadt gesehen.
I saw Hannelore somewhere in town.

Martin fährt morgen **irgendwohin**.
Martin is going somewhere tomorrow.

The negation of **irgendwo** is **nirgendwo** or **nirgends**—*nowhere, not anywhere;* the negation of **irgendwohin** is **nirgend(s)wohin**—*nowhere, not anywhere* (motion to a place).

Wir haben unseren Hund gesucht, konnten ihn aber **nirgends** finden.
We were looking for our dog but couldn't find him anywhere.

Ich fahre dieses Wochenende **nirgendwohin**.
I'm not going anywhere this weekend.

Übung 14-10

ANWENDEN   Create sentences appropriate to the following situations using various **irgend**-prefixed words.

MODEL: Some friends have vacation time, and you want to know if *they are going somewhere.*
<u>Fahrt ihr irgendwohin?</u>

1. A friend asks if you want to go out. You tell him that *you are going nowhere.*
2. You tell your roommate that *you cannot find your glasses anywhere.*
3. You tell a friend that you think your boss isn't happy with you. Your friend asks if *he has made any remarks.*
4. A friend seems really unhappy, and you ask if *you could help somehow.*
5. You tell your parents that *you are definitely going somewhere during the holidays.*
6. And you wonder if *they have any suggestion at all.*
7. A friend asks when a mutual friend has her birthday. You only know that *it is sometime in August.*
8. Your boyfriend called you and he seemed depressed. You asked if *something is not right.*

§6   Uses of *es*

1. Impersonal use of verbs

Verbs used impersonally have **es** as their subject. The inflected verb is always in the third person singular. Compare

USED PERSONALLY	USED IMPERSONALLY
Die Kinder klopfen an die Tür. *The children are knocking at the door.*	**Es** klopft. *There is a knock at the door.*
Der Briefträger klingelt (läutet). *The mailman is ringing.*	**Es** klingelt (läutet). *Someone is ringing the bell.* *The bell is ringing.*
Die Kerzen brennen. *The candles are burning.*	**Es** brennt. *There is a fire.*

Note the use of the impersonal expression **es gibt** (+ accusative).

Es gibt nur **einen ausländischen Studenten** in unserem Studentenheim.

SUBJECT   DIRECT OBJECT

There is only one foreign student in our dormitory.

Es gibt nur **zwei ausländische Studenten** in unserem Studentenheim.
There are only two foreign students in our dormitory.

Es gibt is used with both singular and plural accusative nouns. The English equivalent is *there is* or *there are*.

The following are some idiomatic uses of **es gibt**:

Es gibt heute noch Regen (Schnee, ein Gewitter).
We are going to have rain (snow, a thunderstorm) today.

Was gibt's (gibt es) heute zum Mittagessen (zum Abendessen/Abendbrot)?
What is there (are we having) for lunch (dinner/supper) today?

Gibt's (gibt es) noch Kaffee (Kuchen, usw.)?
Is there any coffee (cake, etc.) left?

Es gibt keinen Kaffee (Kuchen, usw.) mehr.
There is no coffee (cake, etc.) left.

2. Introductory **es** in main clauses

For reasons of style or emphasis (cf. Kap. 17 §5, 4), an introductory **es** may be used in main clauses. Compare

Niemand ist zu Hause geblieben.
  SUBJECT

                          Nobody stayed home.

Es ist niemand zu Hause geblieben.
              SUBJECT

The subject follows the inflected verb.

Note that the verb agrees with the subject, not with **es**.

Drei Studenten fehlen.
Es fehlen drei Studenten. —————> *Three students are absent.*

When another element is placed in first position, **es** may not be used.

Es fehlen drei Studenten.   *Three students are absent.*
Heute fehlen drei Studenten.   *Three students are absent today.*

The introductory **es** cannot be used in questions and dependent clauses.

3. Es anticipating a dependent clause or infinitive phrase

German often uses **es** to anticipate a clause or infinitive phrase where English would use nothing.

Ich kann **es** verstehen, dass er böse auf mich ist.
I can understand that he is angry with me.

Ich hasse **es** morgens um 6 Uhr aufzustehen.
I hate getting up at 6 o'clock in the morning.

Übung 14-11

ANWENDEN Use **es gibt** to describe what *there is* and what *there isn't* in the locations listed below. Give five items for each location. Use **es gibt** in each sentence, but do not begin all the sentences with this phrase.

1. Ihre Küche
2. Ihre Heimatstadt
3. Ihre Universität

Übung 14-12

ZUSAMMENFASSUNG Der- and **ein**-words as pronouns; uses of indefinite pronouns.

A. Formulate follow-up questions that contain demonstrative pronouns + **hier** and **da**.

MODEL: Welcher Wagen gehört Rolf?
          <u>Der hier oder der da?</u>

1. In welchem Haus wohnt Marianne?
2. In welchem Restaurant warst du schon mal?
3. Welche Krawatte soll ich kaufen?
4. Welche Blumen findest du schöner?
5. Welchen Wein soll ich aufmachen?
6. Mit welchem Stift soll ich schreiben?
7. Auf welchen Stuhl möchtest du dich setzen?

B. Respond to the following personalized questions.

1. Welche interessanten Dinge gibt es in Ihrer Heimatstadt? An Ihrer Uni?
2. Gehen Sie heute Abend irgendwohin? Treffen Sie irgendjemanden?
3. Fahren Sie bald irgendwohin? Kennen Sie irgendjemanden dort?
4. Hat ein Freund oder eine Freundin von Ihnen im Moment irgendwelche Probleme?
5. Was sagen Leute oft, wenn jemand zu neugierig ist?
6. Wie ist das Wetter heute? Gibt es Regen, Sonne, Schnee?
7. Was gibt es bei Ihnen heute zum Abendessen? Was gab es gestern?
8. Wie wissen Sie, wann ein Seminar zu Ende ist?

Relative Clauses

§7   In English

Relative clauses are dependent clauses introduced by the relative pronouns *who, which,* or *that*. Relative clauses usually modify nouns, and less frequently pronouns, by giving further information. The nouns or pronouns thus modified are called *antecedents*.

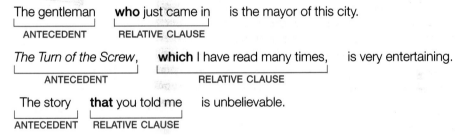

| The gentleman | **who** just came in | is the mayor of this city. |
| ANTECEDENT | RELATIVE CLAUSE | |

| *The Turn of the Screw*, | **which** I have read many times, | is very entertaining. |
| ANTECEDENT | RELATIVE CLAUSE | |

| The story | **that** you told me | is unbelievable. |
| ANTECEDENT | RELATIVE CLAUSE | |

Relative pronouns can have various grammatical functions (e.g., subject, object) within the relative clause.

The student **who** is talking to Mr. Clark is my sister.
　　　　　　　SUBJECT OF THE RELATIVE CLAUSE

The student **whom** you see in this picture is my sister.
　　　　　　　DIRECT SUBJECT OF THE RELATIVE CLAUSE
　　　　　　　OBJECT

In English, the relative pronoun is rarely used as an indirect object. Instead, it occurs more commonly as the object of the preposition *to*.

This is the city councilor   **to whom** the policeman gave a ticket.

                      OBJECT OF   SUBJECT   DIRECT
                      PREPOSITION **to**   OBJECT

In everyday speech, the preposition often stands at the end of the relative clause.

This is the city councilor   **who(m)**   the policeman gave a ticket **to**.

                    OBJECT OF
                    PREPOSITION **to**

When the relative pronoun expresses possession, it is in the possessive (genitive) case.

The student **whose** name is mentioned in the newspaper is my brother.

The English relative pronoun is often omitted.

This is a matter you will never understand.
The figures she quoted are appalling.
This is only one of the inconveniences they will have to contend with.

It is necessary for any student learning German to recognize the function of a given relative pronoun. As a first step, the following exercise will deal with English relative pronouns.

Übung 14-13

VERSTEHEN   State the function of the relative pronouns shown in boldface.

MODEL: This is a remark **that** I resent.
           The relative pronoun *that* functions as direct object.

1. This is a matter **that** you will never understand.
2. I know the artist **who** painted this picture.
3. The figures **that** she quoted are appalling.
4. The lady **whose** picture is on the front page is our neighbor.
5. Professor Johnson, **who** received the Nobel Prize, is the dean of the college.
6. People **who** do such things must be mentally disturbed.
7. The patient **to whom** the nurse gave the wrong medication is recovering.
8. This is a problem **for which** there is no solution.
9. This is only one of the inconveniences **that** they will have to contend with.

§8   Relative Pronouns and Relative Clauses in German

Most forms of the relative pronoun are the same as those of the definite article.

1. a. Der junge Mann, **der** mich angerufen hat, ist Lindas Bruder.
> *who*
> SUBJECT

b. Der junge Mann, **den** ich angerufen habe, ist Lindas Bruder.
> *whom*
> DIRECT OBJECT

2. a. Der Wagen, **der** da vor der Garage steht, gehört meiner Schwester.
> *which/that*
> SUBJECT

b. Der Wagen, **den** Sie da vor der Garage sehen, gehört meiner Schwester.
> *which/that*
> DIRECT OBJECT

The antecedents in the above examples are masculine nouns: **der junge Mann** and **der Wagen**. The relative pronouns refer to both persons and things.

In sentences **1. a.** and **2. a.**, the relative pronoun is the subject of the relative clause and is therefore in the nominative case: **der**.

In sentences **1. b.** and **2. b.**, the relative pronoun is the direct object of the relative clause and is therefore in the accusative case: **den**.

Rule: The relative pronoun agrees in gender and number (singular or plural) with the antecedent. Its case, however, is determined by its function in the relative clause.

The relative clause is a dependent clause; hence, the inflected verb is placed at the end.

Normally, the relative clause immediately follows the antecedent. The relative clause is always set off by commas.

In German, the relative pronoun cannot be omitted.

> *The young man I called is Linda's brother.*
> Der junge Mann, **den** ich angerufen habe, ist Lindas Bruder.

§9   Declension of the Relative Pronoun

	MASCULINE	NEUTER	FEMININE	PLURAL	Depending on context, English equivalents may be:
NOMINATIVE	der	das	die	die	*who, which, that*
ACCUSATIVE	den	das	die	die	*whom, which, that, (who)*
DATIVE	dem	dem	der	**denen**	*(to) whom, which, that,*
GENITIVE	**dessen**	**dessen**	**deren**	**deren**	*whose, of which*

Only the boldface long forms differ from the definite article. (The forms of the relative pronoun are the same as those of definite articles functioning as demonstrative pronouns [cf. §2].)

Examples for all cases

1. The relative pronoun as the subject of the relative clause (nominative)

> Der Student, **der** da drüben steht, ist mein Bruder.
> Das Kind, **das** da drüben steht, ist meine Schwester.
> Die Studentin, **die** da drüben steht, ist meine Freundin.
> Die Leute, **die** da drüben stehen, sind meine Freunde.

2. The relative pronoun as the direct object of the relative clause (accusative)

> Der Student, **den** Sie dort sehen, ist mein Bruder.
> Das Kind, **das** Sie dort sehen, ist meine Schwester.
> Die Studentin, **die** Sie dort sehen, ist meine Freundin.
> Die Leute, **die** Sie dort sehen, sind meine Freunde.

3. The relative pronoun as the indirect object of the relative clause (dative)

> Der Student, **dem** ich das Geld gegeben habe, ist mein Bruder.
> Das Kind, **dem** ich das Geld gegeben habe, ist meine Schwester.
> Die Studentin, **der** ich das Geld gegeben habe, ist meine Freundin.
> Die Leute, **denen** ich das Geld gegeben habe, sind meine Freunde.

4. The relative pronoun showing possession (genitive)

> Der Student, **dessen** Name in der Zeitung steht, ist mein Bruder.
> Das Kind, **dessen** Name in der Zeitung steht, ist meine Schwester.
> Die Studentin, **deren** Name in der Zeitung steht, ist meine Freundin.
> Die Leute, **deren** Namen in der Zeitung stehen, sind meine Freunde.

Remember: The gender and number of the relative pronoun are determined by its antecedent; the case is determined by the pronoun's function in the relative clause.

Note that a relative pronoun referring to **Mädchen** (and also the now seldom used **Fräulein**) must be neuter, though the personal pronoun would often be feminine rather than neuter (cf. Kap. 6 §9).

Keep in mind that some verbs have dative objects, such as **helfen, antworten, danken, folgen, gratulieren**, and **trauen** (cf. Kap. 5 §6, 3).

> Das ist ein Mann, **dem** man nicht trauen kann.
> Das sind Leute, **denen** man nicht trauen kann.

Übung 14-14

VERSTEHEN State the function (e.g., subject, object), the case, and the gender (if singular) or number (if plural) of each relative pronoun in the following sentences.

> MODEL: Ist das die Dame, **die** uns das Museum zeigen soll?
> <u>subject, nominative, feminine</u>
> Sind das die Leute, **die** das Museum sehen wollen?
> <u>subject, nominative, plural</u>

1. Ist das der Herr, **der** uns das Museum zeigen soll?
2. Ist das der Tourist, **dem** wir die Stadt zeigen sollen?
3. Sind das die Touristen, **denen** wir unsere Stadt zeigen sollen?
4. Sind das die Touristen, **die** unsere Stadt sehen wollen?
5. Wie heißen die Leute, **deren** Haus Sie kaufen wollen?
6. Wo ist das Paket, **das** Ihre Eltern geschickt haben?
7. Das große Paket, **das** vor der Tür steht, ist für Hannelore.
8. Wo wohnt Ihre Tochter, **der** Sie dieses Paket schicken wollen?
9. Ist das Mädchen, **das** dich immer anruft, deine feste Freundin?
10. Ist das Mädchen, **das** du immer anrufst, deine feste Freundin?

Übung 14-15

ANWENDEN A. Replace the boldface antecedents with the words given in parentheses. Change the relative pronouns (and, if necessary, the verbs) to match the new antecedents.

> MODEL: **Der Student**, der im Zimmer neben mir wohnt, ist krank.
> (die zwei Studenten)
> <u>Die zwei Studenten, die im Zimmer neben mir wohnen, sind krank.</u>

1. **Das Buch**, das ich für den Kurs in Chemie brauche, ist sehr teuer.
   (die Bücher)
2. **Die Bemerkung**, die Rita gemacht hat, werde ich ignorieren.
   (die Bemerkungen)
3. Das ist **ein Apparat**, der noch nie funktioniert hat. (eine Maschine)
4. Das ist nicht **die Suppe**, die ich bestellt habe. (der Wein)
5. Hast du **das Radio** gesehen, das ich Monika schenken will? (der Ring)
6. Das ist **ein Punkt**, den wir noch besprechen müssen. (eine Sache)
7. **Das Theaterstück**, das ich gestern gesehen habe, ist sehr langweilig.
   (der Film)
8. Das ist **eine Haltung**, die ich nicht verstehe. (ein Problem)
9. Da drüben steht **der Polizist**, dem ich meinen Führerschein zeigen mußte.
   (die Polizistin)
10. **Die Studentin**, der ich bei den Hausaufgaben geholfen habe, hat die Prüfung bestanden. (der Student)
11. Das ist **der Wagen**, dem wir folgen müssen. (die Limousine)

12. Dort sind **Herr und Frau Schreiber**, denen wir für die schöne Party danken müssen. (Frau Krause)
13. **Der Herr**, dem Frau Berger gratuliert, hat eine Gehaltserhöhung bekommen. (die zwei Damen)
14. **Herr Berger**, dessen Vater gestorben ist, hat viel Geld geerbt. (Frau Schiller)
15. Das ist **die Kamera**, die ich geerbt habe. (der Schrank)

B. Combine the following sentences by using a relative clause.

MODEL: Das ist eine Chance. Man bekommt sie nicht jeden Tag.
<u>Das ist eine Chance, die man nicht jeden Tag bekommt.</u>

1. Das ist ein Problem. Ich kann es nicht lösen.
2. Das ist eine grammatische Konstruktion. Ich verstehe sie nicht.
3. Wie gefällt Ihnen der Wagen? Ich habe ihn geerbt.
4. Das sind peinliche Fragen. Man muss sie ignorieren.
5. Karin besucht die Nachbarin. Sie hilft ihr oft im Garten.
6. Da drüben ist der neue Student. Ich möchte ihn kennenlernen.
7. Rainer gibt heute abend eine Party. Seine Freundin hat den ersten Preis gewonnen.
8. Siehst du das kleine Kind? Ich habe ihm ein Eis gekauft.
9. Zimmermanns ziehen nach Köln. Wir haben ihr Haus gekauft.

C. Change each sentence into a complex sentence that contains a relative clause. Use the cued element in parentheses as the antecedent.

MODEL: Gabi hat immer gute Laune. (ein Mädchen)
<u>Gabi ist ein Mädchen, das immer gute Laune hat.</u>
Alle Freunde helfen Rolf gern. (ein Mensch)
<u>Rolf ist ein Mensch, dem alle Freunde gern helfen.</u>

Verschiedene Leute beschreiben.

1. Regina zieht sich immer sehr elegant an. (eine Frau)
2. Alle finden Karl unterhaltsam. (ein Mann)
3. Erika redet immer zu viel. (eine Person)
4. Frau Amerands Mann geht mir auf die Nerven. (eine Freundin von mir)
5. Man kann Tanja und Waleska immer trauen. (zwei Freundinnen)
6. Norberts Verhalten kann niemand verstehen. (ein Bekannter von uns)
7. Margots Verlobter war schon dreimal verheiratet. (eine Freundin von mir)
8. Walter, Ingeborg und Petra gehört ein altes Bauernhaus. (drei Studienkollegen)

D. Now think of five people and describe them using relative pronouns. Try to vary the function of the relative pronoun, i.e., subject, direct object, indirect object, and possessive.

MODEL: <u>Peter ist ein Kollege, den ich in Holland kennengelernt habe.</u>

§10   Relative Pronouns as Objects of Prepositions

Das ist ein Lehrer, **von dem** ich begeistert bin.
                    about whom I am enthusiastic.
            or: *whom I am enthusiastic about.*
Das ist eine Lehrerin, **von der** ich begeistert bin.
Das sind zwei Lehrer, **von denen** ich begeistert bin.

(For cases governed by prepositions, see Kap. 7 §5, §7, §8.)

In German, the preposition always precedes the relative pronoun. Prepositions never occur at the end of a relative clause. As usual, the gender and number of the relative pronoun are in agreement with the antecedent. The case of the relative pronoun is determined by the preceding preposition: **von** governs the dative; thus the relative pronouns are in the dative case in the examples above.

The genitive case—**dessen, deren**—is not affected by any preceding preposition because the object of the preposition is not the relative pronoun but the noun following **dessen** or **deren**.

Das ist Herr Schmidt, **mit dessen** Frau wir verwandt sind.
        (whose wife we are related to)

The masculine form of the genitive is used because its antecedent is **Herr Schmidt**, regardless of the fact that it precedes the feminine noun **Frau**.

For the same reason, the feminine form **deren** is used in the following example:

Das ist Frau Schmidt, **mit deren** Mann wir verwandt sind.
        (whose husband we are related to)

Vokabulartip: Definitionen

Relative clauses are often used to define, categorize, and describe items. Note the following examples:

ein Gerät, mit dem man Teig knetet	*a utensil that you knead dough with*
ein Apparat, dem man Wäsche trocknet	*an appliance that you dry laundry with*
ein Ding, durch das Geschriebenes größer erscheint	*a item through which something written looks bigger*
eine Person, für die ich alles tun würde	*a person I would do everything for*
ein Lebewesen, das in Höhlen lebt	*a creature that lives in caves*

Übung 14-16

ANWENDEN Provide a definition with a preposition + a relative pronoun.

MODEL: eine Videokamera (Gerät)
Eine Videokamera ist ein Gerät, mit dem man etwas filmen kann.

1. ein Teleskop (Gerät)
2. ein Mikroskop (Gerät)
3. ein Handy (Apparat)
4. ein Kompass (Ding)
5. ein echter Freund (Person)
6. ein Walkman (Apparat)
7. ein Modem (Gerät)
8. ein Feind (Person)

Other Forms of Relatives

§11   *welcher, welches, welche*

Welcher, **welches**, and **welche** may function as relative pronouns in the nominative, accusative, and dative cases. These forms have a bookish tone and occur mainly in formal German.

Der Botschafter, **welcher** die Verhandlungen geführt hat, muss den Vertrag unterschreiben.
The ambassador who conducted the negotiations must sign the treaty.

Das war eine Niederlage für die Arbeiter, **welche** keinen Kompromiss schließen wollten.
That was a defeat for the workers who did not want to compromise.

§12   *wo*

Compare the following two sentences that refer to a place:

Das ist der Vorort, **in dem** meine Großeltern wohnen.
Das ist der Vorort, **wo** meine Großeltern wohnen.
That is the suburb where my grandparents live.

In the first sentence, the preposition **in** and the relative pronoun **dem** are used. In the second sentence, **wo** is used instead, as is often done when referring to places. This corresponds to the English use of *where*.

Übung 14-17

ANWENDEN Complete each sentence by using **wo** to refer to the place. Indicate the preposition and the pronoun that **wo** replaces.

Frederike beschreibt Wohn- und Urlaubsorte ihrer Familie.

> MODEL: Meine ganze Familie lebt jetzt in Weimar.
> Die Stadt, wo meine ganze Familie lebt, heißt Weimar. (**in der**)

1. Wir besuchen oft Verwandte in Thüringen.
   Das Bundesland, …
2. Und wir verbringen unsere Ferien oft am Wannsee.
   Der See, …
3. Wir wohnen während dem Urlaub bei Knickes.
   Die Familie, …
4. Wir machen Wanderungen in Brandenburg…
   Die Gegend, …

§13   *was*

Was is used as a relative pronoun in the following instances:

1. When the antecedent is a neuter indefinite pronoun, such as **etwas** (*something*), **nichts** (*nothing*), **alles** (*all, everything*), **wenig** (*little*), **viel** (*much*), or **vieles** (*many things*)

   (English uses the relative pronouns *that* and *which* or omits them completely.)

   > Das ist etwas, **was** ich nicht verstehen kann.
   > *That is something (that) I cannot understand.*

   > Nicht alles, **was** er sagt, ist wahr.
   > *Not everything he says is true.*

   > Es gibt nicht viel, **was** ihm wirklich gefällt.
   > *There is not much he really likes.*

   > Vieles, **was** sie sagt, ist übertrieben.
   > *Many things she says are exaggerated.*

   Note the distinction between **viel** and **vieles** in the chart on the next page.

2. When the antecedent is a neuter adjective in the superlative used as a noun, such as **das Beste** (*the best* [*thing*]), **das Klügste** (*the smartest* [*thing*]), **das Interessanteste** (*the most interesting* [*thing*]) (cf. Kap. 8 §12)

   > Das ist **das Beste**, **was** wir für Sie tun konnten.
   > *That's the best we could do for you.*

   > Das ist **das Klügste**, **was** man in so einer Situation tun kann.
   > *That's the smartest thing one can do in such a situation.*

viel = *much* (refers to something as a whole) **Er weiß viel.** *He knows a lot.* (referring to his knowledge as a whole) **Er sagt nicht viel.** *He doesn't say much.*	vieles = *many things* (refers to a number of individual, separate things, not taken together as one quantity) **Er weiß vieles nicht.** *There are many things he doesn't know.* **Er sagt mir vieles nicht.** *There are many things he doesn't tell me.*

3. When the antecedent is a neuter ordinal, such as **das Erste** (*the first thing*), **das Zweite** (*the second thing*) **das Letzte** (*the last thing*), **das Einzige** (*the only thing*)

> Das war **das Erste, was** er gesagt hat.
> *That was the first thing he said.*

> Das ist **das Letzte, was** ich tun würde.
> *That's the last thing I would do.*

> **Das Einzige, was** mir Sorgen macht, ist meine notorische Faulheit.
> *The only thing that worries me is my notorious laziness.*

4. When the antecedent is an entire clause rather than a single element

> Er will seinen Wagen vor dem Eingang parken, **was** verboten ist.
> *He wants to park his car in front of the entrance, which is forbidden.*

§14   *wo*-Compound Instead of Preposition + *was*

> Das ist etwas, ~~über was~~ er sich immer beschwert.
>   **worüber**

> *That is something about which he is always complaining.*
> or: *That is something he is always complaining about.*

When preceded by a preposition, **was** functioning as a relative pronoun must be replaced by **wo** as part of a **wo**-compound.

Übung 14-18

ANWENDEN Make a statement that is appropriate advice for each of the following situations. Use different introductory phrases such as **Das Erste/Beste/Klügste/ Letzte/Dümmste**.

> MODEL: Sie merken, dass Ihr Eisschrank nicht funktioniert.
>   <u>Das Erste, was man tun soll, ist ihn zu schliessen.</u>

1. Sie stellen fest, dass jemand in Ihr Auto eingebrochen ist.
2. Ein Kind läuft vor Ihrem Auto über die Straße.
3. Sie fahren 75 Stundenkilometer statt 50 und ein Polizeiwagen mit Sirene folgt Ihnen.

4. Sie wachen mitten in der Nacht auf und hören irgendetwas im Haus.
5. Sie schwimmen im Meer und merken, dass Sie sehr weit vom Ufer entfernt sind.
6. Ihre Mutter ruft an und Sie erinnern sich daran, dass gestern ihr Geburtstag war.
7. Ihr/e Freund/in hat den Verdacht, dass Sie ihm/ihr nicht treu sind.

§15   The Relative Pronouns *wer* and *was* with No Antecedent

The relative pronouns **wer** and **was** are used without an antecedent in the sense of

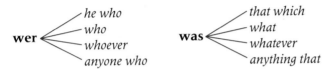

Compare

USED AS INTERROGATIVE PRONOUNS (inflected verb in second position)	USED AS RELATIVE PRONOUNS WITHOUT ANTECEDENTS (inflected verb in last position)
Wer hat einen Wagen?	**Wer** einen Wagen hat, (der) geht selten zu Fuß.
Who has a car?	*He who has a car seldom walks.* or: *Anyone who has a car seldom walks.*
Was sagst du?	**Was** du **sagst**, (das) ist Unsinn.
What are you saying?	*What you are saying is nonsense.*

Note: **Wer** and **was** functioning as relative pronouns introduce dependent clauses; thus, the inflected verb is in final position in the dependent clause.

In the above examples, the demonstratives **der** and **das** are in parentheses because they are generally omitted in sentences with the following combinations:

Wer....	**(der)**
(nom.)	(nom.)
Was....	**(das)**
(nom. or acc.)	(nom. or acc.)

In all other instances, the demonstratives must be added.

Wer nicht arbeiten will, **den** sollte man nicht unterstützen.
He who (Whoever) does not want to work should not be supported.
(literally: one should not support)

Wem das nicht gefällt, **der** kann ja protestieren.
He who (Whoever) does not like it can protest.

The notion of generalization or indefiniteness may be enhanced by adding **immer**, **auch**, or **auch immer**.

> **Wer immer** uns besucht.
> or: **Wer** uns **auch** besucht,   ──────▷ (der) ist willkommen.
> or: **Wer** uns **auch immer** besucht,
>   *Whoever visits us is welcome.*

> **Was immer** sie unternimmt,
> or: **Was** sie **auch** unternimmt,   ──────▷ (das) ist gut überlegt.
> or: **Was** sie **auch immer** unternimmt.
>   *Whatever she undertakes is well thought out.*

The relative pronouns **wer** and **was** frequently occur in advertisements, proverbs, and sayings.

> Wer gesund bleiben will, trinkt Obstsaft.
> *Whoever wants to stay healthy drinks fruit juice.*
> or: *People who want to ...*

> Wer Qualität liebt, kauft bei Merkur.
> *Anyone who loves quality shops at Merkur.*
> or: *People who love quality...*

Proverb: Wer im Glashaus sitzt, soll keine Steine werfen.
           People who live in glass houses shouldn't throw stones.

Übung 14-19

ANWENDEN   A. What do you think each of the following proverbs means? What are English equivalents?

1. Wer zuletzt lacht, lacht am besten.
2. Was ich nicht weiß, macht mich nicht heiß.
3. Wer den Pfennig nicht ehrt, ist des Talers (*coin*) nicht wert.
4. Wer einmal lügt, dem glaubt man nicht, und wenn er auch die Wahrheit spricht.
5. Wer die Wahl hat, hat die Qual (*pain*).
6. Wer A sagt, muss auch B sagen.
7. Wer zuerst kommt, malt zuerst.
8. Was du nicht im Kopf hast, hast du in den Beinen.

B. Rephrase the proverbs using different relative clauses.

MODEL: Wer zuerst kommt, malt zuerst.
         <u>Jemand, der rechtzeitig kommt, hat Vorteile.</u>

§16 Summary of the Main Features of Relative Clauses

1. Relative clauses are dependent clauses that usually modify antecedents, and are always set off by commas.

2. Relative clauses are introduced either by a relative pronoun or by a preposition and its relative pronoun object; neither can be omitted. This pronoun agrees in gender and number with its antecedent in the main clause, but the pronoun's case is determined by its function in the relative clause.

3. Relative pronouns usually resemble the definite article.

4. The alternative forms of the relative pronoun **welcher** occur mainly in formal German.

5. When referring to a place, **wo** is often used instead of a preposition and a form of the relative pronoun **der**, **das**, or **die**.

6. The relative pronoun **was** is used after the following antecedents:

a. indefinite pronouns, such as **etwas, nichts, alles, wenig, viel, vieles**
b. neuter adjectives in the superlative used as nouns, such as **das Beste, das Dümmste**
c. neuter ordinals and **das Letzte, das Einzige**
d. entire clauses

7. **wo**-compounds must be used in place of a preposition + **was**.

8. **Wer** and **was** are used as relative pronouns when there is no antecedent.

Übung 14-20

ZUSAMMENFASSUNG Definite articles as relative pronouns, alone and with prepositions.

A. Restate each sentence as one that contains a relative clause.

MODEL: Ich wurde in diesem Haus geboren.
<u>Das ist das Haus, in dem ich geboren wurde.</u>

Herr Tumm zeigt seinen Kindern, wo er früher gelebt hat.

1. Auf diesem Spielplatz habe ich am liebsten gespielt.
2. Und bei diesem Bäcker hat meine Mutter jeden Samstag Brötchen gekauft.
3. Es gibt den Erdbeerkuchen. Wir haben ihn im Sommer jeden Tag gegessen.
4. Da drüben steht die Kirche. Eure Mutter und ich haben darin geheiratet.
5. Vor diesem Gasthaus haben wir uns oft getroffen.
6. Das Gasthaus gibt es schon über 100 Jahre. Seine Küche ist übrigens berühmt.
7. Ach, und hier sehe ich einen alten Schulfreund. Ich habe ihn schon seit Jahren nicht mehr gesehen.
8. Mit diesem Freund war ich ein Jahr in Frankreich.
9. Er wohnt noch hier. Er ist einer von meinen Klassenkameraden.

B. Imagine now that your are showing someone your hometown and where you grew up. Describe six places, buildings, or people using relative clauses similar to the ones you used in A.

C. Compose five slogans or sayings that promote an item such as food, a vacation destination, an activity. Follow the model (use **wer** or **was**), but otherwise, be creative!

MODEL: Wer gerne wandert, macht in der Alpen Urlaub!
Was Sie auch zum Wohnen brauchen, Sie finden es bei Ikea!

Themen und Vokabular

Kategorien		Personen beschreiben	
der Apparat, -e	*appliance, apparatus*	**die Einstellung** (no pl.)	*attitude*
das Ding, -e	*thing, item*	**der Nerv, -en**	*nerve*
das Gerät, -e	*piece of equipment, utensil, tool*	**jemand(em)** (dat.) **auf die Nerven gehen**	*to get on somebody's nerves*
das Lebewesen, -	*creature, living being*	**jemand(em)** (dat.) **trauen**	*to trust somebody*
der Mensch, -en (weak)	*human, human being*	**unterhaltsam**	*entertaining, amusing*
die Person, -en	*person*	**das Verhalten** (no pl.)	*behavior, conduct*

KAPITEL

15 Reflexives; Reciprocal Pronouns; Uses of *selbst/selber*

Reflexive Pronouns and Reflexive Verbs

Compare the following sentences:

> **John** is defending **his friend**.
> **John** is defending **him**.
> **John** is defending **himself**.

In the first two sentences, the subject and the object are two different persons. In the third sentence, the subject and object are the same person, and the object is expressed with a reflexive pronoun.

In most instances, the reflexive pronoun is the direct object, as in the above example, but it may also function as the indirect object.

> He has to give **himself** more time.
> | |
>   INDIRECT   DIRECT
>   OBJECT   OBJECT

The reflexive pronoun also occurs as the object of a preposition.

> **He** was **beside himself**.
> **He** was talking **to himself**.
> **He** was laughing **at himself**.

There is no difference in form, regardless of whether the reflexive pronoun functions as direct object, indirect object, or object of a preposition.

German reflexive pronouns have the same three functions, but they show some changes in form.

§1   The Reflexive Pronoun in the Accusative Case

The reflexive pronoun is in the accusative when it functions as a direct object.

Hans verteidigt **seinen Freund**.	*Hans is defending his friend.*
Hans verteidigt **ihn**. (personal pronoun)	*Hans is defending him.*
Hans verteidigt **sich**. (reflexive pronoun)	*Hans is defending him.*

The following is a complete set of the reflexive pronouns in the accusative case:

Ich verteidige **mich**.	*I am defending myself.*
Du verteidigst **dich**.	*You are defending yourself.*
Er verteidigt **sich**.	*He is defending himself.*
Sie verteidigt **sich**.	*She is defending herself.*
Es verteidigt **sich**.	*etc.*
Wir verteidigen **uns**.	
Ihr verteidigt **euch**.	
Sie verteidigen **sich**.	

Sie verteidigen **sich**. (second person formal; singular and plural)

Note that the formal reflexive **sich** is the only formal pronoun not capitalized.

Remember: The reflexive pronouns are identical to the accusative personal pronouns except for the form sich in the third person singular and plural, and in the formal address.

All transitive verbs can be used reflexively, for example

sich fragen	*to ask oneself*
sich kennen	*to know oneself*
sich loben	*to praise oneself*
sich täuschen	*to deceive oneself*

Some common verbs are used reflexively in German but not in English.

sich an•stellen	*to get in line*
sich entschuldigen (bei)	*to apologize (to)*
sich erinnern an (acc.)	*to remember*
sich erkälten	*to catch a cold*
sich freuen auf (acc.)	*to look forward to*
sich freuen über (acc.)	*to be happy about*
sich gewöhnen an (acc.)	*to get used to, accustomed to*
sich interessieren für (acc.)	*to be interested in*
sich irren	*to be mistaken*
sich konzentrieren (auf) (acc.)	*to concentrate (on)*
sich langweilen	*to be bored, get bored*
sich rasieren	*to shave*
sich setzen	*to sit down*

sich verfahren (verfährt), verfuhr, hat verfahren	*to lose one's way (driving)*
sich verlaufen (verläuft), verlief, hat verlaufen	*to lose one's way (walking)*
sich waschen (wäscht), wusch, hat gewaschen	*to wash (oneself)*

Because verbs used reflexively are transitive, they form the present perfect and the past perfect with the auxiliary **haben**, even if they are derivatives of verbs that normally employ **sein**, such as **sich verfahren** and **sich verlaufen**.

Wir **sind** in die Stadt gefahren/gelaufen.	*We drove/walked to town.*
Wir **haben uns** verfahren/verlaufen.	*We lost our way (driving/walking).*

Übung 15-1

ANWENDEN A. Restate the sentences using the subjects in parentheses, changing the reflexive pronouns accordingly.

> MODEL: Ich frage mich, ob das wahr ist. (Astrid, wir, meine Eltern)
> <u>Astrid fragt sich, ob das wahr ist.</u>
> <u>Wir fragen uns, ob das wahr ist.</u>
> <u>Meine Eltern fragen sich, ob das wahr ist.</u>

1. Er lobt sich zuviel. (ich, du, ihr)
2. Helga täuscht sich oft. (Herr Berger, wir, Sie)
3. Mein Bruder hat sich noch nie geirrt. (ich, Sie)
4. Konzentrier dich! (ihr, Sie)
5. Ich kenne mich gut genug. (du, ihr)
6. Setzt euch! (du, Sie, wir)

B. Read each situation carefully and supply an appropriate statement or question. Use the reflexive verbs given below. (Use each reflexive verb only once.)

> sich entschuldigen, sich erkälten, sich freuen auf, sich gewöhnen an, sich verfahren, sich verlaufen, sich anstellen, sich waschen, sich langweilen, sich irren

1. Ein Bekannter will Sie besuchen, aber er kann Ihr Haus nicht finden. Von seinem Autotelefon ruft er an und sagt: _____
2. Ein paar Freunde kommen mit viel Verspätung zu Fuß zu einer Party. Sie fragen:_____
3. Sie und Ihr Mann leben erst seit zwei Monaten in Düsseldorf. Sie beide finden das Wetter schrecklich und sagen:_____
4. Ihre kleine Tochter niest und hustet. Sie sagen zu ihr:_____
5. Zwei kleine Kinder sind auf dem Weg ins Bett. Der Babysitter sagt ihnen, was sie vor dem Schlafengehen machen sollen:_____
6. Iris hat den Geburtstag ihrer besten Freundin vergessen. Was macht sie hoffentlich?
7. Morgen beginnen für die Schulkinder die Ferien. Was sagen sie?

8. Ein Mann sitzt neben Ihnen im Konzert. Er hört kaum zu und gähnt die ganze Zeit. Was sagen Sie über ihn?
9. Sie warten in einer Schlange um Karten für ein Konzert zu kaufen. Ein Fremder geht ganz nach vorne. Was sagen Sie zu dieser Person?
10. Ein Freund von Ihnen ist etwas arrogant und glaubt, dass er nie etwas falsch macht. Was sagt er von sich?

The position of the reflexive pronouns

The position of the reflexive pronoun is governed by the same rules as the personal pronoun object (cf. Kap. 6 §10).

In sentences with normal word order, the reflexive pronoun follows the inflected verb form.

> Er hat **sich** gestern auf dem Fußballplatz erkältet.

In sentences with inverted or dependent word order, the reflexive pronoun follows the personal pronoun subject.

> Vielleicht hat er **sich** gestern auf dem Fußballplatz erkältet.
> Es ist möglich, dass er **sich** gestern auf dem Fußballplatz erkältet hat.

The reflexive pronoun precedes all other elements, usually also noun subjects.

> Vielleicht hat **sich** Herr Zimmermann gestern auf dem Fußballplatz erkältet.
> Es ist möglich, dass **sich** Herr Zimmermann gestern auf dem Fußballplatz erkältet hat.

Remember: The reflexive pronoun occurs early in the sentence. It usually *follows* the inflected verb forms or a personal pronoun (subject or object), but *precedes* all other elements.

Particular attention must be paid to verbs associated with a preposition, such as **sich erinnern an** (accusative).

> **Sie erinnert sich noch an meinen Bruder.**
> *She (still) remembers my brother.*

> **Sie erinnert sich noch an ihn.**
> *She (still) remembers him.*
> (**Noch** is commonly added.)

> **Sie erinnert sich nicht mehr an das Picknick.**
> *She doesn't remember the picnic (anymore).*

> **Sie erinnert sich nicht mehr daran, was geschehen ist.**
> *She doesn't remember what happened (anymore).*
> (**Mehr** is commonly added to **nicht**.)

Note the use of the **da**-compound **daran** (cf. Kap. 7 §9).

Übung 15-2

ANWENDEN A. Respond to the questions as cued. Add additional items (e.g., modal verbs) when appropriate.

> MODEL: Habt ihr euch irgendwann verfahren? (ja, einmal)
> <u>Ja, wir haben uns einmal verfahren.</u>
> Hat Viktor sich beim Fahren gut konzentriert? (nein, nicht so gut)
> <u>Nein, er konnte sich nicht so gut konzentrieren.</u>

Ein Telefongespräch. Olga und ihr Bruder sind bei ihrer Großmutter in Salzburg.
Ihre Mutter ruft dort an um mit Olga und ihrem Bruder zu sprechen.

1. Olga, hast du dich schon an das Klima in den Bergen gewöhnt? (ja, ein bisschen)
2. Hat sich eure Kusine noch an euch erinnert? (nein)
3. Hat sich die Oma über das Geschenk gefreut? (ja, sehr)
4. Meinst du, dass sie sich darüber gefreut hat euch alle zu sehen? (ja, sicher)
5. Glaubst du, dass ihr euch irgendwann langweilen werdet? (nein, auf keinen Fall)
6. Erkältet euch abends nicht! (nein, bestimmt nicht)

B. Respond to the personalized questions with either a noun object or a phrase.

> MODEL: Woran erinnern Sie sich gern?
> <u>Ich erinnere mich gern an meinen letzten Urlaub.</u>
> or: <u>Ich erinnere mich gern daran, wie wir zusammen</u>
> <u>skifahren waren.</u>

1. Über welche Dinge freuen Sie sich am meisten? Worüber haben Sie sich vor kurzem gefreut?
2. Wie lange sind Sie schon an der Uni? Woran konnten Sie sich nur schwer gewöhnen?
3. Worauf freuen Sie sich im Moment? Worauf freut sich Ihre Familie?
4. Wann mussten Sie sich das letzte Mal bei jemandem entschuldigen? Warum? Hat sich irgendjemand bei Ihnen entschuldigt? Warum?
5. Woran erinnern Sie sich aus Ihrer Kindheit? Antworten Sie mit ungefähr fünf Sätzen.

C. Ask your parents three questions about their memories. Formulate questions for your mother only, your father only, or for both.

> MODEL: <u>Papa, erinnerst du dich daran, wie du Mutti kennengelernt hast?</u>

§2   The Reflexive Pronoun in the Dative Case

The reflexive pronoun will be in the dative case if there is a direct object in the sentence.

sich etwas überlegen   *to think about something*

Ich überlege **mir die Sache**.   *I am thinking about the matter.*

INDIRECT   DIRECT
OBJECT   OBJECT

Except for the first and second person singular, the dative reflexive pronouns are identical to their accusative counterparts.

Ich überlege **mir** die Sache.
Du überlegst **dir** die Sache.
Er
Sie →überlegt **sich** die Sache.
Es
Wir überlegen **uns** die Sache.
Ihr überlegt **euch** die Sache.
Sie überlegen **sich** die Sache.
Sie überlegen **sich** die Sache. (formal)

Some common verbs with dative reflexive pronouns

sich etwas an•sehen
sich etwas an•schauen   → *to (take a) look at*
sich etwas leisten   *to treat oneself to something*
sich etwas leisten können   *to be able to afford something*
sich etwas überlegen   *to think about something, think it over*
sich etwas vor•stellen   *to imagine something*

When referring to parts of the body, the dative reflexive pronoun is used in combination with the definite article where English uses the possessive.

Ich wasche **mir die Hände/das Gesicht**.   *I'm washing my hands/my face.*
Du kämmst/bürstest **dir die Haare**.   *You are combing/brushing your hair.*

Sie putzen **sich die Zähne**.   *They are brushing their teeth.*
Ich habe **mir den Arm** gebrochen.   *I broke my arm.*

Verbs requiring a dative object (cf. Kap. 5 §4) naturally have a dative rather than an accusative reflexive pronoun.

Ich gefalle **mir** nicht in diesem Kleid.   *I don't like myself in this dress.*
Ich widerspreche **mir**.   *I'm contradicting myself.*

With some verbs, such as **kaufen, bestellen** (*to order*), and **holen** (*to [go and] get, fetch*), the use of the dative reflexive pronoun is optional.

Frau Schmidt hat (sich) einen Wagen gekauft.
Mrs. Schmidt bought (herself) a car.

Was hast du (dir) bestellt?
What did you order (for yourself)?

Ich habe (mir) eine Flasche Mineralwasser aus dem Kühlschrank geholt.
I got (myself) a bottle of mineral water from the refrigerator.

§3 The Imperative of Reflexive Verbs

Reflexive verbs must include the appropriate reflexive pronoun in the imperative. (For the formation of the imperative, see Kap. 2 §12 to §14.) Only the familiar singular imperative distinguishes dative and accusative reflexive pronouns.

REFLEXIVE IN THE ACCUSATIVE CASE		REFLEXIVE IN THE DATIVE CASE
Wasch(e) **dich!**	(familiar singular)	Wasch(e) **dir** die Hände!
Wascht **euch!**	(familar plural)	Wascht **euch** die Hände!
Waschen Sie **sich!**	(formal)	Waschen Sie **sich** die Hände!
Waschen wir **uns!**	(**wir** form = Let's . . .)	Waschen wir **uns** die Hände!

Vokabulartip: morgens und abends

Describing morning and evening grooming routines involves verbs with accusative reflexive pronouns or with dative reflexive pronoun plus parts of the body. Study the following examples:

Zuerst **dusche ich (mich)** und **wasche mir** vor allem **das Gesicht. Ich trockne mich** gründlich **ab** (*to dry oneself off*) und **ziehe mich an**. Dann bürste ich **mir die Haare** (mein Mann hat wenig Haare, **er kämmt sich**). Während **ich mich schminke** (*to make oneself up*), **rasiert sich mein Mann** vor dem Spiegel. Zum Schluss **putze ich mir** noch **die Zähne**.

Übung 15-3

ANWENDEN A. Formulate questions, commands, and statements as cued. Add dative reflexive pronouns when appropriate.

MODEL: Kinder / kämmen! (Haare)
       <u>Kinder, kämmt euch die Haare!</u>

Aktivitäten am Morgen.

1. Waleska / ausziehen! (der Schlafanzug)
2. Waleska und Leo / waschen! (das Gesicht, die Hände)
3. Und Leo / putzen! (Zähne)
4. Ich / schon / holen. (Zeitung [present perfect])

 5. Die Kinder / schon / anziehen? (die Jacken [present perfect])
 6. Waleska / anschauen! (der Stundenplan, die Hausaufgaben)

B. Respond to the personalized questions.

 1. Was machen Sie morgens und abends? (3-4 Aktivitäten)
 2. Was schauen Sie sich regelmäßig im Fernsehen an?
 3. Was können Sie sich jeden Monat leisten? Was können Sie sich nicht leisten?
 4. Was würden Sie sich in einem eleganten Restaurant bestellen?

A note on word order

Compare the following sentences:

Ich kann **mir** diesen Fernseher nicht leisten.	*I can't afford this TV set.*
Ich kann **ihn mir** nicht leisten.	*I can't afford it.*
Ich kann **mir das** nicht leisten.	*I can't afford that.*

As with personal pronoun objects (cf. Kap. 6 §10), the dative reflexive follows the accusative personal pronoun, as in the second sentence. However, it precedes other accusative pronouns, for instance, the demonstrative pronoun **das**, as in the third sentence.

Additional examples

Ich kann **es mir** vorstellen.	*I can imagine it.*
Ich kann **mir das** vorstellen.	*I can imagine that.*
Ich werde **es mir** überlegen.	*I'll think about it.*
Ich werde **mir das** überlegen.	*I'll think about that.*

Übung 15-4

ANWENDEN A. Respond to each question. First, make a statement in the present tense. Then, make a negative statement in the past using the time expression given in parentheses. Replace any noun object with a pronoun.

MODEL: Siehst du dir das Haus an? (gestern)
          Ja, ich sehe es mir an. Gestern habe ich mir das nicht angesehen.

 1. Schaust du dir auch den Garten an? (heute Morgen)
 2. Können wir uns diesen Kauf leisten? (letztes Jahr)
 3. Soll ich mir die Sache nochmal überlegen? (schon vorher [use past subjunctive])
 4. Kannst du dir alles gut vorstellen? (schon immer)

B. Use the cued verb to provide a response that is appropriate to each situation. Use the dative reflexive pronoun + **das**.

 1. Ihre Freundin hat sich ein neues Auto gekauft. Was fragen Sie sie? (sich leisten können)

2. Ein Kollege hasst seine Arbeit und will kündigen. Was sagen Sie? (sich gut überlegen)
3. Ihr Vater ist Fußballfan und heute Abend spielt Deutschland gegen England. Was sagt er? (sich anschauen)
4. Da ab nächstem Jahr alle Kinder aus dem Haus sein werden, planen Ihre Eltern viele Reisen.
   Ihre Eltern sagen zu Ihnen: (sich nicht vorstellen können)

§4 The Reflexive Pronoun as the Object of a Preposition

Compare the following sentences:

Ich habe über **ihn** gelacht.	*I laughed at him.*
Ich habe über **mich** gelacht.	*I laughed at myself.*
Er hat über **sich** gelacht.	*He laughed at himself.*

When the reflexive pronoun is the object of a preposition, as in the second and third sentences, its case is determined by the preceding preposition. (For cases governed by prepositions, see Kap. 7 §1 to 5, §7, and §8.)

Additional examples

Du kannst stolz auf **dich** sein.	*You can be proud of yourself.*
Bist **du** nun zufrieden mit **dir**?	*Are you now content with yourself?*
Ich bin außer **mir**.	*I'm beside myself.*

Note that German uses the reflexive pronoun in the expression **bei sich haben** (*to have on you, to carry with you*)

Haben Sie Ihren Ausweis **bei sich**?	*Do you have your ID card on you?*
Ich habe kein Geld **bei mir**.	*I have no money on me.*

Übung 15-5

ANWENDEN A. Replace the subject in each sentence with the ones given in parentheses. Use the appropriate reflexive pronouns and possessives.

MODEL: Ich bin nicht zufrieden mit mir. (Helga, wir)
   <u>Helga ist nicht zufrieden mit sich.</u>
   <u>Wir sind nicht zufrieden mit uns.</u>

1. Er kann stolz auf sich sein. (Sie, du, wir)
2. Ich bin außer mir. (wir, Bergers)
3. Ich habe kein Geld bei mir. (Herr Berger, die Kinder)
4. Haben Sie Ihren Ausweis bei sich? (du, Klaus, ihr)
5. Leonore hat ihren Führerschein nicht bei sich. (ich, du, Sie)

B. State what you and other people might have on you/them (**bei sich**) in the following situations. Name one or more items.

1. Sie fahren mit dem Auto.
2. Kurt geht zur Uni (viele Bücher).
3. Ihr Freund fliegt nach Deutschland. Was fragen Sie?
4. Sie und ein paar Freunde gehen ins Kino.
5. Ihre Mutter geht in die Stadt zum Einkaufen.
6. Die Direktorin einer Firma geht zur Arbeit.

Reciprocal Pronouns and Uses of *selbst/selber*

§5   Reciprocal Pronouns

1. The reciprocal pronoun **einander** (*each other* or *one another*) is never inflected.

Sie helfen **einander**.	*They help each/one another.*

When following a preposition, **einander** is combined with it.

Wir hören oft **voneinander**.	*We often hear from each other.*
Wir sitzen **nebeneinander**.	*We are sitting next to each other.*

Normally, **einander** and the reciprocal reflexive pronouns are interchangeable; however, after prepositions only **einander** can be used.

2. The reflexive pronouns are often used to express reciprocity.

Sie hassen **sich**.   Possible meanings: *They hate themselves.*
They hate each other.

The context must clarify the meaning.

Übung 15-6

ANWENDEN Paraphrase each of the following statements using one of the verbs listed below and a reciprocal pronoun. You may provide more than one statement for a given situation and use the verbs multiple times.

hassen, schreiben, anrufen, begrüßen, streiten, auskommen, lieben, helfen

1. Anita findet Oskar furchtbar und er mag sie auch nicht.
2. Erika und Christian heiraten. Die Eltern fragen: _____
3. Ute und ihre Freundin haben sich schon lange nicht mehr gesehen und treffen sich beim Einkaufen. Was haben sie zuerst wohl gemacht?
4. Die beste Freundin von Frau Hagen wohnt im Ausland. Was machen die beiden vielleicht um in Kontakt zu bleiben?
5. Die Günthers haben sehr nette Nachbarn. Was sagen die Günthers über ihre Beziehung zu den Nachbarn?
6. Pia liest die Arbeit, die Waltraud geschrieben hat und Waltraud übt English mit Pia.

7. Karin redet und redet mit ihrer Freundin am Telefon. Karins Mutter ist neugierig und fragt: _____
8. Ruth und ihr Mann haben verschiedene Meinungen und reden sehr laut darüber.

§6 Uses of *selbst/selber*

Selbst (*myself, yourself,* etc.) is an intensifier rather than a reflexive pronoun. The form **selber** (*myself, yourself,* etc.) is preferred in colloquial German.

Er glaubt das nicht.	*He doesn't believe that.*
Er glaubt das **selbst** (**selber**) nicht.	*He doesn't believe that himself.*

In the second sentence, **selbst** (**selber**) is used for emphasis. This intensifier has no case endings. English uses the reflexive pronoun as an intensifier.

Additional examples

Waschen Sie Ihren Wagen **selber**?	*Do you wash your car yourself?*
Herr Schreiber macht alle Reparaturen **selbst**.	*Mr. Schreiber does all repair work himself.*
Hast du den Bericht **selber** getippt?	*Did you type the report yourself?*
Kochen Sie **selbst**?	*Do you do your own cooking?*

Selbst (**selber**) may also reinforce reflexives.

Er hat nicht mich, sondern **sich selbst** getäuscht.	*He did not deceive me, but himself.*

When **selbst** (never **selber**) precedes the element it qualifies, it means *even*.

Selbst sie hat kein Geld.	*Even she has no money.*

Übung 15-7

VERSTEHEN Translate the following sentences into English.

1. Machst du alles selber?
2. Der Professor hat es selber nicht gewusst.
3. Selbst ein kleines Kind kann das.
4. Hast du etwas zu mir gesagt oder hast du mit dir selber gesprochen?
5. Du bist die Bescheidenheit selbst! (idiomatic)
6. Sie haben sich einfach selbst bedient.
7. Selbst er musste nachgeben.

§7 Summary of the Main Features

Reflexive pronouns

1. The reflexive pronouns are identical in form to the personal pronouns except for the form **sich** in the third person singular and plural, and in the formal address.

2. The reflexive pronoun occurs more frequently in the accusative than in the dative; dative reflexives are only used when the verb involves a direct object. The forms of the accusative and dative differ only in the first and second person singular.

	ACCUSATIVE	DATIVE
ich	**mich**	**mir**
du	**dich**	**dir**
er		
sie	**sich**	
es		
wir	**uns**	
ihr	**euch**	
sie	**sich**	
Sie		

3. In the imperative, only the familiar singular imperative distinguishes dative and accusative reflexive pronouns.

Wasch **dich!**	Wasch **dir** die Hände!
Wascht **euch!**	Wascht **euch** die Hände!
Waschen Sie **sich!**	Waschen Sie **sich** die Hände!

4. The reflexive pronoun usually follows the inflected verb form or a personal pronoun (subject or direct object), but precedes all other elements.

Reciprocal pronouns

Each other/one another may be expressed by **einander** or by the appropriate reflexive pronoun (except after prepositions).

Uses of selbst (selber)

Selbst (selber) is used as an intensifier and also to strengthen reflexive pronouns. **Selbst** preceding a noun or pronoun corresponds to the English *even*.

Übung 15-8

ZUSAMMENFASSUNG Reflexive pronouns, reflexive verbs, and uses of **selbst**.

A. Using the cues, form statements and questions that fit the context.

> MODEL: Es ist sehr kalt, und ich trage nur eine dünne Jacke. Ich denke:
> (sich erkälten)
> „Vielleicht erkälte ich mich."
> or: „Hoffentlich erkälte ich mich nicht."

1. Margot sitzt vorm Fernseher.
   (sich an•schauen / die Nachrichten)
2. Ich habe Martin beleidigt. Ich denke:
   (müssen / sich entschuldigen)

3. Der Chef ist nicht fair zu Andreas. Warum protestiert Andreas nicht? Ich sage zu ihm:
   (müssen / sich verteidigen)
4. Ich habe Gäste und sage zu ihnen:
   (bitte / sich bedienen!) (familiar plural)
5. Man hat Dieters Brieftasche gestohlen. Dieter sagt:
   (außer sich sein)
6. Annerose fragt mich, was ich am Wochenende gemacht habe. Ich antworte:
   (sich langweilen) (present perfect)
7. Mein Freund sagt, dass das Benzin bestimmt billiger wird. Ich sage:
   (können / das / sich nicht vor•stellen)
8. Ich will einen Scheck einlösen. Leider kann ich es nicht.
   (keinen Ausweis / bei sich haben)
9. Ich habe viele alte Münzen (*coins*) und möchte sie meiner Freundin zeigen. Ich frage sie:
   (sich interessieren / Münzen)
10. Ich niese (*sneeze*) sehr viel. Ich denke:
    (vielleicht / sich erkälten / am Sonntag) (present perfect)
11. Margot und Renate kommen aus der Stadt. Ich frage sie, was sie gekauft haben. Renate sagt:
    (Nichts. Wir / sich an•sehen / nur die Schaufenster) (present perfect)
12. Marlene will ihren Wagen verkaufen. Sie fragt mich, ob ich ihn kaufen will. Ich sage:
    (müssen / sich überlegen)
13. Barbara und Karin haben ein Doppelzimmer im Studentenheim. Im nächsten Semester will Barbara ausziehen (*move out*). Warum? Sie sagt:
    (wir / nicht aus•kommen)
14. Klaus wohnt nicht mehr mit Rainer in einem Zimmer. Helga sagt:
    (sie / nicht aus•kommen) (present perfect)
15. Ich bin bei Barbara. Wir trinken Kaffee und essen Kuchen. Ich frage sie:
    (Kuchen / selbst backen?) (present perfect)
    Sie antwortet:
    (nur Kaffee / selbst kochen) (present perfect)
16. Frank fährt im Sommer nach Kalifornien. Ich frage ihn:
    (sich freuen / Reise?)
    Frank fragt mich, ob ich mitfahren will. Ich habe kein Geld und sage:
    (können / sich leisten / nicht)
17. Andreas Neumann ist ein Freund von mir. Er hat mir eine Karte aus Berlin geschickt. Ich sage zu Käte:
    (du / sich erinnern an? diese Karte / bekommen (present perfect)
    ich / sehr freuen / darüber)

B. Respond to these personalized questions.

1. Welche Dinge machen Sie selbst? Welche Dinge nicht?
2. Fragen Sie einen Freund/eine Freundin über drei Dinge und ob er/sie diese Dinge selbst macht.
3. Ärgern Sie sich manchmal über sich selber? Wann? Warum?

4. Was machen Sie, wenn Sie Ihre Eltern (oder Geschwister, oder Freunde) nach langer Zeit wieder sehen?
5. Beschreiben Sie das Verhältnis zu Ihren Geschwistern. Wie ist es? Streiten Sie sich? Verstehen Sie sich gut?

Themen und Vokabular

Tagtägliches

sich ab•trocknen	to dry oneself off
sich bürsten	to brush oneself
sich (dat.) die Haare bürsten	to brush one's hair
(sich) duschen	to shower, to take a shower
sich kämmen	to comb oneself
sich (dat.) die Haare kämmen	to comb one's hair
sich die Zähne putzen	to brush one's teeth
sich schminken	to put on make-up, to make oneself up
sich rasieren	to shave
sich waschen, wusch, hat gewaschen	to wash up
sich (dat.) die Hände (die Haare, das Gesicht usw.) waschen	to wash one's hands (hair, face, etc.)

Miteinander

(sich) an•rufen, rief . . . an, hat angerufen	to call each other on the phone
gut (nicht) miteinander ausgekommen kam . . . aus	to (not) get along well
(sich) begrüßen	to greet (each other)
sich entschuldigen	to apologize (each other)
(sich) hassen	to hate (each other)
(sich) helfen, half, hat geholfen	to help (each other)

(sich) küssen	to kiss (each other)
(sich) lieben	to love (each other)
(sich) schreiben, schrieb, hat geschrieben	to write (one another)
(sich) streiten, stritt, hat gestritten	to argue (with each other)
(sich) treffen (trifft), traf, hat getroffen	to meet (with each other), to get together
(sich) umarmen	to hug (each other)
sich unterhalten (unterhält), unterhielt hat unterhalten	to converse (with one another), to talk
(sich) gut verstehen, verstand, hat verstanden	to get along, to understand one another

Was man mitnimmt

die Aktentasche, -n	briefcase
der Ausweis, -e	ID card, membership card
das Bargeld	cash
die Brieftasche, -n	wallet
der Führerschein, -e	driver's license
die Geldbörse, -n	purse, wallet
die Gürteltasche, -n	fanny pack
die Kreditkarte, -n	credit card
die Handtasche, -n	(woman's) purse
die Papiere (pl.)	papers, documents
der Pass, ¨e	passport
das Portmonee, -s (also: Portemonnaie, -s)	wallet, purse
der Rucksack, ¨e	backpack
das Scheckheft, -e	checkbook

16 The Passive Voice

Basic Differences between the Active and the Passive Voices

§1 In English

Compare

The policeman caught the thief.	(active voice)
The thief was caught by the policeman.	(passive voice)

In the first sentence the subject, the policeman, does something; it is *active*. The sentence is expressed in the *active voice*.

In the second sentence the subject, the thief, is acted upon by someone, i.e., the policeman. Sentences in which the subject is not active but acted upon are expressed in the *passive voice*. The grammatical term for the element that acts upon the subject of a passive sentence—in the above example, the policeman—is the *agent*. The agent is the element performing the action.

Observe the different subjects and objects between the active and the passive sentence.

ACTIVE: **The policeman** caught **the thief**.
      SUBJECT   DIRECT OBJECT

PASSIVE: **The thief** was caught by **the policeman**.
      SUBJECT   AGENT

The direct object of the active voice becomes the subject of the passive, and the subject of the active voice becomes the agent of the passive.

When you compare the two sentences you will notice a shift of emphasis:

In the first sentence the attention focuses on the fact that the policeman caught the thief.

In the second sentence the focus of attention is the thief and what happened to him.

In many passive sentences, the agent is unknown or unimportant and, therefore, not stated.

> The thief was caught.
> The houses were torn down.
> The Bauers will not be invited.

Stylistically, in formal writing the active voice is preferred in English. The passive voice has less impact and is generally to be avoided. In German, the passive voice lends a more authoritative or intellectual tone to a text and is often preferred in formal writing. The passive voice is used with much greater frequency in German as a result.

Übung 16-1

VERSTEHEN   A. Indicate whether each sentence is in the active or passive voice.

1. The house was built in three months.
2. Why were the children laughing?
3. The spaghetti was eaten by Beppo.
4. Is the road being repaired this summer?
5. The press had been asking for an explanation.
6. Have you seen his latest film?
7. Private Ryan should have been saved.

B. Now identify the agent in each sentence, or state that no agent is stated. Remember that in the passive voice the agent is not the subject of the sentence.

The formation of the tenses in the active and passive voices

Keep in mind that the active and the passive voices use different infinitives.

INFINITIVE OF THE ACTIVE VOICE	INFINITIVE OF THE PASSIVE VOICE
to catch	to be caught
to invite	to be invited
to watch	to be watched

The tenses are based on these infinitives, as seen in the following synopsis.

	ACTIVE VOICE	PASSIVE VOICE
infinitive:	**to watch**	**to be watched**
PRESENT	he watches / is watching	he is (being) watched
PAST	he watched / was watching	he was (being) watched
PRESENT PERFECT	he has watched	he has been watched
PAST PERFECT	he had watched	he had been watched
FUTURE	he will watch	he will be watched
FUTURE PERFECT	he will have watched	he will have been watched

Übung 16-2

VERSTEHEN   A. Restate the following two sentences by using the tenses indicated in parentheses. (In English!)

1. This project is financed by the government. (past, present perfect, past perfect, future)
2. His name was not mentioned. (future, present, present perfect, past perfect)

B. Restate the following sentences in the passive voice. Maintain the tense. (In English!)

1. Many adolescents are reading his latest book.
2. The speaker did not mention this point.
3. A real estate agent has just sold this house.
4. The police had informed the mayor.
5. The interviewer will ask you to give all your qualifications.

§2   In German

Compare

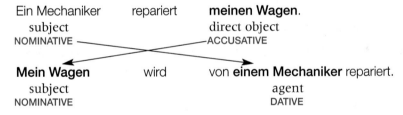

Ein Mechaniker	repariert	**meinen Wagen**.
subject		direct object
NOMINATIVE		ACCUSATIVE

Mein Wagen	wird	von **einem Mechaniker** repariert.
subject		agent
NOMINATIVE		DATIVE

My car is being repaired by a mechanic.

Note:
a. As in English, the direct object of the active voice becomes the subject of the passive voice, which means a switch in German from the accusative **meinen Wagen** to the nominative **mein Wagen**.

b. The subject of the active voice, **ein Mechaniker**, becomes the agent of the passive, **einem Mechaniker** (the dative object of **von**).

c. English uses the auxiliary *to be* + past participle to express the passive; German uses the auxiliary **werden** + past participle. The past participle is in final position.

d. In the German passive infinitive, **werden** follows the past participle: **repariert werden** (*to be repaired*)

(For the formation of past participles, see Kap. 3 §2, §4, §7 to 9.)

Compare the infinitives of the active and passive that will occur in the exercises.

ACTIVE		PASSIVE	
ab•sagen	*to call off, cancel*	abgesagt werden	*to be called off, be canceled*
anerkennen	*to recognize*	anerkannt werden	*to be recognized*
ändern	*to change*	geändert werden	*to be changed*
aus•nutzen	*to exploit*	ausgenutzt werden	*to be exploited*
bauen	*to build*	gebaut werden	*to be built*
bedienen	*to serve, wait on*	bedient werden	*to be served, be waited on*
behandeln	*to treat, deal with*	behandelt werden	*to be treated, be dealt with*
entdecken	*to discover*	entdeckt werden	*to be discovered*
erledigen	*to take care of*	erledigt werden	*to be taken care of*
ernennen	*to appoint*	ernannt werden	*to be appointed*
erwähnen	*to mention*	erwähnt werden	*to be mentioned*
gründen	*to found*	gegründet werden	*to be founded*
loben	*to praise*	gelobt werden	*to be praised*
manipulieren	*to manipulate*	manipuliert werden	*to be manipulated*
unterbrechen	*to interrupt*	unterbrochen werden	*to be interrupted*
untersuchen	*to investigate*	untersucht werden	*to be investigated*
verwöhnen	*to spoil (someone)*	verwöhnt werden	*to be spoiled*
wählen	*to elect*	gewählt werden	*to be elected*
zerstören	*to destroy*	zerstört werden	*to be destroyed*

The Tenses in the Passive Voice

§3   The Present Tense

Compare the following conjugations.

ACTIVE	PASSIVE
infinitive: **fragen**	infinitive: **gefragt werden**
ich frage *I ask, am asking*	ich **werde** gefragt *I am (being) asked*
du fragst	du **wirst** gefragt
er ⎞	er ⎞
sie ⎬fragt	sie ⎬**wird** gefragt
es ⎠	es ⎠
wir fragen	wir **werden** gefragt
ihr fragt	ihr **werdet** gefragt
sie fragen	sie **werden** gefragt
Sie fragen	Sie **werden** gefragt
	werden + past participle
	the past participle remains the same.

Remember:	In passive sentences, **werden** is rendered by a form of *to be*.

Sometimes a German passive construction in the active voice is more appropriately rendered as an active sentence in English. When no agent is stated, the generalizing *they* or *people* are employed as a subject.

Frau Schmidt wird oft angerufen.
lit.: *Mrs. Schmidt is called often.*
idiomatic: *Mrs. Schmidt gets lots of calls.*

Diese Spielzeuge werden gern gekauft.
lit.: *These toys are gladly bought.*
idiomatic: *People like to buy these toys.*

Übung 16-3

VERSTEHEN Determine if the sentence is in the active or passive voice.

1. Das wird oft vergessen.
2. Diese Instrumente werden aus Schweden importiert.
3. Du wirst die Kinder verwöhnen.
4. Wir werden sehr unfair behandelt.
5. Sie werden euch wahrscheinlich ausnutzen.
6. Dieser Punkt wird im ersten Kapitel erwähnt.
7. Werden Sie schon bedient?
8. Diesen Plan werdet ihr ändern.
9. Wie wird die Firma das Projekt finanzieren?
10. Wie wird das gemacht?

Übung 16-4

ANWENDEN State the following information that one might see on signs in the passive voice and the present tense. Begin each sentence with **hier**.

MODEL: Deutsch sprechen
          Hier wird Deutsch gesprochen.

1. Kleidung günstig reinigen
2. Haushaltgeräte schnell reparieren
3. deutsches Essen servieren
4. Verkäuferinnen einstellen
5. Lehrbücher für Medizin verkaufen
6. Deutschkurs für Ausländer anbieten
7. Pilsner Bier ausschenken

§4   The Past, Present Perfect, Past Perfect, Future, and Future Perfect of the Passive Voice

You are familiar with the tenses of **werden** used as the main verb, meaning *to become, get*. When **werden** functions as the main verb, its principal parts are **werden (wird), wurde, ist geworden**.

PRESENT	Sie **wird** nervös.	*She is becoming nervous.*
PAST	Sie **wurde** nervös.	*She became nervous.*
PRESENT PERFECT	Sie **ist** nervös geworden.	*She has become nervous.*
		or: *She became nervous.*
PAST PERFECT	Sie **war** nervös **geworden**.	*She had become nervous.*
FUTURE	Sie **wird** nervös **werden**.	*She will become nervous.*
FUTURE PERFECT	Sie **wird** nervös **geworden sein**.	*She will have become nervous.*

In the passive the auxiliary **werden** governs the tense of the sentence, and the form of its past participle is modified from **geworden** to **worden**.

ACTIVE	PASSIVE
infinitive: **fragen**	infinitive: **gefragt werden**
PRESENT	
Sie fragt nicht.	Sie wird nicht gefragt.
She does not ask.	*She is not (being) asked.*
PAST	
Sie fragte nicht.	Sie wurde nicht gefragt.
She did not ask.	*She was not (being) asked.*
PRESENT PERFECT	
Sie hat nicht gefragt.	Sie ist nicht gefragt worden.
She has not asked. or: *She did not ask.*	*She has not been asked.*
PAST PERFECT	
Sie hatte nicht gefragt.	Sie war nicht gefragt worden.
She had not asked.	*She had not been asked.*
FUTURE	
Sie wird nicht fragen.	Sie wird nicht gefragt werden.
She will not ask.	*She will not be asked.*
FUTURE PERFECT	
Sie wird nicht gefragt haben.	Sie wird nicht gefragt worden sein.
She will not have asked.	*She will not have been asked.*

The past participle of the main verb, i.e., **gefragt**, does not change.

Werden requires **sein**; thus the perfect tenses of the passive voice are formed with **sein**.

In the active voice, the present perfect is frequently used as the conversational past (cf. Kap. 3 §2). This occurs less often in the passive voice. In general, the present perfect is used in contexts where English would use this form.

Examples

> Die Rechnung **ist** noch nicht **bezahlt worden.**
> *The bill has not yet been paid.*
> Die Fernsehsendung **ist** schon wieder **unterbrochen worden.**
> *The TV program has been interrupted again.*

As in the active voice, the future is formed with **werden** + infinitive of the main verb.

Sie **wird** nicht **fragen.**	Sie **wird** nicht **gefragt werden.**
ACTIVE INFINITIVE	PASSIVE INFINITIVE

Keep in mind that in German the present tense is commonly used to express future time if an adverb or the context indicates that the future is referred to (cf. Kap. 2 §6).

Example

> Die Sache **wird** morgen **erledigt.**

The English equivalent is in the future tense.

> *This matter will be taken care of tomorrow.*

The future perfect is rarely used in the passive. It will, therefore, not be practiced.

PATTERN: THE TENSES IN THE PASSIVE VOICE					
PRESENT	sie **wird**	_____ (past part.)		she is (being)	_____ (past part.)
PAST	sie **wurde**	_____ (past part.)		she was (being)	_____ (past part.)
PRESENT PERFECT	sie **ist**	_____ (past part.)	**worden**	she has been	_____ (past part.)
PAST PERFECT	sie **war**	_____ (past part.)	**worden**	she had been	_____ (past part.)
FUTURE	sie **wird**	_____ (past part.)	**werden**	she will be	_____ (past part.)

Übung 16-5

ANWENDEN A. Practice the different tenses by stating each sentence in the past, present perfect, past perfect, and future passive.

1. Nach der Wiedervereinigung / neue Regierung / gewählt worden
   past passive
   present perfect passive
   past perfect passive
   future passive
2. Die neuen Bundesländer / an die Bundesrepublik / anschließen
   past passive
   present perfect passive
   past perfect passive
   future passive

B. Combine the elements into passive constructions, first in the past and then the present perfect.

MODEL: 1961 / die Berliner Mauer / bauen
          Im Jahre 1961 wurde die Berliner Mauer gebaut.
          Im Jahre 1961 ist die Berliner Mauer gebaut worden.

Historische Ereignisse in Deutschland.

1. Deutschland / besiegen / 1945
2. Ab 1949 / Deutschland / als Demokratie / anerkennen
3. 1963 / Freundschaftsvertrag / zwischen Frankreich und Deutschland / abschließen
4. 1989 / die Grenze / öffnen
5. 1990 / Deutschland / offiziell wiedervereinigt

C. Now use similar constructions to mention five historical events of your choosing. State an event in the past and then state a related event in the past perfect.

MODEL: Im Jahre 1871 wurde Frankreich von Preußen besiegt.
          Davor war Bismarck zum Ministerpräsident ernannt worden.

Conjugation of the tenses in the passive

PRESENT

	ich	werde gefragt	*I am (being) asked*
	du	wirst	
er, sie, es	wird		
	wir	werden	
	ihr	werdet	
	sie	werden	
	Sie	werden	

PAST

	ich	wurde gefragt	*I was (being) asked*
	du	wurdest	
er, sie, es	wurde		
	wir	wurden	
	ihr	wurdet	
	sie	wurden	
	Sie	wurden	

PRESENT PERFECT

	ich	bin gefragt worden	*I have been asked*
	du	bist	*I was (being) asked*
er, sie, es	ist		
	wir	sind	
	ihr	seid	
	sie	sind	
	Sie	sind	

PAST PERFECT

	ich	war gefragt worden	*I had been asked*
	du	warst	
er, sie, es	war		
	wir	waren	
	ihr	wart	
	sie	waren	
	Sie	waren	

FUTURE

	ich	werde gefragt werden	*I will be asked*
	du	wirst	
er, sie, es	wird		
	wir	werden	
	ihr	werdet	
	sie	werden	
	Sie	werden	

Übung 16-6

ANWENDEN Restate the sentences in the tenses indicated.

Fragen über diverse Aspekte der Arbeit.

1. Wirst du von deinem Chef ausgenutzt? (past, present perfect, future)
2. Wirst du auch gelobt? (present perfect, past perfect)
3. Werdet ihr von Herrn Kostner manipuliert? (present perfect, past perfect, future)
4. Wie werden die Frauen behandelt? (past, present perfect)
5. Wird alles schnell oder langsam erledigt? (present perfect, past perfect)
6. Werden viele Besprechungen abgesagt? (future)
7. Wird der Chef oft unterbrochen? (past, present perfect, past perfect)
8. Werden viele Dinge geändert? (present perfect, future)

§5   Dependent Word Order

The inflected verb form is in the final position.

> Ich glaube nicht, dass er von seinem Bruder betrogen **wird**.
> betrogen **wurde**.
> betrogen **worden ist**.
> betrogen **worden war**.
> betrogen **werden wird**.

Übung 16-7

ANWENDEN First restate three of the five historical events from Übung 16-5, C., using an introductory clause such as **ich weiß, dass**. . . ; **wusstest du, dass**. . . ; **ich bin nicht sicher, ob**. . . ; **kannst du mir sagen, ob**. . . . Then state three events that you expect to occur in the future and also introduce them with an introductory clause.

Model: Ich weiß, dass im Jahre 1871 Frankreich von Preußen besiegt wurde. Ich glaube, dass nächstes Jahr die Gründung meiner Uni gefeiert werden wird.

Summary and review: the meanings of **werden**

To recognize the meaning of **werden** in a given context, you have to determine first whether it is accompanied by an adjective, a noun, or a verb.

1. werden + predicate adjective or predicate noun

Es **wird** kälter.	*It is getting colder.*
Er **wurde** Präsident.	*He became president.*

Werden is the main verb in the active voice. The English equivalent is *to become, to get.*

2. werden + verb

When **werden** is an auxiliary, the main verb may be an infinitive or a past participle.

If the verb is an infinitive, **werden** is the future auxiliary in the active voice.

Sie **wird** den Fall **untersuchen**. *She will investigate the case.*

If the verb is a past participle, **werden** is the passive auxiliary.

Der Fall **wird untersucht**. *The case is being investigated.*

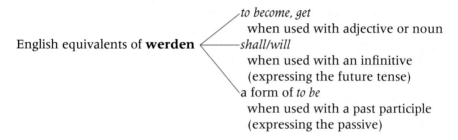

English equivalents of **werden**

to become, get
when used with adjective or noun

shall/will
when used with an infinitive
(expressing the future tense)

a form of *to be*
when used with a past participle
(expressing the passive)

Übung 16-8

VERSTEHEN Analyze the use of **werden** in the following sentences.

MODEL: Ich fürchte, Sie werden mich auslachen.
Werden *plus the infinitive of* auslachen *expresses the future tense.*

1. Niemand wird das glauben.
2. Dein Deutsch wird jeden Tag besser.
3. Das wird anders gemacht.
4. Hoffentlich wirst du das verstehen.
5. Wie werden Sie Ihr Geld investieren?
6. Das Projekt wird von einem Millionär finanziert.
7. Hoffentlich wird es nicht kälter.
8. Ich fürchte, ich werde von Ihnen manipuliert.
9. Das wird nie passieren.

Übung 16-9

ZUSAMMENFASSUNG Tenses in the passive voice. Dependent word order.
A. Formulate two statements in the present passive for each location or situation.

MODEL: in einem Hotel
In einem Hotel wird Frühstück serviert.
In einem Hotel werden die Zimmer jeden Tag saubergemacht.

Was wird hier gemacht?

1. im Kino
2. am Flughafen

3. im Krieg
4. in einem Konzert (in der Oper, im Theater)
5. während einer Diskussion
6. in der Schule

B. State five promises that a candidate for mayor or governor might make. Use the future passive.

MODEL: Öffentliche Gebäude werden renoviert werden.

Additional Features of Passive Sentences

§6   The Agent Preceded by *von, durch,* or *mit*

In most passive sentences the agent is preceded by the preposition **von** (+ dative). Occasionally **durch** (+ accusative) is used to indicate the intermediary or the inanimate means by which an action is brought about.

> Wir wurden **durch einen Boten** benachrichtigt.
> *We were notified by a messenger.*
> Die Kirche wurde **durch Bomben** zerstört.
> *The church was destroyed by bombs.*

The preposition **mit** (+ dative) is used when the reference is to an instrument or a tool. This parallels the English use of *with*.

> Die Tür wurde **mit einem Hauptschlüssel** geöffnet.
> *The door was opened with a master key.*

§7   Introductory *es* in Passive Sentences

Es is often placed at the beginning of passive main clauses. It cannot be used in questions or dependent clauses.

> **Viele Fabriken** werden geschlossen.
>   SUBJECT
>
> *Many factories are being closed.*
>
> **Es** werden **viele Fabriken** geschlossen.
>   SUBJECT

Naturally, the verb agrees with the subject **viele Fabriken** rather than with **es**. (The use of introductory **es** with active verbs is explained in Kap. 14 §6, 2.)

Es is omitted if another element is placed at the beginning of the sentence:

Einige Fragen wurden nicht beantwortet.	*Some questions were not*
Es wurden einige Fragen nicht beantwortet.	*answered.*
Leider wurden einige Fragen nicht beantwortet.	*Unfortunately, some questions were not answered.*

§8   Dative Objects in Passive Sentences

1. English permits either the direct or indirect object of an active sentence to become the subject of a passive sentence.

ACTIVE   They awarded **this inventor the Nobel prize**.
                       INDIRECT OBJECT   DIRECT OBJECT

PASSIVE   a. **The Nobel prize** was awarded to this inventor.
               SUBJECT

          b. **This inventor** was awarded the Nobel prize.
             SUBJECT

In German, only the accusative (direct) object of the active sentence may become the subject (nominative case) of the passive voice.

ACTIVE   Sie verliehen **diesem Erfinder den Nobelpreis.**
                       INDIRECT OBJECT   DIRECT OBJECT

PASSIVE   a. **Der Nobelpreis** wurde diesem Erfinder verliehen.
              SUBJECT

          b. **Diesem Erfinder** wurde **der Nobelpreis** verliehen.
           INDIRECT OBJECT   SUBJECT

          or: Es wurde **diesem Erfinder der Nobelpreis** verliehen.

In contrast to the English passive sentence b., the subject in the German passive sentence b. is **der Nobelpreis**, the direct object of the active sentence. It is marked by the nominative case.

The indirect object **diesem Erfinder** is retained in the dative case. It may be placed in first position, or follow the inflected verb when an introductory **es** is used.

Additional examples

    Ihm wurde auch eine französische Medaille verliehen.
or: Es wurde **ihm** auch eine französische Medaille verliehen.
    He was also awarded a French medal.

    Mir wurde eine zweite Chance gegeben.
or: **Es** wurde **mir** eine zweite Chance gegeben.
    I was given a second chance.

    Uns wurden nur die Vorteile gezeigt, nicht die Nachteile.
or: **Es** wurden **uns** nur die Vorteile gezeigt, nicht die Nachteile.
    We were shown only the advantages, not the disadvantages.

2. Dative verbs that lack accusative objects (cf. Kap. 5 §7), such as **danken, drohen** (*to threaten*), **gratulieren, helfen,** and **widersprechen** (*to contradict*), can form only subjectless passives, since there is no accusative object in the active sentence to become the subject in the passive. The verb is in the third-person singular. An introductory **es** is frequently added. Compare

ACTIVE   Man gratuliert ihr.
PASSIVE   **Ihr** wird gratuliert.
or: **Es** wird **ihr** gratuliert.
She is being congratulated.

ACTIVE   Man dankte ihm nicht dafür.
PASSIVE   **Ihm** wurde nicht dafür gedankt.
or: **Es** wurde **ihm** nicht dafür gedankt.
He was not thanked for it.

Note that the English equivalents have nominative subjects, *he* and *she*, respectively.

3. In German, the implied subject of a passive verb may be a dependent clause or an infinitive phrase.

Mir wurde gesagt, ⸺⸺⸺⸺ dass sie Margot Bauer heißt.
or: **Es** wurde **mir** gesagt, ⸺
I was told that her name is Margot Bauer.

Ihm wurde geraten, ⸺⸺⸺⸺ weniger aggressiv zu sein.
or: **Es** wurde **ihm** geraten, ⸺
He was advised to be less aggressive.

Übung 16-10

VERSTEHEN   State whether the element in the first position is the subject or a dative object.

1. Ihnen wurde nicht geholfen.
2. Die Stelle wurde dem letzten Bewerber gegeben.
3. Den Eltern wurden viele Karten geschickt.
4. Dem Kind wurde alles dreimal gesagt.
5. Alles ist dreimal gesagt worden.
6. Das Gemälde wurde mitten am Tag gestohlen.
7. Uns war die Information zu spät zugekommen.

Übung 16-11

ANWENDEN Restate the following sentences twice, first using the dative object and then **es** in the first position. Maintain the tense.

> MODEL: Man hilft mir nicht.
> <u>Mir wird nicht geholfen.</u>
> <u>Es wird mir nicht geholfen.</u>

1. Man wird dir nicht dafür danken.
2. Man hatte ihm selten widersprochen.
3. Man gab ihm eine zweite Chance.
4. Man hat mir das Geschenk für Marlene nicht gezeigt.
5. Man hat mir das Getränk geholt.
6. Man gratuliert ihr nicht.

§9 Passives That Lack both Subject and Object

The following sentences illustrate a peculiar passive construction.

Es wurde nicht applaudiert.	*There was no applause.*
Leider wurde nicht applaudiert.	*Unfortunately, there was no applause.*

Since **es** or some other element can occupy the subject position, a passive sentence in German may lack both subject and object. Note that the introductory **es** is not used when another element is in the first position.

These sentences are sometimes difficult to render in English. A subject may be supplied according to the context.

> Es wird hier viel gestohlen.
> or: Hier wird viel gestohlen.
> *There is a lot of stealing going on around here.*
> *They steal a lot around here.*

> Es wurde viel gegessen und getrunken.
> or: Da wurde viel gegessen und getrunken.
> *There was a lot of eating and drinking going on.*
> *They ate and drank a lot.*

> Heute wird gefaulenzt.
> *Today we are loafing. (No one is working today.)*
> *Today I am loafing.*

Occasionally, this construction has the force of a command:

> Hier wird nicht geraucht!
> *No smoking here.*

Übung 16-12

ANWENDEN

A. Restate the commands in the passive voice. Begin each sentence with **hier**.

> MODEL: Macht mit!
> <u>Hier wird mitgemacht!</u>

1. Arbeitet heute!
2. Passt auf!
3. Faulenzt nicht!
4. Redet nicht!
5. Alles aufessen!

B. Use the cues to respond in the passive voice to each question. Use time and place expressions or **es** in the initial position, i.e., do not supply a subject or objects.

1. Warum ist es so laut im Nachbarhaus? (da / feiern)
2. Wie feiern die Leute Silvester? (viel tanzen, viel essen und trinken)
3. Und was machen sie noch? (bis zum Morgen / reden)
4. Und am nächsten Tag? (lange schlafen / wenig arbeiten)

§10   Modal Auxiliaries in Passive Sentences

In passive sentences modal auxiliaries usually occur in two tenses: the present and the simple past.

The present tense

ACTIVE   Detektive **müssen** diesen Fall **untersuchen.**
ACTIVE INFINITIVE

PASSIVE   Dieser Fall **muss** von Detektiven **untersucht werden.**
PASSIVE INFINITIVE

This case has to be investigated by detectives.

Note: a. The direct object of the active sentence, **diesen Fall**, becomes the subject of the passive sentence, **dieser Fall**.

b. The modal must agree with the passive subject; thus **müssen** becomes **muss**.

c. The infinitive **untersuchen** becomes **untersucht werden**, which is the passive infinitive.

Keep in mind: The modal is not in the passive, but it is complemented by a passive infinitive.

Here are some active and passive infinitives which occur in the exercises:

ACTIVE		PASSIVE	
benachrichtigen	*to notify*	benachrichtigt werden	*to be notified*
ein•reichen	*to hand in*	eingereicht werden	*to be handed in*
klären	*to clarify*	geklärt werden	*to be clarified*
lösen	*to solve*	gelöst werden	*to be solved*
stören	*to disturb*	gestört werden	*to be disturbed*
übersehen	*to overlook*	übersehen werden	*to be overlooked*
vergessen	*to forget*	vergessen werden	*to be forgotten*
vermeiden	*to avoid*	vermieden werden	*to be avoided*
voraus•sehen	*to foresee*	vorausgesehen werden	*to be foreseen*

The simple past

The modal as the inflected verb is in the past tense (cf. Kap. 4 §2); the passive infinitive remains unchanged. Compare

ACTIVE	PASSIVE
Ich **musste** ihn **benachrichtigen.**	Er **musste benachrichtigt werden.** *He had to be notified.*
Ich **konnte** ihn **benachrichtigen.**	Er **konnte benachrichtigt werden.** *He could be notified.*
Ich **wollte** ihn **benachrichtigen.**	Er **wollte benachrichtigt werden.** *He wanted to be notified.*
Ich **sollte** ihn **benachrichtigen.**	Er **sollte benachrichtigt werden.** *He was supposed to be notified.*

Übung 16-13

ANWENDEN A. Formulate sentences with the correct form of the modal and the passive infinitive.

> Model: Nichts vergessen (dürfen)
> <u>Nichts darf vergessen werden.</u>
> or: <u>Es darf nichts vergessen werden.</u>

Ein Kriminalfall. Was muss (soll, darf, kann) getan werden?

1. den Kommissar benachrichtigen (müssen)
2. ihn stören (dürfen)
3. den Fall genau untersuchen (soll)
4. Informationen schriftlich einreichen (können)
5. Fehler vermeiden (sollen)
6. nichts übersehen (dürfen)
7. den Fall lösen (müssen)

B. Now restate the sentences in the simple past.

C. Make three statements in the past about what had (could, should, was allowed) to be done in the following situations. Use modals in the simple past and passive infinitives.

> MODEL: Vor einer Party
> Es musste eingekauft werden. Das Haus sollte saubergemacht werden. Viele Leute konnten eingeladen werden.

1. ein Autounfall
2. eine Wohnung vor dem Unzug
3. das Haus (die Pflanzen, die Katze) der Nachbarin versorgen
4. Semesterbeginn

Dependent word order

The inflected modal is in final position in dependent word order.

> Ich nehme an, dass er benachrichtigt werden **muss**.
> Schade, dass er nicht benachrichtigt werden **konnte**.

The present perfect, past perfect, and future

As you have seen, passive sentences with modal auxiliaries in the present and simple past parallel their active counterparts. The passive sentences are distinguished merely by the presence of a passive infinitive in place of the active infinitive of the main verb.

This applies also the present perfect, past perfect, and future, as the following table illustrates.

ACTIVE INFINITIVE:	**fragen**	PASSIVE INFINITIVE:	**gefragt werden**
	to ask		*to be asked*

PRESENT PERFECT

Ich **habe** ihn nie **fragen müssen**.	Er **hat** nie **gefragt werden müssen**.
DOUBLE INFINITIVE	DOUBLE INFINITIVE
I have never had to ask him.	*He has never had to be asked.*

PAST PERFECT

Ich **hatte** ihn **fragen müssen**.	Er **hatte gefragt werden müssen**.
DOUBLE INFINITIVE	DOUBLE INFINITIVE
I had had to ask him.	*He had had to be asked.*

FUTURE

Ich **werde** ihn **fragen müssen**.	Er **wird gefragt werden müssen**.
DOUBLE INFINITIVE	DOUBLE INFINITIVE
I will have to ask him.	*He will have to be asked.*

These awkward passive constructions are rarely used and will therefore not be practiced.

§11   The Statal Passive

Ordinarily, passive sentences describe a process: something is, was, or will be taking place. For many passive sentences, there is also a statal counterpart or completed action, called the *statal passive.*

1. a. Die Tür **wird geschlossen**.   *The door is being closed.*
   b. Die Tür **ist geschlossen**.   *The door is closed* (not open).
2. a. Mein Wagen **wird repariert**.   *My car is being repaired.*
   b. Mein Wagen **ist repariert**.   *My car is repaired*
      (back in working order).

Sentences 1. a. and 2. a. indicate the *process* of closing and repairing; sentences 1. b. and 2. b. denote the *result* of that process, i.e., a state or completed action. *Statal passives* employ **sein**: the past participles **geschlossen** and **repariert** function as predicate adjectives.

Übung 16-14

ANWENDEN   The following sentences in English express a process or a condition. Express them in German with the passive in the present tense, or as a statal passive with **sein**.

1. Do you know if the museum is closed on Monday?
2. Are the restaurants open late at night?
3. Is the church being renovated the whole month?
4. At what time will the stores close?
5. Is wine sold on Sundays?

A note on the use of geboren werden *and* geboren sein

a. Wann **wurde** Lincoln **geboren**?   *When was Lincoln born?*
b. Wann **sind** Sie **geboren**?   *When were you born?*
   (lit. *When are you born?*)
c. Ich **bin** 1960 **geboren**.   *I was born in 1960.*

The three English sentences are in the simple past of the passive voice. German uses the simple past of the passive voice for people no longer living, as in a., and the present statal forms for the living, as in b. and c. However, a living person frequently uses the simple past of the passive voice when listing biographical data in a personal report, such as a curriculum vitae:

Ich **wurde** am 5. Mai 1960 in Düsseldorf **geboren**.

Alternatives to the Passive Voice

The passive voice is used less in conversational German than in English. The following are some German alternative constructions.

§12   The Use of *man*

The most common alternative to the passive is the use of **man** as the subject of a sentence in the active voice. It may be used to avoid the occurrence of numerous passive constructions.

PASSIVE	**Der Autor** wird nicht erwähnt.	The author is not mentioned.
ACTIVE	**Man** erwähnt den Autor nicht.	*They don't mention the author.*
		(lit.: One doesn't mention the author.)

The subject of the passive sentence becomes the direct object of the active sentence with **man** as the subject (cf. Kap. 14 §4).

Übung 16-15

ANWENDEN   Restate the following sentences in the active voice using **man** as the subject. Maintain the tense.

1. Ich werde hier nie gelobt.
2. Der Chef wurde immer ignoriert.
3. Georg und Franz sind schlecht behandelt worden.
4. Die Chefin wird manipuliert werden.
5. Du warst nicht eingeladen worden.
6. Die Kinder werden sehr verwöhnt.

The following alternatives to the passive are far less common than the **man**-construction.

§13   The Use of *sein* + *zu* + Infinitive

Hunde **sind** an der Leine **zu führen**.
Dogs are to be kept on a leash.
or: *Dogs must be kept on a leash.*

Ist Fräulein Berger telefonisch **zu erreichen**?
Can Miss Berger be reached by phone?

Such constructions indicate that something *is to be done, must be done,* or *can be done.* They also occur in the past tense.

Die Katastrophe **war** nicht **vorauszusehen**.
The catastrophe could not be foreseen.

Note that verbs with separable prefixes insert **zu** between the prefix and verb, as in the example above.

§14   The Use of Reflexive Verbs

1. lassen + **sich** + infinitive is frequently used as a substitute for **können** + passive infinitive.

Das **kann** nicht **vorausgesehen werden.**
Das **lässt sich** nicht **voraussehen.** — *That cannot be foreseen.*

Das **konnte** nicht **vorausgesehen werden.**
Das **ließ sich** nicht **voraussehen.** — *That could not be foreseen.*

Idiom:
> **Das/Es lässt sich nicht ändern.**   *That/It cannot be helped.*
> **Das/Es ließ sich nicht ändern.**   *That/It could not be helped.*

2. Some other verbs permit the reflexive to substitute for the passive.

Dieses Wort wird anders geschrieben.
Dieses Wort schreibt sich anders. — *This word is spelled differently.*

Wie wird Ihr Name ausgesprochen?
Wie spricht sich Ihr Name aus? — *How is your name pronounced?*

Expression:

Das versteht sich. — *That is understood. That goes without*
or: **Das versteht sich von selbst.** — *saying.*

Übung 16-16

ANWENDEN A. Respond to the following sentences using **sein** and **zu** plus infinitive, or **lassen** plus infinitive as an alternative to the passive.

MODEL: Wann muss die Miete bezahlt werden? (am ersten Tag des Monats)
<u>Die Miete ist am ersten Tag des Monats zu bezahlen.</u>
Konnte seine Schuld bewiesen werden? (nein)
<u>Nein, seine Schuld ließ sich nicht beweisen.</u>

1. Wann sollen die Eltern benachrichtigt werden? (sofort)
2. Können Fehler vermieden werden? (nicht immer)
3. Wann muss das Ziel erreicht werden? (nächsten Monat)
4. Kann man die Entwicklung vorraussehen? (ja)
5. Konnte der Wunsch erfüllt werden? (leider nicht)
6. Können die Punkte geklärt werden? (ja, leicht)
7. Kann der Rechtsanwalt telefonisch erreicht werden? (nur schwer)

B. Restate the following sentences, using the reflexive verb as alternative to the passive.

> MODEL: Hoffentlich wird bald eine Lösung gefunden.
> <u>Hoffentlich findet sich bald eine Lösung.</u>

1. Hoffentlich wird bald ein Ausweg aus diesem Dilemma gefunden.
2. Dieses Wort wird anders ausgesprochen.
3 Wie wird Ihr Name geschrieben?
4. Diese Tür wird automatisch geschlossen.
5. Solche Gerüchte werden schnell verbreitet.

Übung 16-17

ZUSAMMENFASSUNG   Various features of the passive voice and its alternatives.

A. Form sentences that fit the context from the cues that are given. Use the passive voice and appropriate tense forms.

1. Sie sind froh, dass das Semester bald zu Ende ist. Sie sagen zu ihren Freunden: . . .
   (das Semesterende / müssen / gefeiert)
2. Ihre Freundin Anne sagt, dass sie älter ist als Sie. Sie können das nicht glauben und fragen sie: . . .
   (in welchem Jahr / geboren?)
3. Sie sind in einer Buchhandlung und schauen ein paar Bücher an. Ein Verkäufer kommt und fragt Sie: . . .
   (schon / bedient?)
4. Sie besuchen einen Freund und stellen Ihr Fahrrad hinters Haus. Dann fragen Sie Ihren Freund: . . .
   (hier / gestohlen?)
5. Sie haben einen Eimer Farbe gekauft, können ihn aber nicht aufmachen. Sie fragen Ihre Schwester: . . .
   (wie / aufgemacht?)
6. Ihr Freund fragt Sie, warum Sie nicht gern zu politischen Versammlungen gehen. Sie antworten . . .
   (zuviel geredet / nicht genug gehandelt)
7. Sie mussten das ganze Wochenende für eine Prüfung lernen. Sie sagen: . . .
   (das / schrecklich / sein, aber es / sich nicht ändern lassen [past])
8. Ihr Freund fragt Sie, ob Sie ihn verteidigen würden, wenn jemand etwas schlechtes über ihn sagt. Sie antworten: . . .
   (das / von selbst / sich verstehen)

B. Answer the following questions by using the active voice with **man**.

1. Wann ist Ihre Universität gegründet worden?
2. Was wird an der Uni angeboten, was für Sie interessant ist?
3. Was wird in Ihrer Heimatstadt gerade renoviert oder repariert?
4. Wann wurde das Haus Ihrer Eltern gebaut?
5. Wann sind Ihre Großeltern geboren? Wann und wo sind Sie geboren?

C. Find five English newspaper headlines written in the passive voice and express them in German. Be aware that headlines often lack elements which the reader understands from the context. State the implied elements in your German sentences.

MODEL: Mayor reelected
Der Bürgermeister (die Bürgermeisterin) wurde wiedergewählt.

For the use of subjunctive forms in the passive voice, see Kapitel 18 §14 and §15.

Themen und Vokabular			
Geschichte		der Ministerpräsident, -en	prime minister (m.)
die Allierten (pl.)	the Allied Forces	der Ministerpräsidentin, -nen	prime minister (f.)
der Krieg, -e	war	der Vertrag, ⸚e	treaty
die Mauer, -n	wall (also: the Berlin Wall)	die Wiedervereinigung	(re)unification

KAPITEL

17 Word Order Variations

This chapter supplements what has been said already about German word order in previous chapters (Kap. 1; Kap. 5 §6, 3; Kap. 6 §10; Kap. 7 §9; Kap. 11 §1 to §3; Kap. 15 §3 [Note on word order]).

The Position of Objects

§1 The Sequence of Direct and Indirect Objects

The indirect object, usually a person, precedes the direct object, usually a thing, unless the direct object is a personal pronoun.

	INDIRECT OBJECT (DATIVE/PERSON)	DIRECT OBJECT (ACCUSATIVE/THING)	
Ich habe	**Daniel**	**das Gerücht**	erzählt.
Ich habe	**ihm**	**das Gerücht**	erzählt.
Ich habe	**ihm**	**alles** **etwas** **nichts** **das**	erzählt.

When the direct object is a personal pronoun, the sequence is reversed. (For the cases of personal pronouns, see Kap. 6 §10.)

	DIRECT OBJECT	INDIRECT OBJECT	
Ich habe	**es**	**Daniel**	erzählt.
Ich habe	**es**	**ihm**	erzählt.

Note: Ich habe **es ihm** erzählt.
  but: Ich habe **ihm das** erzählt.

Because **das** is a demonstrative pronoun rather than a personal pronoun, it follows the personal pronoun indirect object.

Übung 17-1

ANWENDEN A. Respond logically to each question. Add an appropriate time expression such as **gestern, letzte Woche, morgen,** or **heute Abend** and replace elements as directed in parentheses.

> MODEL: Hast du deiner Mutter Blumen gekauft? (pronouns)
> <u>Ja, ich habe sie ihr gestern gekauft.</u>

Renate hatte ein paar Dinge zu erledigen.

1. Hast du den Kindern ein paar Brötchen geholt? (pronouns)
2. Hast du Dieter die Post nachgeschickt? (pronouns)
3. Und hast du ihm auch die Zeitungen nachgeschickt? (alles)
4. Möchtest du Helga ein Geschenk kaufen? (etwas)
5. Und bringst du der Nachbarin das Paket? (pronouns)

B. Respond by replacing the object given in parentheses with a pronoun and replacing the direct object with **das.** Use the verb given in parentheses in place of the verb in the question.

> MODEL: Hast du die Zeitung geholt? (der Chef / bringen)
> <u>Ja, ich habe ihm das schon gebracht.</u>

Klaus arbeitet in einem Büro und musste Dinge für die Angestellten erledigen. Er beantwortet die Fragen seiner Chefin.

1. Hast du die Bücher gekauft? (Herr Engel / geben)
2. Und hast du die Informationen bekommen? (die Kollegen / mitteilen)
3. Hast du die Disketten besorgt? (Frau Petri / auf den Schreibtisch legen)
4. Und hast du Kaffee gekocht? (alle / hinstellen)
5. Und hast du den Handy geholt? (ich / hinlegen)

§2   The Position of Prepositional Objects and *da*-Compounds

Prepositional objects and **da**-compounds usually follow pronoun objects and noun objects.

	PERSONAL OR REFLEXIVE PRONOUNS	OTHER PRONOUNS OR NOUNS	PREPOSITIONS + PRONOUNS OR NOUNS; DA-COMPOUNDS	
Ich habe		**ein Paket**	**von meinen Eltern**	bekommen.
Ich habe	**es**		**von ihnen**	bekommen.
Ich habe		**das** **alles** **etwas** **nichts**	**von ihnen**	bekommen.
Ich habe	**ihnen**		**dafür**	gedankt.
Er hat	**sich**		**über die Einladung**	gefreut.

Übung 17-2

ANWENDEN Insert the elements in parentheses in the proper sequence.

1. X: Haben Sie _____ besprochen? (mit Ihrer Frau / diesen Plan)
   Y: Ja, ich bespreche _____. (mit ihr / alles)
2. X: Hast du _____ gewarnt? (Herrn Berger / vor dieser Gefahr)
   Y: Ich habe versucht _____ zu warnen. (davor / ihn)
3. X: Hat Barbara den Führerschein bekommen?
   Y: Ja. Du kannst _____ gratulieren. (dazu / ihr)
4. X: Haben Sie _____ entschuldigt? (sich / bei Andreas)
   Y: Ich habe vergessen _____ zu entschuldigen. (bei ihm / mich)
5. X: Leider habe ich vergessen _____ mitzubringen. (für Helga / das
   Geburtstagsgeschenk)
   Y: Und ich habe vergessen _____ mitzubringen. (für sie / die
   Geburtstagskarte)
6. X: Michael hat _____ erzählt. (von dieser Sache / nichts / mir)
   Y: Und du? Hast du _____ erzählt? (etwas / davon / ihm)
7. X: Hoffentlich gewöhnen Sie _____ . (sich / an dieses Klima)
   Y: Ich glaube, es ist nicht sehr schwer _____ zu gewöhnen. (daran / sich)

The Position of Adverbial Modifiers and Complements

§3   The Position of Adverbial Modifiers

Adverbial modifiers include simple adverbs, such as **heute**, **dort**, and **gut**, or phrases, such as **diesen Freitag**, **in diesem Monat**, **in der Stadt**, and **mit dem Bus**. For simplicity's sake, both will be called *adverbs* here.

An adverb often stands at the beginning of a main clause.

> **Gestern** war ich nicht in der Vorlesung.
> **Dort** steht mein Wagen.

Otherwise, adverbs normally take the following positions:

1. Adverbs of time (answering the question **wann?**), such as **oft**, **manchmal**, **immer**, **vorher** (*before*), **nachher** (*afterward*), **heute**, **nach der Deutschstunde**, and **vor ein paar Minuten** (*a few minutes ago*), occur early in the sentence, follow personal pronouns, and usually precede all other elements.

> Ich rufe dich **nach der Deutschstunde** an.
> *I am going to call you after German class.*

> Haben Sie **manchmal** Schwierigkeiten mit Ihren Nachbarn?
> *Do you have trouble with your neighbors sometimes?*

> Ich habe vor Sie **morgen** zu besuchen.
> *I am planning to visit you tomorrow.*

2. Adverbs of place (answering the question **wo?**), such as **dort**, **da drüben** (*over there*), **vorn** (*in front*), **hinten** (*behind, in the back*), **oben** (*at the top, upstairs*), **unten** (*at the bottom, below, downstairs*), **bei Müllers** (*at the Müllers'*), and **auf einer Party** (*at a party*), come toward the end of the sentence and follow adverbs of time. This is unlike English, in which adverbs of place precede adverbs of time.

> Wir sind nur ein paar Tage **in Hamburg** geblieben.
> *We stayed in Hamburg only a few days.*

> Ich war gestern abend **bei Köhlers**.
> *I was at the Köhlers' last night.*

Do not confuse the following adverbs and prepositions:

ADVERBS
vorn—hinten
> Frank sitzt **vorn** and Käte sitzt **hinten**.
> *Frank sits in front and Käte sits in the back.*

oben—unten
> Helga wohnt **oben** und Ute wohnt **unten**.
> *Helga lives upstairs and Ute lives downstairs.*

PREPOSITIONS (PRECEDING NOUNS OR PRONOUNS)
vor—hinter
> Frank sitzt **vor mir** und Käte sitzt **hinter mir**.
> *Frank sits in front of me and Käte sits behind me.*

über—unter
> Helga wohnt **über mir** und Ute wohnt **unter mir**.
> *Helga lives above me and Ute lives below me.*

The prepositional phrases **vor mir**, **hinter mir**, **über mir**, and **unter mir** function as adverbs of place.

3. Other adverbs generally follow pronouns and nouns. When they occur with adverbs of time and place, they usually follow expressions of time but precede expressions of place. In our examples, we will concentrate on adverbs of manner (answering the question **wie?**). Many such adverbs are identical to adjectives, for instance, **schnell**, **langsam**, **gut**, **schlecht**, **freundlich**, and **höflich** (*polite*). They also include prepositional phrases, such as **mit dem Bus (Wagen, Zug)**, **zu Fuß** (*on foot*), and **mit lauter (leiser) Stimme** (*in a loud [low] voice*).

> Sie hat mich **gestern höflich** gegrüßt.
>   TIME   MANNER
> *She greeted me politely yesterday.*

> Wir sind **langsam durch den Park** gelaufen.
>   MANNER   PLACE
> *We walked slowly through the park.*

Wir sind **heute Nachmittag langsam durch den Park** gelaufen.

| | | |
| TIME | MANNER | PLACE |

We walked slowly through the park this afternoon.

Note that these are rule-of-thumb guidelines. The complements may, of course, occur in different orders depending on the context and the emphasis a speaker wishes to place on them (cf. §5). Remember also that any single complement may be placed at the very beginning of the sentence.

Übung 17-3

ANWENDEN Respond to each question. Add a time, place, or manner adverb in your response, paying special attention to their position.

1. Wo haben Sie letztes Jahr gewohnt?
2. Wohin ist Ihre Familie letztes Jahr gefahren?
3. Wann sind Sie das letzte Mal spazieren gegangen? Wo und wie lange?
4. Wie lange waren Sie das letzte Mal im Urlaub?
5. Wann und wo haben Sie gearbeitet?
6. Wann werden Sie zum Supermarkt gehen?
7. Seit wann wohnen Sie in _____?
8. Wie kommen Sie jeden Tag zur Uni?
9. Wie sprechen Ihre Professoren mit Ihnen? Freundlich? Höflich?
10. Wie spricht Ihre Lehrerin/Ihr Lehrer während der Deutschstunde? Laut? Leise? Schnell? Langsam?

§4   The Position of Verb Complements

In this book, the term *verb complements* is used for certain sentence elements that have a particularly close relationship to the verb and may be said to complement or complete its meaning. These verb complements stand at the end of a clause, immediately before the final verb elements (if any). The main complement types are listed below.

1. Predicate adjectives and predicate nouns (cf. Kap. 1 §7)

Rainer ist **krank**.
Rainer ist schon eine Woche **krank**.   *Rainer has been ill for a week.*

Sie ist **Journalistin**.
Sie ist seit einem Jahr **Journalistin**.   *She has been a journalist for a year.*

Er ist **Lehrer** geworden.
Er ist vor zwei Jahren **Lehrer** geworden.   *He became a teacher two years ago.*

Note that most other sentence elements must precede the predicate adjective or noun. However, prepositional phrases may often stand either before or after a predicate adjective (cf. Kap. 7 §8).

Sie ist **zu mir** sehr nett.

or: Sie ist sehr nett **zu mir**.

She is very nice to me.

2. Necessary adjuncts of verb phrases

Many common noun objects, adjectives, adverbs, and prepositional phrases are used as verb complements and therefore stand at the end of the clause, followed only by closing verb forms.

Tennis (Fußball, Karten, Schach, Klavier) spielen

Wir haben gestern hinter dem Studentenheim **Fußball** gespielt.
We played soccer behind the dormitory yesterday.

zu Mittag (zu Abend) essen   *to have lunch (dinner)*

Wir haben in einem kleinen Restaurant **zu Mittag** gegessen.
We had lunch in a little restaurant.

die Wahrheit sagen   *to tell the truth*

Haben Sie bei der Polizei **die Wahrheit** gesagt?
Did you tell the truth at the police station?

auswendig lernen   *to learn by heart, memorize*

Ich nehme an, dass wir das Gedicht **auswendig** lernen müssen.
I assume that we have to memorize the poem.

ernst nehmen   *to take seriously*

Man kann nicht alles, was er sagt, **ernst** nehmen.
One can't take everything he says seriously.

einen Kompromiss schließen   *to compromise*

Ich werde versuchen mit meinem Vater **einen Kompromiss** zu schließen.
I'll try to compromise with my father.

eine Rede halten   *to make a speech*

Dr. König hat im Auditorium **eine Rede** gehalten.
Dr. König made a speech in the auditorium.

einen Heiratsantrag machen   *to propose (marriage)*

Er hat ihr in Wien **einen Heiratsantrag** gemacht.
He proposed to her in Vienna.

Adverbs of place that merely provide locations, as in some of the examples above, are not verb complements. However, when adverbs of place denote motion to or from a place, they are called *directionals*. As necessary adjuncts of the verbs of motion, they are verb complements and stand at the end of the clause followed only by final verb forms.

in die Stadt (nach Hause, nach Bremen) fahren   *to go into the city (home, to Bremen)*

> Möchten Sie mit uns **in die Stadt** fahren?
> *Would you like to go to town with us?*

auf eine Party gehen   *to go to a party*

> Inge ist vor ein paar Minuten mit Erika **auf eine Party** gegangen.
> *Inge went to a party with Erika a few minutes ago.*

nach oben (nach unten, nach vorn, nach hinten) gehen   *to go upstairs (downstairs, to the front, to the back)*

> Herr und Frau Berger sind soeben mit ihren Gästen **nach unten** gegangen.
> *Mr. and Mrs. Berger have just gone downstairs with their guests.*

> Bitte kommen Sie mit Ihrem Freund **nach vorn**!
> *Please come to the front with your friend.*

A note on the position of nicht

Nicht precedes verb complements in sentences with normally accented negation (cf. Kap. 1 §7).

> Ich habe meinem Freund **nicht** die Wahrheit gesagt.
> Wir haben **nicht** Fußball gespielt.

Übung 17-4

ANWENDEN A. Form sentences in the present perfect, arranging the elements in the proper sequence.

MODEL: ich / gehen / in den Zirkus / mit ein paar Freunden / gestern Abend
<u>Ich bin gestern Abend mit ein paar Freunden in den Zirkus gegangen.</u>

Martin und seine Freunde haben in den letzten Tagen viel unternommen.

1. Ich / fahren / in die Stadt / mit einer Freundin / gestern Nachmittag
2. Und ich / gehen / ins Theater / mit Inge / am Sonnabend
3. Helga / gehen / auf eine Party / mit Rainer / gestern Abend
4. Leider / wir / spielen / Tennis / nicht
5. Aber / wir / spielen / Fußball / auf dem neuen Sportplatz / am Freitag Nachmittag
6. Du / spielen / Karten / mit deinen Freunden / oft?
7. Klaus / gehen / nach unten / mit dem Hund
8. Inge / gehen / zum Friseur / vor ein paar Minuten / mit Margot

B. Form sentences using the cues given and adding a logical time, manner, or place expression. Use various subjects and tenses.

MODEL: zu Abend essen
Ich habe gestern mit meiner Familie zu Abend gegessen.

1. zu Mittag essen
2. Fußball (Tennis, Squash, Karten, Klavier usw.) spielen
3. einen Kompromiss schließen
4. eine Rede halten
5. etwas auswendig lernen

Variations in the Sequence of Elements

§5 Shifting Elements Further to the End of a Sentence

Important elements are placed close to the end or beginning (cf. Kap. 1 §2) of a German sentence. You have already seen that the complement, which is vital, is placed immediately before the final verb forms. Any other element to which special importance is attached in a given context may also be placed close to the end of the sentence, particularly if it represents new information.

1. Changes in the order of adverbial modifiers

Compare the following two sentences:

Monika ist fünf Tage in Hamburg geblieben.
　　　　TIME　　PLACE
Monika stayed in Hamburg for five days.

Soviel ich weiß, ist sie in Hamburg **nur drei Tage** geblieben.
　　　　　　　PLACE　　TIME
As far as I know, she stayed in Hamburg for only three days.

The first statement is a sentence with normal intonation, i.e., every element carries its natural stress. No element is given more emphasis than usual, and thus the adverb of time precedes the adverb of place.

In the second sentence, the response (the place expression, **in Hamburg**) is the known element; the time expression, **nur drei Tage**, is more important, for it provides new information. It is more heavily stressed than usual and moves closer to the end of the sentence. The normal order of time before place is thus reversed.

The same change may occur in questions, dependent clauses, and infinitive phrases.

Ist sie in Hamburg wirklich **nur drei Tage** geblieben?
Ich habe gehört, dass sie in Hamburg **nur drei Tage** geblieben ist.
Sie hatte vor in Hamburg **nur drei Tage** zu bleiben.

2. Alternative order of objects

Compare the following two sentences:

Er hat seiner Freundin einen Kalender gegeben.

INDIRECT OBJECT DIRECT OBJECT

He gave his girlfriend a calendar.

Er hat den Kalender **seiner Freundin** gegeben.

DIRECT OBJECT   INDIRECT OBJECT

He gave the calendar to a girlfriend.

The first sentence shows the regular order of noun objects: indirect object before direct object. In the second sentence, the direct object, **den Kalender**, represents old information, while the indirect object, **seiner Freundin**, is new information and is therefore placed toward the end of the sentence. A similar ordering of the objects occurs in English, although the English indirect object is used with a preposition (*to*, sometimes *for*) when placed after the direct object.

Note the shift from **einen Kalender** in the first sentence to **den Kalender** in the second. Objects preceded by the definite article usually refer to something that is known and, therefore, they have less news value than those objects preceded by the indefinite article.

3. Alternative order of prepositional phrases

Klaus hat tausend Mark von seinem Vater bekommen.
Ich glaube, er hat von ihm **nur fünfhundert Mark** bekommen.

Prepositional phrases usually follow direct and indirect objects. However, when an object represents new information, it may be placed after a prepositional phrase that communicates old information (as in the second sentence) or is less important.

4. Alternative position of subjects

Es ist soeben auf dem Marktplatz **ein schwerer Autounfall** passiert.
Soeben ist auf dem Marktplatz **ein schwerer Autounfall** passiert.
A serious car accident happened just now at the marketplace.

The subject, **ein schwerer Autounfall**, has been moved to the end of each sentence for greater emphasis. The first sentence begins with an introductory **es**, which is omitted in the second sentence because another element is in first position (cf. Kap. 14 §6, 2).

The standard beginning of a fairytale contains such a "delayed" subject:

Es war einmal **eine schöne Prinzessin** (ein armes Mädchen, ein weiser König).
Once upon a time, there was a beautiful princess (a poor girl, a wise king).

Übung 17-5

ANWENDEN Formulate sentences placing the boldface elements toward the end.
Use the present perfect tense unless otherwise indicated.

MODEL: X: Ich habe gestern einen Brief an Renate geschrieben.
Y: du / ab•schicken / **auch gestern** / das Paket für Renate? (pres. perf.)
Hast du das Paket für Renate auch gestern abgeschickt?

1. X: Ich habe vorige Woche jeden Tag in der Bibliothek gearbeitet.
    Y: du / arbeiten / **auch am Sonntag** / da?
2. X: Wir sind um 9 Uhr in Frankfurt angekommen.
    Y: ihr / an•kommen / **wirklich schon um 9 Uhr** / in Frankfurt?
3. X: Ich glaube, Helga hat vier Semester in Wien studiert.
    Y: sie / studieren / **nur zwei Semester** / in Wien
4. X: Wer hat Margot das Gerücht erzählt?
    Y: Das war Rainer. Er / erzählen / **allen Leuten** / das Gerücht.
5. X: Wer hat der Polizei den Tip gegeben?
    Y: Unsere Nachbarin: sie / geben / **auch einem Rechtsanwalt** / den Tip
6. X: Hast du das Paket von deinen Eltern bekommen?
    Y: Ja, und ich / bekommen / **auch einen Scheck** / von ihnen.
7. X: Hat der Polizist Renate einen Strafzettel gegeben?
    Y: Nein, er / geben / **Renates Freundin** / den Strafzettel.
8. X: Bitte geben Sie der Dame die Speisekarte!
    Y: warum / Sie geben / **dem Herrn und nicht der Dame** / die
    Speisekarte?
9. X: Bitte sagen Sie dem Polizisten, was gestern abend passiert ist.
    Y: Es war gegen 10 Uhr. Ich ging von der Garage zur Haustür.
    Plötzlich / **ein Mann** / stehen / vor mir. (past)
10. X: Das ist ein Bild von mir, als ich zehn Jahre jünger war.
    Y: Wie im Märchen; es / **ein schöner Prinz** / sein / einmal (past)

A note on the use of stress in spoken German

In spoken German, there is an additional way of indicating the unusual importance of
a particular element: stressing it without moving it (indicated here in boldface). Thus
in spoken German, the example of §5, item 1, could be

Monika ist fünf Tage in Hamburg geblieben.
Soviel ich weiß, ist sie nur **drei** Tage in Hamburg geblieben.

§6 Placing Elements after the Final Verb Forms

1. Als and **so...wie** phrases in comparisons

In comparisons, **als** and **so...wie** phrases (cf. Kap. 9 §3) are normally placed
after all other sentence elements, including separable prefixes and final verb
forms.

Compare

> a. Ich rufe nicht oft zu Hause **an**.
> b. Ich rufe nicht so oft zu Hause **an wie mein Bruder**.
> c. Er ruft mehr **an als ich**.

In sentence **a.** the separable prefix occupies its normal position at the end of the sentence. In sentences **b.** and **c.** it is followed by the **als** and **wie** phrases.

Additional examples

> Du kannst sehr schnell laufen.
> Du kannst schneller laufen **als ich**.
> Du weißt doch, dass du schneller laufen kannst **als ich**.

> Ich bin dicker geworden.
> Ich bin nicht so dick geworden **wie Renate**.
> Ich bin froh, dass ich nicht so dick geworden bin **wie Renate**.

Übung 17-6

ANWENDEN Use an appropriate comparison with **als** or with **so ... wie**. Follow the model.

> MODEL: Kai: Ich helfe oft in der Küche.
>   <u>Also, ich helfe in der Küche mehr als du!</u>
>   or: <u>Also, du hilfst in der Küche nicht so oft wie ich!</u>

Konkurrenzkampf. Die zwei Geschwister Jutta und Kai vergleichen, wer was besser oder schlechter macht.

> 1. Jutta: Dein Freund Lars ist früh mit den Hausaufgaben fertig.
> 2. Jutta: Ich bin sicher, dass er bei seinem Job viel Geld verdient.
> 3. Kai: Du redest ewig am Telefon.
> 4. Jutta: Und du bist ganz schön rund geworden.
> 5. Kai: Und ich weiß, dass du oft die Schule schwänzt!
> 6. Jutta: Ich entdecke immer interessante Dinge auf dem Internet.

2. Other elements

> Wir sind trotz des schlechten Wetters an den Strand gegangen.
> Wir sind an den Strand gegangen **trotz des schlechten Wetters**.
> *We went to the beach in spite of the bad weather.*

In the first sentence, the past participle is in its usual final position. In the second sentence, the prepositional phrase **trotz des schlechten Wetters** is placed after the past participle. Such an extraposition is sometimes done for special emphasis, but often the extraposed element (usually a prepositional phrase) is a mere afterthought.

Additional examples:

Ich bin aus finanziellen Gründen nicht nach Florida geflogen.
Ich bin nicht nach Florida geflogen **aus finanziellen Gründen**.
I didn't fly to Florida for financial reasons.

Mein Vater ist nach vielen Jahren harter Arbeit in den Ruhestand getreten.
Mein Vater ist in den Ruhestand getreten **nach vielen Jahren harter Arbeit**.
My father retired after many years of hard work.

Übung 17-7

ZUSAMMENFASSUNG Word order with various elements.

Write a paragraph that contains various time, manner, and place expressions. Choose one of the topics given below.

First, write down the information using the common word order for time and place elements in (time before place; manner before pronouns and nouns, and after time), then, rearrange these elements depending on such factors as emphasis, old vs. new information, and importance.

1. Erzählen Sie etwas von Ihrem letzten Urlaub.
2. Beschreiben Sie einen Besuch in einem Museum.
3. Beschreiben Sie eine Feier (Geburtstag, Semesterende, usw.).

18 Additional Features of German Grammar

This chapter focuses on several grammatical features that are better treated separately than in the context of the preceding chapters. The discussion of each feature is self-contained to allow instructors to select only those sections that are of particular value for given classes.

The German Equivalent of *another*

§1 The German Equivalent of *another: ein ander-* or *noch ein*

Dieser Kaffee ist kalt.	Bitte geben Sie mir **eine andere Tasse Kaffee**.
	*Please give me **another cup of coffee**.*
Dieser Kaffee ist gut.	Bitte geben Sie mir **noch eine Tasse Kaffee**.
	*Please give me **another cup of coffee**.*

In the first sentence, *another cup of coffee* means "a different cup of coffee." The German equivalent is **eine andere Tasse Kaffee**. In the second sentence, *another cup of coffee* means "one more cup" or "an additional cup of coffee." The German equivalent is **noch eine Tasse Kaffee**.

Remember: another — **ein ander-** meaning: a different (one)
noch ein meaning: one more, an additional (one)

In both expressions **ein** has its usual **ein**-word endings; **ander-** has normal adjective endings (cf. Kap. 8 §3 and §10). Do not confuse **ein ander-** with the reciprocal **einander** (cf. Kap. 15 §5)

Übung 18-1

VERSTEHEN Explain the choice of **ein ander-** or **noch ein** in the following sentences.

1. Diese Handschuhe gefallen mir. Vielleicht kaufe ich noch ein Paar.
2. Diese Bluse ist schmutzig. Ich muss eine andere anziehen.

3. Der Kuchen schmeckt ausgezeichnet. Könnte ich noch ein Stück haben?
4. Leider habe ich die Stelle nicht bekommen. Sie haben sie einem anderen Bewerber gegeben.
5. Dieser Verkäufer hat mich nicht bedient. Es war ein anderer.

Another with the plural:

another three weeks
= three more weeks ⟶ **noch drei Wochen**

Übung 18-2

ANWENDEN A. Insert the logical equivalent of *another*—**ein ander-** or **noch ein**.

1. Ich wollte Herrn Klein meinen Wagen verkaufen. Leider hat er _____ gekauft.
2. Schmidts haben schon zwei Wagen. Wissen Sie, warum sie _____ kaufen wollen?
3. Ich habe schon zwei Semesterarbeiten getippt. Leider muss ich _____ tippen.
4. Diese Fernsehsendung ist schrecklich langweilig. Können wir uns nicht _____ anschauen?
5. Wir haben nur ein Kind und möchten gern _____ haben.

B. Respond with a logical phrase that contains **noch**, and a number plus the cued element in the plural.

MODEL: Was wollen wir noch anschauen? (Museum)
        Schauen wir uns noch zwei Museen an.

Lotte und Regine besprechen ihren Auftenthalt in Wien.

1. Wie lange wollen wir noch in Wien bleiben? (Tag)
2. Müssen wir noch etwas schreiben? (Postkarte)
3. Wie lange übernachten wir noch in diesem Hotel? (Nacht)
4. Willst du noch mehr kaufen? (Schokoladenpralinen)
5. Und wollen wir noch ein paar Restaurants ausprobieren? (Café)

German Equivalent of *to like*

§2 To Like Doing Something

1. The most frequent expression uses the adverb **gern** with a verb.

Ich singe **gern**.	*I like to sing.*
Ich singe **sehr gern**.	*I like to sing very much.*
Er tanzt **nicht gern**.	*He doesn't like to dance.*

When English adds (*very*) *much/a lot*, German uses **sehr**.

2. The modal **mögen** + infinitive is not common. Only the subjunctive **möchte** (*would like*) is used frequently (cf. Kap. 4 §14).

> Ich **mag** sie nicht um Geld bitten.
> *I don't like to ask her for money.*
> more common: Ich **möchte** sie nicht um Geld bitten.

§3   To Like Something or Someone

1. The verb **gefallen** expresses pleasure or displeasure in an unemotional fashion.

> Dieses Bild **gefällt mir**.   *I like this picture.*
> Dieses Bild **gefällt mir sehr.**
> or: Dieses Bild **gefällt mir gut.**   *I like this picture very much.*
> or: Dieses Bild **gefällt mir sehr gut.**
> Dieses Bild **gefällt mir nicht**.   *I don't like this picture.*

For emphasis, **sehr**, **gut**, or **sehr gut** can be added; all correspond to *very much, a lot*.

Remember:

> The verb **gefallen** is used like the English *to please*. Its subject is the thing or person that is liked or disliked. Its dative object is the person who has these feelings (cf. Kap. 6 §9). **Das gefällt mir**. *I like that.* (*That pleases me.*)

2. Mögen is more emotional in tone than **gefallen**.

> Ich **mag** dieses Bild nicht.   *I don't like this picture.*
> Wir **mögen** unsere neuen Nachbarn   *We don't like our new neighbors.*
> nicht.

Used with food or drink:

> **Mögen** Sie Käse?   *Do you like cheese?*
> **Mögen** Sie Tomatensaft?   *Do you like tomato juice?*

It is very common to use **gern** with the verbs **essen** and **trinken** instead.

> **Essen** Sie **gern** Käse?
> **Trinken** Sie **gern** Tomatensaft?

3. Gern haben is used in the sense of *to be fond of*.

> Ich **habe** Barbara **sehr gern**, aber ich liebe sie nicht.
> *I am very fond of Barbara, but I don't love her.*

4. People one finds pleasant and likeable are often said to be **sympatisch**.

> Sie ist mir **sympatisch**.   *I like her (in the sense of I find her pleasant/likeable).*
>
> Sie ist mir **nicht sympatisch**.
> or: Sie ist mir **unsympatisch**.   *I don't like her.*

Occasionally **sympatisch** is used with things.

> Dieser Vorschlag ist mir **nicht sympatisch.**
> *I don't like this suggestion.*
> *This suggestion doesn't appeal to me.*

§4   The Position of *gern*

Gern is an adverb of manner; it usually follows adverbs of time and precedes adverbs of place (cf. Kap. 17 §3, 3).

> Ich habe vorigen Sommer **gern** im Garten gearbeitet.

It follows pronoun objects.

> Ich helfe Ihnen **gern.**

It follows or precedes noun objects.

> Essen Sie **gern** Fisch?
> Essen Sie Fisch **gern**?

It usually precedes prepositional phrases and verb complements.

> Ich spreche **gern** mit ihm.
> Sie spielt **gern** Tennis.

Exception: With **haben**, **gern** is a verb complement and stands at the end of the clause, followed only by the closing verb forms (cf. Kap. 17 §4).

> Ich habe als Kind diesen Teddybär **sehr gern** gehabt.
> *As a child I was very fond of this teddy bear.*

Übung 18-3

ANWENDEN Respond to the following questions.

1. Was machen Sie gern? Was machen Sie nicht gern?
2. Wer ist Ihnen sympathisch? Wer ist Ihnen unsympathisch?
3. Wen haben Sie sehr gern?
4. Welcher Schauspieler oder welche Schauspielerin gefällt Ihnen? Welche(r) nicht?
5. Was gefällt Ihnen an Ihrer Uni? Was nicht?
6. Nennen Sie drei Dinge, die Sie gern essen und drei, die Sie gern trinken.
7. Nennen Sie drei Aktivitäten, die Sie gern machen.

Uses of *hängen, legen, stellen, setzen,* and *liegen, stehen, sitzen*

§5   *Hängen* Used Transitively and Intransitively

A transitive verb can take a direct object in the accusative case.

> Ich schreibe **einen Brief**.
> Sie trinkt **keinen Kaffee**.

An intrasitive verb cannot take a direct object but is often complemented by a prepositional phrase.

> Wir reisen **durch Deutschland**.
> Ich bleibe **in Frankfurt**.

Some verbs are used either transitively or intransitively. One of them is **hängen**.

Used transitively: expressing an activity	Used intransitively: expressing a condition

PRESENT

Sie hängt **das Bild an die Wand**.	Das Bild hängt **an der Wand**.
(DIRECT (PREPOSITIONAL OBJECT) PHRASE)	(SUBJECT) (PREPOSITIONAL PHRASE)

PAST

Sie **hängte** das Bild an die Wand.	Das Bild **hing** an der Wand.

PRESENT PERFECT

Sie **hat** das Bild an die Wand **gehängt**.	Das Bild **hat** an der Wand **gehangen**.

──────── PRINCIPAL PARTS ────────

hängen—hängte—hat gehängt Used transitively, **hängen** is a <u>weak</u> verb.	**hängen—hing—hat gehangen** Used intransitively, **hängen** is a <u>strong</u> verb.

A good rule of thumb: When **hängen** is used in the sense of *to put*, it is weak; otherwise, it is strong.

Übung 18-4

VERSTEHEN   State whether the following sentences express an activity or a condition.

1. Frau Braun hängt die Wäsche auf die Leine.
2. Frau Zimmermanns Wäsche hängt auf der Leine.
3. Klaus und Petra hängen ihre Jacken an den Haken.
4. Mein Mantel hängt am Haken neben der Tür.
5. Ingrids Mantel hängt auf einem Bügel.
6. Dieter hängt den Anzug auf den Bügel.
7. Wo hängt die Fahne?
8. Hängt die Wäsche auf dem Wäschegestell?

Übung 18-5

ANWENDEN   A. Put the sentences from Übung 18-4 into the past and the present perfect.

B. Answer the following questions.

1. Was hängt in Ihrem Zimmer an der Wand?
2. Was würden Sie gern an die Wand hängen?
3. Was hängt in Ihrem Klassenzimmer an der Wand?
4. Was hängt in einem Museum an der Wand? In einem Restaurant?
5. Welche Kleidungsstücke hängen Sie auf einen Kleiderbügel? Was hängt bei Ihnen zu Hause an einem Haken?

Forms of hängen *with a prefix*

TRANSITIVE (WEAK)	INTRANSITIVE (STRONG)
erhängen *to hang someone*	**ab•hängen** *to hang up (phone)*
Sie haben ihn **erhängt**. *They hanged him.*	Sie hat einfach **abgehängt**. *She just hung up.*
sich erhängen *to hang oneself*	**ab•hängen von** (dat.) *to be dependent on*
Er hat **sich erhängt**. *He hung himself.*	Bergers wollen nicht von ihren Kindern **abhängen**. *The Bergers don't want to be dependent on their children.*

EXPRESSION:

Das hängt von dir ab. ⟨ *That depends on you.*
That's up to you.

Das hing von dir ab.
Das hat von dir abgehangen.

§6   The Use of the Transitive Verbs *legen, stellen,* and *setzen*

The English verb *to put* has no single German counterpart. Instead, one uses specialized verbs of placing, such as **hängen**, or the following (cf. Kap. 7 §3).

legen   *to put* (in a horizontal position), *lay, place horizontally*
Bitte **legen Sie** das Buch auf den Schreibtisch!
Please put (lay) the book on the desk (down flat).

stellen   *to put* (in an upright position), *place vertically*
Bitte **stellen Sie** das Buch ins Regal!
Please put the book on the shelf (upright).

setzen   *to put, set, make sit*
Bitte **setzen Sie** das Kind auf die Couch!
Please put (set) the child on the couch.

Since these verbs imply motion toward a goal, two-way prepositions used with them require accusative objects. The three transitive verbs are weak.

legen — legte — hat gelegt
stellen — stellte — hat gestellt
setzen — setzte — hat gesetzt

Übung 18-6

ANWENDEN Form sentences with the appropriate verbs and locations.

MODEL: die Milch / Eisschrank
Sie hat die Milch in den Eisschrank gestellt.

Nicola war gerade einkaufen. Wohin hat sie alles gestellt und gelegt?

1. das Kind / Stuhl
2. ihre Tasche / Tisch
3. die Zeitung / Regal
4. das Obst / Korb
5. der Saft / Eisschrank
6. die Kekse / Teller
7. der Sprudel / Balkon

§7   The Uses of the Intransitive Verbs *liegen*, *stehen*, and *sitzen*

Just as German uses specialized verbs of placement, it often prefers to use specialized verbs of location. Compare

transitive verbs (weak): expressing an activity	intransitive counterparts (strong): expressing a condition
legen — **legte** — **hat gelegt** **stellen** — **stellte** — **hat gestellt** **setzen** — **setzte** — **hat gesetzt**	**liegen** — **lag** — **gelegen** **stehen** — **stand** — **hat gestanden** **sitzen** — **saß** — **hat gesessen**

Examples:

a. Sie **legt** das Buch auf den Tisch.
legte
hat...gelegt

She lays (laid) the book on the table.
(principal parts: *to lay—laid—laid*)

or: *She puts (put) the book on the table.*

b. Sie **stellt** die Bücher ins Regal.
stellte
hat...gestellt.

She puts (put) the books up on the shelf.

c. Sie **setzt** das Kind aufs Sofa.
setzte
hat...gesetzt.

She puts (put) the child on the sofa.

Das Buch **liegt** auf dem Tisch.
lag
hat...gelegen

The book lies (lay) on the table.
(principal parts: *to lie—lay—lain*)

or: *The book is (was) on the table.*

Die Bücher **stehen** im Regal.
standen
haben...gestanden.

The books are (were) up on the shelf.

Das Kind **sitzt** auf dem Sofa.
saß
hat...gesessen.

The child sits (sat) on the sofa.

TWO-WAY PREPOSITIONS

Note: require the accusative   require the dative

Übung 18-7

VERSTEHEN State whether the following sentences express an activity or a condition.

1. In seinem Zimmer liegen alle Sachen auf dem Boden.
2. Der Teddybär sitzt auf Helgas Schreibtisch.
3. Rainer legt alle Sachen auf den Boden.
4. Monika stellt den neuen Sessel neben die Couch.
5. Helga setzt den Teddybären neben die Schreibtischlampe.
6. Der alte Sessel steht in der Ecke.

Übung 18-8

ANWENDEN Use both transitive and intransitive verbs to discuss where items are currently located and where you placed them.

Beschreiben Sie irgendeinen Raum, z.B. Ihr Zimmer, ein Restaurant, ein Kinderzimmer, ein Arbeitszimmer, ein Büro, ein Klassenzimmer. Schreiben Sie ungefähr acht Sätze.

Übung 18-9

ZUSAMMENFASSUNG A. Form sentences that fit the context. Use the verbs discussed in §7 and 8.

MODEL: Hannelore gibt Ihnen ein Glas Milch. Sie ist nicht kalt, sondern lauwarm.
Sie denken : „Milch / nicht / Kühlschrank" (present perfect)
<u>Die Milch hat nicht im Kühlschrank gestanden.</u>

1. Ingrid sucht wieder einmal ihre Brille. Sie sehen die Brille und sagen:
„neben / Zeitung"
2. Warum ist Ihr Mantel so zerknittert (*creased*)? Sie sagen:
„nicht / auf Bügel" (present perfect)
3. Meine Eltern erwarten Gäste. Ich frage, ob ich irgendwie helfen kann. Meine Mutter sagt:
„du / können / Teller* und Gläser / auf Tisch"
4. Die Gäste wollen nach Hause gehen. Meine Mutter sagt:
„mein Mann / alle Mäntel / auf Bett" (present perfect)
5. In Reiners Zimmer liegen die meisten Bücher auf dem Boden. Sie fragen ihn:
„warum / du / Bücher / nicht / Regal"
6. Meine neue Freundin hat mir ein Foto von sich geschenkt.
„ich/ auf Schreibtisch" (future)

---

*__Teller__ is used with __stellen__ (*to put the plates on the table*), because a plate usually rests on a base rather than lying completely flat.

7. Frank sagt, dass er gestern im Konzert war. Sie haben ihn nicht gesehen. Sie fragen:

   „wo / du / sitzen?" (present perfect)

8. Sie wollten gestern Sabine etwas fragen, sind aber nicht in ihr Zimmer gegangen. Warum nicht?

   Schild / „Bitte nicht stören!" / Tür (present perfect)

9. Wenn man mich fragt, ob ich den Magister machen will, antworte ich:

   „das / von Noten / abhängen"

10. Ich frage Barbara, wie oder wo sie ihren neuen Freund kennengelernt hat. Sie antwortet:

    „ich / Inserat / Zeitung / setzen" (present perfect)

B. Answer the personalized questions.

Was machen Sie mit diesen Dingen, wenn Sie nach Hause kommen? Wohin stellen, legen oder setzen Sie sie?

Was machen sie mit...

1. Ihrem Auto oder Ihrem Fahrrad?
2. Ihrem Mantel?
3. Ihrem Rucksack? Ihrer Tasche? Ihrer Aktentasche?
4. den Lebensmitteln (nach dem Einkaufen)?
5. der Zeitung?
6. Ihrem Hund oder Ihrer Katze?
7. Ihren Büchern?
8. Ihrem Hut oder Regenschirm?

Double Infinitive Constructions with *sehen, lassen, hören,* and *helfen*

§8   Formation

When accompanied by another verb, **sehen**, **lassen**, **hören**, and **helfen** occur with double infinitive constructions in compound tenses. They follow the example of the modal auxiliaries (cf. Kap. 4 §3 to §5).

WITHOUT A DEPENDENT INFINITIVE	WITH A DEPENDENT INFINITIVE

1. sehen

Wir **sehen** ihn.	Wir **sehen** ihn **kommen**
We see him.	*We see him coming.*
Wir **sahen** ihn.	Wir **sahen** ihn **kommen**.
Wir haben ihn **gesehen**.	Wir haben ihn **kommen sehen**.
Wir hatten ihn **gesehen**.	Wir hatten ihn **kommen sehen**.
Wir werden ihn **sehen**.	Wir werden ihn **kommen sehen**.

The accompanying verb precedes **sehen**.

WITHOUT A DEPENDENT INFINITIVE	WITH A DEPENDENT INFINITIVE

2. lassen

Wir haben den Koffer im Wagen **gelassen.**	Wir haben Klaus nicht allein **fahren lassen.**
We left the suitcase in the car.	*We didn't let Klaus drive alone.*

EXPRESSIONS:

Lass mich ausreden!	*Let me finish!*
Lasst mich in Ruhe!	*Leave me alone!*

3. hören and **helfen**

Ich habe ihn nicht **gehört.**	Ich habe ihn nie **lachen hören.**
I didn't hear him.	or: Ich habe ihn nie **lachen gehört.**
	I have never heard him laugh.
Ich habe ihr **geholfen.**	Ich habe ihr **packen helfen.**
I helped her.	or: Ich habe ihr **packen geholfen.**
	I helped her pack.

The use of the past participle **gehört** or **geholfen** has become more common.

Übung 18-10

ANWENDEN Restate the sentences with **sehen**, **hören**, **helfen**, or **lassen**. Use the subject cued in parentheses.

> MODEL: Ein Baby weint. (ich)
>   <u>Ich höre das Baby weinen.</u>

1. Arbeitet Peter im Garten? (Sie [second person singular; formal])
2. Andreas schleppt schwere Möbel. (Klaus)
3. Der Hund bellt jede Nacht. (du)
4. Unser Nachbar singt laut. (wir)
5. Ich darf nicht rauchen. (man)
6. Ich kann nicht schlafen. (unser Baby)
7. Die Kinder winken von der Brücke. (ihr)

The causative meaning of lassen

In German **lassen** is used to express both permission and causation; the meaning must be determined from context. The sentences in the preceding section use **lassen** in the sense of "to leave and to let." In this section we will deal with the causative use of **lassen**.

> **Ich lasse ihn den Wagen waschen.**
> *I let him wash the car.* (expressing permission)
> or: *I'm having him wash the car.* (expressing causation)

In German, as in English, the person who actually carries out the action need not be mentioned. When this person is omitted, German continues to use the complementary infinitive, whereas English uses the past participle.

PRESENT	Ich lasse meinen Wagen **waschen**.	*I am having my car washed.*
	Ich lasse ihn **waschen**.	*I am having it washed.*
PRESENT PERFECT	Ich habe meinen Wagen **waschen lassen**.	*I had my car washed.*
	Ich habe ihn **waschen lassen**.	*I had it washed.*

Übung 18-11

ANWENDEN Respond to each question with a logical response that contains **lassen**.

MODEL: Kannst du den Fernseher selbst reparieren?
Nein. Ich lasse ihn von einem Elektriker reparieren.

Uwe und seine Freunde machen nichts selber!

1. Uwe, kannst du die Bewerbung selbst auf dem Computer tippen?
2. Mäht Ihr euren Rasen selbst?
3. Hans, putzt du dein Haus selber?
4. Und Walter, kochst du dein Essen selbst?
5. Macht ihr irgendetwas selber?

Lassen is also used reflexively: **sich etwas machen lassen** means to have something done to or for oneself.

sich die Haare schneiden lassen   *to have one's hair cut, get a haircut*

PRESENT	Ich lasse mir die Haare schneiden.	*I'm having my hair cut.*
		I'm getting a haircut.
PRESENT PERFECT	Ich habe mir die Haare schneiden lassen.	*I had my hair cut.*
		I got a haircut.

Note that the reflexive pronoun is in the dative case because the sentence contains a direct object: **die Haare** (cf. Kap. 15 §2).

Übung 18-12

ZUSAMMENFASSUNG Double infinitive constructions. Form sentences that fit the context. Use the tense cued in parentheses.

MODEL: Frank hat gestern wunderbar Flöte gespielt. Ich frage Margot (present perfect)
„Hast du ihn Flöte spielen hören?"

1. Neumanns haben seit gestern einen Hund. Er hat die ganze Nacht gebellt. Ulrich fragt sie: _____

2. Ich gehe mit Susanne spazieren. Ihre Schwester fährt an uns vorbei.
   Susanne fragt mich: _____ (present perfect)
3. Hartmut hat schlechte Laune. Er will nichts mit mir zu tun haben und sagt
   sehr unfreundlich: _____
4. Martin unterbricht mich immer. Ich sage: _____
5. Mein Wagen läuft jetzt ausgezeichnet. Warum? _____ (present perfect)
6. Wir haben unser Wochenendhaus nicht selbst gestrichen, sondern _____.
   (present perfect)
7. Irene hat eine neue Frisur. Was sagt sie? _____ (present perfect)

German Equivalents of Two Special Meanings of *would*

§9   *Would* Expressing Past Habitual Occurrences

Compare the following two sentences.

> *If she heard such nonsense, she **would laugh** about it.*
> Wenn sie so einen Unsinn hörte, **würde** sie darüber **lachen**.

> *When she heard such nonsense, she **would laugh** about it.*
> ***(used to)***
> Wenn sie so einen Unsinn gehört hat, **hat** sie immer darüber **gelacht**.

The first sentence is a contrary-to-fact statement. The German sentence uses **würde** + infinitive in the conclusion. (cf. Kap. 12 §5)

The second sentence expresses a past habitual occurrence: *would laugh* means *used to laugh*. German uses the adverb **immer** (*always*) or, less frequently, **gewöhnlich** (*usually*), and expresses the sentence in the past.

Additional examples for the expression of past habitual occurrences.

> *My grandfather **would/used to get** very nervous when he could not find his pipe.*
> Mein Großvater **wurde immer** sehr nervös, wenn er seine Pfeife nicht finden
>   konnte.
> *To save money, we **would/used to** stay overnight in cheap motels.*
> Um Geld zu sparen, **haben** wir **immer** in billigen Motels **übernachtet**.

§10   *Would* Having the Meaning of *was/were willing to*

When *would* has the meaning of *was/were willing to,* it is expressed in German by **wollte**, as the following example illustrates.

> *The case was hopeless, but nobody **would/was willing** to give it up.*
> Der Fall war hoffnungslos, aber niemand **wollte** ihn aufgeben.

For greater emphasis English often adds the adverb *just* in such sentences. Here the German equivalent of *just* is **einfach**.

We asked Bettina what was bothering her, but she just **wouldn't/wasn't willing to** tell us.

Wir haben Bettina gefragt, was ihr Sorgen macht, aber sie **wollte** es uns **einfach** nicht sagen.

Übung 18-13

VERSTEHEN Indicate if *would* establishes an unreal condition, describes a past habitual occurrence, or has the meaning of *willing to*.

1. The children just wouldn't eat the salad.
2. Whenever I served salad the kids would not eat it.
3. My sister would do the dishes when we lived at home.
4. I would not do the dishes if I hadn't cooked.
5. Sam just wouldn't help.
6. He would read the newspaper after he came home.
7. When I was at the airport nobody would help me.
8. I would not do that if I were you.

Übung 18-14

ANWENDEN Express the sentences in Übung 18-13 in German.

The Subjective Use of Modal Auxiliaries

§11   Comparing the Uses of *müssen*

Thomas sucht eine bessere Stelle. Er **muss** mehr Geld verdienen.
Thomas is looking for a better job. He must make more money.

Unser Nachbar hat ein großes neues Haus gekauft. Er **muss** viel Geld verdienen.
Our neighbor bought a big new house. He must make a lot of money.

In the first sentence the modal **müssen** expresses the necessity of making more money. In the second sentence the speaker concludes that his neighbor is making a lot of money based on the fact that he has bought a big new house. That is his judgment, a subjective sizing up of the situation. **Müssen** is used subjectively rather than objectively, as in the first sentence.

Structurally, the objective and subjective uses look identical. When used in the present tense, the meaning of the modal must be derived from the context. However, when the subjective modal refers to a past act or state, it differs structurally from the objective modal.

In the following sentence, the objective modal is in the simple past.

Thomas **musste** mehr Geld verdienen.   *Thomas had to make more money.*

The next sentence is a present inference about a past situation. The modal is in the present tense and the accompanying verb in the perfect infinitive.

> Herr Berger hat einige Jahre in Alaska gearbeitet. Als er zurückkam, hat er ein Hotel gekauft.
> Er **muss** viel Geld **verdient haben**, als er in Alaska war.
> ⎣___PERFECT INFINITIVE___⎦

> *Mr. Berger worked in Alaska for a few years. When he came back, he bought a hotel.*
> He **must have made** *a lot of money when he was in Alaska.*
> ⎣___PERFECT INFINITIVE___⎦

Additional examples of the subjective use of **müssen**:

PRESENT	Das **muss** ein Missverständnis **sein**. *That **must be** a misunderstanding.*
PAST	Das **muss** ein Missverständnis **gewesen sein**. *That **must have been** a misunderstanding.*
PRESENT	Er **muss** Schwierigkeiten in Chemie **haben**. *He **must have** problems in chemistry.*
PAST	Er **muss** Schwierigkeiten in Chemie **gehabt haben**. *He **must have had** problems in chemistry.*

Keep in mind:

> The modal is in the present tense; the dependent infinitive is either a simple infinitive (referring to a present action or state) or a perfect infinitive (referring to a past action or state).

Examples of the objective and subjective uses of **können**, **mögen**, **sollen**, and **wollen**:

können

objective: expressing ability

> Ich **kann** (**konnte**) das verstehen.
> *I can (could) understand that.*

expressing objective possibility

> Wir **können** (konnten) mit dem Bus vom Flughafen in die Stadt fahren.
> *We can (could) go by bus from the airport to town.*

subjective: expressing a subjectively perceived possibility

PRESENT	Das **kann** wahr **sein**. *That may be true.*
PAST	Das **kann** wahr **gewesen sein**. *That may have been true.*

mögen

objective: expressing liking

Ich **mag (mochte)** ihn nicht fragen.
I don't (didn't) like to ask him.

subjective: expressing a subjectively perceived possibility similar to the use of **können**. (**Mögen** has a more literary connotation.)

PRESENT   Das **mag** sein.
That may be so.

PAST   Das **mag** eine gute Idee **gewesen sein**.
That may have been a good idea.

sollen

objective: expressing obligation

Der Bürgermeister **soll (sollte)** eine Rede halten.
The mayor is (was) expected to make a speech.
or: *The mayor is (was) supposed to make a speech.*

subjective: expressing rumors, hearsay

PRESENT   Sie **soll** sehr reich **sein**.
She is said to be very rich.
or: *She is supposed to be very rich.*

PAST   Sie **soll** sehr reich **gewesen sein**.
They say she was very rich.
or: *She is supposed to have been very rich.*

Note that English *to be supposed to* has similar dual function. It has both objective meaning (*to be expected to*) and subjective meaning (*to be said to*).

wollen

objective: expressing a wish or an intention

Hannelore **will (wollte)** das erledigen.
Hannelore wants (wanted) to take care of that.
or: *Hannelore intends (intended) to take care of that.*

subjective: expressing the speaker's or writer's reservation about someone's claim

PRESENT   Er **will** ein großer Musiker **sein**.
He claims to be a great musician.
(But I have my doubts.)
or: *He claims that he is a great musician.*

PAST   Er **will** ein großer Musiker **gewesen sein.**
He claims to have been a great musician.
(But I have my doubts.)
or: *He claims that he was a great musician.*

Übung 18-15

ANWENDEN Express the sentences in English.

Möglichkeiten

1. Das kann nicht wahr sein!
2. Das kann Absicht (*intention*) gewesen sein.
3. Das mag ein Fehler sein.
4. Das mag eine Ausrede (*excuse*) gewesen sein.

Hörensagen

5. Sabine Richter soll eine gute Schauspielerin sein.
6. Herr Bachmann soll in seiner Jugend ein guter Fußballspieler gewesen sein.
7. Schreibers sollen ein Haus an der Riviera haben, aber das glaubt niemand.
8. Rainer will zwei Jahre in Rom studiert haben.

Annahme

9. Renate schreibt mir nicht mehr. Sie muss mich vergessen haben.
10. Der junge Tenor aus Hamburg hat nicht gut gesungen. Er muss Lampenfieber (*stage fright*) gehabt haben.
11. Petra und Martin wollen eine fliegende Untertasse gesehen haben.
12. Gregor will auf einem Elefanten geritten sein.

The modal in the subjunctive

To make a statement seem more tentative and cautious, the subjective modal may be expressed in the subjunctive mood. This is particularly true with **können**.

PRESENT	Das **könnte** wahr **sein**.
	That might (could) be true.
PAST	Das **könnte** wahr **gewesen sein**.
	That might (could) have been true.

Übung 18-16

ANWENDEN Respond by using the subjunctive form of the modal **können** and the cued elements.

MODEL: Warum hat Walter dich nicht gegrüßt? (nicht gesehen haben)
        <u>Er könnte mich nicht gesehen haben.</u>

1. Warum spricht der Redner so leise und so schnell? (nervös sein)
2. Warum hat Marianne gestottert, als sie dich gesehen hat? (aufgeregt gewesen sein)
3. Warum sagt Jürgen seinen Eltern nicht die Wahrheit? (Angst haben)
4. Warum hat er seiner Freundin nicht die Wahrheit gesagt? (unsicher gewesen sein)
5. Warum hat Ruth mich nicht angerufen? (vergessen haben)

Appositives

§12 Appositive: An Explanatory Noun Phrase Which Immediately Follows the Noun or Pronoun It Modifies

Peter Stein, **der berühmte Pianist**, hat den Beethoven-Preis gewonnen.
SUBJECT   NOMINATIVE
NOMINATIVE

*Peter Stein, **the famous pianist,** won the Beethoven Prize.*

The *appositive* is normally in the same case as the element it modifies. In the above example, the appositive, **der berühmte Pianist**, is in the nominative because it modifies the subject of the sentence, **Peter Stein**.

Examples in other cases

Wir haben **ihm, dem berühmten Pianisten**, zu seinem Erfolg gratuliert.
DATIVE   DATIVE
We congratulated him, the famous pianist, on his success.

Wir haben **ihn, den berühmten Pianisten,** um ein Autogramm gebeten.
ACCUSATIVE   ACCUSATIVE
We asked him, the famous pianist, for an autograph.

Sie ist die Tochter **Peter Steins, des berühmten Pianisten**.
GENITIVE   GENITIVE
She is the daughter of Peter Stein, the famous pianist.

Sie kommt **aus Rossau, einem kleinen Dorf** in Sachsen.
DATIVE   DATIVE
She comes (is) from Rossau, a little village in Saxony.

Diese Blumen sind **für meine Großmutter, die Mutter meines Vaters**.
ACCUSATIVE   ACCUSATIVE
These flowers are for my grandmother, my father's mother.

Übung 18-17

ANWENDEN Respond to the questions by giving a name and then an appositive to identify the person.

MODEL: Wen haben Sie kürzlich getroffen?
Ich habe Frau Rosner, eine Freundin von mir, getroffen.

1. Wen haben Sie kürzlich zum Essen eingeladen? Und wer hat Sie eingeladen?
2. Wem haben Sie mit irgendetwas geholfen? Wer hat Ihnen geholfen?
3. Mit wem waren Sie im Konzert, im Kino oder im Theater?
4. Für wen haben Sie kürzlich ein Geschenk gekauft?
5. Wen haben Sie schon lange nicht mehr angerufen? Wer hat Sie schon lange nicht mehr angerufen?

Extended Adjective Constructions

§13   Adjectives Preceding Nouns Extended by Additional Modifiers

Herr Krause hat die **schon lange überfällige** Entschädigung noch nicht erhalten.
Mr. Krause has not yet received the long overdue compensation.

In this sentence, the adjective **überfällig** is modified by a time expression, **schon lange**. Because this expression is relatively short, both English and German permit the modified adjective to precede the noun. But if the modification of the adjective is more extensive, only German permits the construction to precede the noun. English requires that the adjective construction be placed after the noun, often as part of a relative clause.

Herr Krause hat die **schon seit mehr als drei Monaten fällige** Entschädigung noch nicht erhalten.
Mr. Krause has not yet received the compensation due for more than three months.
or: *Mr. Krause has not yet received the compensation that has been due for more than three months.*

These extended adjective constructions occur frequently in written German (literary and scientific texts, newspapers, and periodicals). In most instances, the adjective is a present or past participle (cf. Kap. 8 §13).

PRESENT PARTICIPLE

Der **schon seit Monaten steigende** Preis für Benzin hat zu wirtschaftlichen Schwierigkeiten geführt.
The price of gas, which has been rising for months, has led to economic difficulties.

When preceded by **zu**, the present participle has passive meaning and implies obligation or possibility. There are several English equivalents: *to be, can be, may be, must be, should be* + past participle, depending on the context.

die heute **zu** bezahlenden Rechnungen

the bills to be paid today
or: *the bills that must be paid today*
or: *the bills that should be paid today*

Note the position of **zu** if the participle has a separable prefix.

die nicht voraus**zu**sehenden Schwierigkeiten

the difficulties that cannot be foreseen
or: *the difficulties that may not be foreseen*

PAST PARTICIPLE

Der im vorigen Jahr so hoch **gestiegene** Preis für Treibstoff hat zu wirtschaftlichen Schwierigkeiten geführt.

The price of gasoline, which has climbed so high in the past year, has led to economic difficulties.

Alle noch nicht **bezahlten** Rechnungen sind in dieser Mappe vorzufinden.
All bills that have not yet been paid can be found in this folder.

Note that many features of these sentences, not only the extended adjective constructions, are more formal. Usually, when something is uttered in a more formal context, formal lexical and grammatical features co-occur, i.e., are used together. To progress in learning a language it is important to be aware of what constitutes formal and informal language. In German, the conversational past, the subjunctive with **würden**, and the possessive with **von**, are more informal, and the simple past for verbs other than **haben**, **sein**, the modals, the present subjunctive, and the genitive case are more formal.

Vokabulartip: übersetzen

Rendering extended adjective constructions into idiomatic English often poses considerable problems. Here are a few hints as to how to proceed.

$$\begin{array}{cccc} 1 & 4 & 3 & 2 \end{array}$$

Auf Seite 10 finden wir die bei jungen Leuten sehr beliebten Fernsehsendungen.

First bring together the beginning and the end of the extended adjective construction, i.e., the article **die** (1) and the noun **Fernsehsendungen** (2). Then proceed backward: First take the adjective that immediately precedes the noun, i.e., **beliebten** (*popular*). It is modified by the adverb **sehr**. Thus **sehr beliebten** is the third unit. It is preceded by the fourth unit, **bei jungen Leuten**. The result is

On page 10 we find the TV programs that are very popular with young people.

Übung 18-18

ANWENDEN Express the sentences in acceptable English.

Meldungen in der Zeitung und im Fernsehen.

1. Die Lohnerhöhungen blieben hinter den von Monat zu Monat steigenden Lebenshaltungskosten (*cost of living*) weit zurück.
2. Der in eine Seitenstraße einbiegende Bus stieß mit einem Lastwagen zusammen.
3. Die bei diesem Unfall verletzten Fahrgäste wurden in das Albert-Schweitzer-Krankenhaus gebracht.
4. Die Bürgermeisterin gab einen Überblick über die in diesem Jahr zu lösenden Probleme.

5. Die Diskussionen über die noch zu klärenden Fragen beginnen am Montag.
6. Die am Anfang des zwanzigsten Jahrhunderts viel gelesenen Romane dieses Autors sind jetzt ganz in Vergessenheit geraten.

Vokabulartip: erweiterte Adjektivkonstruktionen

Often there is more than one extended adjective construction in a sentence. If they modify the same noun, translate the first one completely, then add the next one, etc. In the following example, the two constructions A and B modify the noun **Fernsehsendungen**.

Auf Seite 10 finden wir die bei jungen Leuten sehr beliebten

A

aber von den Eltern oft kritisierten **Fernsehsendungen**.

B

On page 10 we find the TV programs that are very popular with young people, but are often criticized by parents.

If the constructions modify different nouns, each is translated directly after the corresponding noun. In the following sentences, the construction A modifies **Seite 10** and the construction B modifies **Fernsehsendungen**.

Auf der weitere Auskunft erteilenden **Seite 10** finden

A

wir die bei jungen Leuten sehr beliebten **Fernsehsendungen**.

B

On page 10, which gives further information, we find the TV programs that are very popular with young people.

Übung 18-19

ANWENDEN Express the sentences in acceptable English as best you can. Hint: First identify the noun or nouns that are modified, and then identify the meaning of the words. Then, translate as suggested above. View the exercise as a fun challenge in the realm of more formal German, not as something you are expected to do easily.

1. Die schon seit mehr als drei Monaten fällige und trotz wiederholter Mahnungen (*reminder*) noch nicht erhaltene Bezahlung wird durch SUMA kassiert werden.
2. Der bei dem Autounfall vor der Sporthalle schwer verletzte und per Hubschrauber (*helicopter*) in die Zentralklinik gebrachte Fahrer hat das Bewusstsein noch nicht wiedererlangt (*to regain consciousness*).

3. Die schon seit Jahren mit Erfolg auf dem Gebiet (*area, field*) der Genetik tätige Forscherin hat jetzt ein sehr kompliziertes und an ihr Können (*ability*) hohe Ansprüche stellendes (to *place demands on*) Projekt in Angriff genommen (to *tackle, embark on*).
4. Die mit fieberhaftem (*feverish*) Eifer (*zeal*) und höchster Konzentration arbeitenden Mechaniker tun alles, was menschenmöglich ist (*all that is humanly possible*), damit die mit den modernsten Geräten ausgestattete (to *equip*) Jacht im nächsten Rennen erfolgreich konkurrieren (to *compete*) kann.

The Passive in the Subjunctive Mood

Chapters 12 and 13 treated only the active forms of the subjunctive. Passive subjunctive forms also occur, principally in indirect discourse and in unreal conditions and conclusions. They are much less common, since in general the passive voice is used far less frequently than the active voice.

§14   Subjunctives in Indirect Discourse

(For their use in the active voice, see Kap. 13 §6 and §7.)

In indirect discourse the subjunctive occurs in three tenses: present, past, and future. The following synopsis shows two different auxiliaries for each tense: the general subjunctive (first form) and the special subjunctive (second form). The two forms have the same meaning.

DIRECT QUOTATION	INDIRECT QUOTATION
PRESENT INDICATIVE	PRESENT SUBJUNCTIVE
Der Polizist sagte: „Der Fall wird untersucht."	Der Polizist sagte, der Fall **würde** untersucht. **werde**
ANY PAST INDICATIVE	PAST SUBJUNCTIVE
„Der Fall wurde untersucht." „Der Fall ist untersucht worden" „Der Fall war untersucht worden."	der Fall **wäre** untersucht worden. **sei**
FUTURE INDICATIVE	FUTURE SUBJUNCTIVE
„Der Fall wird untersucht werden."	der Fall **würde** untersucht werden. **werde**

Note: The auxiliaries **würde/werde** and **wäre/sei** signal the subjunctive.

Examples:

> Die Kandidatin sagte: „Mein Name wird nicht erwähnt."
> Die Kandidatin sagte, ihr Name **würde/werde** nicht erwähnt.

Der Architekt sagte: „Das Projekt wird von der Regierung finanziert werden."
Der Architekt sagte, das Projekt **würde/werde** von der Regierung finanziert werden.

Die Polizistin sagte: „Der Dieb wurde gestern verhaftet."
Die Polizistin sagte, der Dieb **wäre/sei** gestern verhaftet worden.

Übung 18-20

ANWENDEN Change the statements to indirect quotations stating both subjunctives, as in the examples in §14.

1. Eine Beamtin sagte: „Ich werde wohl auch nicht befördert."
2. Eine andere Beamtin sagte: „Ich werde wohl auch nicht befördert werden."
3. Frau Köhler sagte: „Ich wurde nicht gefragt."
4. Herr Köhler sagte: „Meine Frau wird doch immer gefragt."
5. Der Reporter sagte: „Der Redner wird zu oft unterbrochen."
6. Die Zuhörer sagten: „Der Redner ist noch nie so oft unterbrochen worden."
7. Frau Martin sagte: „Der Bürgermeister wurde zu viel kritisiert."
8. Ihr Mann sagte: „Seine Vorgängerin (*predecessor*) war noch mehr kritisiert worden."
9. Die Agentin sagte: „Diese Reise wird vom Chef bezahlt."
10. Die Chefsekretärin sagte: „Die Reise wird wohl nicht von ihm bezahlt werden."

In the plural, the form **werden** of the special subjunctive is identical to the indicative form **werden** (cf. Kap. 13 §6). It is therefore replaced with the general subjunctive form **würden**. Thus the synopsis for plural forms is as follows:

PRESENT INDICATIVE	PRESENT SUBJUNCTIVE
Der Polizist sagte:	Der Polizist sagte,
„Die Fälle werden untersucht."	die Fälle **würden** untersucht.

ANY PAST SUBJUNCTIVE	PAST SUBJUNCTIVE
„Die Fälle wurden untersucht."	
„Die Fälle sind untersucht worden."	die Fälle **wären** untersucht worden
„Die Fälle waren untersucht worden."	**seien**

FUTURE INDICATIVE	FUTURE SUBJUNCTIVE
„Die Fälle werden untersucht werden."	die Fälle **würden** untersucht werden.

Remember: In the plural, only the **würde** forms are used in the present and future.

Übung 18-21

ANWENDEN Change the sentences to indirect quotations stating both subjunctives, as in the examples in §15.

MODEL:	Sie sagte:	Sie sagte,
	„Diese Uhren werden exportiert."	diese Uhren würden exportiert.
	„Viele Fehler wurden übersehen."	Sie sagte, viele Fehler wären/seien übersehen worden.

1. „Einige Schecks sind noch nicht eingelöst worden."
2. „Die Arbeiter von MAFRASA werden nicht gut bezahlt."
3. „Die Arbeiter werden wohl ausgenutzt werden."
4. „Diese Sachen sind noch nicht erledigt worden."
5. „Zwei Straßennamen werden geändert."
6. „Die Hausnummern sind schon geändert worden."

§15 Subjunctives and Contrary to Fact Conditions and Conclusions

In contrary to fact conditions and conclusions in the passive voice, only the general subjunctive is used. (For the use of subjunctives in the active, see Kap. 12.) The general subjunctive occurs in two tenses in the passive voice:

a. the present subjunctive referring to the present and future,
b. the past subjunctive referring to the past.

1. Wenn-clauses expressing contrary to fact conditions

The **wenn**-clause is a dependent clause; thus the inflected auxiliary is in last position.

a. Wenn der Fall **untersucht würde**...
PRESENT SUBJUNCTIVE

If the case **were investigated . . .**

b. Wenn der Fall **untersucht worden wäre**...
PAST SUBJUNCTIVE

If the case **had been investigated . . .**

Pattern		
present SUBJUNCTIVE	**Wenn**... _____ **würde** PAST PARTICIPLE	*If . . . were* _____ PAST PARTICIPLE
past SUBJUNCTIVE	**Wenn**... _____ **worden wäre** PAST PARTICIPLE	*If . . . had been* _____ PAST PARTICIPLE

Übung 18-22

ANWENDEN A. Write down five things that happened to you (or a person close to you) in the past. Use the passive voice.

> MODEL: <u>Mein Fahrrad wurde gestohlen.</u>
> <u>Meinem Bruder wurde der erste Preis in einem</u>
> <u>Klavierwettberwerb verliehen.</u>

B. Now speculate what might have happened if the events you mentioned in part A had not taken place. Keep the **wenn**-clause in the passive, but use the active voice in the conclusion.

> MODEL: Wenn mein Fahrrad nicht gestohlen worden wäre, dann wäre ich fitter geblieben.
> <u>Wenn meinem Bruder nicht der erste Preis verliehen worden wäre,</u>
> <u>dann hätten ihm nicht alle Freunde gratuliert.</u>

2. Contrary to fact conclusions

Referring to the present and future

> Wenn es nach mir **ginge**, (dann) **würde** der Fall **untersucht (werden)**.
> *If it were up to me, (then) the case **would be investigated**.*

Referring to the past

> Wenn es nach mir **gegangen wäre**, (dann) **wäre** der Fall **untersucht worden**.
> *If it had been up to me, (then) the case **would have been investigated**.*

The conclusion (main clause) has inverted word order because it is preceded by the dependent **wenn**-clause.

Pattern		
present **würde** _____		*would be* _____
SUBJUNCTIVE PAST PARTICIPLE		PAST PARTICIPLE
past **wäre** _____ **worden wäre**		*would have been* _____
SUBJUNCTIVE PAST PARTICIPLE		PAST PARTICIPLE

Übung 18-23

ANWENDEN A. Write down five events that you consider negative. Then restate each sentence beginning with the introductory clause **wenn es nach mir ginge**. Put the conclusion in the subjunctive.

> MODEL: <u>Die neue Mensa an meiner Uni wird nicht gebaut.</u>
> <u>Wenn es nach mir ginge, würde die neue Mensa gebaut werden.</u>

B. Write down five such negative events that occured in the past. Then restate the sentence, beginning with the introductory clause **wenn es nach mir gegangen wäre** and concluding it in the subjunctive.

MODEL: Meine beste Freundin wurde nicht zu Sams Geburtstagsparty eingeladen.
Wenn es nach mir gegangen wäre, wäre sie eingeladen worden.

Appendix

§1 The German Spelling Reform

After the governments of Germany, Austria, and Switzerland had agreed to a number of changes in German spelling in 1990, the German **Rechtschreibreform** (*spelling reform*) took effect on August 1, 1998. The reform is intended to simplify many of the arbitrary and confusing spelling rules.

The old and the new systems will officially co-exist until the year 2005 to facilitate the eventual transition to the new system. Schools are teaching the new system, but students will not be penalized for using old rules.

Students of German will encounter, for quite some time, texts that follow the old system alongside materials that have converted to the new one.

The following sections will summarize the major features of the new system.
Note: This book generally follows the new system as much as possible. However, much like speakers and writers in the German-speaking countries, the writers are only beginning to use, and become used to, the new conventions.

Spelling: ss *or* ß?

ß is used only between vowels if the preceding vowel is long or is a diphthong.

> grüßen heißen schließen Preußen außer

ss is used in all other positions.

ss must also be used in compounds if the two s's belong to different parts of the compound.

> aussprechen (aus + sprechen) diesseits (dies + Seite)

Note that in Switzerland, the ß is usually replaced with ss.

Capitalization

Along with nouns, nominalized adjectives are now capitalized.

> Rad fahren, im Allgemeinen, heute Abend, morgen Vormittag, aufs Höchste erfreut

Noun compounds

When nouns are compounded and the same consonant occurs three times, all three are retained. In the old system, only two were allowed.

OLD	NEW
Schiffahrt	Schifffahrt
Ballettruppe	Balletttruppe
Misstand	Missstand

Foreign words

For foreign words, both the foreign and the German spelling are possible, although the German spelling will be considered the preferred one.

FOREIGN SPELLING	GERMAN SPELLING
Joghurt	Jogurt
Ketchup	Ketschup
Portemonnaie	Portmonnee
Soufflé	Soufflee
Spaghetti	Spagetti
Trekking	Trecking

Words in the same family

When words belong to the same etymological family, the tendency is to make their spellings uniform.

OLD	NEW
fönen (*to blow dry* [hair])	föhnen (like Föhn)
numerieren	nummerieren (like Nummer)
überschwenglich (exuberant)	überschwänglich (like Überschwang [*exuberance*])

Verb, adjective, and participle compounds

Compounds consisting of verbs, adjectives, or participles will be written as separate words where before they often occurred as one word.

Auto fahren, spazieren gehen, kennen lernen, hier bleiben, gut gelaunt

Comma placement

For more punctuation rules, including the comma, see also §6 below.

Infinitival clauses are no longer set off with a comma (cf. Kap.11 §6)

> Er ging in die Küche **um sich ein Glas Milch zu holen.**
> Sie hat abgehängt **ohne ein Wort zu sagen.**

All dependent clauses continue to be set off by a comma (cf. Kap. 11 §3).

> Sabine hat Peter kennengelernt, **als sie in München studiert hat.**
> Leider hat es immer geregnet, **wenn wir ein Picknick machen wollten.**

Appositives are also set off by commas (cf. Kap.18 §12)

> Peter Stein, **der berühmte Pianist,** hat den Beethoven-Preis, gewonnen.

Note: Generally speaking, the comma rules have been relaxed. Comma placement is now more at the discretion of the writer and his or her intent. That is, the addition (or omission) of a comma allows the writer to mark the relation between elements, for example, whether an element is merely an additive or not.

> Er ist(,) ohne ein Wort zu sagen(,) gegangen.

The commas mark the phrase **ohne ein Wort zu sagen** as an additive. By not setting it off with commas, however, the writer places more significance on the phrase.

§2   Principal Parts of Strong and Irregular Verbs

The third person singular forms of verbs with a vowel change in the present tense are shown in parentheses after the infinitive. The third person singular forms are also shown for the general subjunctive present, many of which are felt to be stilted or obsolete. They are usually replaced with **würde** + infinitive (cf. Kap. 12 §6). Verbs that <u>are</u> still used in the general subjunctive present form are listed in Kap.12 §4, 4 and 5.

INFINITIVE (3RD-PERSON SINGULAR)	SIMPLE PAST	PRESENT PERFECT	GENERAL SUBJUNCTIVE PRESENT (3RD-PERSON SINGULAR)	MEANING
backen (bäckt)	backte	hat gebacken	backte	*to bake*
befehlen (befiehlt)	befahl	hat befohlen	beföhle or: befähle	*to command*
beginnen	begann	hat begonnen	begänne or: begönne	*to begin*
beißen	biss	hat gebissen	bisse	*to bite*
betrügen	betrog	hat betrogen	betröge	*to deceive*
beweisen	bewies	hat bewiesen	bewiese	*to prove*
biegen	bog	hat gebogen	böge	*to bend*

INFINITIVE (3RD-PERSON SINGULAR)	SIMPLE PAST	PRESENT PERFECT	GENERAL SUBJUNCTIVE PRESENT (3RD-PERSON SINGULAR)	MEANING
bieten	bot	hat geboten	böte	to offer
binden	band	hat gebunden	bände	to bind, tie
bitten	bat	hat gebeten	bäte	to ask (for), request
blasen (bläst)	blies	hat geblasen	bliese	to blow
bleiben	blieb	ist geblieben	bliebe	to stay, remain
braten (brät)	briet	hat gebraten	briete	to roast, fry
brechen (bricht)	brach	hat gebrochen	bräche	to break
brennen	brannte	hat gebrannt	brennte	to burn
bringen	brachte	hat gebracht	brächte	to bring
denken	dachte	hat gedacht	dächte	to think
empfangen (empfängt)	empfing	hat empfangen	empfinge	to receive
empfehlen (empfiehlt)	empfahl	hat empfohlen	empföhle or: empfähle	to recommend
empfinden	empfand	hat empfunden	empfände	to feel (about something)
erlöschen (erlischt)	erlosch	ist erloschen	erlösche	to go out (light, fire)
erschrecken (erschrickt)	erschrack	ist erschrocken	erschräke	to be startled
essen (isst)	aß	hat gegessen	äße	to eat
fahren (fährt)	fuhr	ist gefahren	führe	to drive, travel
fallen (fällt)	fiel	ist gefallen	fiele	to fall
fangen (fängt)	fing	hat gefangen	finge	to catch
finden	fand	hat gefunden	fände	to find
fliegen	flog	ist geflogen	flöge	to fly
fliehen	floh	ist geflohen	flöhe	to flee
fließen	floss	ist geflossen	flösse	to flow
fressen (frisst)	fraß	hat gefressen	fräße	to eat (animals)
frieren	fror	hat gefroren	fröre	to freeze, be cold
geben (gibt)	gab	hat gegeben	gäbe	to give
gehen	ging	ist gegangen	ginge	to go
gelingen	gelang	ist gelungen	gelänge	to succeed
gelten (gilt)	galt	hat gegolten	gölte or: gälte	to be valid, carry weight

INFINITIVE (3RD-PERSON SINGULAR)	SIMPLE PAST	PRESENT PERFECT	GENERAL SUBJUNCTIVE PRESENT (3RD-PERSON SINGULAR)	MEANING
genesen	genas	ist genesen	genäse	*to recover (from illness)*
genießen	genoss	hat genossen	genösse	*to enjoy*
geschehen (geschieht)	geschah	ist geschehen	geschähe	*to happen*
gewinnen	gewann	hat gewonnen	gewönne or: gewänne	*to win*
gießen	goss	hat gegossen	gösse	*to pour*
gleichen	glich	hat geglichen	gliche	*to equal, resemble*
gleiten	glitt	ist geglitten	glitte	*to glide, slide*
graben (gräbt)	grub	hat gegraben	grübe	*to dig*
greifen	griff	hat gegriffen	griffe	*to grip, seize*
haben (hat)	hatte	hat gehabt	hätte	*to have*
halten (hält)	hielt	hat gehalten	hielte	*to hold, stop*
hängen	hing	hat gehangen	hinge	*to hang (intransitive)*
heben	hob	hat gehoben	höbe	*to lift*
heißen	hieß	hat geheißen	hieße	*to be called*
helfen (hilft)	half	hat geholfen	hülfe or: hälfe	*to help*
kennen	kannte	hat gekannt	kennte	*to know, to be acquainted with*
klingen	klang	hat geklungen	klänge	*to sound*
kneifen	kniff	hat gekniffen	kniffe	*to pinch*
kommen	kam	ist gekommen	käme	*to come*
kriechen	kroch	ist gekrochen	kröche	*to crawl*
laden (lädt)	lud	hat geladen	lüde	*to load*
lassen (lässt)	ließ	hat gelassen	ließe	*to leave, let, cause to*
laufen (läuft)	lief	ist gelaufen	liefe	*to run, walk*
leiden	litt	hat gelitten	litte	*to suffer*
leihen	lieh	hat geliehen	liehe	*to lend*
lesen (liest)	las	hat gelesen	läse	*to read*
liegen	lag	hat gelegen	läge	*to lie, be situated*
lügen	log	hat gelogen	löge	*to (tell a) lie*
meiden (vermeiden)	mied	hat gemieden	miede	*to avoid*

INFINITIVE (3RD-PERSON SINGULAR)	SIMPLE PAST	PRESENT PERFECT	GENERAL SUBJUNCTIVE PRESENT (3RD-PERSON SINGULAR)	MEANING
messen (misst)	maß	hat gemessen	mäße	to measure
nehmen (nimmt)	nahm	hat genommen	nähme	to take
nennen	nannte	hat genannt	nennte	to name, call
pfeifen	pfiff	hat gepfiffen	pfiffe	to whistle
preisen	pries	hat gepriesen	priese	to praise
raten (rät)	riet	hat geraten	riete	to advise, guess
reiben	rieb	hat gerieben	riebe	to rub
reißen	riss	ist gerissen	risse	to tear
reiten	ritt	ist geritten	ritte	to ride (on an animal)
rennen	rannte	ist gerannt	rennte	to run
riechen	roch	hat gerochen	röche	to smell
rufen	rief	hat gerufen	riefe	to call
saufen (säuft)	soff	hat gesoffen	söffe	to drink (animal)
scheiden	schied	hat geschieden	schiede	to separate
scheinen	schien	hat geschienen	schiene	to shine, seem
schelten (schilt)	schalt	hat gescholten	schölte	to scold
schieben	schob	hat geschoben	schöbe	to shove, push
schießen	schoss	hat geschossen	schösse	to shoot
schlafen (schläft)	schlief	hat geschlafen	schliefe	to sleep
schlagen (schlägt)	schlug	hat geschlagen	schlüge	to hit, beat
schleichen	schlich	ist geschlichen	schliche	to creep
schließen	schloss	hat geschlossen	schlösse	to close
schmelzen (schmilzt)	schmolz	hat geschmolzen	schmölze	to melt
schneiden	schnitt	hat geschnitten	schnitte	to cut
schreiben	schrieb	hat geschrieben	schriebe	to write
schreien	schrie	hat geschrie(e)n	schreie	to shout, scream
schreiten	schritt	ist geschritten	schritte	to stride
schweigen	schwieg	hat geschwiegen	schwiege	to be silent
schwimmen	schwamm	ist geschwommen	schwömme or: schwämme	to swim
schwingen	schwang	hat geschwungen	schwänge	to swing
schwören	schwor	hat geschworen	schwöre	to swear, vow
sehen (sieht)	sah	hat gesehen	sähe	to see
sein (ist)	war	ist gewesen	wäre	to be
senden	sandte	hat gesandt	sendete	to send
singen	sang	hat gesungen	sänge	to sing
sinken	sank	ist gesunken	sänke	to sink

INFINITIVE (3RD-PERSON SINGULAR)	SIMPLE PAST	PRESENT PERFECT	GENERAL SUBJUNCTIVE PRESENT (3RD-PERSON SINGULAR)	MEANING
sitzen	saß	hat gesessen	säße	*to sit*
spinnen	spann	hat gesponnen	spönne	*to spin*
sprechen (spricht)	sprach	hat gesprochen	spräche	*to speak*
springen	sprang	hat gesprungen	spränge	*to jump*
stechen (sticht)	stach	hat gestochen	stäche	*to prick, sting*
stehen	stand	hat gestanden	stünde	*to stand*
stehlen (stiehlt)	stahl	hat gestohlen	stähle	*to steal*
steigen	stieg	ist gestiegen	stiege	*to climb, rise*
sterben (stirbt)	starb	ist gestorben	stürbe	*to die*
stinken	stank	hat gestunken	stänke	*to stink*
stoßen (stößt)	stieß	hat gestoßen	stieße	*to push*
streichen	strich	hat gestrichen	striche	*to paint*
streiten	stritt	hat gestritten	stritte	*to quarrel*
tragen (trägt)	trug	hat getragen	trüge	*to carry; wear*
treffen (trifft)	traf	hat getroffen	träfe	*to meet*
treiben	trieb	hat getrieben	triebe	*to drive (cattle) pursue (an activity)*
treten (tritt)	trat	ist getreten	träte	*to step, tread*
trinken	trank	hat getrunken	tränke	*to drink*
tun	tat	ist getan	täte	*to do*
verderben (verdirbt)	verdarb	hat verdorben	verdürbe	*to spoil*
vergessen (vergisst)	vergaß	hat vergessen	vergäße	*to forget*
verlieren	verlor	hat verloren	verlöre	*to lose*
verschwinden	verschwand	ist verschwunden	verschwände	*to disappear*
verzeihen	verzieh	hat verziehen	verziehe	*to pardon*
wachsen (wächst)	wuchs	ist gewachsen	wüchse	*to grow*
waschen (wäscht)	wusch	hat gewaschen	wüsche	*to wash*
weichen	wich	ist gewichen	wiche	*to yield, give way*
wenden	wandte	hat gewandt	wendete	*to turn*
werben (wirbt)	warb	hat geworben	würbe	*to recruit; woo*
werden (wird)	wurde	ist geworden	würde	*to become*
werfen (wirft)	warf	hat geworfen	würfe	*to throw*
wiegen	wog	hat gewogen	wöge	*to weigh*
winden	wand	hat gewunden	wände	*to wind, twist*
wissen (weiß)	wusste	hat gewusst	wüsste	*to know*
ziehen	zog	hat gezogen	zöge	*to pull*
zwingen	zwang	hat gezwungen	zwänge	*to force*

§3   Adjectives That Add an Umlaut in the Comparative and Superlative

The following monosyllabic adjectives add an umlaut in the comparative and superlative (cf. Kap. 9 §2):

alt	älter	ältest-
arg (*bad*)	ärger	ärgst-
arm	ärmer	ärmst-
dumm	dümmer	dümmst-
grob (*coarse, rude*)	gröber	gröbst-
groß	größer	größt-
hart	härter	härtest-
hoch	höher	höchst-
jung	jünger	jüngst-
kalt	kälter	kältest-
klug	klüger	klügst-
krank	kränker	kränkst-
kurz	kürzer	kürzest-
lang	länger	längst-
nah	näher	nächst-
oft	öfter	(öftest-) häufigst-
scharf (*sharp*)	schärfer	schärfst-
schwach (*weak*)	schwächer	schwächst-
schwarz	schwärzer	schwärzest-
stark	stärker	stärkst-
warm	wärmer	wärmst-

The following adjectives have comparative and superlative forms with and without umlauts. If two forms are possible, the boldface marks the one that is more common.

blass (*pale*)	**blasser** blässer	**blassest-** blässest-
fromm (*religious, devout*)	frommer frömmer	frommst- frömmst- (either form)
gesund (*healthy*)	gesunder **gesünder**	gesundest- **gesündest-**

glatt	**glatter**	**glattest-**
(*smooth, slippery*)	glätter	glättest-
nass (*wet*)	**nasser**	**nassest-**
	nässer	nässest-
rot (*red*)	roter	rotest-
	röter	**rötest-**
schmal (*narrow*)	**schmaler**	**schmalst-**
	schmäler	schmälst-

§4 Flavoring Particles

Certain adverbs and conjunctions, such as **doch**, **schon**, **aber**, and **denn** are often used as flavoring particles. They express the speaker's attitude toward what is said and are difficult to translate into English in any consistent way. Nevertheless, it is possible to state when, and often why, they are used. Here are some frequently occurring flavoring particles and their most common uses.

aber

Aber merely strengthens the thought expressed.

> Das hast du **aber** fein gemacht.
> *You really did a fine job.*
> *You did a fine job, I must say.*

auch

1. Auch may confirm that a possibility or supposition is reality.

> Köhlers hatten vor ein Haus zu kaufen.—Sie haben **auch** eins gekauft.
> *The Köhlers were planning to buy a house—They did buy one.*

> Frau Schreiber soll sehr nett sein.—Sie ist **auch** sehr nett.
> *Mrs. Schreiber is supposed to be very nice—She indeed is very nice.*

2. Auch used in questions may express a certain doubt.

> Hast du mich **auch** verstanden?
> *Did you really understand me?*

> Kann man sich **auch** auf dich verlassen?
> *Can one really rely on you?*

3. Auch used in commands reinforces them.

> Vergiss das **auch** nicht!
> *Be sure not to forget that.*

> Komm **auch** nicht zu spät!
> *Be sure not to be late.*

denn

1. Denn used in questions may imply special interest, impatience, or surprise on the part of the speaker.

> Wann ist **denn** der Unfall passiert?
> *When did the accident happen? (I'd like to know.)*

> Warum kommt **denn** der Bus nicht?
> *Why isn't the bus coming? (We've been waiting at least 15 minutes.)*

> Kommst du **denn** nicht mit?
> *Aren't you coming along? (I thought you would.)*

2. Denn may make questions less abrupt.

Wieso **denn**?	*How so?*
Wo **denn**?	*Where?*
Wann **denn**?	*When?*

doch

1. Doch is frequently used for emphasis.

> Das ist **doch** die Höhe!
> *That is the limit. (stress on is)*

> Das ist **doch** kaum zu glauben.
> *That certainly (indeed) is hard to believe.*

2. Doch may express opposition; what is said is opposite to what one would have expected.

> Wir haben Müllers **doch** noch eingeladen.
> *We invited the Müllers after all (contrary to what we said or planned to do before).*

Such a statement is often strengthened by adding **noch.**

3. Doch may express the opposition to a negative statement, i.e., a positive.

> Kommst du nicht mit?
> **Doch**! (Ich komme mit.)

einmal (mal)

1. Nun einmal (nun mal) indicates acceptance of something that cannot be helped.

> Ich bin **nun einmal (nun mal)** sehr unbeliebt.
> *I am very unpopular (and there is nothing to be done about it).*

> Das ist **nun einmal (nun mal)** so.
> *That's how it is. That's how it goes.*

2. Mal (seldom **einmal**) usually makes a sentence sound more casual and less abrupt or blunt.

> Komm **mal** her!
> *Come here, will you?*

> Ich muss mir das **mal** überlegen.
> *I have to think about that.*

ja

1. Ja is frequently used when stating facts that are known or when making assertions with confidence. **Ja** either remains untranslated, or remarks such as *you know, as is known,* are added.

> Das ist **ja** kein Geheimnis.
> *That's no secret, you know.*

> Das weiß **ja** jeder.
> *Everybody knows that.*

2. Ja conveys admonition in imperatives.

> Vergiss das (**nur**) **ja** nicht!
> *Be sure not to forget that.*

> Machen Sie das (**nur**) **ja** nicht wieder!
> *Don't ever do that again.*

> **Ja** is stressed in these cases; **nur** is frequently added for reinforcement (see the following section).

nur, bloß

Colloquially, **bloß** is frequently used instead of **nur**.

1. Nur (**bloß**) may express intense interest in learning the answer to some puzzling question.

> Warum hat er **nur** (**bloß**) gelogen?
> *Why did he lie? (I'd really like to know.)*

> Wie konntest du **nur** (**bloß**) soviel Geld verschwenden?
> *How on earth could you waste so much money?*

2. In imperative sentences **nur** may express encouragement and reassurance.

> Kommen Sie **nur** herein!
> *Do come in.*

> Haben Sie **nur** keine Angst!
> *Don't be afraid.*

It may also express admonition, frequently reinforcing **ja**.

Beleidige ihn **nur** nicht!

Beleidige ihn **nur** ja nicht!

> Don't insult him. (by all means)

schon

1. Schon may express reassurance that something will be so, although it may seem to be doubtful.

Du wirst es **schon** schaffen.
Don't worry, you'll make it.

Wir werden **schon** eine Lösung finden.
Don't worry, we'll find a solution.

2. Schon may express a concession.

Das ist **schon** richtig, aber das ist nicht die ganze Wahrheit.
That's correct, I admit (I grant you), but that's not the whole truth.

In den Ferien hast du doch genug Zeit zum Schreiben.—Das **schon**, aber ich
habe keine Lust dazu.
*During vacation you do have enough time to write.—That's true, I admit, but I don't
(have the urge to do it) feel like it.*

As the above sentences illustrate, this concessive use can easily be recognized by the conjunction **aber** introducing a qualifying remark, frequently a counter-argument.

3. Schon is used in rhetorical questions in the sense of "after all, but then."

Ich habe nichts gesagt. Was kann man **schon** in so einem Fall sagen?
I said nothing. After all, what can one say in such a case?

Natürlich ist das eine herrliche Jacht. Aber wer kann sich **schon** so einen
Luxus leisten?
Of course, that is a magnificent yacht. But then, who can afford such a luxury?

§5 Common German Measurements and Their English Equivalents*

Most measures (except those ending in -e) add no ending in the plural when they follow a numeral.

das Pfund, -e	zwei Pfund	*two pounds*
der Grad,-e	zwei Grad	*two degrees*
die Meile,-n	zwei Meilen	*two miles*
die Gallone,-n	zwei Gallonen	*two gallons*

---

*Data and illustrations from "These Strange German Ways," courtesy Atlantik-Brücke e. V., Hamburg.

German	English Equivalents	English	German Equivalents
1 Zentimeter (1 cm)	0.4 inch	1 inch	2,5 Zentimeter
1 Meter (1 m)	3.3 feet	1 foot	0,3 Meter
	or: 1.1 yard	1 yard	0,9 Meter
1 Kilometer (1 km)	0.62 mile	1 mile	1,6 Kilometer

Illustration of how many miles correspond to 1–500 km

Mile	0.6 1.8 3.1 4.9 6.2 9.3	12.4	15.5	18.6	21.7	24.8	27.9	31.0	62.1	93.1	124.2	155.2	186.4	217.4	248.5	279.5	310.6
Kilometer	1 3 5 8 10 15 20	25	30	35	40	45	50	100	150	200	250	300	350	400	450	500	

1 Quadratmeter (1 qm) = 10.8 square feet 1 Quadratkilometer (1 qkm) = 0.39 square mile	1 square foot = 0,092 Quadratmeter (qm) 1 square mile = 2,6 Quadratkilometer (qkm)
1 Liter (1 l) = 2.1 U.S. pints 1.05 U.S. quarts	1 U.S. pint = 0,47 Liter (l) 1 U.S. quart = 0,94 Liter (l) 1 U.S. gallon = 3,76 Liter (l)
1 Gramm (1 g) = 0.04 ounce 1 Pfund (1 Pfd) = 1.1 pounds 1 Kilogramm (1 kg) = 2.2 pounds or: Kilo	1 ounce = 28 Gramm (g) 1 pound = 454 Gramm (g)

Some practical hints

A **Meter** is a little more than a yard.

A **Pfund** is a little more than a pound.

A **Liter** is a little more than a quart. **3 3/4 Liter** = 1 gallon.

A **Kilometer** is 5/8 of a mile. **5 Kilometer** = approx. 3 miles.

When you weigh yourself on a German scale, your weight is 10 percent less than on an American scale; for example, Barbara weighs 120 pounds in America, but **108 Pfund** in Germany.

Fahrenheit and Centigrade (Celsius)

Wieviel Grad haben wir heute?
Heute haben wir zehn Grad Celsius. (written: 10 C)

If you have the centigrade reading and want to find out
the temperature in Fahrenheit, multiply the centigrade
reading by 9, divide by 5, and add 32.

Formula: $F = \dfrac{9C}{5} + 32$

If you have the Fahrenheit reading and want to find
out the temperature in centigrade, deduct 32 from the
Fahrenheit reading, multiply by 5, and divide by 9.

Formula: $C = \dfrac{5(F - 32)}{9}$

The dual scales on the thermometer shown
on the right give you some equivalents.

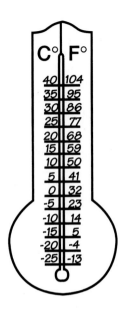

C°	F°
40	104
35	95
30	86
25	77
20	68
15	59
10	50
5	41
0	32
-5	23
-10	14
-15	5
-20	-4
-25	-13

Conversion Tables

SKIRTS, DRESSES, COATS		SHIRTS		SHOES		SUITS	
U.S.	EUROPE	U.S.	EUROPE	U.S.	EUROPE	U.S.	EUROPE
10	38	14	36	6	37	36	46
12	40	14 1/2	37	7	38	38	48
14	42	15	38	8	39	40	50
16	44	15 1/2	39	9	40	42	52
18	46	16	41	10	41	44	54
20	48	16 1/2	42	11	42	46	56
		17	43	12	43	48	58
				13	44		

BLOUSES		HATS		KITCHEN HINTS	
U.S.	EUROPE	U.S.	EUROPE	U.S.	EUROPE
30	38	7	57	1 cup sugar	200 g
32	40	7 1/8	58	1 cup flour	150 g
34	42	7 1/4	59	1 tsp.	5 g
36	44	7 3/8	60	1 tbsp.	12 g
38	46	7 1/2	61		
40	48				

§6   Punctuation

The following punctuation rules differ from English usage.

The comma

1. In enumerations, the last item is not set off by a comma if preceded by
und or **oder**.

> Klaus, Margot **und Renate** haben einen Preis gewonnen.
> *Klaus, Margot, and Renate won a prize.*

> Klaus, Margot **oder Renate** hat den ersten Preis gewonnen.
> *Klaus, Margot, or Renate won first prize.*

2. All dependent clauses are set off by commas (cf.§1).

> Ich weiß, **dass er jetzt zu Hause ist.**
> *I know that he is at home now.*

> Das ist ein Film, **der mir gefällt.**
> *That's a film I like.*

> Die Zeitung, **die ich heute Morgen gekauft habe**, ist verschwunden.
> *The newspaper I bought this morning has disapppeared.*

3. Adverbs and prepositional phrases are normally not set off by commas.

> **Natürlich** weiß er das.
> *Of course, he knows that.*

> **Zum Glück** war Margot zu Hause.
> *Luckily, Margot was at home.*

> **Nach vielen Jahren schwerer Arbeit** ist mein Vater endlich in den
> Ruhestand getreten.
> *After many years of hard work, my father finally retired.*

4. The comma is used as a decimal point (cf. Kap. 10 §1).

> **3,50** (read: drei Komma fünf null) = 3.50 (three point five O)

Keep in mind

> German leaves a space or uses a period to separate thousands
> and millions (cf. Kap. 10 §1).
> 10 000 or 10.000 = English 10,000
> 1 000 000 or 1.000.000 = English 1,000,000

Punctuation of direct quotations

Direct quotations are preceded by a colon. Except in typing, the opening quotation mark is set on the line.

>Er sagte: „Ich habe keine Zeit."
>*He said, "I don't have time."*

As in English, the end quote follows a period, question mark, or exclamation point, but in contrast to English, it precedes a comma.

>„Ich habe keine Zeit", sagte er.   *"I have no time," he said.*

Typewriters and computers that do not have the opening quotation mark use the end quote instead.

>"Ich habe keine Zeit", sagte er.

The exclamation point

Imperative sentences end with an exclamation point or, if there is no special emphasis, with a period.

>Bitte kommen Sie.   *Please come.*
>
>Komm jetzt!   *Come now!*

The hyphen in compounds

German often omits an element belonging to two different compound nouns. The hyphen is then used to show where it has been omitted.

>Er ist Mathematik- und Physikprofessor.
>(for: Mathematikprofessor und Physikprofessor)
>
>Ich habe den Sonnenaufgang und -untergang fotografiert.
>(for: Sonnenaufgang und Sonnenuntergang)

§7   Writing Letters and Addresses

For writing the date, see Kapitel 10 §4, 5.

Formal letter

>Sehr geehrter Herr Krause,
>Sehr verehrte Frau Rießland,
>Sehr geehrte Damen und Herren,
>für Ihren Brief vom 23. August danke ich Ihnen… Ich verstehe natürlich, dass …
>Mit freundlichen Grüßen,
>
>*Maria Schoeuber*

The salutation **Sehr geehrter Herr Krause** (lit.: *Very esteemed Mr. Krause*) corresponds to the English *Dear Mr. Krause*. When the letter is directed to a woman, it may begin with **Sehr verehrte Frau Rießland**; a company may be addressed with **Sehr geehrte Damen und Herren** or no salutation.

Some people hesitate to begin a formal letter with **ich** because it is considered impolite. Thus they begin with another element and use inversion.

> Sehr geehrter Herr Krause,
> für Ihren Brief danke ich Ihnen ...

Note that there are no indentations.

Informal letters

When a comma follows the salutation, the first word of the letter is not capitalized.

> Liebe Monika,
>
> lange habe ich nichts von dir und deiner Familie gehört.
> Hast du meinen Brief vom. 1 September nicht erhalten?...
>
> Mit herzlichen Grüßen,
> deine
> *Sabine*

If an exclamation mark instead of a comma is used, the first letter is capitalized.

> Liebe Barbara und lieber Dietmar!
>
> Ich habe lange nichts von euch gehört. Habt ihr meinen Brief vom 30. Juli nicht erhalten?...
>
> Beste Grüße,
> von eurem
> *Klaus*

Addresses (*die Anschrift*)

Familie	Frau
Martin Schramm	Dr. Käte Wolf
Beethovenstraße 21	Ringstraße 171
D-60001 Frankfurt/Main	D-04029 Leipzig
Fräulein	Herrn
Maria Renner	Professor Dr. H. Spörli
Schubertring 2	Mainaustr. 12
A-1011 Wien	CH-8008 Zürich

Note: a. The house number follows the street.

b. The 5-digit ZIP code (**die Postleitzahl**) precedes the city name.

c. Letters sent to another country have a country symbol prefixed to the ZIP code. Some of the common ones are

A	Austria (**Österreich**)
CH	Switzerland (**die Schweiz**)
D	Federal Republic of Germany (**Deutschland**)
FL	Fürstentum Liechtenstein
LUX	Luxemburg

d. Senders usually place their name and address on the back of the envelope.

§8   The German Alphabet

Modern German books and newspapers use the same type fonts that are used in English, and German handwriting is similar to ours. Until the second quarter of the twentieth century, Gothic type (**Fraktur**) was commonly used in Germany. Because you may encounter this type in older books, the following table provides Roman and Gothic styles, together with handwritten Gothic forms.

ROMAN TYPE		GOTHIC TYPE AND GERMAN SCRIPT				PRONUNCIATION OF LETTER NAME
A	a	𝔄	*A*	a	*a*	ah
B	b	𝔅	*B*	b	*b*	beh
C	c	ℭ	*C*	c	*c*	tseh
D	d	𝔇	*D*	d	*d*	deh
E	e	𝔈	*E*	e	*e*	eh
F	f	𝔉	*F*	f	*f*	eff
G	g	𝔊	*G*	g	*g*	geh
H	h	ℌ	*H*	h	*h*	hah
I	i	ℑ	*I*	i	*i*	ee
J	j	𝔍	*J*	j	*j*	yot
K	k	𝔎	*K*	k	*k*	kah
L	l	𝔏	*L*	l	*l*	ell
M	m	𝔐	*M*	m	*m*	em
N	n	𝔑	*N*	n	*n*	en
O	o	𝔒	*O*	o	*o*	oh
P	p	𝔓	*P*	p	*p*	peh
Q	q	𝔔	*Q*	q	*q*	coo
R	r	𝔕	*R*	r	*r*	err
S	s	𝔖	*S*	ſ ß	*ſs*	ess
T	t	𝔗	*T*	t	*t*	teh
U	u	𝔘	*U*	u	*u*	oo
V	v	𝔙	*V*	v	*v*	fow (*as in* fowl)
W	w	𝔚	*W*	w	*w*	veh
X	x	𝔛	*X*	x	*x*	iks
Y	y	𝔜	*Y*	y	*y*	üpsilon
Z	z	𝔷	*Z*	z	*z*	tset

UMLAUTE

Ä	ä	*Ä*	*Ä*	*ä*	*ä*	ah umlaut
Ö	ö	*Ö*	*Ö*	*ö*	*ö*	oh umlaut
Ü	ü	*Ü*	*Ü*	*ü*	*ü*	oo umlaut

DIPTHONGS

Au	au	*Au*	*Au*	*au*	*au*	= ow (as in owl)
Äu	äu	*Äu*	*Äu*	*äu*	*äu*	= ow umlaut
Eu	eu	*Eu*	*eu*	*eu*	*eu*	= oy (as in boy)
Ai	ai	*Ai*	*Ai*	*ai*	*ai*	
Ei	ei	*Ei*	*ei*	*ei*	*ei*	} = eye

EXAMPLES

ROMAN TYPE

Herbstlied

Bunt[1] sind schon die Wälder,
Gelb die Stoppelfelder,[2]
Und der Herbst beginnt.
Und die Blätter fallen,
Und die Nebel[3] wallen,[4]
Kühler weht[5] der Wind.
— Salis-Seewis

GOTHIC TYPE

Herbstlied

Bunt sind schon die Wälder,
Gelb die Stoppelfelder,
Und der Herbst beginnt.
Und die Blätter fallen,
Und die Nebel wallen,
Kühler weht der Wind.
—Salis-Seewis.

GERMAN SCRIPT

Herbstlied
Bunt sind schon die Wälder,
Gelb die Stoppelfelder,
Und der Herbst beginnt.
Und die Blätter fallen,
Und die Nebel wallen,
Kühler weht der Wind.

1	bunt	*many-colored*
2	das Stoppelfeld, -er	*stubble field*
3	der Nebel, -	*fog*
4	wallen	*to surge*
5	wehen	*to blow*

German-English Vocabulary

A

abartig (8) abnormal, deviant
abstoßend (8) revolting
der/die **Abgeordnete, -n** (13) representative (m./f.)
ab•sagen (16) to call off, cancel
abscheulich (8) disgusting, repulsive
die **Abtreibung, -en** (7) abortion
sich ab•trocknen (15) to dry oneself off
die **Aktentasche, -n** (15) briefcase
die **Alliierten** (pl.) (16) Allied Forces
an•erkennen, erkannte an, hat anerkannt (16) to recognize, to acknowledge
der/die **Angestellte, -n** (3) employee (m.f.)
der **Anorak, -s** (6) parka, windbreaker
anwesend (3) present, in attendance
der/die **Anwesende, -n** (adj. noun) (3) attendee (m.f.)
der **Anzug, ⁝e** (6) suit (men's)
an•rufen, rief an, hat angerufen (4) to call on the phone
der **Apparat, -e** (14) equipment, appliance
die **Arbeitsstelle, -n** (2) job, position
das **Argument, -e** (11) argument
argumentieren (11) to argue, to present arguments
die **Arroganz** (9) arrogance
der **Arzt, ⁝e** (6) doctor, physician (m.)
die **Ausdauer** (9) endurance, stamina
die **Auseinandersetzung, -en** (11) controversy, argument, fight
die **Auskunft** (10) directory information
die **Aussage, -n** (13) testimony
aus•sagen (13) to state, to make a statement
aus•sehen als ob (i), sah aus, hat ausgesehen (13) to look as if
aus•statten (18) to equip
der **Ausweis, -e** (15) ID card, membership card
aus•nutzen (16) to exploit, to take advantage
das **Auto, -s** (3) car, automobile
ändern (13) to change
die **Ärztin, -nen** (6) doctor, physician (f.)

B

der **Bach, ⁝e** (7) creek
die **Bahn** (3) rail, train
bald (3) soon
das **Bargeld** (15) cash
bauen (16) to build
bedienen (16) to serve, to wait on
begabt (9) talented
behandeln (16) to treat, to deal with
behaupten (13) to claim, to state
der/die **Bekannte, -n** (adj. noun) (6) acquaintance (m./f.)
benachrichtigen (16) to notify
das **Benzin** (2) gasoline
der **Berg, -e** (7) mountain
der **Bericht, -e** (3) report
der **Beruf, -e** (4) occupation
  von Beruf (4) as an occupation, by trade
bescheiden (9) modest, humble
die **Bescheidenheit** (9) modesty
besorgen to get, buy
bringen, brachte, hat gebracht (5) to bring
mit•bringen (5) to bring along
  (also: to bring as a token or gift)
besprechen (i), besprach, hat besprochen (11) to negotiate, to discuss
die **Besprechung, -en** (3) meeting, conference
betonen (13) to emphasize, to stress
der **Betrieb, -e** (2) company, business
die **Betriebsfeier, -n** (2) company party
die **Betriebswirtschaft** (2) business (academic subject or major)
die **Beziehung, -en** (7) relationship
das **Bier, -e** (4) beer
das **Bild, -er** (5) picture (also: photo)
das **Buch, ⁝er** (5) book
der **Bildband, ⁝e** (5) photo book
  (der **Band** = volume)
der **Blazer, -** (6) blazer
die **Bluse, -n** (6) blouse
der **Braten, -** (4) roast
der **Brief, -e** (5) letter
die **Brieftasche, -n** (15) wallet
  (usually men's)
das **Brot, -e** (4) bread
das **Brötchen, -** (4) roll
der **Bruder, ⁝** (5) brother
das **Bundesland, ⁝er** (7) federal state
die **Butter** (4) butter
der **Bürgermeister, -** (13) mayor (m.)
die **Bürgermeisterin, -nen** (13) mayor (f.)

A-21

sich (acc.) **bürsten** (15) to brush oneself
  sich (dat.) **die Haare bürsten** (15) to brush
  one's hair

C

der **CD-Spieler**, **-** (5) CD-player
der **Chef**, **-s** (3) boss, supervisor (m.)
die **Chefin**, **-nen** (3) boss, supervisor (f.)
der **Christ**, **-en** *weak* Christian (m.)
die **Christin**, **-nen** Christian (f.)
der **Computer**, **-** (5) computer
der **Cousin**, **-s** (5) cousin (m.)

D

die **Demokratie**, **-n** (7) democracy
dies- (3) this
das **Ding**, **-e** (14) thing, item
diskutieren (11) discuss
das **Dorf**, **¨er** (7) village
drohen (13) to threaten
sich (acc.) **duschen** (15) to shower,
  to take a shower

E

die **E-mail** (5) e-mail
egoistisch (9) egotistical, selfish
freundlich (9) friendly
der **Eifer** (18) zeal, enthusiasm
sich (dat.) **etwas ein•bilden** (13) to exist
  in one's imagination
der **Einfall**, **¨e** (9) insight, idea
die **Einladung**, **-en** (4) invitation, company
einmalig (8) unique
der **Einwohner**, **-** (6) inhabitant (m.)
die **Einwohnerin**, **-nen** (7) inhabitant (f.)
ein•kaufen (2) to go shopping,
  to go to the store
ein•reichen (16) to hand in
die **Einstellung** (14) attitude
die **Eltern** (5) parents
entdecken (16) to discover
sich (acc.) **entschuldigen** (15) to apologize
entsetzlich (8) dreadful, horrible
der **Erfinder**, **-** (6) inventor (m.)
die **Erfinderin**, **-nen** (6) inventor (f.)
erklären (13) to explain
die **Erklärung**, **-en** (3) explanation
erledigen (16) to take care of
ernennen, ernannte, hat ernannt (16)
  to appoint
erwähnen (16) to mention
erzählen (13) to tell, to narrate

das **Essen** (4) food, das **Essen**, **-** (4) meal
das **Examen**, **-** (2) comprehensive exam

F

die **Fahne**, **-n** (18) flag
fahren (ä), fuhr, ist gefahren (3) to ride,
  drive
das **Fahrrad**, **¨er** (3) bicycle
faszinierend (8) fascinating
die **Fähigkeit**, **-en** (4) ability, skill
die **Fähre**, **-n** (3) ferry
feiern   to celebrate
das **Feld**, **-er** (7) field
der **Fernseher**, **-** (5) TV set
das **Fest**, **-e** (4) party, fest
der **Fisch**, **-e** (4) fish
fliegen, flog, ist geflogen (3) to fly
das **Flugzeug**, **-e** (3) airplane, plane
der **Fluss**, **¨e** (7) river
folgen (3) to follow
formulieren (13) to phrase, to formulate
der **Fotoapparat**, **-e** (5) camera
die **Fremdsprache**, **-n** (4) foreign language
der **Freund**, **-e** (6) friend (m.); boyfriend
die **Freundin**, **-nen** (6) friend (f.); girlfriend
freundlich (2) friendly
die **Freundschaft**, **-en** (7) friendship
früher (3) in earlier times
furchtbar (8) frightful, awful
der **Führerschein**, **-e** (2) driver's license

G

der **Gast**, **¨e** (4) guest
geben (i), gab, hat gegeben (5) to give, to
  hand
das **Gebiet**, **-e** (18) area, field
der **Geburtstag**, **-e** (2) birthday
die **Geburtstagsfeier**, **-n** (2) birthday party
die **Geduld** (9) patience
geduldig (9) patient
die **Gegenwart** (4) present
gehen, ging, ist gegangen (3) to go
  (also: to leave)
  wenn es nach mir (dir, uns, usw.) ginge
  (11) if it were up to me (you, us, etc.)
die **Geldbörse**, **-n** (15) purse, wallet
das **Gemälde**, **-** (5) painting
das **Gemüse** (4) vegetable
die **Gemüsesorte**, **-n** (4) vegetable
gerade (3) just, at the moment (also: straight)
das **Gerät**, **-e** (14) device, appliance
das **Gericht** (13), court **vor Gericht** (13)

in court
das **Gerücht, -e** (13) rumor
die **Geschichte** (16) history
die **Geschichte, -n** story
die **Geschwister**, (pl.)   (5) siblings
gestern (3) yesterday; **gestern Morgen**
  (3) yesterday morning; **gestern Nachmittag**
  (3) yesterday afternoon
das **Getränk, -e** (2) beverage, drink
die **Gewerkschaft, -en** (7) union
glänzend (8) brilliant
grausig (8) ghastly
die **Grenze, -n** (7) border
die **Großeltern** (pl.) (5) grandparents
die **Großmutter, ⸚**(5) grandmother
der **Großvater, ⸚** (5) grandfather
der **Grund, ⸚e** (11) reason
(sich) grüßen (15) to greet (each other)
gründen (16) to found
die **Gürteltasche, -n** (15) fanny pack

H

der **Haken, -** (18) hook
die **Handtasche, -n** (15) (woman's) purse
der **Handy, -s** (5) cellular phone
hassen (15) to hate
das **Haus, ⸚er** (5) house
hässlich (8) ugly
helfen (i), half, hat geholfen (15) to help
das **Hemd, -en** (6) shirt
hervorragend (8) outstanding, superb
heute (3) today **heute Morgen** (3)
  this morning **heute Nachmittag** (3)
  this afternoon
hochinteressant (8) highly interesting
der **Hubschrauber, -** (18) helicopter
das **Huhn** (4) chicken
der **Hügel, -** (7) hill

I

die **Idee, -en** (9) idea
sich (acc.) **informieren über** (13)
  to inform oneself about
intelligent (9) intelligent

J

die **Jacke, -** (6) jacket
das **Jacket, -s** (6) coat
das **Jahr, -e** (3) year
die **Jahreszeit, -en** (10) season
das **Jahrhundert, -e** (10) century
die **Jahrhundertwende** (10)
turn of the century
das **Jahrzehnt, e-** (10) decade
der **Jogurt, -s** (4) yogurt
der **Jude, -n** *weak* (5) Jew
der **Junge, -n** *weak* (5) boy

K

der **Kaffee** (4) coffee
kassieren (18) to collect
kaufen (5) to buy
sich kämmen (15) to comb oneself
  sich (dat.) die **Haare kämmen** (15)
  to comb one's hair
der **Käse** (2) cheese
das **Kind** (4) child; als **Kind** (4) as a child
klären (16) to clarify
das **Kleid, -er** (6) dress
der **Kleiderbügel, -** (18) clothes hanger
die **Kleidung** (5) clothing, clothes (sing. only)
das **Kleidungsstück, -e** (5) article of clothing
klingen als ob, klang, hat geklungen (13)
  to sound as if
kommen, kam, ist gekommen (3) to come
  (gut) miteinander aus•kommen (13) to
  get along (well)
der **Kompromiss, -e** (11) compromise
  einen **Kompromiss schließen** (11)
  to compromise
konkurrieren (18) to compete
das **Kostüm, -e** (6) suit (women's)
das **Können** (18) ability
köstlich (8) delicious
krankhaft (8) sick, sickening
die **Krawatte, -n** (6) tie
die **Kreditkarte, -n** (15) credit card
der **Krieg, -e** (16) war
der **Kuchen, -**(2) cake
die **Kusine, -n** (5) cousin (f.)
(sich) küssen (15) to kiss (each other)

L

das **Land, ⸚er** (7) country, nation, land
  (also: federal state); **auf dem Land** (7)
  in the country
landen (3) to land
laufen (ä), lief, ist gelaufen (3) to walk, jog
das **Lebewesen, -** (14) living being,
  living creature
lecker (8) tasty
legen (7) to lay down, place (horizontal)
leihen, lieh, hat geliehen (5) to loan
  something to somebody

letzt- (3) last
(sich) lieben (15) to love (each other)
liegen, lag, hat gelegen (7) to lie (no motion)
die **Limo, -s** (4) soft drink
die **Lobby, -s** (7) (political) lobby
loben (16) to praise
lösen (16) to solve
die **Lösung, -en** (11) solution

M

die **Mahnung, -en** (18) reminder
manipulieren (16) to manipulate
der **Mantel, ⁻** (6) coat, overcoat
der **Marktplatz** (7) market square
marschieren (ist) (3) to march
die **Mauer, -** (16) wall (also: the Berlin wall)
der **Mensch, -en** *weak* (14) human, human being
menschenmöglich (18) humanly possible
die **Milch** (4) milk
das **Mineralwasser, -** (4) sparkling water, club soda
der **Ministerpräsident, -en** *weak* (16) prime minister (m.)
die **Ministerpräsidentin, -nen** (16) prime minister (f.)
mit•teilen (13) to share, tell (something to somebody)
die **Monarchie, -n** (7) monarchy
der **Monat, -e** (3) month
morgen (3) tomorrow; **morgen früh** (3) tomorrow morning; **morgen Abend** (3) tomorrow evening
das **Motorrad, ⁻er** (5) motorcycle
die **Mutter, ⁻** (5) mother

N

der **Nachbar, -n** *weak* (5) neighbor (m.)
die **Nachbarin, -nen** (5) neighbor (f.)
nächst, - (3) next
der **Neffe, -n** *weak* (5) nephew
nehmen (i), nahm, hat genommen (18) to take **in Angriff nehmen** (18) to tackle, embark on
der **Nerv, -en** (14) nerve
 jemand(em) (dat.) **auf die Nerven gehen** (14) to get on somebody's nerves
das **Neujahr** (10) new year, New Year's Day
die **Nichte, -n** (5) niece
die **Nudel, -n** (4) noodle, pasta

O

das **Oberhemd, -en** (6) dress shirt
das **Obst** (pl.) (4) fruit, fruits
die **Obstsorte, -n** (4) fruit, fruits
der **Onkel, -** (5) uncle
ordentlich (9) neat, orderly
der **Ort, -e** (7) town (also: place, location)

P

das **Paket, -e** (5) package
die **Papiere** (pl.) (15) papers, documents
der **Park, -s** (7) park
der **Parka, -s** (6) parka
die **Partei, -en** (7) (political) party
die **Party, -s** (4) party
der **Pass, ⁻e** (15) passport
passieren (ist) (3) to happen, to occur
das **Päckchen, -** (5) small package
die **Person, -en** (14) person
der **Pfad, -e** (7) path
der **Platz, ⁻e** (7) square
das **Portmonee, -s** (also: **Portemonnaie, -s**) (15) wallet, purse
die **Postkarte, -n** (5) postcard
das **Problem, -e** (11) problem
der **Professor, -en** (6) professor (m.)
die **Professorin, -nen** (6) professor (f.)
prophezeien (13) to predict, to prophesy
der **Prozess, -e** (13) trial
 den **Prozess verlieren, verlor, hat verloren** (13) to lose the case, to lose the trial

R

das **Rad, ⁻er** (5) bike **Rad fahren** to bicycle
sich rasieren (15) to shave
die **Raststätte, -n** (2) highway stop, restaurant
der **Rechtsanwalt, ⁻e** (13) lawyer (m.)
die **Rechtsanwältin, -nen** (13) lawyer (f.)
die **Rede, -n** (11) speech, talk
 jemanden (acc.) **zur Rede stellen** (11) to confront somebody
reisen (ist) (3) to travel
der **Reisepass, ⁻e** (7) passport
das **Rennen, -** (18) race, run
rennen, rannte, ist gerannt (3) to run
der **Richter, -** (13) judge (m.)
die **Richterin, -nen** (13) judge (f.)
der **Rücktritt, -e** (13) resignation
 mit dem Rücktritt drohen (13) to threaten to resign

der **Rock**, **¨e** (6) skirt
der **Rucksack**, **¨e** (15) backpack

S

der **Saft**, **¨e** (4) juice
sagen (13) to say
der **Salat**, **-e** (4) salad (also: lettuce)
die **Sandale**, **-n** (6) sandal
das **Sandwich** (4) sandwich
der **Schal**, **-s** (6) scarf
der **Scheck**, **-s** (5) check
das **Scheckheft**, **-e** (15) checkbook
scheinen als ob, **schien**, **hat geschienen**
  (13) to seem as if
schenken (5) to give (as a gift)
scheußlich (8) ugly, hideous
schicken (5) to send, to mail
das **Schiff**, **-e** (3) ship
das **Schild**, **-er** (18) sign
der **Schilling**, **-e** (2) shilling
  (Austrian currency)
der **Schlips**, **-e** (6) tie
sich schminken (15) to put on make-up
schockierend (8) shocking
schon (3) already
schrecklich (8) terrible
sich schreiben, **schrieb**, **hat geschrieben**
  (15) to write one another
der **Schuh**, **-e** (6) shoe
schwänzen (2) to skip class
die **Schwester**, **-n** (5) sister
schwimmen, **schwomm**,
  ist geschwommen (3) to swim
der **See**, **-n** (7) lake
segeln (3) to sail
sehen (i), **sah**, **hat gesehen** to see
der **Seidenschal**, **-s** (6) silk scarf
sein (ist), **war**, **ist gewesen** to be
die **Selbstbeherrschung** (9) self-control
streng (9) strict
das **Seminar**, **-e** (2) seminar, class
sich setzen (7) to sit down
das **Silvester** (10) New Year's Eve
sitzen, **saß**, **hat gesessen** (7) to sit
  (no motion)
die **Socke**, **-n** (6) sock
der **Spaziergang**, **¨e** (7) walk
der **Spazierweg**, **-e** (7) walking trail
der **Sportplatz**, **¨e** (7) sports field
der **Sprudel** (4) sparkling water, club soda
die **Stadt**, **¨e** (7) city

der **Stadtrat**, **¨e** (13) town councilor,
  councilman (m.) (also: city council)
die **Stadträtin**, **-nen** (13) town councilor,
  councilwoman (f.)
starten (ist) (3) to take off, start
stehen, **stand**, **ist gestanden** (7) to stand
  (upright)
die **Stelle**, **-n** (11) position, place,
  an jemands Stelle sein (11) to be in
  someone's place, **wenn ich (du, er, usw.)**
  an seiner (ihrer, deiner, usw.) Stelle
  wäre if I (you, he, etc.) were in his (her,
  your, etc.) place
stellen (7) to place (upright),
  an jemanden (acc.) **Ansprüche stellen**
  (18) to make demands (on someone)
die **Stereoanlage**, **-n** (5) stereo
die **Steuer**, **-n** (7) tax
stören (16) to disturb
die **Straßenbahn**, **-en** (3) trolley
der **Streik**, **-s** (7) strike
der **Streit**, **-s** (11) quarrel, fight
(sich) streiten, **stritt**, **hat gestritten** (11)
  to fight, quarrel (with each other)
der **Strumpf**, **¨e** (6) sock, stocking
der **Studienkollege**, **-n** weak (2)
  co-student (m.)
die **Studienkollegin**, **-nen** (2) co-student (f.)
sympatisch (18) pleasant, likeable

T

der **Tag**, **-e** (3) day
die **Tageszeit**, **-en** (10) time of the day
die **Tankstelle**, **-n** (2) gas station
die **Tante**, **-n** (5) aunt
tätig sein (an) (18) to work at
der **Tee** (4) tea
der **Teenager**, **-e** (4); **als Teenager** (4)
  as a teenager
der **Teich**, **-e** (7) pond
die **Telefonnummer**, **-n** (10)
  telephone number
die **Todesstrafe** (7) capital punishment
tolerant (9) tolerant, accepting
die **Toleranz** (9) tolerance
toll (8) great, super
jemandem (dat.) **trauen** (14) to
  trust somebody
(sich) treffen (i), **traf**, **hat getroffen** (15)
  to meet each other, to get together
(so) tun als ob, **tat**, **hat getan** (13)
  to act as if

U

die **Uhrzeit, -en** (10) clock time, time
die **U-Bahn, -en** (3) subway
(sich) umarmen (15) to hug (each other)
unabhängig (2) independent
unfreundlich (9) unfriendly
ungeduldig (2) impatient
unordentlich (9) messy, disorderly
unterbrechen (i), unterbrach, hat unterbrochen (16) to interrupt
sich unterhalten (ä), unterhielt, hat unterhalten (15) to converse, to talk (to each other)
unterhaltsam entertaining, amusing
untersuchen (16) to investigate, check
übermorgen (3) the day after tomorrow
übersehen (ie), übersah, hat übersehen (16) to overlook

V

der **Vater, ⁻** (5) father
die **Vergangenheit** (4) past
vergessen (i), vergaß, hat vergessen (16) to forget
das **Verhalten** (14) behavior
vermeiden, vermied, hat vermieden (16) to avoid
(sich) verstehen, verstand, hat verstanden (15) to get along, to understand (one another)
der **Vertrag, ⁻e** (16) treaty, contract
die **Verwandten** (pl.) (5) relatives
jemanden (acc.) **verwöhnen** (16) to spoil someone
verwöhnt (16) spoiled
die **Videokamera, -s** (5) video camera
voraus•sehen (ie), sah voraus, hat vorausgesehen (16) to foresee
vorgestern (3) the day before yesterday
vorher (3) earlier
jemandem (dat.) (so) **vor•kommen als ob, kam vor, ist vorgekommen** (13) to appear to someone as if
das **Vorlesungsverzeichnis, -se** (2) course catalog, schedule
die **Vorwahl** (10) area code, country code
der **Vorwand, ⁻e** (13) pretense

W

der **Wagen, -** (3) car
die **Wahl, -en** (7) election
der **Wald, ⁻er** (7) forest
der **Waldweg, -e** (7) hiking trail
die **Wanderkarte, -n** (7) hiking map, guide
wandern (ist) (3) to hike
die **Wanderung, -en** (7) hike
sich (acc.) **waschen (ä), wusch, hat gewaschen (15)** to wash up **sich (dat.)** die **Hände**/die **Haare**/das **Gesicht** (acc.) **waschen** (15) to wash one's hands/hair/face
wählen (16) to elect, chose
die **Wäscheleine, -n** (18) clothes line
das **Wäschegestell, -e** (18) cloth drying rack
der **Weg, -e** (7) trail
der **Wein, -e** (4) wine
widerlich (8) disgusting, nauseating
(sich) widersprechen (i), widersprach, hat widersprochen (13) to contradict (oneself)
das **Bewusstsein wieder•erlangen** (18) to regain consciousness
die **Wiedervereinigung** (16) (re)unification
die **Wiese, -n** (7) lawn, meadow
die **Willensstärke** (9) will power
die **Woche, -n** (3) week
der **Wochentag, -e** (10) week day
das **Wochenende, -n** (10) weekend
wunderbar (8) wonderful, miraculous
wunderschön (8) beautiful
die **Wurst** (2) cold cuts die **Wurst, ⁻e** (2) sausage die **Wurstplatte, -n** (2) platter with cold cuts

Z

der **Zahn, ⁻e** (15) tooth
sich (dat.) die **Zähne putzen** (15) to brush one's teeth
zerstören (16) to destroy
der **Zeuge, -n** *weak* (13) witness (m.)
die **Zeugin, -nen** (13) witness (f.)
das **Zitat, -e** (13) citation, quote
zitieren (13) to cite, quote
der **Zug, ⁻e** (3) train
die **Zukunft** (4) future
zurück•treten (tritt), trat zurück, ist zurückgetreten (13) to resign
der **Zweck, -e** (11) use, purpose
es hat keinen Zweck (11) it's no use

Glossary of Grammatical Terms Used in the Book

Accusative Case   The **Case** that marks a **Noun** or noun equivalent as the **Direct object** of the **Clause** or **Sentence**; *see also* **Cases**

Accusative object   *See* **Direct object**

Accusative prepositions *See* **Prepositions**

Active voice   Asserts that the **Subject** of the sentence is carrying out the action expressed by the **Verb**

Adjective   A lexical category of words that semantically modify **Nouns** or **Verbs** and that can be marked to represent degrees of comparison (**Comparative, Superlative**); *see also* **Attributive adjectives** *and* **Predicative adjectives**

Adverb   The element that specifies the time, manner, or place of an event

Affix   An element that attaches to the **Root** or **Stem** of a word most commonly as a **Prefix** to the beginning or as **Suffix** to the end; example of prefix in English: *im* in *im*-possible

Agent   The performer of an action

Agreement   The marking of a word, most commonly a **Verb,** with an **Affix** to indicate its relationship to another word, usually the **Subject**

Antecedent   A word or group of words replaced and referred to by a substitute

Appositive   A modifying noun phrase that immediately follows the noun or noun equivalent it modifies

Article   The element that denotes the definiteness and the **Case, Gender,** and

Number of the **Noun** it precedes; *see also* **Definite** *and* **Indefinite Article**

Attributive adjective   The **Adjective** that modifies the **Noun** and takes endings according to the **Case, Gender,** and **Number** of the noun it precedes or follows

Auxiliary verb   A verb that serves as the specifier of the **Main verb;** for example *hat* in *er hat gegessen*

Cardinal number   The number used in counting; *see also* **Ordinal number**

Case   A grammatical category associated with **Articles, Adjectives, Nouns** and **Pronouns** that marks the grammatical functions of **Subject, Object** and **Possessive**

Clause,   A group of words containing at least a **Subject** and a **Verb;** *see also* **Dependent** and **Independent clauses**

Compound   The joining together of elements; *see also* **Noun compound**

Comparative   Degree of comparison to denote increase in quality or quantity expressed by an **Adjective** or **Adverb**

Complex sentence   A sentence that consists of a main, or **Independent** clause and one or more subordinate, or **Dependent clauses**

Conjugated verb   *See* **Conjugation**

Conjugation   Refers to a class of **Verbs** having the same inflectional forms; *see also* **Inflection**

Conjunction   A small set of words that join **Sentences, Clauses, Phrases** or **Words;** *see also* **Coordinating** *and* **Subordinating conjunctions**

Coordinating conjunction   An element that joins together two Independent clauses

Consonants   One of the two major classes of sounds produced by constriction or closure at one or more points in the oral cavity to create audible friction; *see also* **Vowels**

Dative case   The Case that marks the Noun or noun equivalent as the Indirect object of the Clause or Sentence; *see also* **Cases**

Dative object   *See* **Indirect Object**

Dative prepositions   *See* **Prepositions**

Declarative   Having the form of a statement; *see also* **Imperative** *and* **Interrogative**

Declension   Articles, Adjectives, Nouns and Pronouns that take the same set of inflectional forms

Definite article   The element that denotes Gender, Case and Number in reference to a specific noun; *see also* **Article** *and* **Indefinite article**

Demonstrative pronoun   A Definite article used as a Pronoun

Dependent clause   The clause that depends on another clause and cannot stand alone; introduced by a **Subordinating conjunction.** The element that introduces a **Subordinate** or **Dependent** clause

Diminutive   A Word, Affix or name that indicates small size and sometimes the state of being familiar

Direct discourse   The exact quoting of a person's words; marked by quotation marks; *see also* **Indirect discourse**

Direct object   The one of two grammatical relations known as Object; the direct object is the noun or noun equivalent that receives the direct action

expressed by the Verb; *see also* **Indirect object**

Directional   An Adverb of place that denotes motion to or from a place

Feminine   *See* **Gender**

Flavoring particle   Certain elements that express the speaker's attitude toward what is said

Future   The tense that marks an event as taking place at a time yet to come

Future perfect   The tense that marks an event or state as being completed at some point in the future

Gender   The subclass within a grammatical class such as **Noun** or **Pronoun** that is arbitrary (**Grammatical gender**) or based on certain characteristics such as sex (**Natural Gender**); German has grammatical gender with three classes, masculine, feminine and neuter

Genitive case   The Case that marks an element as the possessor of another; *see also* **Cases**

Grammatical relation   The role, for example **Subject**, that a noun or noun equivalent plays within in a clause; *see also* **Direct** *and* **Indirect objects**

Imperative   The verb form that expresses commands, requests, or directives

Indefinite article   The element that denotes Case, Gender, and Number in reference to a nonspecific noun

Indicative mood   The verb form that indicates that an utterance is factual or relatively likely; *see also* **Subjunctive mood**

Indirect discourse   The reporting of a person's utterance without quoting the person directly; *See also* **Direct discourse**

Indirect object   (Usually) the person to whom something is given or for whom something is done

Infinitive   The basic form of the verb that is found in a dictionary

Inflection   The change of form that words undergo to mark **Case, Gender, Number, Person, Tense, Mood,** or **Voice;** *see also* **Conjugation** *and* **Declension**

Interrogative   Having the form or force of a question

Interrogative pronoun   A **Pronoun** that introduces a question

Intransitive verbs   The category of verbs that do not take **Direct objects**

Main clause   *See* **Independent clause**

Main verb   A verb other than the **Auxiliary verb;** for example *leave* in *they must leave*

Masculine   *See* **Gender**

Modal verb or Auxiliary   Used to modify a sentence, typically with a **Verb** or **Predicate**

Modality   *See* **Mood**

Mood   A grammatical category of **Verbs** marking speakers' attitude toward the truth of their assertions or obligation, permission, or suggestion; *see also* **Indicative** *and* **Subjunctive mood** *and* **Modal verb**

Neuter   *See* **Gender**

Nominative case   The **Case** that marks the **Noun** or noun equivalent as the **Subject** of the **Clause** or **Sentence;** *see also* **Cases**

Noun   Words that name persons, things, actions, qualities and can be characterized by inflections for **Case, Gender** and **Number**

Noun compound   The combination of two or more nouns

Number   Denotes whether a word form, usually a **Noun** or **Pronoun,** is one (singular) or more than one (plural)

Object   The noun or noun equivalent (**Pronoun, Clause**) that is the goal or result of the action of the **Verb;** *see also* **Direct** *and* **Indirect Object**, *and* **Subject**

Ordinal (number)   A number designating the place (first, second, third) of an item in a sequence

Participle   A verb form that shows characteristics of both **Verb** and **Adjective;** *see also* **Present** *and* **Past participle**

Passive voice   Asserts that the Subject of a sentence is the receiver of the action expressed by the **Verb;** *see also* **Active voice**

Past participle   One of the three principal parts of Verbs; *see also* **Infinitive** *and* **Past tense**

Past perfect   The **Tense** that refers to an action or event in the remote past

Past tense   A verb tense that expresses a time period before the present; *see also* **Simple past tense**, **Present perfect**, *and* **Past perfect**

Person   A grammatical category principally associated with **Pronouns** that marks the speaker in the first person, the addressee in the second person, a third party in the third person or a combination of these; **Verbs** in a **Clause** may be marked for person **Agreement,** usually with their subject

Personal pronoun   A **Pronoun** that expresses distinction of **Person**

Phrase   A group of two or more grammatically related words

Plural   *See* **Number**

Possessive pronoun   A **Pronoun** that derives from a **Personal pronoun** and denotes possession

Predicate   The part of a **Clause** or **Sentence** that makes a statement about the **Subject** and consists of a **Verb** with or without **Objects** or **Complements**

Predicate adjective   An **Adjective** that completes the meaning of the **Verb** in a **Clause** and predicates, or states something about the **Subject**; *see also* **Attributive adjective**

Prefix   An element attached to the beginning of a word to produce a derived form; *see also* **Affix** *and* **Suffix**

Preposition   An element that combines with a **Noun** or noun equivalent to form a phrase

Present participle   A participle that expresses present action in relation to the time expressed by the **Conjugated verb** and is often used as an **Adjective**

Present perfect A verb tense that refers to the completion of a state or action at the time of speaking or merely to a state or action before the present

Present tense   The tense of a verb that typically expresses state or action in the present time and is sometimes used to refer to state or action in the past or in the future

Pronoun   A word that is used in place of a **Noun** or noun equivalent and refers to persons or things understood in the context; *see also* **Demonstrative**, **Interrogative**, **Personal**, **Reciprocal**, **Reflexive**, *and* **Relative pronouns**

Question   *See* **Interrogative**

Reciprocal pronoun   A **Pronoun** (e.g. *each other*) that denotes mutual action

between the members of a plural **Subject**

Reflexive pronoun   A **Pronoun** referring to the **Subject** of the **Clause**, **Sentence** or phrase in which it occurs

Relative clause   A **Clause** introduced by a **Relative pronoun** that modifies a noun or noun equivalent

Relative pronoun   The **Pronoun** that refers to an element in the preceding clause and introduces a **Relative clause**

Root   The part of the word that functions as the basis from which its other forms are derived

Sentence   A self-contained speech unit consisting of a word or a syntactically related group of words that expresses a statement, question, wish, command, exclamation and the like; *see also* **Simple** *and* **Complex sentences**

Simple past tense   The **Past tense** that is formed by attaching a **Suffix** to the **Root** of the **Main verb** or with a **Stem vowel** change

Simple sentence   A sentence that contains only one **Clause**

Singular   *See* **Number**

Statement   *See* **Declarative**

Stem   The part of an inflected word that remains unchanged except for phonetic changes and to which an inflectional **Affix** is added

Stem vowel   The vowel contained in the **Stem** that is often subject to change, for example in the formation of the **Simple Past tense**

Subjunctive mood   The verb form that indicates that something is relatively unlikely, implausible, conjectural, or contrary to fact

Subject   The noun or pronoun, or group of nouns plus modifiers, that generates the action of the verb and takes the **Nominative case**

Subordinate clause   *See* **Dependent clause**

Subordinating conjunction   The element that introduces a subordinate or **Dependent clause**

Suffix   An element that attaches to the end of the word

Superlative   Refers to the degree of grammatical comparison that denotes an extreme level or extent expressed by an **Adjective** or **Adverb**

Syllable   A unit of one or more sounds

Tense   The forms of the verb that express distinctions of time or durations of time; *See also* **Present** *and* **Past tense**

Transitive verb   The category of verb that can take a **Direct object**; *see also* **Intransitive verb**

Verb   A lexical category of words that form the center of the **Predicate**; they express an act, state, or event, and can be marked for categories such as **Tense, Modality, Person** and **Number**; *see also* **Conjugation**

Verb complement   Sentence elements that have a close relationship to the verb such as **Predicate adjectives** and **nouns**, and **Directionals**

Voice   *See* **Active** *and* **Passive voice**

Vowels   One of two major classes of sounds, produced without constriction in the oral cavity; *see also* **Consonants**

Index